# THE GREAT BOOK OF
# WORLD
# WAR II

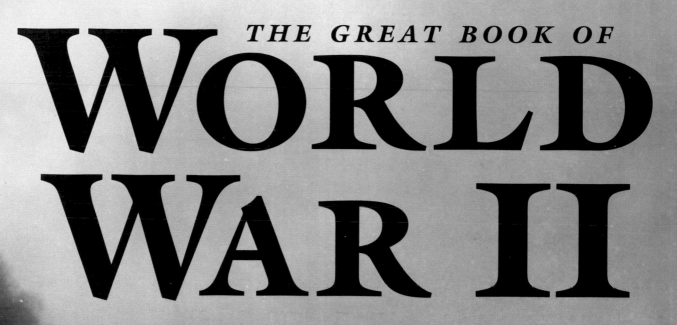

# THE GREAT BOOK OF
# WORLD WAR II

### THE COMPLETE STORY OF THE WEAPONS,
### THE BATTLES, AND THE FIGHTING MEN

### EDITED BY DAVID MILLER

THUNDER BAY
P·R·E·S·S

San Diego, California

**Thunder Bay Press**
An imprint of the Advantage Publishers Group
5880 Oberlin Drive, San Diego, CA 92121-4794
www.thunderbaybooks.com

Copyright © Salamander Books Ltd, 2003

A member of **Chrysalis** Books plc

All notations of errors or omissions should be addressed to Thunder
Bay Press, Editorial Department, at the above address. All other
correspondence (author inquiries, permissions) concerning the
content of this book should be addressed to Salamander Books Ltd,
The Chrysalis Building, Bramley Road, London W10 6SP, U.K.

ISBN 1-59223-062-8

Library of Congress Cataloging-in-Publication Data
available on request.

Printed in China

1  2  3  4  5  07  06  05  04  03

**CREDITS**
**Project Manager:** Ray Bonds
**Editor:** David Miller
**Designer:** John Heritage
**Commissioning Editor:** Antony Shaw
**Production:** Don Campaniello
**Reproduction:** Anorax

# CONTENTS

# INTRODUCTION

WORLD WAR II was fought by mass armies, but, unlike World War I, the strategies were more flexible, the tactics more fluid, and the major leaders more forceful and charismatic. Indeed, the European war was caused

by one man, Adolf Hitler, and was essentially a prolonged operation to crush him and his armed forces. Having come to power in August 1934, Hitler, known to his followers as *"der Führer"* (the leader), used his growing military power to test the resolve of other European leaders. He took the Rhineland, then Austria and then Czech Sudetenland without a shot being fired, but when the Poles refused to give way over Danzig, and reassured by the nonaggression pact with the Soviet Union, he became even more daring and on September 1, 1939, he invaded Poland.

The course of the war was determined by the leadership at the top. The strategic direction of the major European powers—Britain, Germany, and the Soviet Union—was undertaken by the political heads of each government, who also acted as the generalissimos of their armed forces. Each approached his enormous problems in a characteristically different way, the requirement being to be sufficiently dictatorial to set and maintain the aims while remaining sufficiently open-minded to admit some argument and be receptive to unpalatable information. This proved to be Hitler's Achilles' heel and his leadership lacked rationality—indeed, what he really thought he could do with Russia had his invasion succeeded

remains a mystery to this day. As it was, he cut himself off from all advice and led his country inexorably to disaster.

In dealing with the army Hitler deeply resented the combination of Junker aristocracy, arrogance, and intellectual strength that was the hallmark of the Great General Staff. He believed himself to be a better general than any of those professionals and took control at both the strategic and operational levels, becoming a "pins in the map" general, who delighted in regrouping armies and drawing arrows showing thrust lines and encirclements. A clever man, he was sometimes dangerously proficient, but it distracted him from economic and political questions.

Churchill's anti-Hitler strategy was based on a very simple plan, which was firmly rooted in reality; he had to keep the war going until the United States was drawn in, his aims being survival followed by liberation. To achieve this he needed to retain a springboard for reentry into Europe; Britain itself and the eastern Mediterranean together with the north African coast. Unlike Stalin and Hitler, Churchill was worried about expenditure of life, his views being strongly influenced by the grim casualties of World War I, and by the inherent shortage of manpower in the United Kingdom. All his strategy favored a long-range, encircling counteroffensive from the southern flank as opposed to cross-Channel assault followed by a head-on clash with the main German forces in France. He may have been a nuisance to his

Below: The three Allied leaders meet in Tehran, Iran, November 28 to December 1, 1943. From the left: Soviet leader Josef Stalin, U.S. president Franklin D. Roosevelt, and British prime minister Winston Churchill.

Inset: Germany shows its military might to celebrate Hitler's fiftieth birthday on April 20, 1939. Six years later, Hitler was dead, Germany was defeated, and the dreams of an empire had gone to dust.

Left: Italian dictator Benito Mussolini (second from right) was a guest of Adolf Hitler (center) and the German government at the 1937 *Wehrmacht* maneuvers. Hitler and Mussolini hoped to divide up all of Europe between them and for a time it seemed that they just might get away with it.

Above: Two of the forgotten preludes to World War II were the skirmishes between the Soviets and Japanese in 1938 and 1939. In both cases, the expansionist Japanese penetrated Soviet territory, first near Lake Khalsan and later in the Khalkin Gol area. In this picture from the Khalkin Gol battle, Soviet BT-7 tanks and infantry charge forward to repel the invaders.

generals and tended occasionally to meddle with operations, but his advisers were the best he could find and not afraid to speak their minds.

Stalin succeeded where Hitler failed, functioning as the supreme head of state and generalissimo. His problems were appalling, although some, such as the purging of the top army leadership in the 1930s, were of his own making. The Red Army's doctrine and plans were in disarray as late as 1940 and the overwhelming fact facing Stalin in 1941 was that nowhere could the ill-led Soviet divisions stand up to the magnificent German armies; indeed, they surrendered in droves. Thus, Stalin had first to check Hitler's advance while concurrently building up Soviet industry and reequipping and retraining new armies; only then would he be able to assume the offensive and destroy the invaders. Stalin had a complete grip of the operational picture and, above all, he grasped the fact that the only way a generalissimo can influence the battle is by having an uncommitted reserve; thus, he created a huge one that he used with decisive effect.

The Americans kept a more orthodox balance between their president, both the head of state and, constitutionally, the commander in chief, and his service advisers. There was a clear-cut division between national policy and military operations and while Roosevelt had no ambition to play the generalissimo, he inevitably had to take the most important decisions.

The least understood leadership element was that of the Japanese. The head of state was Emperor Hirohito, who was regarded as divine by his people. As described in more detail below, during the 1920s Japanese domestic politics became increasingly nationalistic and when the global depression inflicted particular hardship on Japan, the perceived solution was territorial expansion, first into Manchuria, then China and thereafter across Asia and the Pacific. During its long war with China, Japan signed two pacts with the other fascist powers, Germany and Italy. The first was in 1936, but the more significant was the Tripartite Pact (also known as the "Axis Pact") in 1940. There was a civilian prime minister, Konoe, but the real power lay with the army, supported by the navy (there was no separate air force). The Japanese military insisted on occupying French Indochina in July 1941 and when General Tojo took over as prime minister in October, he, like Hitler, became a virtual dictator (although not head of state) and commander in chief, and was thus able to implement advances both eastward and southward in order to establish the "Greater East-Asian Co-Prosperity Sphere"—another name for an expanded Japanese empire.

## LAND WARFARE

The military instruments available to the belligerents differed markedly in character. The German army was monolithic, with a common loyalty and a strong *esprit de corps*. It was divided, tactically speaking, into two wings: one, the modernized Panzer element, all motorized on either tracks or wheels, the other, the infantry divisions, with marching soldiers and horse-drawn artillery little changed from World War I.

The army (*das Heer*) was highly trained and, despite all its setbacks, remained loyal right up to the end of the war. The officer corps was dominated by the General Staff, which prided itself on its strategic vision and ability to make the most complicated plans and then carry them out smoothly and efficiently. The generals themselves were, in most cases, very capable, the most distinguished including men such as von Rundstedt and Model, although the most famous of them all, Rommel, was not quite in the same class, and probably peaked in performance as a corps commander. For all

German generals, however, the great complicating factor was Hitler, whose interference became more intrusive and reached ever lower levels as the war progressed.

A unique feature during the war years was the *Waffen-SS*, which grew from some 18,000 men in a large number of small units at the outbreak of war into a force a million strong in 1944. Essentially a private army manned by dedicated Nazi party members, its organization followed the same lines as *das Heer*, although it had its own uniforms, ranks, and badges. The Waffen-SS formations (i.e., divisions and corps) were subordinated to the army chain of command and complied with the army's operational plans, but within its areas of responsibility it made its own rules. During the war, the Waffen-SS could not recruit sufficient ethnic Germans for its needs, so it raised units

Below: An anxious Waffen-SS trooper seeks to explain himself to a U.S. 82nd Airborne Division interrogator. The highly trained and highly motivated Waffen-SS existed in parallel to the German army and was a totally new phenomenon for the Allies, who found that its units always fought very hard and to the very end.

composed of volunteers from national groups such as Belgians, Croatians, Danes, Dutch, Estonians, French, Latvians, and Norwegians.

The Red Army was made up of a vast mass of illiterate peasant levies dragooned into action by the discipline of the Communist Party machine, and thus lacking much of the Germans' initiative and *élan*. Further, the 1937–38 leadership purge, in which three marshals and some 400 generals were "liquidated," left a nervous group of generally second-rate officers. On the other hand, the Red Army's equipment was not as backward as is sometimes portrayed: it had excellent tanks and guns in ever-increasing quantities, and its tactical doctrine was well-founded. There were

eventually whole armies of tanks, but artillery was the Red Army's principal weapon—"The God of War," as Stalin called it. Discipline was draconian and commanders were expected to drive their troops into action as long as even one man remained standing.

Despite the dominance and all-pervading influence of the Communist Party, and the draconian measures it sometimes used against its own people, there can be no doubt that the vast bulk of the Soviet Army was loyal to Mother Russia. The officers and soldiers in the units underwent extraordinary hardships and in the end they outmaneuvered and outfought the Germans who, in 1941–42, had held them in such low esteem.

"territorials," although these were rapidly supplemented by conscripts as the war progressed. The second element was the very large, all-volunteer Indian Army, which, although a separate organization, was under British direction, and British and Indian units served side-by-side in formations from brigade upwards. There were also similar but much smaller forces raised in the British colonial territories, such as Burma, Malaya, and various African colonies. In a separate category were the forces from the "old Dominions" such as Australia, Canada, New Zealand, and South Africa, which owed allegiance to their home government but were generally placed under British command. Toward the end of the war, Australian and New Zealand forces also came under United States command.

Above: General Dwight D. Eisenhower speaks with U.S. paratroopers before they take off for France, June 5, 1944. Eisenhower was promoted rapidly, but proved to be an ideal Supreme Allied Commander.

Below: British general Bernard Montgomery was a highly professional officer. He was sometimes difficult, particularly with Eisenhower, but he won battles, which is what generals are paid to do.

The British Army had carried out many tactical experiments during the interwar years, but, even so, the war started in a period of self-inflicted confusion about military doctrine and with the task of transforming an imperial police force into a modern army. This was done with remarkable success, and the most flattering tributes paid to it came from its German opponents, but it took time.

It is important to note that what were described as "British land forces" were actually composed of a number of separate elements. First, there was the British Army proper, which was recruited and based in the United Kingdom; at the start of the war this was a relatively small, all-volunteer force, backed by part-time

The latecomer to the conflict, the U.S. Army, was regarded by the Germans as over-civilized and soft, but the basic U.S. doctrine was to have the best weapons available and to use equipment and munitions to save lives. The U.S. Army was highly successful, being admirably designed to make the best use of American technological know-how and of its well-educated, technically minded soldiers.

U.S. Army generals were among the most outstanding in the war, and while some were inexperienced at the outbreak of hostilities, that was quickly cured. Among the very best were Bradley, MacArthur, and Patton, but in a quite separate class of his own was Eisenhower. Known everywhere as "Ike," he was a little-known colonel at the outbreak of war and had never commanded anything larger than a battalion. Despite this, he was personally selected by General Marshall, the U.S. Army's chief of staff, to be Supreme Allied Commander in Europe, jumping over the heads of several hundred more senior officers. This step was triumphantly vindicated by his success

in the post, where his tact and diplomacy played a major role in keeping a bunch of fractious sub-ordinates, such as the British Montgomery and the American Patton, concentrating on fighting the Germans rather than each other. At the fighting level the junior officers and the GIs proved in all the campaigns in which they participated, whether in Europe, the Mediterranean, or the Pacific, that they learned very fast, and could fight as long and as hard as any other soldier in the world.

In the Far East the Japanese army was initially seriously underrated by the American and British armies, and territories such as the Philippines and Malaya were quickly overrun. However, both armies regrouped and retrained and were then able to defeat various Japanese armies in the field, before the atomic bombs brought the war to an end.

## TECHNOLOGICAL ADVANCES

Study of land warfare in the years 1919–39 reveals a number of advances. First was the

Below: PzKpfw IV tank of the German Afrika Korps. The desert war was famous for its fast movement, rapid reversals of fortune, and the militarily correct way in which it was fought. It was, however, a sideshow, in particular for the Germans, who often found themselves dragged into these situations by their Italian allies.

increase in the basic speed of warfare in the land battle, which had been predicted by military thinkers such as the British J. F. C. Fuller and the American W. Mitchell. Such men outlined their ideas in the 1920s for fast-moving, deep-penetration attacks with wide outflanking movements directed against headquarters and communications centers in the rear areas. Twenty years later this theory became reality as the Germans showed how it should be done in the *blitzkrieg* (lightning war), which overwhelmed Poland in 1939 and western Europe in 1940.

While tanks and motorized transport were the manifestations of such operations, it was radio that made it possible to give instant orders over long distances, while reductions in size made it possible to carry a set inside the turret of a tank. Thus, field commanders could move with their formations, but remain in contact with superior headquarters; all levels of command could be continuously fed with up-to-date information; and, perhaps the most important of all, plans could be changed while forces were on the move. The tank became the symbol of mobile warfare, but it was radio that told it what to do and when to do it.

The infantry gained little from interwar developments and went into battle in 1939 with few changes from the equipment they had used in 1918, still marching on foot and carrying a heavy rifle. In gunnery there had been advances in range but the most significant development, as with the tanks, was the use of radio to direct and control the guns. Progress had also been made in making the guns more mobile.

One of the most significant operational developments was the introduction of airborne troops, in which the Soviet Red Army played a major role, making the first experiments and showing the way. Germany developed the idea and brought it to the point where airborne attacks formed a substantial and decisive part of the blitzkrieg, and their example was followed by Britain, the U.S., and Japan, but there were different organizational patterns. In Germany, the paratroops belonged to the *Luftwaffe*, while in America, Britain, and Russia, they were part of the army, but the Japanese found their own answer with both the army and the navy raising their own airborne forces.

## NAVAL FORCES

When the German High Seas Fleet steamed into captivity on November 21, 1918, Britain's

Above: The British battlecruiser HMS *Hood* was the epitome of British naval power for twenty years, but its mighty and graceful appearance camouflaged some serious weaknesses.

*15*

The prospect of such an economically crippling armaments race was so daunting that U.S. President Harding called a conference of the major naval powers at Washington and on February 6, 1922, a Naval Limitations Treaty was signed (usually known as the "Washington Naval Treaty"). This established a ratio in overall naval strengths of Britain—5: United States—5: Japan—3: France—1: and Italy—0.75. Further limitations on individual types of ships, both by tonnage and gun caliber, were also laid down; cruisers, for example, were limited to 10,000 tons displacement and guns to no more than 8 in. (203 mm) caliber. Aircraft carriers were similarly limited, both in total and in individual characteristics.

The German navy was in an unusual position, since it was restricted by the Versailles Treaty to surface warships of not more than 10,000 tons (and no U-boats at all), but since it had not been invited to attend, it was unaffected by either the Washington or London treaties. In the 1920s it made a modest revival with a few light cruisers and then built the 12,000-ton "pocket battleships," which were intended for employment as commerce raiders. However, since 1934, following Hitler's rise to power, Germany had been secretly evading the clause of the Versailles Treaty that forbade it to build submarines.

## THE END OF THE BATTLE CRUISER

Until the 1930s, capital ships were divided into two classes. One was the battleship, which had heavy armor and heavy guns, but was not particularly fast. The other was the battle cruiser, which had a similarly heavy armament, but was capable of much higher speeds, which was achieved by a very light armored protection; it was described as being able to outshoot any ship that could catch it, but outrun any ship that could outshoot it. However, technological advances in marine propulsion and hull design meant that the final generation of battleships could be fast, as well as heavily gunned and well armored, and the day of the battle cruiser—always a dangerous hybrid—was over. Prime examples were the Italian battleships *Littorio* and *Vittorio Veneto* laid down in 1934, which had a displacement of 41,167 tons and an armament of nine 15 in. guns, and were well-armored, but were able to travel at 30 knots.

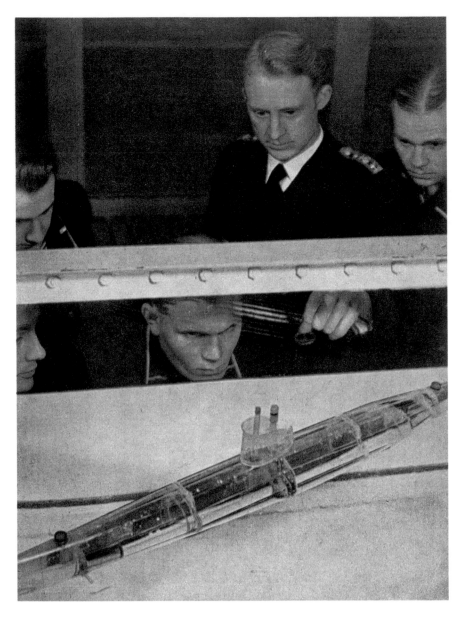

Above: German submariners under instruction at a prewar training school. Such men and the U-boats they manned were to have strategic effects out of all proportion to their numbers.

Previous pages: All but a very few World War II battleships were built under the restrictions of the Washington and London Naval Treaties, which imposed strict limits on individual and collective tonnages, as well as the caliber and number of main guns.

Royal Navy, with a strength of 41 Dreadnought battleships and battle cruisers, was incomparably the most numerous and powerful in the world. This was not, however, to last for long, since in 1916 both the United States and Japan had announced huge naval building programs, the former firmly stating its intention to acquire a "navy second to none." Thus, before World War I had even ended a naval arms race was already underway.

Japan's intention was to build a fleet of eight battleships and eight battle cruisers, to which the United States responded with a plan for ten new battleships and six battle cruisers over the next five years, together with many cruisers and more than 80 destroyers. Great Britain could not at first accept even equality of naval strength with any other single power, and its naval estimates for 1921 provided for four new battle cruisers and a number of battleships.

Such fast battleships made all existing battleships obsolete just as the Dreadnought had done thirty years earlier. When the Washington Treaty and the London Naval Treaty of 1930 lapsed at the end of 1936, therefore, America and Britain both embarked upon a program of fast battleships.

## RAEDER'S PLAN Z

The Germans signed a Naval Agreement with Britain in 1935, but this was a subterfuge designed to disguise their long-term intentions, which were embodied in the top-secret Plan Z. In this plan, it was intended to abrogate the Anglo-German agreement at a suitable moment, following which the fleet would be built up into to an ultramodern force of eight battleships, five battle cruisers, four aircraft carriers, over 200 submarines, and a large number of cruisers and destroyers. Fortunately for Germany's enemies, Plan Z was geared to a completion date of 1944 or 1945, so that when war broke out on September 3, 1939, only the two battleships, five cruisers, and one aircraft carrier were under construction (and, in the event, the carrier was never to be completed). Further, the U-boat arm had only 57 submarines in commission on the outbreak of war, of which 27 were ocean-going and the remainder coastal types

Even more than in World War I, therefore, the German surface fleet would not be able directly to challenge the British and, as will be seen, it was deployed instead on commerce raiding operations except for the brief interlude of the Norwegian Campaign. In the Mediterranean, on the other hand, Mussolini's Italian fleet, centered on four modernized Dreadnought battleships and including a powerful force of armored 8 in. cruisers, would in theory be superior to any fleet the British could deploy there, and distinctly so when the battleships *Littorio* and *Vittorio Veneto* were commissioned in 1940.

In 1918, the British absorbed their naval and military air services into a single, independent Royal Air Force, but by the 1930s had come to realize that shipborne naval aviation needed to be under naval command and control. Thus, in 1937 these air assets returned to the Admiralty as the Fleet Air Arm. By the outbreak of war, the Royal Navy had seven carriers in commission and more building, and

these were recognized as an integral and essential part of any naval force.

As regards submarine warfare, the British lulled themselves into a false sense of security as a result of the invention of the "Asdic" system of using sound pulses to detect and direct attacks on a submerged submarines.[1] This was thought to provide a complete answer to the submarine threat, but experience of its use in war showed that, while a very major advance, it was not quite the infallible system it was originally made out to be.

---

[1]Asdic was short for "Anti-Submarine Detection and Interception Committee," the body responsible for the device. Its more modern term is Sonar (SOund Navigation And Ranging), which will be used in this book.

Above: British naval aircraft were provided by the RAF from 1918 to 1937, when they passed to Admiralty control as the Fleet Air Arm. Even so, some wartime aircraft were of obsolete design, such as this Albacore biplane torpedo bomber.

Below: In the interwar years the German navy was determined to restore at least part of its might, which had been destroyed by the Versailles Treaty. The first fruits of this expansion were the "pocket battleships."

Above: A kamikaze pilot adjusts his *hachimaki*, a traditional headband wrapped around the head by a sumurai before donning his helmet, both as extra padding and to keep sweat from running into his eyes. Suicide pilots became a great menace for Allied warships, although, with hindsight, the actual damage they inflicted was not as great as it appeared at the time.

grievous losses, including the battle cruisers *Hood* and *Repulse*, battleship *Prince of Wales*, and aircraft carrier *Ark Royal*. One of its finest moments, however, came in the Normandy invasion when, in company with the U.S. Navy, a vast naval force of warships, landing craft, and ships succeeded in placing a huge army safely ashore in France, in the most daring and complicated amphibious operation ever undertaken.

The sailors of the U.S. Navy started the war under the shadow of the devastating blow of Pearl Harbor, but their natural resilience quickly turned that name into a rallying cry. The expansion was very rapid and vast numbers of men were produced to crew the armadas in the Atlantic and Pacific Oceans. Of greatest

The other main technological advance during the interwar years was the development of radar (RAdio Detection And Ranging), which was initially used to detect approaching aircraft far beyond visible range. However, it was also found to be able to detect surface ships and then to control ships' guns, the latter revolutionizing the science of naval gunnery.

The Royal Navy started the war as the largest in the world, but its global commitments and heavy early losses meant that it was steadily overhauled by the U.S. Navy, which by 1943 had become the predominant partner. The officers and sailors of the Royal Navy fought hard throughout the war, their engagements ranging from the big ship battles in which German ships such as *Graf Spee* and *Bismarck* were sunk to the corvettes, sloops, and frigates that defeated the German U-boats in the Atlantic. The Royal Navy also suffered some significance was the development of airpower, which included the carriers, the aircraft, and, even more important, the trained manpower to operate them effectively and efficiently.

The only other major naval power, Japan, was manned by tough and resilient officers and sailors. Their navy had played only a limited part in World War I, but every one of them knew of the Japanese triumph over the Russians at the Battle of the Straits of Tsushima in 1905. As a result, they had great pride in both their service and themselves, which seemed to be warranted in the early successes at Pearl Harbor and the victories in early 1942. Thereafter, they continued to be determined, but now it was in the face of impending defeat, and it was the Imperial Japanese Navy that introduced the word *kamikaze* (suicide missions) to the international lexicon. One branch of the Imperial Navy that failed to distinguish itself was the submarine service, whose strategy of attacking mainly warships was flawed, and its tactics were poor, primarily because the submarines were so large and lacking in maneuverability. Submarine captains were also responsible for some shocking atrocities, particularly against the crews of American and British merchant ships.

## AIR FORCES

The enormity of the conflict that followed Germany's invasion of Poland in the fall of 1939 caught even the German Luftwaffe unprepared. But the air forces of all the other countries

Left: During the interwar years the Japanese navy built a large submarine fleet ranging from some of the biggest boats in the world to the smallest, such as this Type C two-man midget. During the war they achieved some successes, but overall their results were very disappointing.

involved were even more inadequately equipped. Biplanes were still front-line fighters in both America and Britain, and Germany and Japan led the fighter field in their theaters. But in the end it was the foresight of the Allied powers, who had not neglected the development of heavy bombers, that was to expose the fatal flaws in the strategic planning of their enemies. Nonetheless, there were some strange aircraft types among that motley array that lined up on each side in 1939, ready to do battle in the first major war in the air.

## THE SITUATION IN 1939

What mattered in 1939 was that the Luftwaffe had been given numbers of operational aircraft that none of its immediate opponents could hope to match. It did not matter at the time (nor was it apparent to either the leaders or the aircrew) that those numbers had been delivered at the expense of far more important, long-term designs. The Luftwaffe's lineup in September 1939 was perfectly capable of beating the air arms of every single neighbor of Germany, and its aircraft had more than enough range for the job. But the watchword for the entire German Wehrmacht had always been "one target at a time." Every single international crisis in Hitler's expansionist policy since the occupation of the Rhineland in 1936 had left no reserves to spare, and the same applied to the Polish campaign in 1939. There was not even a central fighter force for the defense of the Reich, although this oversight was as much due to Hermann Göring's arrogance as to Adolf Hitler's refusal to sanction

the earmarking of any resources for purely defensive duties.

Of the Western Allies, France was undoubtedly in the worst state as far as its air arm was concerned and as a result the French placed a wildly exaggerated confidence in the capacity of the RAF to launch heavy bombing attacks on Germany. The fact was, however, that the trio of twin-engined British bombers then in service—Hampden, Wellington, and Whitley—were inadequate for the task, although the first two of the crucial four-engined bombers were in an advanced stage of development.

The Luftwaffe of September 1939 was more than a match for the Allied opposition, but it, too, had much to learn. The dive-bombing units—later to contribute one of the most dreaded words of the war, Stuka (from SturzKAampfflugzeug = dive-bomber)—had yet to be tried in action in close collaboration with mobile ground troops, while the other ground-attack aircraft was an obsolescent biplane. The most serious weakness in the fighter arm still lay concealed: the concept of the "destroyer" fighter. Meanwhile, Germany's partner, Italy, was unready for war in any shape or form and its air force, the Regia Aeronautica, lacked any aircraft, either fighters or bombers, that could be described as "world-class."

In Britain the RAF was reequipping with monoplane fighters, and on the outbreak of war there were fourteen Hurricane and nine Spitfire squadrons operational, although the biplane Gladiator was still in service, while the Boulton Paul Defiant, a fighter with a rear turret, was in service but about to be exposed by the Messerschmitt Me 109 in the skies over Dunkirk as a death trap.

Due to the nonaggression pact it had signed with Germany in August 1939, Soviet Russia remained neutral until attacked by Germany in mid-1941. Although it had taken part in the Spanish Civil War, the Soviet Air Force operated a mixed bag of obsolescent aircraft and it was as well that it did not have to face the full might of the Luftwaffe in 1939 or 1940.

Japan, the third member of the Axis bloc in September 1939, had been involved in all-out war with China for over two years, but this was no polite war, respecting civilian lives and property, but the full, brutal experience. By September 1939, the Japanese forces had a number of excellent designs, including the Zero fighter and the Mitsubishi G3M Nell and Ki-21 Sally twin-engined bombers. These gave an indication of the shape of things to come in the Far East by their impressive operations against Chinese coastal cities, flying from southern Japan and Formosa.

## THE VITAL FUEL FACTOR

One of the vital long term problems for all three Axis powers was that of fuel to keep the tanks and land transport moving and aircraft flying, and here the scales were bound to tip against them in the longer term.

It seemed inconceivable that Germany would be able to wage a war on all fronts, although the genius of Albert Speer created an almost incredible output of synthetic fuel in the latter years of the war. At the start of the war, however, the Allies were totally unable to mount any kind of efficient bombing offensive against the main sources of German oil supply. Fuel problems were even greater where Italy and Japan were concerned—indeed, America's economic cold-shouldering of Japan in 1940–41 was the factor that determined Japanese strategists to make an all-out bid to seize and hold the oil-producing regions of the Pacific before it was too late. The situation at the end of the war—both in the European and Pacific theaters—proved this to the hilt, with German and Japanese tanks stationary and aircraft constantly grounded (and training of replacement crews drastically cut) for a lack of fuel.

Above: Brigadier General James H. Doolittle, U.S. Army Air Corps (foreground, left), and Admiral Marc A. Mitscher (foreground, right) aboard USS *Hornet* (CV-8), April 1942. They are en route to the launching of Doolittle's B-25 bombers for their attack on Japan—a daring, imaginative, and very courageous raid that demonstrated to the Japanese that their homeland was not immune to retribution.

## THE AIRMEN

All the major air forces involved in the war fought hard and well, and all produced fighter "aces," although none in such numbers, and with such high scores, as the German Luftwaffe. These fighter aces deserved the acclaim they received, but they also overshadowed other aircrew, such as those manning level bombers, dive-bombers, and antisubmarine aircraft, whose missions were not only equally as hazardous and demanding of a high a level of professional skill, but which also required dogged and sustained endurance not usually necessary in the much shorter and less frequent fighter missions. In most air forces the short-comings were almost always more the result of poor equipment—particularly aircraft—rather than problems with the aircrew themselves. Thus, Italy never produced a successful fighter in meaningful quantities, while the Germans had excellent fighters but relatively poor twin-engined bombers and no effective four-engined bombers at all.

Probably the finest all-around air commanders were found in the United States forces, and included such men as Spaatz, Doolittle, Le May, and Chennault. In the Royal Air Force, the great fighter leaders were at group and wing levels, although Dowding towers over other higher commanders for his exceptional leadership during the Battle of Britain. Similarly, Harris, the leader of RAF Bomber Command,

was among the great air commanders, although it is worth noting that both Harris and Dowding were treated shabbily once their usefulness had passed. The success of air leadership in Germany was distorted by the activities of Hermann Göring, who was both the architect of the Luftwaffe and one of its main problems, as he used it to achieve his political ends in the maneuvering within the upper levels of the Nazi party.

## THE WAR IN THE PACIFIC

The war with Japan was quite different in nature from that against Germany and Italy in Europe, and to achieve a greater understanding it is necessary to examine the background in more detail. The United States and Japan sided with the Allies in World War I. Japan seized the

Above: One of the numerous conflicts during the buildup to World War II was the Sino-Japanese War, in which the numerically inferior but militarily far superior Japanese inflicted humiliating defeats on their enemy. Here Japanese infantrymen celebrate their conquest on top of the walls of Nanking. After taking the city they then undertook a program of rape and pillage that ranks as one of the major war crimes of World War II.

Left: For Axis and Allies alike, each armored regiment, such as this Free French unit, required large amounts of fuel every day and the total requirement was enormous. But the Allies had ready access to unlimited sources of gasoline, the shipping to bring it to Europe, and the organization and trucking capacity to deliver it to the front line. Germany enjoyed no such advantages and by 1944 fuel shortages were commonplace; by 1945 aircraft and tanks were increasingly immobilized by a complete lack of fuel.

Above: Japan acquired numerous small territories under League of Nations mandates in the early 1920s, but was hungry for a far larger prize—China. Here, Japanese marines arrive in Shanghai aboard a cruiser on August 18, 1937.

opportunity to absorb German holdings in China as well as the central Pacific islands that Germany had bought from Spain. The United States, however, had no territorial ambitions and concentrated its attention on restoring the power balance in Europe, although it did, of course, have an interest in maintaining its lines of communication to the Philippines. The Treaty of Versailles that officially ended World War I in 1919 awarded Japan "trusteeship" over Tinian and Saipan in the Marianas, as well as the Palaus, the Carolines, and the Marshalls. This was confirmed by League of Nations mandate. Meanwhile, having taken over the German possessions in China, the Japanese asserted economic control over Manchuria, although it

still paid lip service to the "open door" policy, which supposedly ensured equal economic opportunity in China for all foreign nations.

One consequence of the League of Nations trusteeship agreements was that the Pacific islands now controlled by Japan lay athwart the United States' vital routes between Hawaii and the Philippines, causing concern to the government in Washington. Meanwhile, Great Britain was worried that the emergence of Japan as a major naval power would jeopardize British colonial territories in Hong Kong, Malaya, and Burma. China, however, was threatened even more directly and feared for its very existence.

Against this backdrop, U.S. President Harding convened the 1921 Washington Naval

mainland, and in September 1931 started the invasion of Manchuria. China protested to the League of Nations, which issued a very mild reprimand to Japan, but even that was too much for the Japanese militarists and their country withdrew from the league.

The 1921 Washington Naval Treaty included a review after ten years, and new negotiations started in London in 1930, with a brilliant young officer named Yamamoto serving as Japan's technical adviser. The outcome was the London Naval Treaty, which extended the agreements for a further five years, but with some concessions to the Japanese, although the proportion of 5:5:3 for battleships and aircraft carriers remained unaltered. As the 1930 pact drew to an end, Yamamoto took part in another attempt to modify the hated ratio, but when the U.S. and Great Britain refused, Japan broke off the talks and in 1937 approved the construction of the world's largest battleships, the 72,000-ton *Yamato* and *Musashi*.

In July 1937 the Japanese army used Manchukuo as a springboard for an assault on China, and Roosevelt tried to maintain correct, though not cordial, relations with Japan, in the hope that the mounting costs of the war would discredit the Japanese militarists and bring to power a government willing to write off the venture as a bad gamble. Unfortunately, the United States had little influence on Japanese behavior, and there was a series of incidents which led the U.S. president to allow the commercial treaty with Japan to expire. He also extended credit to China and imposed an embargo on a lengthening list of war materials

Below: The scale of Japanese ambitions was exemplified by the two Yamato-class battleships, which were the largest and most powerful ever built. They took a long time to build and consumed vast resources, but proved to be abysmal failures, designed to fight a type of naval warfare that had disappeared, and were destroyed by the very airpower that had overtaken them.

Conference with the aim of preventing a naval armaments race, keeping Great Britain from siding with Japan in any Pacific war, and reducing the possibility of such a conflict. As mentioned above, the treaty established a tonnage ratio of 5:5:3 among the U.S., Great Britain, and Japan and also prevented them from fortifying their outlying possessions, although the British naval base at Singapore, then under construction, was excluded.

Japanese attitudes hardened as the decade wore on and the 5:5:3 ratio came to be seen as a national humiliation; indeed, a group of aggressive army officers branded it as "the navy's failure." This army group was intent upon seizing a bridgehead on the Asian

Above: A British antiaircraft gun battery in Hong Kong, early 1942. The gun position is well laid out and spotlessly clean, and the troops smart and efficient, but they represented a way of life that had disappeared and were quickly overwhelmed by the vigorous and unconventional Japanese troops.

Previous pages: The attack on Pearl Harbor took place on December 7, 1941. At the time the Japanese thought it to be a national triumph, but in reality it was the first step on a long and painful road to national disaster.

destined for Japan, including aluminum for aircraft production and aviation gasoline.

In April 1940 Roosevelt decided to reinforce his measures in the Pacific with a modest show of force by directing that the Pacific Fleet should remain in Hawaiian waters after completing its annual exercises, shifting its base from California to Pearl Harbor. Even this did not deter the Japanese and in the following month, when France collapsed in the face of German might, Japan extorted the first in a series of concessions in French Indochina, which included the right to build airfields, access to the rice harvest, and use of the airport at Saigon.

Meanwhile, events in Europe caused even more complications for Japan, when the Germans signed the nonaggression pact with the USSR in August 1939. Then, in September 1940, Japan, Germany, and Italy signed the Tripartite Pact, each agreeing to go to the other's aid in the event of an attack by a power not already involved in the European conflict or the war in China. Japan also obtained further assurance of a free hand in Asia by negotiating a nonaggression treaty with the Soviet Union, which was signed in April 1941.

Yamamoto, now an admiral, warned that, "A war between Japan and the United States would be a major calamity for the world, and for Japan it would mean, after several years of war already [in China], acquiring yet another powerful enemy—an extremely perilous matter for the nation. . . . It is necessary, therefore, that both Japan and America should seek every means to avoid a direct clash." But the German alliance was made and as Japan drifted closer to war with the United States, Yamamoto became convinced that every Japanese, himself included, had to fall in line behind the emperor, whatever the risk to the nation.

Perhaps as early as January 1941, Yamamoto concluded that the best strategy would be to attack the American Pacific Fleet at Pearl Harbor in order to gain time to seize the Philippines, Malaya, Burma, and the Netherlands East Indies, thus acquiring an empire rich in oil, ore, rice, and other resources. Other officers, especially in the army, believed that Japan would prevail in such a conflict, since the Americans lacked the discipline and courage to recover from the initial Japanese victories; the U.S. would not pay the price in blood and

treasure to roll back the tide, and the war would end in a negotiated settlement.

In July 1941, Japan, after nibbling away at French Indochina, decided to grab what remained and Roosevelt reacted by imposing an embargo on supplying American oil to Japan and freezing Japanese assets in the United States. The United Kingdom and the Netherlands government-in-exile also impounded Japanese funds, so that Japan could no longer buy oil from the usual Dutch or American suppliers. Imports of crude oil and petroleum products, which totaled almost 40 million barrels during the year ending in March 1941, slowed overnight to a comparative trickle from Latin America and the Near East. In the fall of 1941, Japan's oil reserves amounted to some 50 million barrels, and the temptation to invest that reserve in a war of conquest to gain the vast output of the Netherlands East Indies proved irresistible; thus, the economic pressure, designed to discourage aggression, actually accelerated the movement toward war.

On October 17 General Tojo took over as prime minister, while, in Washington, the Japanese ambassador, Admiral Nomura,

persisted in his negotiations with the U.S. government but was not permitted to offer any concessions. American intelligence was intercepting, decoding, and translating Japanese diplomatic traffic, so that American officials sometimes read Nomura's instructions from Tokyo before he did; no wonder the product of the cryptanalysts was called "Magic"!

Unfortunately, American cryptanalysts were unable to break the Japanese naval codes, making them ignorant of the content of Yamamoto's messages. Thus, they had to try to draw conclusions from the volume and source of the traffic and the call signs and transmitting characteristics of the radio operators, and were unaware that the Japanese fleet was closing in for its fateful attack on Pearl Harbor.

As the Japanese steamed toward Hawaii, peacetime routine prevailed on the ships of America's Pacific Fleet, and in the offices and workshops on the base. It was a normal Saturday morning until all hell broke loose as the Japanese planes dropped their bombs and launched their torpedoes, aided by attacks from surface ships and submarines. The Pacific war had begun, noisily, early on December 7, 1941.

Above: Newspapers in both the United States and Great Britain report the Japanese attack and the United States's declaration of war. There were major disasters to come, but there could be no turning back now.

31

# WAR
# IN
# EUROPE

## Chapter 1

# THE WAR ON LAND

In 1939 AND 1940 THE GERMAN ARMIES swept all before them with unstoppable speed. But then Hitler turned against Russia, leaving Great Britain undefeated and determined in his rear. Hitler's gamble in Russia seemed to have paid off at first. But the arrival of winter in 1941 halted his forces and, while the following year proved moderately successful, then came disaster at Stalingrad. Meanwhile, in the heat of Africa and southern Europe, Hitler's armies came up against the battle-hardened Allied opponents who proved as forceful, skilled, and well-equipped as his own. Ultimately overcoming the stalemate, the Allies set about the liberation of Europe from the German yoke, and in June 1944 came the greatest seaborne invasion of all time: the landings in Normandy, otherwise known as Operation Overlord. With the Western Allies pushing on from France and the Russians surging from the east, Germany's end in the spring of 1945 was certain. But its death throes exacted a terrible cost on both sides. Hitler committed suicide on April 30, and within days his war machine was finally destroyed, with the unconditional surrender taking place on May 8.

Right: An American Sherman tank grinds its way through a ruined town in Italy during the battle for Rome. The German army rarely surrendered a city without a fight, resulting in bitter close-quarter engagements and the type of damage seen here.

Previous pages: Troops of the U.S. 3rd Armored Division in the streets of the German city of Cologne in 1945. The devastation that Hitler and the Nazis brought upon the German people is only too apparent, although the twin towers of the cathedral remain to inspire hope in the future.

Was there some secret to the successes of the German army in 1939–41? Some suggest that Hitler's Germany was geared to aggression and that his armored divisions, with close support from dive-bombers, were bound to carve through old-fashioned, infantry-based armies deployed in linear defense. But, as far as the tactics were concerned, the Germans had devised a new form of attack in 1917–18, which was based on small groups of elite troops—the *Stosstruppen* and *Sturmabteilungen*—whose mission was to thrust as deeply as their momentum would carry them into the heart of the enemy defense system, with the officers leading from the front, and without regard for flank security. Then, too, there was the invention of the tank and the tactical theories of British military thinkers such as Fuller, Broad, and Liddel Hart, whose writings caught the imagination of the men rebuilding the German army, notably Heinz Guderian, who never again wished to see the stagnation of trench warfare.

The tactics of the blitzkrieg[1] were the result of uniting infiltration tactics with the tank and then substituting dive-bombers for slow-moving heavy artillery. But the real secret was the combat training of the German soldier, and it was not the tanks or aircraft that counted so much as the men inside, and the infantry of the motorized divisions who worked with them.

Below: In their first major conquest of the war, these German PzKpfw II Ausf. C. light tanks advance through the streets of Warsaw, the Polish capital. In this campaign German tanks established a reputation for effectiveness, which was more the result of brilliant handling than technical excellence.

It is said that a fish rots from the head first and in 1939–40 the leadership of France had neither the will nor the knowledge to fight a modern war; moreover, this weakness was compounded by vain (and totally misplaced) confidence in the superiority of the French army over all others. The leadership of the French army and air forces was equally decayed, the generals being cautious and expecting a repetition of the 1914–18 war. Their theory of war was based on a linear defense centered upon a fortified belt of frontier bulwarks, the Maginot Line, whose main weakness was that it went no further north than the Belgium-Luxembourg frontier for fear of offending the Belgians.

Further, although some 22 divisions were not committed to the front line, they were not organized into a large, properly organized reserve army, or *mass de manoeuvre*, for decisive use once the enemy's point of main effort had become clear. As for modern weapons, the tanks were of mixed quality and not properly organized or deployed, there were few aircraft suitable for cooperation with the army, and the inept command system in any case did not cater for it.

In May 1940 some 2,500,000 German troops stood poised on the country's western borders: Army Group B (Bock) with 30 divisions

[1]Curiously, the name, which means "lightning war," was coined by an American war reporter and was not the German army's own name for these tactics.

Above: German eight-wheeled, armored command vehicle advancing through Luxembourg in 1940, epitomizing the speed of advance that totally outwitted British and French commanders. The frame is a high-frequency radio antenna.

Below: During the early campaigns of the war, the German Ju-87—the dreaded Stuka—established an awesome reputation, but experience was to show it was only effective when the Nazis had air supremacy.

Right: A Char B1 lies abandoned in a street in a French town during the German attack in 1940. These were good tanks for their time, but were handled badly. They also suffered from their very small turrets, which required one man to command the tank as well as load and fire the gun.

Below: A German PzKpfw II and an infantryman during the campaign in France in 1940. A poorly trained, badly led, and demoralized French army provided little resistance to the German advance.

in the north; Army Group A (Rundstedt) with 44 divisions in the center; and Army Group C (Leeb) with 17 divisions in the south. The key element in the coming campaign was to be the 2,574 Panzers (tanks), most of which were in Army Group A. The other key element was the Luftwaffe, which fielded some 3,500 aircraft in two air fleets. Hitler was in overall command, with Army General Brauchitsch in direct control of the battle.

Opposing the Germans were some 2,000,000 men of the French forces and the British Expeditionary Force (BEF), under the overall command of French General Georges. These consisted of First Army Group (Billotte) in the north, Second Army Group (Pretelat)

behind the Maginot Line in the center, and Third Army Group (Besson) actually manning the Maginot Line defenses. The Allies deployed in the expectation that the Germans would rerun the World War I Schlieffen plan with an attack through Belgium. But, unknown to them, a new plan, devised by General von Manstein, involved the main thrust coming through the heavily wooded Ardennes, an area which the Allies considered to be impassable to tanks. The Belgian (600,000 men) and Dutch (400,000 men) national armies had been mobilized, but in compliance with their neutral status neither had discussed their defense plans either with each other or with anyone else.

The French army had 3,100 tanks, of which 2,285 were modern, including 800 of the powerful Char B and Somua types, armed with 75 mm and 47 mm guns. These were pitted against some 2,500 German tanks of all types, but 1,400 were lightly armed PzKpfw IIs,[2] eked out by obsolete PzKpfw Is; thus only 627 of the attacking Panzers were the really battle worthy PzKpfw IIIs and IVs, armed with 37 mm and a short 75 mm gun respectively. The German tanks, however, were grouped into hard-hitting, highly mobile Panzer divisions, whereas the great majority of French tanks were distributed throughout the army formations, apart from a few in the newly formed *Divisions Cuirassiers*, but these were wrongly organized. To add to the French shortcomings, the whole command-and-control system was defective, slow-moving, and unresponsive, right down to the tanks, few of which had radio sets.

At least some of the French weaknesses could have been remedied by determined leadership and vigorous training between the declaration of war in 1939 and the German onslaught on May 10, 1940. Instead, absolutely nothing was done, with no apparent attempt to evaluate the lessons of the Polish campaign, nor were any staff exercises or maneuvers conducted. The staff, although intelligent and full of theory, sat at their desks and tried to prepare for and run a war using peacetime office

[2] 'PzKpfw' is the German abbreviation for *Panzerkampfwagen*, the German name for a tank. Different types were denoted by a Roman numeral (i.e., PzKpfw IV) and some of the later models also had names (e.g., Tiger).

Below: Any watching Frenchman would have been humiliated by this scene as German soldiers parade in captured French Somua tanks, which were designated PzKpfw 35C 739(f) by the Wehrmacht.

Right: A German *fallschirmjäger* (paratrooper) leaps from a Junkers Ju-52 during the attack on the Netherlands in 1940. Note his spread-eagle position and the static line that will deploy his parachute automatically. All German World War II paratroops belonged to Göring's Luftwaffe and not to the army, as was the case in most other nations.

methods, with the result that the French formations proved to be incapable of the simplest maneuvers. Worst of all, the vast mass of conscripts and reservists called up to the colors in 1939–40 were none too pleased to be in uniform nor were they very clear about what this *"drôle de guerre"* was about; then, to make matters even worse, they were left idle for months in a very cold winter.[3] So, when battle was joined the bulk of the officers were ill-informed and arrogant, while the majority of the troops were bored, disillusioned, sullen, and ill-disciplined— it was a recipe for disaster.

The "phony war" ended dramatically on May 10, 1940, when the Germans opened their campaign with four paratroop landings in the

Netherlands and a glider-borne assault on Fort Eben Emael in Belgium, while on the ground Army Groups A and B crossed the Belgian and Dutch borders. The main weight of the German offensive was in the Ardennes, which, because of its assumed impassability, was defended by category B divisions, mostly reservists, of the 2nd (French) Army (Corap). Corap sent a recon force of cavalry and light tanks forward, which met the main German armored force advancing on May 11, and was severely mauled.

The Germans quickly advanced to the Meuse, a rapidly flowing river some 200 ft. wide and considered unfordable, while Corap and his subordinate commanders indulged in some wishful thinking, persuading themselves that, despite evidence to the contrary, the Germans would not cross the river. Their error became clear at precisely noon on May 13, when German Stuka dive-bombers began a large-scale attack on the French 2nd Army. The explosions, noise, and, above all, the characteristic howl from the windmills under the Stukas' wings had a dramatic effect on French morale, even though their actual casualties were surprisingly light. The air attack ceased at 4:00 P.M. as suddenly as it had begun, but German 88 mm antiaircraft guns then came into play, using direct fire to demolish those concrete bunkers that had resisted the Stukas' bombs. After all this, the forward French troops did little to resist the German attack, which swept over the river.

Any French counterattacks that were attempted were only halfhearted.

By dawn the first German armor was across the river and inevitably suffered a period of vulnerability in the first hours as its strength slowly built up, but the French totally failed to exploit their opportunities. The Panzers started to advance at about 7:30 A.M. and met a French counterattack near the town of Chemery; the German tanks destroyed the French tanks, whereupon the defending infantry fled.

The same occurred further to the north, where the 7th Panzer Division crossed the Meuse on May 13, led from the front by its dynamic but then-unknown commander, Major General Erwin Rommel. The French counterattacked but, after some initial success, they ran out of momentum and failed.

French problems were now becoming cyclical. Morale was low, many units were disintegrating, rumors were rife, and confusion abounded, leading to yet further lowering of morale. In the center, the inept Corap was sacked, but his relief, Giraud, one of the best of the French generals, was captured by a German patrol only five days later.

In such a situation, the Germans swept on, reaching the Channel coast at Abbeville and then swinging north, arriving at Boulogne on May 25 and cutting the northern Anglo-French

[3]By contrast, the British Expeditionary Force was worked incessantly.

Above, right: The surface of the Belgian fortress at Eban-Emäel after the German attack by *Oberleutnant* Witzig and his parachute engineers. The fort was manned by a large garrison, but they were split up into many small groups manning individual guns, and once the Germans were inside the defenders were picked off, section by section.

Above, left: A German DFS-230 glider. This was the standard glider in 1939–40 and was towed by a variety of tugs. It carried a crew of two and a maximum of eight fully equipped troops. It had a braking parachute, which could be deployed either in the air to enable it to dive steeply, or on the ground to shorten the landing run.

Above: British soldiers take a last look at France and the blazing port of Dunkirk as their ship begins its passage back to England. Even now they were still not safe, as Luftwaffe aircraft bombed and machine-gunned many ships on their short voyage across the English Channel.

Previous page: German parachute engineers relaxing after their epic battle for Fort Eban-Emäel, May 12, 1940. As usual in such events, the man with the cigarette packet has an instant circle of friends. Note the Luftwaffe collar patches worn by the soldier in the center and the smiling man behind him.

armies off from the rest of France. The Germans pressed northward and were temporarily held up by a brave resistance from British troops in Calais, but with the Belgian surrender (the Dutch had already capitulated on May 14) the circle around the Allied forces was closed, their only escape being the sea at their backs.

At this point, the British government decided to withdraw as many men as possible across the beaches at Dunkirk. In Operation Dynamo, a miscellaneous mixture of Royal Navy ships and civilian boats of all shapes and sizes was assembled to do what they could to save both the BEF and the French troops confined within the perimeter. Initially, the German army ceased its attacks on the encircled troops, having been ordered to halt by Hitler (May 26) in response to an appeal from Göring, who wanted the Luftwaffe to have the honor of finishing off the British, although the order was rescinded on May 28 and the Panzer attacks resumed. The RAF, operating from bases in southeast England, was able to hold off the German aircraft and in the nine days ending on June 4, 226,000 British and

112,000 French and Belgian troops were transported to the U.K.

While this was going on both German and French forces were regrouping for the final phase of the Battle of France, which lasted from June 5–25. On the French side morale was very low and most of the regular troops had already been badly mauled and much equipment lost. On the other side, the Germans were elated at their unexpectedly rapid and overwhelming successes, which inspired them to yet greater endeavors. Army Group B smashed its way through the French 10th Army, reaching the River Seine on June 9, while in the north the Panzer divisions trapped France's IX Corps and the British 51st Division against the sea, the latter being compelled to surrender at St. Valery on June 12.

Hoping to share in the fruits of this astonishing victory, the Italian dictator, Mussolini, declared war on June 10, but the somewhat halfhearted attempt at invasion of southeastern France by no fewer than 32 Italian divisions was totally defeated by six French divisions on June 21.

The series of disasters that were inflicted by the Germans caused political turmoil in France. Ministers came and went with even more rapidity than usual and in the end an aged World War I hero, Marshal Petain, was appointed. He immediately requested an armistice on June 17, which was implemented on June 21. Salt was rubbed into the French wounds when the Germans insisted that the armistice be signed at the same location and in the identical railway coach that had been used when the Germans signed their humiliating armistice in 1918.

The defeat of France was a triumph of military skill and professionalism, Hitler's army having succeeded in weeks where the Imperial German army had failed over a period of four years in World War I. For the French it was an unmitigated disaster, with only the lone voice of a relatively obscure professional army officer, Brigadier General Charles de Gaulle, offering a vision of redemption. For the British the evacuation at Dunkirk became part of British folklore, although it is often dismissed as an example of a national trait for retrospectively turning disasters into triumphs. Two facts contradict this view. First, with the collapse of the French armies in the center and the surrender of the Belgians, the Germans were able to encircle the BEF, which then had little alternative but to withdraw by sea. Secondly, the

Above: General Guderian in his command vehicle in France in June 1940. The radio operator (with earphones) is immediately in front of Guderian, and nearest the camera are the operators for the Enigma code machine, which is on the desk (bottom left).

Left: They had quarreled often enough during the war, but here in a June 1945 ceremony French general Charles de Gaulle presents a sword once owned by Napoleon to the Supreme Allied Commander, General Dwight D. Eisenhower.

BEF represented a substantial proportion of the British Army and over the next three years the survivors provided the experienced foundation upon which was built the army that carried out the 1944 Normandy invasion.

The Germans had won a resounding victory. Indeed, in the whole history of war there had never been a comparable occasion when a new philosophy of warfare had been carefully thought out, the correct military instrument to realize it created, and the philosophy then so triumphantly carried out, a process that was not to be repeated until Operation Desert Storm in 1991.

Despite this overall success, one valid military question remained: would the blitzkrieg work against an opponent who also had effective tanks in sufficient numbers, powerful antitank guns, effective air defenses against the terrifying Stukas and, above all, commanders and staffs who did not become hysterical at the

first disaster? A careful analysis of the campaign revealed that not all the defenders had panicked and in many places there had been determined French resistance. As a result—and again it seems to have been largely unnoticed at the time—the Germans incurred 156,492 casualties, of whom 27,074 were killed. If military history is studied and the lessons correctly interpreted, it will show that any new and challenging doctrine eventually produces both the correct response and the weapons with which to achieve it. However, so arrogant were Hitler and his generals that they were to learn the hard way in Russia that their much vaunted blitzkrieg was by no means invincible.

Indeed, Hitler was so euphoric about his military victory that he totally failed to exploit the immediate strategic or political opportunities that were open to him and he even damped down arms production and released some army manpower to industry. He certainly considered

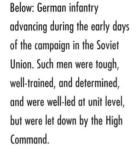

Below: German infantry advancing during the early days of the campaign in the Soviet Union. Such men were tough, well-trained, and determined, and were well-led at unit level, but were let down by the High Command.

invading England with what was to be called "Operation Sea Lion," but only in a somewhat halfhearted way. Later studies suggest that Operation Sea Lion would probably not have succeeded, although nothing is absolutely certain in war and there was always a chance that it might have done so had some anticipatory planning been done and the English Channel crossing mounted as soon as possible after the evacuation of Dunkirk. Certainly those British soldiers who can remember the state of the British Home Forces in the early fall of 1940 would not have backed them confidently against the veterans of Poland and France. In fact, it was the German navy that was most opposed to Sea Lion because during the Norwegian campaign it had lost one of its few cruisers and half its destroyers. In addition, it had a healthy respect for the Royal Navy, which, it knew, would make every sacrifice to cut the sea communications behind the landing. As for getting the troops to England by water, the German navy feared that the river and canal barges commanded by civilian freshwater skippers would all founder in the strong tides of the English Channel. Great as the risks were, however, they did not compare with the dangers of following Napoleon's road to Moscow, but without any coherent plan in his brain or an effective subordinate to counsel him otherwise, it was toward the loathed Soviet Union that Hitler's thoughts turned.

First, however, he had to consolidate his position in the remaining portions of Europe. He sought to draw Franco's Spain into the Axis alliance, or at least to obtain right of passage for his troops to enable them to capture Gibraltar and block off the whole Mediterranean. In this, and despite Germany's help to Franco during the recently concluded civil war, he failed signally, which meant that the British were able to keep open a precarious lifeline across the Mediterranean to Malta and Egypt. Hitler had better success in eastern Europe, and by March 1941 Hungary, Romania, and Bulgaria were all firmly in the Axis camp. (Czechoslovakia had already been annexed as a German "protectorate" in March 1939.) That left Greece, which was already at war with Germany's Axis partner, Italy, and Yugoslavia, whose people had revolted against their rulers when the latter had agreed to accommodate Hitler. Enraged by their resistance, Hitler declared war on both Greece and Yugoslavia on April 6, 1941.

## RESISTANCE IN AFRICA

Meanwhile, a British Commonwealth and Imperial army (Australians, Africans, British, Indians, New Zealanders, and South Africans) in the Middle East was conducting a minor blitzkrieg of its own and was dismembering the Italian-African empire and removing the

Above: German paratroops watch an attack by Stuka dive-bombers on a Dutch artillery position during the invasion of the Netherlands in May 1940. Somewhat unusually, the man in the center wears a civilian scarf, an unusually informal touch in the World War II Wehrmacht.

Right: Hitler and his somewhat unreliable ally, Benito Mussolini, in the *Wolfsschanze* (wolf's lair), one of the German leader's wartime headquarters. Others in the picture include the sinister Martin Bormann (on left) and General Keitel (second from right in side view), who, despite being an old-school *junker* and an officer of the General Staff, was subservient to Hitler's every wish.

threat to Britain's Middle East bases. Hitler's ally, the Italian dictator, Mussolini, was in deep trouble, being unable to make any headway in Greece, and routed and humiliated by the British in Africa. As a result, Hitler decided to reinforce the Italian forces in Tripolitania (modern Libya) and on April 14 the first reconnaissance unit of the German 5th Light Division disembarked in Tripoli and the German Theater commander, Erwin Rommel, who had done so well during the invasion of France and was now a lieutenant general, immediately seized command of military operations from the Italians.

Despite their many commitments in the various Middle Eastern campaigns, the British government decided to go to the help of Greece with some 100,000 men. These arrived in Greece but were then "blitzed" by the advancing Germans and forced to make an ignominious reembarkation after just 13 days, leaving all their equipment and some 11,000 casualties behind. Yugoslavia had fallen in a separate campaign, so the Balkans were now completely in Hitler's hands.

The British still hoped to hold the island of Crete, from where they would be able to exercise control over the Aegean, and a garrison was hastily organized from the troops evacuated from Greece under a redoubtable New Zealander, Major General Bernard Freyberg, VC. The German reaction was a unique operation and their first—and last—major airborne assault. On May 20, heavy bombing was the prelude to a landing by some 1,500 troops and more bombing stifled the counter-attacks to recapture the landing ground. This enabled the German buildup to continue under cover of more intense bombing, using para-chutists, gliders, and finally troop-carrying Junkers Ju 52 aircraft.

The Royal Navy destroyed every seaborne convoy bringing reinforcements and supplies, but lost no fewer than three cruisers and six destroyers in the process. The overall outcome was that after ten days' fierce fighting the Germans won a narrow and costly victory, but it was, nevertheless, a victory, while for the British and Commonwealth forces it was yet another defeat and another evacuation. The Germans

Left: The legendary General Erwin Rommel (with hat) in his desert headquarters. Rommel shot to prominence as a divisional commander in the invasion of France and went on to become one of the best-known German commanders of the war. The officer second from left is wearing the Afrika Korps insignia on his right sleeve.

Below: Two crash-landed Junkers Ju-52s on Maleme airfield in Crete. The losses suffered by the German paratroops during this invasion were so great that Hitler never again allowed a similar operation.

lost 5,670 (excluding losses on the sea voyage) while the British lost some 13,000, of whom 3,573 were Australians. Hitler, however, was so shocked by the German losses that he never again permitted a major airborne assault.

For the British, things went almost as badly in Tripolitania, where the effect of the diversion of so many good troops to Greece had left the Italians with a foothold that should have been liquidated long before. Following his arrival in March, Rommel seized the opportunity to probe the British defenses, and finding them weak, he rapidly converted what had started as a reconnaissance in force into an all-out offensive and fairly routed them, capturing two generals in the process and surrounding the 7th Australian Division in Tobruk, while his advanced units drove the British back to the Egyptian frontier. For the first, but by no means last time, the Suez Canal seemed to be almost within his grasp.

Right: The often-overlooked third land-based element in the German blitzkrieg was the artillery, which gave close and continuous support to the panzers and infantry. At the start of the war, most German artillery was wheeled, as shown here, and towed by trucks or, in some cases, by horses. Such guns had difficulty in keeping up with rapid advances, so an increasing proportion of artillery was self-propelled, sometimes on wheels but more often on tracks.

Despite Rommel's undoubted success, however, it began to appear to those prepared to consider such things that the blitzkrieg might not be such a magical formula for success after all, and that it was only really effective against poorly trained and badly led troops who lacked much morale.

At first sight, the port of Tobruk seemed impossible to defend, lying in a basin that was overlooked from all sides once the long

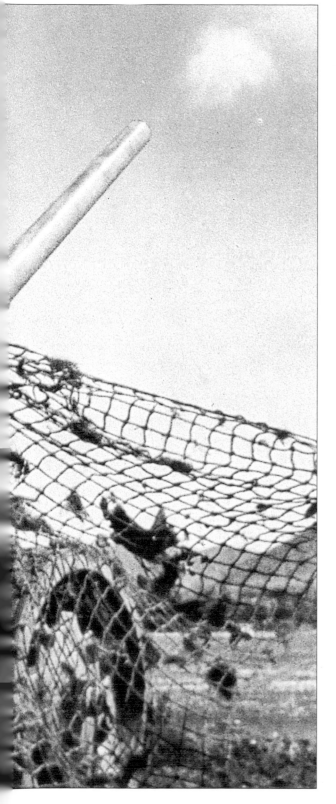

perimeter had been breached. Thus, following the disorganized British withdrawal, the defending troops should by rights have been easy prey for the typical Panzer rush ordered by Rommel on April 14. However, to his chagrin, the Australian infantry refused to budge and kept the attacking infantry pinned down forward, while the German tanks careered on unsupported until they ran into the British and Australian artillery, plus a few British tanks, in the heart of the defenses. The Germans incurred heavy losses and after three days the survivors withdrew. Another and better organized attack made later fared little better. These were minor

Above: German PzKpfw V, the Panther, developed in response to the Soviet army's T-34. One of the outstanding tanks of the war, its major weakness was the interleaved suspension, which could freeze solid in the Russian winter.

Below: A German PzKpfw III in the North African desert. One of the main designs at the start of the war, it was quickly outclassed.

actions but straws in the tactical wind. Rommel, as it turned out, was not to march to Suez but to spend the rest of 1941 defending himself against British counteroffensives.

### BARBAROSSA AND THE BATTLES IN THE SOVIET UNION

By midsummer 1941 Hitler's land empire extended from the Norwegian coastline in the north to the Egyptian desert in the south, and from the Pyrenees in the west to the shores of the Black Sea in the east. It is tempting to speculate what might have been the outcome had Hitler chosen to make his next major effort in the Middle East with all the glittering strategic prizes that it offered, but he was obsessed by the perceived danger from Communist Russia. Thus, on June 22 he embarked on Operation Barbarossa, leaving the British hanging on to the cornerstones of their land strategy—the British Isles and Egypt.

Long before he came to power, Hitler had concluded that one of the central parts of his self-imposed mission was the destruction of Communism and its base in Russia. Although there were many races in the Soviet Union, Hitler's lumped them together as one inferior race that was to be eradicated and enslaved under German rule. The oil and agricultural wealth of the Ukraine and the Caucasus were to be exploited for the sole benefit of Germany. His notional strategic goal was Russia as far east as a line running from Archangel to Astrakhan, but he seemed incapable of considering what might happen in the vast expanse of the Soviet Union that extended into Asia, it being typical of his mental condition that no doubts from the real world were allowed to challenge his fantasies.

Nor did Hitler or other members of his high command seem to have any appreciation of Soviet industrial and economic capabilities and its vast manpower resources. In reality, the Soviet armaments industry was capable of producing 12,000 tanks and 21,000 aircraft per year. Further, the peacetime strength of the Red Army was some 5 million men organized into 303 divisions, plus other field formations, fortress troops, and frontier guard units, 24,000 tanks of all types. In addition, the air force had some 7,000 largely obsolete but still useful aircraft, with much better ones on the way.

Below: Soviet army BT-7 tanks drive through the streets of snowbound Moscow on their way to the front, November 7, 1941. The move was meant to raise morale, but most civilians on the street seem to have other things to worry about, the most important of which was almost certainly just finding the food they needed for survival.

The western defenses of the Soviet Union were soundly planned on conventional lines, bearing in mind that the first strategic aim in defense is to retain intact as much of the national territory as possible. Spread out along the frontier was a covering force consisting of three elements: special frontier troops; a fortified belt consisting of machine gun and artillery emplacements in concrete, which were arranged in depth and manned by fortress troops; and these were backed by the field divisions stationed in each military district and ready to deploy to their battle stations on mobilization. Behind this covering force stood 28 divisions, organized into three armies and a rifle corps, whose task was an immediate counteroffensive. The role of this numerically formidable defense system was to gain time for general mobilization. Its total strength in the frontier defense zone was some 2.9 million men, 12,000 modern tanks plus some 12,000 obsolete ones, 35,000 guns and heavy mortars (excluding pieces less than 50 mm caliber). It should be noted that the Soviet T-34 and KV-1 tanks with their long 76.2 mm guns outclassed and outgunned the German battle tanks, although few of these latest Russian vehicles were available at the outset of the Russo-German war.

The Soviet weakness lay in the quality of these troops at every level. The terrible Stalin purges had reduced the numbers of the officer corps and left the more senior survivors badly shaken and nervous about their future. The junior officers were of poor quality, the training of the armed forces had lagged, and some war games held under Stalin's own eye had revealed that the Red Army's tactical doctrine was confused, notably over the question of the organization and use of armored formations.

Stalin was a realist and feared war because he understood the terrible damage Hitler's war machine might inflict on his country. He also knew that 24 years of Bolshevik rule had not been enough to weld the diverse Russian peoples together or to develop fully the country's economic potential. No one knew better than he its political, economic, and military weaknesses. So, while preparing for the inevitable war he did his best to delay its premature outbreak.

Stalin was not deaf to the various warnings of the impending attack that reached him from both his own intelligence apparatus and friendly

Below: Elderly Russian peasants return to their home in 1944. They totally ignore the German PzKpfw IV, but note the long barrelled gun, additional armor on the sides and turret, and the hull machine gun. The tank appears undamaged and may simply have run out of fuel.

countries, but he delayed mobilization and the deployment of the covering force to its battle stations for fear of provoking Hitler. This meant that orders only went out on the night of June 21, just a few hours before Hitler launched Operation Barbarossa at dawn the following morning. The result was that the Panzer spearheads rolled unresisted across a peaceful countryside, with the Soviet defenders being caught in their barracks or, at best, en route to their battle stations. Tactical surprise was

complete and the collapse of the covering force and the first deep penetrations by the German army were the fault of Stalin's vacillation, but it was the only moment in the war that followed when he faltered.

The German operational plan ignored the problems of time, space, topography, and relative strengths, and these were crucial, because at the back of Hitler's cloudy notion of warfare was the hope that the strategic absurdities of his plan would be covered by its

Right: German soldiers stand alongside a captured Soviet T-35 heavy tank. One of the largest tanks in the world in the late 1930s, it was armed with one 76 mm gun, two 45 mm guns, and seven machine guns. It required a crew of eleven men. About sixty were built and a few were used in the very early days of the German invasion, but it was not a success.

Previous pages: A grieving Russian woman surveys her burning house. The Germans were ruthless in their destruction of the towns and villages in their path, which was one of the main reasons for the harshness of the Soviet occupation of Germany from 1945 onward.

operational success. Western Russia was a backward forest and arable country whose towns were connected by dirt roads that were impassable to wheeled vehicles at the first burst of rain. It was, however, somewhat ironic that almost all the German army's logistical second- and third-line support was provided by horsed transport, which was very backward and anachronistic by the standard of the day, but a positive advantage when tracked and wheeled transport were all immobilized by the mud.

The lines of communication of the invading force eventually stretched 600 miles from Brest-Litovsk on the border eastward to Moscow and southeastward 1,200 miles to Stalingrad on the Volga. The front was 900 miles wide at the start line but expanded to 1,500 on the proposed final pause line. It was a logistical nightmare.

In terms of time, the whole conquest of western Russia had to be complete before the fall rains, which were themselves the prelude to the Russian winter. For the whole of this gigantic task, the smashing of the Soviet war machine and the subjugation of half a continent, the operational plan relied upon 3,550 tanks (the bulk upgunned 50 mm PzKpfw IIIs and PzKpfw IVs with the short 75 mm) and some 2,000 aircraft. Reserves of all sorts were deficient, and if the Russian railways were to be used, they had to be converted from broad to narrow gauge to accommodate German trains.

Above: A Soviet T-34 tows a German tank off the battlefield. At the time of the 1941 invasion, the Germans despised the Russians and their capabilities, so the technical excellence of the T-34 and the tactical skills of its crews came as a great surprise.

Below: Soviet T-34 in action. Note the well-sloped armor, low turret, and Christie suspension, which was developed by the Red Army from tanks bought from the United States in the 1930s. The original gun, seen here, was 76 mm in caliber, but was later increased to 85 mm.

Above: The German PzKpfw VI Tiger II was not suitable for mobile warfare, but with its 88 mm gun and thick armor it was an excellent ambush weapon. A small number of such tanks, suitably sited, particularly in close country and urban areas, could hold off large numbers of enemies for long periods.

The invasion was conducted by three army groups: Army Group North under Field Marshal Wilhelm von Leeb was directed through the Baltic states on Leningrad; Army Group South under Field Marshal Gerd von Rundstedt was to advance through Bessarabia on Kiev; and Field Marshal Fedor von Bock's Army Group Center was to push along the line of main effort—the axis Minsk-Smolesnk-Moscow. Of the 19 Panzer and 14 motorized divisions, Bock was allotted two Panzer groups (equivalent to armies, as indeed they were later designated) out of four, one under General Hermann Hoth, the other commanded by Guderian, the architect of the Panzer arm. (Guderian subsequently denied that there was a point of main effort and criticized the plan, as he criticized any plan that did not use the whole Panzer might in one concentrated blow.) A significant part of the plan was that Bock was not to drive all out for Moscow, which was both

strategically and operationally the real prize, but had first to turn aside to help Leeb mop up and capture Leningrad, to which, for some reason, Hitler attached great importance. Behind the Panzer spearhead came 116 marching infantry divisions with horse-drawn artillery and transport, plus one seeming anachronism, a cavalry division, which was to prove particularly useful in the trackless Pripet Marshes.

The tactics to be followed were the "double envelopment," or to use the graphic German phrase *Keil und Kessel* (literally "wedge and kettle," or *Kesselring*, a hunting term in which a shrinking circle of beaters drives the game on to the waiting guns). The idea was to break through in a few narrow Panzer *Schwerpunkte* (point of main effort) whose heads would meet far behind the enemy defensive positions, cutting them off. The infantry divisions would then destroy or pound the mass caught in the "kettle." These were to be really bold maneuvers: the junction point for the first of Bock's encirclements was to be Minsk, and the second Smolensk.

By July 16 these vast operations had three parts succeeded, and in terms of sheer numbers the Germans might have concluded that the war was won. Some of the Russian units fought hard, but a great many simply dissolved under Panzer and air attack after the Russian command-and-control system broke down from top to bottom, leaving the Germans the tactical problem of mopping up and marching on.

The encirclements in the center netted 590,000 prisoners and 5,500 tanks, while Rundstedt in the south pulled in another 130,000 prisoners. The German casualties by this date were 102,000, or 3 percent. It seemed as if all Hitler's predictions were being borne out, but the view from closer to the front was less encouraging. Only Army Group Center had

Below: German tanks in the Soviet Union in 1941. Note that the nearest tank is fitted with spare track section, either bolted or welded into place, which improved protection against incoming antitank rounds.

totally destroyed its opposing Soviet west front. (A "front" was the Russian equivalent of an army group.) Leeb had advanced successfully and was approaching the outskirts of Leningrad but having to fight hard, while Rundstedt in the south was facing two battered but unbroken fronts and threatened by a major counter-offensive from his left, or northeast.

To harvest the fruits of the operational victory it was essential to keep moving and give the Soviet high command no respite to stabilize the front or mount counterattacks, but the supply and replacement situation was beginning to cause anxiety, especially in tanks and tank spares. The German range of tanks was mechanically reliable, but grinding along in low gear in dust and soft ground for hundreds of miles was inevitably taking its toll. Artillery ammunition was running short, and sooner or later, when there was bound to be some protracted, static fighting, this was going to make a difference.

It is clear, with the advantage of hindsight, that the German invasion was historically doomed from the start, but it was at this point that Hitler, sticking his pins in his map far away in his headquarters in East Prussia, took the

Right: *Generaloberst* (colonel-general) von Manstein (left) talking to Colonel von Choltitz (with peaked hat), who had just led his infantry regiment in a dramatic breakthrough of Soviet lines, resulting in the Germans taking Sevastopol on July 6, 1942.

fatal step that ensured the eventual defeat of his armies—he turned away from Moscow. In all operations it is a good rule to reinforce success, and in this case success had been in the center, where Bock's division was only 200 miles from Moscow with nothing in front—and its soldiers, flushed with success, were eager to continue.

The capital had great symbolic value in war, and it also was the main rail communication focus in western Russia. Its capture would split north from south and make the movement of reserves and the building-up of fresh fronts extremely difficult. These advantages were thrown away for the sake of an operational success. One of Bock's Panzer groups (Hoth) was ordered to break way and march 400 miles north to assist in the capture of Leningrad (which was never achieved), and the other (Guderian) sent 400 miles in the opposite direction to assist Rundstedt to trap and destroy the Southwest Front in a great *kessel* 130 miles wide and deep northeast of Kiev. It is true that some 665,000 prisoners were taken, but it was a barren victory, for while theoretically it is sound sense to make the enemy armies, and not places, the objective, there remained the stubborn facts

Below: Albert Speer (right) on a briefing visit to the Eastern front. An architect, Nazi party member, and Hitler favorite, he was appointed head of Organization Todt in his thirties, eventually becoming armaments supremo. He made wide-scale use of slave labor, one reason for the twenty-year jail sentence given to him at Nuremberg in 1946.

Above: Soviet infantrymen practice the skill of crawling toward the enemy's position. Such men proved to be tough, brave, and resilient, and, like any soldier, they responded to good leadership. In addition, they were accustomed to Russian winter conditions. In the end, these infantrymen, in cooperation with their comrades in the tank corps and artillery, outfought the Germans and drove them all the way back to the river Elbe.

of military arithmetic. Enormous as Soviet losses were, there were still vast reserves of manpower and yet more armies would stream out of Siberia in a seemingly endless procession.

The significant thing about the whole battle of Moscow was its date: September 9, 1941. Bock's total success against the Western Front was completed by July 16, but it was not until August 23 that Hitler decided to scatter his Panzer striking force and declare that his true strategic objectives lay far away to the southeast. Then, while the battle of Kiev was in progress, he abandoned his aim of capturing Leningrad and ordered a frontal attack to capture Moscow.

The preliminary break-in battle of Vyazma-Bryansk was fought in the first week of October. As has happened for centuries, the first rain and snow of the fall arrived at the beginning of the second week of October, leading into the prelude to winter, which was marked by mud that arrested all movement. Then winter arrived with unimaginable cold, which froze unprotected men to death and stopped the machinery, with lubricants solidifying into gum.

It is astounding that in that first winter the German army did not crumble. It was not as if the Germans and Russians were wearing each other down equally: the same German army, aided by few reinforcements, fought successive, fresh Russian contingents. However great the defeat inflicted on each, it cost both sides casualties in terms of men, tanks, and, what is often forgotten, thousands of overworked horses that died in harness, until the whole forward transport system was almost paralyzed. From an initially desperate position the Russian defense recovered by superhuman exertions to the point that by November the militarily frugal Stalin could once more pull out formations to build up his reserves. By mid-November massive reinforcements, including 2,000 guns, were available for the Western Front, whose counteroffensive was to go on throughout the winter.

Above: Soviet infantry doubling across flat terrain during the Battle of Stalingrad.

Hitler had lost six weeks of dry weather, partly as a result of undertaking the campaigns in Yugoslavia and Greece, but also due the delays to Bock's efforts, and all the track mileage wasted in motoring Hoth and Guderian on a round trip of 1,000 miles in opposite directions. In a static position, or when attacking after careful and systematic preparation, the Red Army could fight well, but, at least in this early stage of the war, its commanders seemed unable to cope with rapidly maneuvering German forces, and once enveloped or surrounded the Red Army command tended to collapse.

But the onset of the fall rains meant that German wheeled transport got bogged down, supply vehicles could not get through with petrol for the tanks, and the war became an infantry/artillery affair fought at foot pace, and as many as 16 horses were needed to drag a single 105 mm howitzer through the mud. To exploit the Vyazma-Bryansk victory, where some 670,000 men, 1,200 tanks, and 4,000 guns had been trapped, proved impossible. Thus, the Germans lost the battle of Moscow and, in retrospect, it is clear that this was the first milestone on the way to Hitler's defeat, with two more to come—Stalingrad and Kursk.

The final phase of the battle for Moscow concluded with German army Group Center overextended, below strength, and exhausted, driven back some 60 miles by furious counter-attacks converging from either side of Moscow. Military experience dictated that the only sensible course open to the Germans once the Moscow offensive had failed was to break cleanly away to a shortened defensive line to rest, reorganize, and reequip, but Hitler would have none of that and on December 29 he sacked Field Marshal von Brauchitsch and assumed direct operational control. He forbade withdrawal and the upshot was that his exhausted armies were driven slowly back in a costly retreat to the line their commanders had asked to occupy in the first place.

Above: German troops engaged in street fighting in the Russian city of Rostov. Soviet troops knew exactly how to make such fighting very costly for the German army.

and not only depriving the Soviet armies of their oil supplies, but also gaining them for the use of his own armies.

Hitler insisted on the need for large-scale operations to acquire grain from the Ukraine, iron ore from the Donets, and oil from the Caucasus, being encouraged in this view by local German successes on the Soviet front in early 1942. The plan involved two army groups. Army Group A, consisting of one Panzer and one marching army, was to race to the line of Baku-Batum, while Army Group B, with one Panzer and two marching armies, was to drive all before it and establish a defensive flank over 600 miles long from Voronezh along the upper Don River as far as Stalingrad and thence along the Volga River. These spearheads were to be all-German, but following them would be three

The bitter fighting continued as Stalin realized that his troops knew how to fight in the winter and the Germans did not. He was right, and it is doubtful if the German army, which had so brilliantly won the "three weeks' offensive" of that summer, was ever to be the same instrument again. After much confused and bitter fighting, in which the encirclers were themselves encircled and then the encircling rings broken once again, the battle for Moscow ended with the Russians victorious and both sides immobilized by sheer exhaustion and the return of the mud in the spring thaw.

This was a great victory, but the actual turn of the tide was at Stalingrad. Having been frustrated completely in the north, Hitler decided that his 1942 campaign would be based on a sweep down into the Caucasus, thus cutting off all Soviet resources in the Don basin

additional armies, one Italian, one Hungarian, and one Romanian. Thus, the whole expedition involved 60 German divisions (ten Panzer, six motorized, and 44 infantry), plus 43 non-German divisions, the latter being a grim indicator of the increasingly serious German manpower situation.

This total of 103 divisions seems enormous, but at the maximum point of advance this front alone, measured from end to end, would be some 1,200 to 1,400 miles in length, with tenuous lines of communication stretching over some 1,000 miles and exposed to constant partisan attack. Hitler may have been correct in his assumption that the Soviet army could not yet stand up to the Panzers, but he seemed unable to comprehend that the vast distances diluted the latters' strength, that fighting caused casualties on such a huge scale that he was unable to replace them, and that the further this rash invasion advanced the more it was exposed along its long northeastern flank to a deadly counteroffensive.

These operations started with Army Group A (List) attacking in the Caucasus, while Army Group B (Bock) attacked on its left, to protect its flank. Army Group B's attack, designated "Blau I," was launched on June 28, 1942, and was intended to be a double encirclement, using 2nd Army (Weichs) in the north and 4th Panzer Army (Hoth) in the south. To increase Soviet problems, the attack was aimed at the junction of two Soviet fronts—always a military weak point—and Stalin, despite concerns about a possible drive on Moscow, released three armies from the reserve, which deployed along the Don

Below: Soviet infantry in the Battle of Stalingrad.

Right: A German 37 mm antitank gun in action against Soviet tanks during the attack on Smolensk. The smoke plume makes it clear that it has hit its target.

River north of the German incursion. Soviet countermoves were unsuccessful, however, and Stalin sacked several of his top generals.

At first, the sequence of events seemed to be repeating the pattern of 1941. The Crimea fell to Manstein and his German-Romanian group. Army Group A under Field-Marshal List and Army Group B under Bock rolled forward overcoming all opposition, and again the Red Army suffered enormous losses with two of its armies and part of another being encircled in May. The Germans took Voronezh in July, crossed the Don in force, and by late August List's Army Group A had reached Maykop and Krasnodar in the Caucasus; the following month they were in Novorossiysk.

The German 6th Army (von Paulus) started its drive southeastward on June 30, to join up with the 4th Panzer Army, which was moving south along the west bank of the Don. Progress became confused when Hitler intervened directly in the battle, reorganizing corps and armies when the battle failed to progress to his satisfaction, and issuing orders that changed the original plan. Hitler's Directive No. 45, issued on July 23, ordered the 6th Army to advance and capture Stalingrad, and the confusion was compounded when Hitler dismissed the commander of Army Group B and moved his headquarters to Vinnitsa in the Ukraine.

As the 6th Army edged closer to Stalingrad, Soviet counterattacks were piecemeal and were defeated in detail. By mid-September, however, Hitler's summer offensive was at a standstill with the 6th Army still not at Stalingrad, while the southern push into the Caucasus had also

Left: It is generally thought that the German armies were fully motorized, but this was certainly not the case, as made clear by this photograph taken shortly after the German invasion of the Soviet Union, June 22, 1941. Panzer divisions had motorized logistic support, enabling them to travel fast, but most infantry units had horse-drawn supply carts right up to the end of the war. Such horse-drawn logistic units were not only slow moving, but their horses needed vast amounts of food and water, and were very susceptible to the winter conditions.

been brought to a standstill. Hitler fired the commander of Army Group A, List, and took personal command of the group. Closer to home, he sacked Halder as Chief of Army General Staff, replacing him with Zeitzler.

Stalingrad was a city of some 500,000 people, extending for some 30 miles along the west bank of the Volga. Its main importance was as an industrial center and the people remained at their jobs until the encirclement by the Germans was virtually complete, when a small proportion managed to escape. The city was defended by the 62nd and 64th Armies under the overall command of General Chuikov. These two armies were desperately under strength, together mustering some 100,000 men and several dozen tanks, with negligible air support.

Once the German 6th Army was on the outskirts of Stalingrad a tremendous battle with the Soviet defenders began. The Germans were full of confidence and Paulus launched four major attacks on the city between early September and mid-November. As always in built-up areas, however, the conflict rapidly deteriorated into a myriad of small engagements as desperate men fought for a street, a house, a cellar, or even, perhaps, a wall. The Soviet garrison was attacked by Luftwaffe aircraft by day, and all around the clock by artillery and mortars, although some reinforcements managed to cross the river under cover of darkness. During this phase of the battle,

various features of the city took it in turn to become the focus of attention: at one stage it was the *Mamayev kurgan*, a small hill in the center of the city, while at another it was the "Red October" factory.

Most of Army Group B was sucked into the battle, leaving the Germans very thinly stretched elsewhere, with much of the line being held by formations from Hungary, Italy, Romania, and Spain. One of Paulus's most severe problems was logistics, with his supplies dependent upon one railway line. Command, too, was a problem, with Hitler issuing orders to Paulus direct, bypassing the army group commander. Eventually, the Soviet forces were pinned down in a long, thin line along the western bank of the Volga, and were divided into three groups, since the Germans had managed to break through to the riverbank in two places.

Seeing such huge forces concentrated around Stalingrad, the Soviets launched a pincer movement to entrap the Germans. Commanded by Zhukov, this was timed to coincide with the frost, which hardened the ground and enabled tanks to move. On November 19, the Southwest Front (Vatutin) attacked the Germans out of two bridgeheads across the Volga to the north of the city, using armored spearheads backed up by cavalry and infantry. The attacks were concentrated on very narrow frontages against Romanian and weak German divisions, which were quickly pushed aside. On November 20,

Left: German infantry advance cautiously up a street in a Russian town, keeping to the sides to avoid presenting targets to any snipers who may have been missed.

Below: A mixed armor-infantry team advances toward Moscow. The swastika flag on the tank turret is to prevent attacks by Luftwaffe dive-bombers.

the Stalingrad Front (Yeremenko) to the south of the city also defeated two Romanian divisions, and then the Don Front (Rokossovsky) joined in the north with a pincer movement involving two armies. On November 23, the Southwest Front and Stalingrad Front met to the west of Stalingrad and the tables had truly been turned on the Germans: some 20 besieging divisions were now themselves surrounded and fighting for their lives.

Paulus proposed that the 6th Army should fight its way out before the noose was too tight, a plan endorsed by the 2nd Army's Weichs, but Hitler told him to remain in place, having been assured by the bombastic Göring that the Luftwaffe could fly in 500 tons of supplies per day. (The Luftwaffe never exceeded 140 tons per day, reduced to 60 tons per day in January when it lost its forward airfields.) However, General Manstein was ordered from the north on November 27, to create Army Group Don, with the task of relieving the 6th Army.

Manstein launched an attack on December 12 by the 57th Panzer Corps, which consisted of three understrength Panzer divisions. Attacking from the southwest, the corps got to within 25 miles of Stalingrad but was then forced to halt. Manstein told Paulus to break out but again Paulus awaited orders from Hitler. Matters then got even worse when two Soviet armies attacked the 57th Panzer Corps on December 24, driving it back in confusion beyond its start line.

Above: The German army's PzKpfw III, here fitted with a long 50 mm gun. This vehicle did well against the British in the Western Desert, but was much less effective against Soviet armor during the invasion of Russia.

territory. German intelligence indicated that it contained approximately one million men and vast amounts of equipment, and it was clear to both sides that a German pincer movement across the base of the salient would not only straighten the German line, but would also cut off and eliminate vast numbers of Soviet troops. Hitler, while agreeing to such a plan, imposed a

Meanwhile, an attack by the Red Army launched on December 16 by the Southwest Front surrounded the Italian 8th Army, which surrendered on December 25. With the front now disintegrating, the Germans seeking to relieve their forces around Stalingrad now found that they were fighting for their lives. The Hungarian Army also fell apart, while the 1st Panzer Army, which had invaded the Caucasus, was forced to withdraw to avoid being cut off and trapped, as had happened to the 6th Army.

By the end of January, the 6th Army was starving: resupply by the Luftwaffe had fallen from 140 tons to under 70 tons per day and the garrison had long since eaten their horses. Under intense Soviet pressure and with an ever-diminishing perimeter, the first Germans surrendered on January 30, followed by the remainder on February 2, 1943.

Three armies and 26 German divisions were destroyed in this action. The Stalingrad garrison comprised some 400,000 Germans and 100,000 Allies, mostly Romanian. Of those, 120,000 surrendered and 40,000 escaped, indicating that some 340,000 must have died. Nor was that the end: of the 120,000 prisoners, just 6,000 returned to Germany in the early 1950s.

The German surrender at Stalingrad on February 2, 1943, and the Soviet drive across the Donets River (February 2–20, 1943) were partially offset by von Manstein's successful counterattack at Kharkov (February 18–March 20). However, von Manstein's victory left Soviet forces in a huge salient, roughly semicircular in shape, 100 miles across at the base and penetrating some 75 miles into German-held succession of delays, so that by the time it was actually implemented in July the Soviets were fully prepared.

The German plan, designated *Zitadelle* (citadel) was on a vast scale, involving no fewer than 17 tank (Panzer) divisions; three armored infantry (Panzergrenadier) divisions, and 16 infantry divisions. The northern pincer was the responsibility of Model's 9th Army, with seven Panzer, two Panzergrenadier, and nine infantry divisions. The southern pincer was the responsibility of the 4th Panzer Army (Hoth), with ten Panzer, one Panzergrenadier, and seven infantry divisions. Together these represented the largest tank force ever committed to battle and included large numbers of the Panther tank, as well as

Below: A German airfield, situated west of the Don river, under Soviet attack in early 1943.

two battalions of the latest Tiger tanks. There was considerable air support, including numerous "tank busters."

The opposing forces comprised the eleven Soviet armies (equivalent in numbers and firepower to a German corps) of the Voronezh Front (General Vatutin). Their main weapon was the T-34 tank, arguably the finest of its generation. As usual, the Soviet artillery was also very strong, including some 20,000 howitzers, 1,000 Katyusha rocket launchers, and 6,000 antitank weapons. The Soviets always laid strong minefields, but on this occasion, suspecting the German intentions, they were particularly dense, especially at the shoulders of the salient.

The ground was open, rolling countryside, with scattered woods and rivers, and numerous small villages—what soldiers call "good tank country." It was high summer and conditions varied between two extremes. Most of the time the ground was very dry and extremely dusty, and the tank crews suffered from extreme heat inside their vehicles, while the dust clouds became so dense that opposing tanks sometimes collided head-on, having failed to see the other approach. If it rained—and sometimes there were cloudbursts of tropical intensity—the ground turned into a muddy morass in which tanks became bogged down and thus sitting targets for enemy ground-attack aircraft.

Hitler several times postponed the start of what was to become known as the Battle of Kursk, mainly to allow two more battalions of the new Tiger tank to take part, but finally settled for July 4, 1943. H-hour was presaged by a four-hour Soviet artillery barrage, suggesting that they were privy to German plans, but the Germans still crossed the start line at 3:00 P.M., as planned. Despite the heavy concentration of German troops over a relatively narrow frontage, progress was very slow. A frequently used Soviet tactic in the early stages was to allow the Germans to penetrate lightly held positions until they were stopped by the real Soviet positions. The Germans, elated by the

Above: A Soviet divisional commander addressing his troops in July 1943.

ease of the advance, then held on, not realizing that they were occupying ground that the Soviets had chosen for them and where they became victims of deliberate, planned Soviet counterattacks, and suffered accordingly.

In the north, the attack was led by 100 Tiger tanks, operating in conjunction with medium Mark IIIs and Mark IVs in a *Panzerkeil* (tank wedge), which protected the flanks of the slower-moving, heavy tanks. However, the Tigers had been rushed from the factory specifically for this operation and were not fully combat-ready; as a result, they suffered numerous breakdowns. Ninth Army's 47 Panzer Corps advanced some ten miles in seven days, suffering heavy losses in the process and, despite Model's well-known aggressiveness, never managed to get much further.

Hoth's forces in the south did somewhat better, although the attack was led by some 90 *Ferdinand* (also known as *Elefant*) self-propelled assault guns, which were slow-moving and lacked any machine guns, so they were frequently picked off by aggressive Soviet infantry using flamethrowers. One commander who did well was *Oberstgruppenführer* (the Waffen-SS equivalent to lieutenant general) Sepp Dietrich, commander of the *Leibstandarte* Adolf Hitler Panzer Division, which advanced seven miles and destroyed 27 T-34s on July 5. Dietrich was not renowned for his intelligence, but on this occasion he showed some skill by stopping short of villages at dusk, which were then heavily bombarded by the Soviets throughout the night. Dietrich's troops then advanced, relatively unscathed, at dawn. Despite this, his division was at a standstill by the third day, due as much to mechanical problems with his tanks as to Soviet action.

On July 7, 48 Panzer Corps on the left of the southern sector pushed forward and began to wheel to the left. This move was initially successful and the Soviets were off-balance until the afternoon, when they counterattacked. In a unique encounter some 300 tanks on each side faced each other in the open and continued to fire at each other until darkness fell. In the north the Soviet 3rd Army added to the German 9th Army's problems by making a strong attack toward Orel, in effect by closing a pincer on Model's pincer, while the Soviet 7th Guards Army attempted a similar tactic in the south, attacking toward Belgorod. The Soviet objective, however, was not to take ground but to exert such strong pressure that the Germans would be forced to deploy resources to fight off these attacks, thus hampering the planned pincer operations.

After seven days' fighting the German troops were extremely tired, a situation made worse by shortages of ammunition, supplies, and rations. This was due, at least in part, to Soviet air attacks on the main German logistics center at Poltava and on railway lines vital to the German supply system.

On July 12 Hoth's 4th Panzer Army again attempted to breakthrough. It was a particularly hot and dry day and the German advance created a huge dust cloud as it advanced. Suddenly the Soviet 5th Armored Army, fresh from being in reserve, counterattacked. A muddled battle ensued in which the two armored forces slugged it out—the greatest

tank-on-tank battle of the war. Tigers and Panthers could defeat T-34s at up to 2,000 yards (1,830m) range, but this was of little value when the mass of T-34s closed to point-blank range. The Soviets cut off the whole of 3rd Panzer and part of the *Grossdeutschland* divisions and the day ended with Soviet tanks swarming across the battlefield, penetrating into the German rear areas and isolating many pockets of resistance.

Hitler realized that the battle was lost and was also distracted by the Allied invasion of Sicily, which had taken place on July 9. He therefore ordered that *Zitadelle* be brought to a close, although it took another week and yet more losses for this to be achieved.

The two great German pincers never came closer than some 60 miles (96km) and their losses were immense—20 Panzer divisions had virtually ceased to exist; 70,000 men had been killed or wounded; 3,000 tanks, 1,000 guns, 5,000 motor vehicles, and 1,400 aircraft had been lost. Soviet losses have never been properly documented but were probably of the same order. The difference was that the Soviets, particularly with the supplies now coming from their Western Allies, could afford them while the Germans could not.

Below: T-34/76s advance in tactical formation across an almost featureless snowscape, although a solitary traffic sign suggests a road beneath the snow. Western Russia's open terrain was ideal tank country and immense battles were fought there.

## FROM ALAMEIN TO THE ALPS

Meanwhile in North Africa, an unbroken run of Allied victories began on November 3, 1942, when the British and Commonwealth 8th Army under Lieutenant General Bernard Montgomery cracked the Axis defenses at El Alamein and began its long advance westward. The newly arrived Montgomery had fought in France throughout World War I and had long pondered his experiences there. Among his many conclusions were that: he would always minimize casualties; he would only fight when he had superiority in men, tanks, and in the air; his men would always be fully in the picture; the men would know who their generals were—and he would always win. Montgomery's forces consisted of 30th Corps (Leese) in the north, 13th Corps (Horrocks) in the south, with the armor concentrated in 10th Corps (Lumsden). The Desert Air Force (Coningham) was in support. Montgomery quickly imposed his will on this force, although a few old desert hands had reservations about the brash and self-confident newcomer.

The Axis forces were commanded by Field Marshal Erwin Rommel, an infantryman who had excelled as a Panzer commander in France in 1940 and in some of the earlier desert battles, but he was not well and on September 22, 1942, had flown back to Germany to recuperate at home, leaving General Stumme temporarily in command. As with the British, the German position rested on the sea and the Qattara Depression, and consisted of an unbroken line of infantry divisions—alternating German and Italian. These Axis positions were protected by a complex system of minefields, known to the British as "Devil's Gardens." There were two armored reserve forces, the 15th Panzer Division and Littorio (Italian) Division in the north, and the 21st Panzer Division and Ariete (Italian) Division in the south, with the German 90th Light Division and Italian Trieste Division in general reserve near El Daba. The Axis supply position was not good: it had 11 days of fuel, 21 days of fresh bread, but very little fresh fruit.

Montgomery resisted strong political pressure for an early attack and gave the order only when he was convinced that all was ready. The Desert Air Force, with help from USAAF B-24 Liberators, started the attack on enemy airfields on October 19 and the British had air superiority during the battle. Montgomery's

Below: In the Western Desert, Indian soldiers in a Bren gun carrier watch the advance of a surrendering German soldier, whose tank burns in the background. These carriers were very fast and maneuverable and gave good mobility to infantry battalions of the Commonwealth and Imperial forces.

initial intention was to break through the enemy line, with the main effort in the north, where the infantry would clear two corridors through the minefields and Axis positions as far as a line designated "Oxalic." This would let the armor pass through to form a shield against counter-attacks along a line designated "Pierson." The infantry would then crumble the Axis infantry.

The first attack, on the night of October 23–24, 1942, was preceded by a barrage of 589 guns, which started at 9:40 P.M. Although they knew that an attack was imminent, the Axis forces were taken by surprise and the initial confusion was increased when General Stumme went forward to see the situation for himself and

died of a heart attack. By dawn most 30th Corps units were near their objective (the Oxalic line) while the 10th Corps' armored units were following down the two cleared corridors. However, the Italian infantry resisted strongly and the 15th Panzer Division counterattacked, slowing down the British operations, and the armor failed to reach the Pierson line.

In the south, the 13th Corps undertook a diversionary attack, which was sufficiently strong to persuade the Germans not to move their armored reserve to the north. On the Axis side, Stumme's death resulted in von Thoma taking over at 12:00 P.M. and sending an urgent message to Rommel to return to the desert.

Below: British armored units of the 8th Army advance on El Hamma, March 29, 1943. The nearest tank is a Lee/Grant, the other tank is the later Sherman; both were supplied by the United States under lend-lease.

In the morning of October 24, Montgomery ordered the break-in phase to continue and that night he called a meeting of his corps commanders to reiterate his determination to continue with the plan. On the morning of October 25, however, he recognized that the thrust in the southern corridor was getting nowhere and that night he sent the Australian 9th Division to cut the coast road behind enemy lines, which they achieved with great speed.

Rommel had returned late on October 25 and carried out a personal reconnaissance in the north on October 26. He sent in counterattacks on October 27: The 90th Light Division attacked the Australians while the 21st Panzer

Division (which had, at last, been brought up from the south) attacked the British 1st Armored Division in the northern corridor; but both attacks failed.

Sensing that his troops were tired after the incessant fighting, Montgomery gave the 30th Corps the chance to recuperate and withdrew some frontline units to create a new reserve for a new plan, named "Operation Supercharge." This reserve consisted of the New Zealand 2nd Division (Freyberg) reinforced by two British infantry and two British armored brigades. The new attack was launched at 1:00 A.M. on November 2 with the two British infantry brigades leading, followed by the 9th Armored Brigade. All reached their objectives, although the armored brigade lost 70 of its 94 tanks, but destroyed 35 Axis tanks and self-propelled guns, seriously weakening the Axis forces in the area. Rommel withdrew the 90th Light Division from its attack on the Australians and combined it with the remnants of the 21st Panzer Division for a counterattack on Freyberg's thrust. The British tanks and the aircraft of the Desert Air Force combined to inflict heavy damage; the Germans lost 70 tanks and the Italians another 47. That night the British 51st Division carried out a successful attack on Trieste Division.

On November 3, the Germans were reduced to 35 tanks and in the evening Rommel sent two messages to *Oberkommando der Wehrmacht* (OKW) outlining the disaster that had befallen

Above: These Foreign Legionnaires, part of the 13th Demi-Brigade serving with the British in the Western Desert, have transferred their 75 mm field gun into a very elementary self-propelled weapon. Note the famous kepis.

Above: Following the Battle of Alamein, a British armored unit, mounted in U.S.-supplied Sherman tanks, pushes forward across the desert in pursuit of Rommel's retreating army.

Previous pages: The Afrika Korps in the desert. The tanks are PzKpfw II light tanks armed with a 20 mm main gun.

him and announcing his intention to withdraw. It is worth mentioning that these two signals give a good example of the effectiveness of Britain's "Ultra" electronic interception system. They were transmitted from the desert at 7:50 P.M. on November 2 and were in Hitler's hands by 9:00 A.M. the following morning; the same messages, completely decrypted by Ultra, were also in the hands of both Montgomery in the desert and General Brook in London by 12:00 P.M.—just three hours after they reached Hitler! The Führer, of course, had no idea that such messages were being red by the Allies, and he issued a "stand-or-die" order, but he was too late, as the German infantry had long since departed and the German armor withdrew on November 3–4, leaving the Italians in the lurch; four divisions were rounded up by the British.

Montgomery was later criticized for failing to follow up with swift annihilation, but the facts were that his troops were exhausted and heavy rain turned the desert sand into a muddy morass. However, his victory was indisputable.

The victory at Alamein was closely followed by Operation Torch (November 7), the first of the four major landings in the Mediterranean, in which some 850 naval vessels and transports disembarked American and British armies on the shores of French North Africa. Soon afterward, paratroopers and a small mechanized force were sent off to capture Tunis.

The German General Staff, or rather the Commander in Chief South, Field Marshal Albert Kesselring, reacted with their usual speed to block the Allies and to establish their own bridgehead in Tunisia by forming, in their

Left: A German *Spähpanzer* eight-wheeled reconnaissance vehicle during the campaign in Tunisia. The gun is a short-barrelled 75 mm Stu.K L/24.

Far right: U.S. Army paratroops aboard a C-47 transport plane for a combat jump. Note the reserve parachutes carried across their chests. The Americans and British carried out far more parachute operations than the Germans, and generally with much greater success.

Below: U.S. infantry searching the town of Bizerta, May 8, 1943. The town has clearly been damaged by air attack or artillery fire, but the soldiers are still on their guard.

inimitable way, small battle groups from every available unit or individual as fast as they could be flown in. After some dashing operations by both sides the Germans won the race by a week or so, just as the fall rains began. But, in spite of all their efforts, the Axis venture in Africa was doomed. The Allies had control of the air, the Axis sea routes were cut, and their armies were trapped between Montgomery's and General Dwight D. Eisenhower's forces advancing irresistibly from east and west. There was much hard fighting yet to be done, but today the final battles are of interest only to historians. Long before the Axis forces were liquidated, the Allied staffs were preparing for the landings in Sicily and the Italian mainland.

## SICILY AND ITALY

On July 9–10, 1943, the British 8th and the U.S. 7th Armies invaded Sicily. A pointer to the extreme complexity of such operations, and to

the room for error inherent in them, was the terrible mishap on the part of the airborne forces, which inadvertently flew over the supporting fleet en route to its dropping zones and was engaged by the naval guns. Tactically, Sicily was a warning of the defensive potential of the Italian terrain, so different from the flat expanses of Russia or the undulating western desert. The tank was no longer supreme, and time-consuming attacks by infantry with powerful artillery support were required to turn the skilled and dogged German battle groups out of the little villages or off the rocky ridges where they were ensconced. This pattern was to persist for month after long month until the spring of 1945.

All Axis resistance in Sicily ended on August 17, the very day on which Churchill and Roosevelt met in Quebec to agree on the final strategy for the liberation of Europe.

Despite the immediacy of the ongoing operations, Churchill managed to take a long

view and saw military strategy as a preparation for the political goals in the ensuing peace, the foremost of which was to prevent central Europe from falling under Soviet control. At an operational level, he favored the indirect approach and never ceased to press for a far-reaching encircling thrust from the south with perhaps Vienna as its objective.

To the Americans, both these ideas were anathema on two grounds. It was politically unacceptable to use American lives and war materiel to further Britain's aims—always suspect—in Europe, and strategically the United States chiefs of staff favored the exact opposite: invasion by the shortest, cross-Channel route and a deliberate clash with the enemy's main forces, which would be destroyed in the field, thus freeing the United States to concentrate on the war against Japan. Coming from the major partner, the American view inevitably prevailed,

and, as many would argue, rightly so. The agreed aim of the Italian campaign was to contain or distract as many Axis troops away from the main area of decision in France after which, in due course, a proportion of the Allied divisions in Italy would be switched to the subsidiary invasion of the French Riviera. This was the general idea. There was never a master plan for Italy with precise objectives, and there continued to be a tug between a purely holding operation and the ambitions of the theater commanders to inflict as much damage as possible—perhaps penetrating into Austria. After all, generals in command of large forces are seldom content to accept a secondary role, and the British Field Marshal Sir Harold Alexander and the American General Mark Clark were no exceptions.

As it happened, Hitler was himself an "indirect approach" man and viewed the Italian

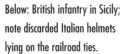

Below: British infantry in Sicily; note discarded Italian helmets lying on the railroad ties.

situation and its dangers to his position the same way as did Churchill. As a result, he decided to reinforce Italy regardless of its sudden surrender on September 8, from then on treating his former ally as just another occupied country.

Two German armies were organized, initially of 16 divisions, eight in the south to fight a long delaying action, and eight to prepare a final defensive position in the Appenines, running across Italy from approximately La Spezia on the Mediterranean coast to Pesaro on the Adriatic; this was known as the "Green Line" to the Germans and, rather more grandly, as the "Gothic Line" to the Allies. These 16 divisions were later reinforced to 19, but the Germans were understrength, with divisions holding frontages of ten miles or more; outgunned in artillery, but not in tanks and antitank guns; and had lost control in the air.

The German defense in Italy was to prove one of the most remarkable professional feats in military history, bearing in mind that it was not simply superior firepower and a mass of materiel that drove them back. The German infantry, who only two to three years previously had been the terrors of Europe and Russia, now met opponents who, platoon for platoon, were as good at the game as themselves. To take the 8th Army alone, its forcing of the Gothic Line defenses in the fall of 1944 was one of the finest feats of its multinational infantry, for the credit was not confined to the Americans and British: there were 26 nationalities in the 5th and 8th Armies—including Brazilians, Canadians, French, French Moroccans and Algerians, Gurkhas, Indians of a dozen castes and ethnic groups, New Zealanders, and Poles. Allied strength fluctuated, but after four French and three U.S. divisions had been withdrawn, Alexander still had 20 divisions.

From the Allied side Italy can be seen as the war of lost opportunities. After Sicily the 8th Army hopped over the Straits of Messina and established bridgeheads around the foot of Italy and then began, rather slowly, to work inland. On September 9 the 5th (U.S.) Army landed in strength south of Salerno, initially lightly opposed, but the German reaction was characteristically rapid and Clark was not able to break out until the 24th. Thereafter the fall and winter were spent with the 8th Army in the east and the 5th in the west slowly grinding away against the German intermediate lines and

through a maze of mines and demolitions. Every river line and every ridge ran athwart the Allied line of advance; each was skillfully defended and determinedly forced. It was an engineer's war as well as an infantryman's war and, surprisingly in the mid-century, a muleteer's war as well—by the end of the campaign no fewer than 30,000 mules were occupied in frontline supply and casualty evacuations from ground where not even a jeep could go.

In October the Allies came up against a solid belt of defenses based in the west on Cassino and the Rapido River, and then what the German commanders feared more than anything else happened. On January 22, 1944, the Allies used their amphibious capability to land behind the German right flank, at Anzio, and so turn their whole position. This opportunity was muffed through feeble leadership, and the Anzio detachment was kept penned up in its bridgehead until May 23, when it broke out as the 5th Army broke through the Gustav intermediate line at Cassino. (None of these lines, it must be said, was seen as "intermediate" by the troops on the ground: to clear each required an intense bombardment by 1,000 or more guns, massive air strikes, and costly hand-to-hand combat.)

Another chance to trap the southern echelon of the German armies was then lost through a

Above: U.S. Sherman tanks come ashore from a U.S. Navy LST (landing ship, tank) Anzio. The relaxed attitude of the sailors make it clear that there was little air threat at the time the picture was taken, but the Battle of Anzio quickly became a very hard-fought conflict.

Right: During the advance up the Italian peninsula, British infantry take the opportunity offered by a lull in the fighting to press forward through a shattered town. The soldier nearest the camera is a lance-corporal, armed with a Thompson submachine gun, an ideal weapon for such close-quarter fighting.

decision by Clark to go for Rome instead of swinging from the Anzio perimeter around behind the defenders of the Gustav Line and so cutting off a major portion of the 10th Army. From then on the two Allied armies were committed to a laborious northward crawl, led by their engineers building bridges, with one frontal attack after another until they at last came up against the Gothic Line.

The decision to force the Gothic Line was a bold one. Alexander had only a marginal superiority in numbers (although by the nature of mountain warfare he could concentrate at will against one pass after another), it was late in the season and he had no reserve. Moreover, his planners were mistaken in the notion that

Above: A German paratrooper runs across open ground in the ruins of the Benedictine monastery at Monte Cassino. The Allied decision to destroy the monastery was, and remains, a controversial issue.

Below: The ruins of Monte Cassino, showing just how accurate and devastating Allied bombing had become by this stage of the war.

behind the Appenines there was country suited for a classical armored breakthrough, and they continued to believe that such a breakthrough might yet after all permit a glorious strategic thrust through the Ljubljana gap to Vienna.

It was a vain hope, for once the divisions for the landings in southern France were withdrawn, there were no reserves for rapid exploitation. The Gothic Line was indeed pierced in a series of company and battalion battles in which both sides showed self-sacrifice and heroism, but the British armor was stopped cold, there were no replacements for casualties, the supplies of artillery ammunition were cut down to keep the insatiable guns in France

supplied, and then it began to rain. Napoleon's "fifth element," the mud, stopped the war until the spring of 1945. Kesselring, the German commander in chief and an airman who proved one of the best German commanders of the war, could at least grimly congratulate himself that he had kept his word to Hitler and held the Allies penned in Italy.

## OVERLORD—THE GERMANS ARE SWEPT FROM FRANCE

Allied plans for the liberation of Europe from the German yoke led in June 1944 to the greatest seaborne invasion of all time: the

Below: D-Day, June 6, 1944, as U.S. infantry storm ashore from a U.S. Coast Guard landing craft. The infantry already ashore are pinned down by machine gun fire from German positions in the high ground behind the beach.

landings in Normandy, known to the military as "Operation Overlord" and to history, quite simply, as "D-Day." There was never any doubt that the shortest and surest way to defeat Hitler and liberate Europe was to launch an invading army across the English Channel, but all involved perceived that the dangers were immense. Churchill was not a man given to fear, yet he dreaded the prospect. On a lower plane, late in 1943 during a Staff College discussion of the technical issues, one speaker joked about "Operation Bloodbath," and a shudder went around a room full of veteran officers.

How it was done—and done so successfully—was a triumph of imaginative planning

and technology applied to apparently insoluble military problems.

The German defense in France and the Low Countries, under Rundstedt, totaled ten Panzer and *Panzergrenadier*[4] divisions—as ever the elite and spearhead of the army—and 38 other divisions. The coast was guarded along its whole length and the most likely landing areas strongly fortified in depth, with underwater obstacles, mined beaches, tank traps, and ditches, with a checkerboard pattern of heavy antiship guns and antitank guns in concrete emplacements, infantry pillboxes and field artillery. This was the so-called Westwall. Only one uncertainty divided the minds of the German command. Was the best plan to hold the perimeter and maintain the bulk of the armor in reserve so as to mount a counteroffensive when it became clear which landings were feints and which were the ones on the point of main effort? Or should the defense forces rely on a rigid linear defense of the beaches, gambling on eliminating the attackers when they were most vulnerable?

Rommel, whose Army Group B was to defend the invasion coast, believed that the Allied air forces could interdict any large-scale

Above: An extraordinary scene on Omaha beach, with shipping stretching as far as the eye can see, while infantry, artillery, and engineers hasten to get off the beach and join the fighting units further inland.

[4]Panzergrenadiers were German Army infantry units mounted on tracked or wheeled personnel carriers

Above: A soldier of the United States 8th Infantry Regiment of 4th Infantry Division carrying a Browning machine gun. He had landed on Utah beach and is now advancing northward up the Cotentin peninsula toward the port of Cherbourg, June 9, 1944.

Previous pages: British infantry disembark from a landing craft assault (LCA), with larger Mark IV landing craft tanks behind. The wheeled trailer on the left being pushed ashore by a bulldozer is loaded with bundles of fascines, used by tanks to cross ditches and small gaps.

enormous industrial potential of the United States. The fortified assembly area was provided by the whole island of Britain, and the artillery preparation and covering fire on the vast scale and intensity required were provided by aircraft based on aircraft carriers. The success of Overlord, the most famous of operational code names, rested on four technological bases:

• Specialized landing craft were produced so that tanks, guns, infantry, and trucks could be carried up to the very beach, where the craft were deliberately run aground to allow the

move by a central reserve, and Hitler supported him, so the second course—the more favorable from the attacker's point of view—was adopted, with one reservation: the armored reserve, Panzer Group West under General Geyr von Schweppenburg, was held back for use at the high command's discretion.

The difficulties of an opposed landing can be simply explained by comparing it with a purely land attack on a highly organized defensive system. The attackers in the latter case could—exactly as their ancestors had when attacking a fortress—start from the cover of their own defense works with massive preplanned supporting fire, and were then faced with only a short advance across open ground before close combat inside the enemy defenses began. If checked, they could try again or, at worst, disengage and dig in. By contrast, an amphibious attack was like attacking the same system across an open plain, without any cover, and from assembly areas 50 or 100 miles away.

This was the accepted picture, and in classical strategy its worst elements were to be avoided by a surprise landing on some undefended stretch remote from the objective, then swinging around to take the coastal defenses from behind and capture a working port through which the buildup of the invaders could continue.

It was not tactics that were to provide the solution to the problem but technology and the

troops to wade ashore or the vehicles to drive over the lowered ramp.

- The second was airpower, which was used offensively on a vast scale.
- The third was a very simple British invention called a "DD," or duplex-drive, tank. These were ordinary battle tanks fitted with canvas floating gear and a marine propeller, which swam in until their tracks touched bottom. They were supported by engineer-manned specialty tanks used for breaching obstacles and clearing minefields, and self-propelled armored artillery, which started firing as their

landing craft ran in. Without the DD tanks it is doubtful whether the infantry could have survived on the beach, let alone moved inland in a decisive way.

- The fourth was a breathtaking piece of lateral thinking. Capturing a port and putting it in working order would take too long; instead, two prefabricated ports were prepared in England and towed across the Channel to serve the British and American beachheads.

To these technological factors can be added a fifth: it was not possible to outflank the

Left: Soldiers of No. 4 Commando advancing into Ouistrehan on D-Day, June 6, 1944. They have fire support from Sherman tanks, which are the "DD" (duplex drive) version, with collapsible screens and twin propellers, which enabled them to swim ashore during the actual landings.

Westwall, but it was possible to jump over it. Thus, an effective part of the operational plan was the use of three airborne divisions—one British, two American—to land in the Germans' rear and block the likely routes for immediate counterattack.

The operation plan was simple enough, but as always in war the problems lay in the details of managing and maneuvering such large forces in a novel operation of such size and complexity. The essentials of the plan were as follows.

The first phase was a sustained air offensive prior to D-Day, which was designed to cripple the German transportation system and wreck the coastal batteries and radars.

The second phase was the amphibious assault itself, which would be made on a 70-mile front with 15 divisions organized into two armies, plus other combat troops amounting to two equivalent divisions, and the three airborne divisions. The actual assault was to be conducted by five divisions: the 1st and 4th U.S. divisions, the 3rd and 5th British divisions, and the 3rd Canadian division.

Then, once the beaches had been joined up and the bridgehead deepened to achieve its first

Below: Sherman tanks of the British Army's Nottinghamshire Yeomanry advance past a knocked-out Tiger tank of the Waffen-SS's 101st Heavy Tank Battalion. The scene is the village of Rauray on the road to Tilly-sur-Seulles.

objectives, the British and Canadians on the left were to pound and grind away around Caen in order to draw in all the German reserves in a battle of attrition, while the Americans on the right broke out westward, clearing the Contentin peninsula and thrusting down to Brittany until the German forces containing the beachhead were outflanked, thus allowing a great armored operation to develop in the open and then move east.

Finally, and as soon as time and space permitted, another U.S. army was to be deployed and General Eisenhower would then

take command of all the operations in France, with Montgomery reverting to command of the 21st Army Group.

This was the master plan, which was developed by Montgomery and his staff and then given to him to execute as the overall commander in the field. There has been much controversy about the Battle of Normandy, but, allowing for the accidents of war and the fact that the enemy does not always oblige, it went almost exactly according to plan and Montgomery can be fairly credited as both the planner and victor. It was his greatest feat and one of the great battles of the war.

Only figures can give some idea of that vast operation. Before D-Day on June 6, 1944, the combined air forces dropped 66,000 tons of bombs, of which some 14,000 tons were directed on the coastal defenses, knocking out most of the heavy guns and radar stations. Some 14,600 offensive sorties were flown by the Allied air forces on D-Day itself. The airborne assault was carried in 2,395 aircraft sorties and 867 gliders. Then, when it was light enough at dawn on June 6, the astonished defenders could see some 4,000 landing craft in the bay, only part of a combined fleet of 6,000 vessels.

The fire plan for the run-in used 7,600 tons of bombs, augmented by naval bombardment, followed up by landing craft fitted with multirail rocket launchers and the self-propelled field

Above: American soldiers William Boyd (left) and Jesse Volasquez inspect a German PzKpfw IV tank that has been almost completely demolished by a U.S. Army tank destroyer, December 16, 1944.

batteries that fired while still afloat in the approaching landing craft. By June 12 there were 326,000 troops, 54,000 vehicles of all kinds, and 104,000 tons of supplies on the beachhead, which was then protected against any counteroffensive.

The reaction was typically dour and determined, but unfortunately for the Germans, the harder they fought and the more sustained their forward defense, the more they became trapped in Montgomery's meat-grinder and the more they served to further his master plan. Their only hope would have been a phased withdrawal keeping their armies in being, but this was vetoed by Hitler when he actually made one of his very rare visits (on June 17) to a theater commander.

On July 3 Lieutenant General Omar Bradley's 1st (U.S.) Army began to clear space for a breakout at St. Lo, while the British and Canadians went for Caen, the anchor position of the German right, which Rommel and Rundstedt saw as their most dangerous flank.

The British attacks were made after intense bombing, with results similar to the ponderous artillery bombardments of World War I: the craters and the damage done blocked the advance of the assaulting troops and provided cover for the defenders. On July 18 another advance was attempted under cover of another huge aerial bombardment, which was to be followed up this time by three British armored divisions. But the bombing failed to include the German antitank belt deployed in depth and, as was now the trend in armored warfare, the guns won the day and stopped the British tank attack with heavy losses. Nevertheless, these attacks served their purpose in attracting the German reserves and wearing them down.

The 1st (U.S.) Army, using similar tactics at St. Lo, made better progress against reduced resistance. On July 28 Coutances was captured and Lieutenant General George Patton's newly formed 3rd Army took up the hunt. He captured Avranches, by August 10 Nantes was in Allied hands, and the whole of the Brittany peninsula

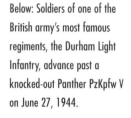

Below: Soldiers of one of the British army's most famous regiments, the Durham Light Infantry, advance past a knocked-out Panther PzKpfw V on June 27, 1944.

was cut off. Patton was now directed to turn east and set off with Paris as the objective.

It was at this point that Hitler, looking at his map as usual and playing military chess, perceived the theoretical vulnerability of the inner, or left-hand, flank of Patton's eastward-swinging hook, and ordered every Panzer formation that could be disengaged to attack from Mortain westward toward Avranches. Bradley rapidly and competently countered this, deploying eight U.S. divisions, and as General Paul Hausser's German 7th Army threatened to cut into Patton's flank, the Americans in turn cut into Hausser's with an attack directed on Vire.

Away to the east, the British had cleared as far south as Villers Bocage on one side of Caen and on the other the Canadians had thrust down toward Falaise. It was slow progress, but they achieved their objectives and Montgomery's objectives by bashing and battering away, supported by massive air and land firepower. Meanwhile Patton, out in the open, was already south of Hausser's left rear.

Germany's 7th Army, with its head at Mortain and its communications running back 40 miles to the narrow gap between Falaise and Argentan, was therefore doomed. That the net was not pulled tight has been the subject of much military criticism, but in fact it was partly due to the accidents of battle, what the 19th century German military thinker, Clausewitz, calls "friction," and the disobliging behavior of the 2nd Panzer Division, which, battered though it was, refused to play the part of the passive enemy to oblige theoretical strategists. This German division tore a gap in the enclosing Allied cordon and held it open for just long enough to enable a substantial fraction of the wrecks of the 7th Army formations to slip through to temporary freedom. Those that remained inside this *kessel* of Hitler's own creation became the victims of some of the most horrifying scenes of destruction of the whole war. All the roads were jammed three abreast and miles deep with tanks, artillery, and transport from 15 German divisions, and up and

Below: Armored troops and infantrymen of the British Guards Armored Division in an orchard near Caen, France, July 18, 1944. The infantry will dismount short when nearing the enemy and go into battle on foot, leaving the tanks free to maneuver on their own.

Above: The Allied invasion of southern France, with heavy transport ships standing offshore and cargo being brought ashore near Cavalaire by DUKWs. The DUKW was essentially a 2½-ton truck wrapped in a watertight shell to make it amphibious. It was equally at home on land or water.

down them the combined air forces flew remorselessly, bombing, rocketing, and firing cannons. The Germans left west of the Seine some half million men, 3,000 guns, 1,500 tanks, 2,000 wrecked aircraft, and 20,000 vehicles. The Falaise pocket was full of wrecked tanks and guns, and of dead men and horses. Such was the end of the Battle of Normandy.

Hitler's other contribution, apart from ordering the hopeless Mortain counterattack, had been to sack Field Marshal Rundstedt, who, when asked on June 23 what should be done, with disasters occurring thick and fast, replied, "Make peace, you fools!" Another to go was Geyr von Schweppenburg, the Panzer corps commander. These were replaced by one of Hitler's stooges, Field Marshal Guenther Hans von Kluge, who was, in his turn, later replaced by General Walther Model. Field Marshal Rommel was *hors de combat*, wounded, the victim of an Allied air attack. Thus, not only were the German defenses in France smashed but its effective leadership had also been

removed. All France was now open to Eisenhower and the victorious Allied armies.

As a battle, Overlord lives up to its resounding title. It was a masterpiece that the British Major General J. F. C. Fuller described in his book *The Decisive Battles of the Western World* as among the most decisive battles in history, but there is, however, less agreement over its strategic exploitation.

The next phase of the Allied assault came on August 15 with the landings in the French Riviera, which had been elaborately planned in every detail and executed with barely a shot fired. This operation, some argue, was a classic violation of the principle of economy of force: the resources taken from Italy rendered the Gothic Line battles sterile for lack of power to exploit them, and landed so late in France that they had no effect on the operations raging in the north. Indeed, the chief advantage was the gain in port facilities to speed the U.S. buildup.

Others again argue that Patton's spectacular dash could have been better directed to a deep encirclement of the remaining German formations instead of motoring off to register a glittering list of liberated French cities. The chief critics of Eisenhower's strategy, of which Montgomery was the most vocal, argue that if all the logistic resources had been concentrated on one selected army, stripped down to its fighting echelons so as to make it fully mobile, a rapid pursuit in classical style might have prevented the shattered German forces from ever rallying again, allowing the war in the West to be ended in 1944.

In order to be effective such a move would have had to be planned long before Overlord began, commanders briefed and acclimatized to the idea, and national rivalries concerning who was to have the leading role assuaged. There were also purely technical considerations. The western divisions were so lavishly equipped with vehicles that they had reached a point at which overmechanization had actually made them less mobile than leaner formations.

After bitter argument the Eisenhower strategy was followed, and the five armies rolled forward against light resistance in line abreast. The 7th (U.S.) Army came up from the south of France directed on the Vosges, the 3rd (Patton) headed for Verdun, the 1st Army headed for the Ardennes via Paris, while the 2nd (British) Army crossed the Somme at Amiens and the 1st (Canadian) moved along the Channel coast. In this way the Germans were swept out of France tidily, but were given what no prudent commander ever gave German generals—time. Thus, with their great resilience they were able to organize another defensive front and even stage a counteroffensive before the year was out.

## UNCONDITIONAL SURRENDER

With the Western Allies pushing on from France and the Russians from the east, Germany's end in the spring of 1945 was certain, but its death throes exacted a terrible cost on both sides. An examination of the whole strategic picture of the war in Europe in August 1944 inevitably gives rise to the question as to why should it have taken another eight months of bitter fighting to subdue the German war machine? Why did the Germans fight on and not follow Rundstedt's brutal advice to make peace; or why would the Allies not choose some less uncompromising alternative to unconditional surrender?

The German defensive system in the West had ceased to exist. Even the original Westwall, also known as the "Siegfried Line," was without a proper garrison and its weapons, shifted to the Atlantic Wall (the later Westwall), had all been lost. In eastern Europe there had been a series a appalling disasters, starting with the then-unheard-of surrender of a whole German army at Stalingrad in 1943, the retreat from the Caucasus, and the defeat at Kursk (an event as significant as Stalingrad). Offensives up and down the Eastern Front, checked only with great difficulty, were followed in the last week of July 1944—when the Normandy battle was at its height—by the virtual destruction of the German Army Group Center, which momentarily left a great gap in the line running from Riga to Sandomierz.

Top: British general Sir Bernard Montgomery (in beret) with another British general atop a haystack in Normandy. Montgomery was sometimes difficult to deal with, but he was a very effective commander and won his battles.

Above: German infantry advancing during the Ardennes offensive, December 17, 1944. This bitterly fought battle was the last major undertaking by the Germans in the West.

The Germans no longer had any true reserve. The best they could do was to shuttle divisions from one part of a front to another, or between the two major fronts, the latter becoming increasingly costly in the West in the face of overwhelming Allied air superiority.

The short and simple answer to these questions is that the war was not being fought for any coldly weighed considerations of political profit and loss, but to destroy a wholly evil and destructive entity. With the benefit of hindsight, it is possible to regret a military outcome that divided Europe and Germany, but it must be remembered that as far as the Soviet Union was concerned, an unprovoked aggression had devastated their country and cost untold lives, and so they were certainly not going to stop until the last German soldier was dead or disarmed and Berlin in their hands. The British and American leaders were equally determined to destroy Hitler and his war

machine, and talked of the dismemberment of the German Reich. There can be no doubt that this echoed the feeling of the vast majority of ordinary people in the West.

Hitler himself in any case was both immovable and irremovable, since he still held all but a very few of his followers in a hypnotic grip. By 1944 he was completely demented and thus determined to immolate the Germans as a punishment for what he saw as their failure to achieve the aim he had given them. He still possessed a huge and extraordinarily responsive army whose leaders were driven by a complex variety of motives ranging from faith in *Der Führer* to bring off yet another miracle, through their own soldierly traditions, to fear of defeat. All these ensured that they grimly continued to fight battles that their professional judgment told them they could not possibly win.

It must also be remembered that in the summer of 1944 the German army still had

*Below: During the advance through Germany, U.S. infantrymen run past an M4 Sherman armed with a 76 mm gun.*

Left: British paratroop mortar section in action, September 20, 1944. The weapon is a 3 in. mortar, and its very high angle indicates that it is firing at very close range. The radio operator (right) is receiving ranging and target information from the MFC (mortar fire controller).

some 325 divisions. Admittedly they were understrength and there was a dearth of ammunition, petrol, and (as a result of chaotic planning policies) weapons in general and tanks in particular. But these divisions carried little administrative fat; their middle and junior leaders, in spite of frightful losses, were still very good and the extraordinary alchemy of German training turned at least some of their last remaining recruits—many of them mere boys, while others were elderly and often sick men— into tough and resilient fighters. Right to the end no Allied soldier in his senses ever tackled a German position except with great circumspection and maximum fire support.

In 1944 the Russians appreciated that they faced 179 of these divisions, together with 49,000 guns and 5,250 tanks. They knew of only one way of dealing with this huge and still-formidable force, which was to build up their own resources. In 1943 alone the Russians had raised 78 new divisions, which were organized into tank and infantry divisions, as well as specialized formations such as artillery divisions intended to provide the enormous bombardments that preceded every attack. In 1944 their armaments industry produced 90 million shells, 29,000 tanks, and 40,000 combat aircraft. These were to be used in a succession of well-planned, deliberately mounted offensives, first on one sector and then on another, with local

Right: A grinning British tank crew looks on as their gunner makes his way with some difficulty across a churned-up German farmyard. His mission, however, is an important one: to obtain water for tea.

superiority of 4:1 and 100–250 guns and mortars per kilometer of front, until the last German reserves were used up, their whole Eastern Front cracked, and the way to Berlin was open.

As for the Allied armies in the West, it is argued to this day whether or not they could have conquered Germany in 1944; all that is certain is that their victory in France caught them unprepared both militarily, mentally, and logistically.

Some German generals believed that a dash at the Rhine crossings before a defensive crust had time to harden might have reached the Ruhr. This was the policy advocated by Montgomery but, as has been said, for perfectly

breathing space for Hitler's last operational plan to be put in hand. First, both fronts had to be stabilized, using every possible expedient, then an armored force was to be assembled for a spoiling attack through the Ardennes against the long, weak cordon Eisenhower's broad-front policy had lined along the German frontier. After that, when the British and Americans had been thrown back on their heels, the main effort would be switched back to the east.

## ARNHEM

Following D-Day, 16 separate airborne plans were made and canceled, but when the Allied 21st Army Group reached the Low Countries, Montgomery, realizing that the highly trained Allied airborne army was still sitting in England and still awaiting a practicable mission, decided on a bold advance northeastward, which would enable him to drive into northern Germany, free Antwerp, and eliminate the V-1 and V-2 launching sites. Operation Market required the 101st (U.S.) Airborne Division to capture two canal bridges north of Eindhoven, the 82nd (U.S.) Airborne Division to capture bridges over the Maas and the Waal, and the 1st (British) Airborne Division the bridges across the Lower Rhine at Arnhem. The ground element, Operation Garden, required the 30th (British) Corps to advance, relieving each airborne bridgehead in turn until, once past Arnhem, it could head for the Zuider Zee.

In detail, the 1st Airborne Division was to capture the two bridges at Arnhem, establish a

Below: British paratroops land among gliders at a landing/ dropping zone outside the town of Arnhem, September 17, 1944. The gliders are all Airspeed Horsas and have made good landings. Note the invasion stripes carried by all Allied aircraft, and how the tails have been detached to enable the aircraft to be unloaded rapidly.

good political and logistic reasons Eisenhower, as soon as he had assumed command in the field, had decided on a broad-fronted advance.

This at first was against the lightest of resistance. The British arrived in Brussels on September 3 and the U.S. armies reached the Dutch and German frontiers by the 11th. Then there was the pause that gave the Germans

Above: U.S. troops advance under fire from German artillery, October 9, 1944.

Below: The scene on the Dutch river Waal at Nijmegen, September 30, 1944. The bridges are unusable but the DUKWs continue to operate.

82nd Airborne Division to Grave, and the British 1st Airborne Division to Arnhem: a massive air operation involving 3,887 aircraft. The British 1st Para Brigade was carried in C-47s of the U.S. 9th Troop Carrier Command, while the 1st Airlanding Brigade was in 358 British Army–crewed gliders, towed by RAF tugs. Intense preliminary Allied air attacks ensured that the enemy was in no position to

bridgehead on the south side, and secure and hold the dropping zones (DZs) and landing zones (LZs). Aircraft shortages meant that only one para brigade and one glider-borne brigade —plus divisional headquarters—could fly in on the operation's D-day (September 17, 1944), with the third brigade following on D+1, and the Polish brigade in reserve. A fatal decision was to site the DZs and LZs some seven miles from the bridges.

On September 17 the assault waves of the 101st Airborne Division flew to Eindhoven, the disrupt the flight, and pathfinders dropped the 21st Independent Parachute Company to mark and hold the DZ/LZs, closely followed by the paratroops and gliders. On landing, the 1st Parachute Brigade set off for the bridges, with 2nd Battalion, Parachute Regiment (2 Para) reaching the Arnhem road bridge approach by dark, although the railway bridge was demolished before they arrived. Opposition was stronger than expected and, once at the bridge, 2 Para was cut off from the remainder of the brigade. Meanwhile, the 1st Airlanding Brigade secured the DZs and LZs as planned. In the afternoon divisional headquarters lost communications with 1 Para Brigade, so Major General Urquart set off to discover how things were going, but he was trapped in a house by enemy snipers, and nobody knew where he was.

Below: Men of 1st Parachute Battalion in a shell hole during the fighting at Arnhem. The soldier on the left is armed with a Bren light machine gun; the others have short magazine Lee-Enfield rifles.

Right: Having just landed on the east bank of the Rhine, U.S. paratroopers dig in, some of their camouflaged parachutes still caught up in the trees.

On D+1 (September 18) bad weather caused delays and when 4 Para dropped on DZ "Y" and units of the 1st Airlanding Brigade landed on LZ "S," they were five hours late, a delay that enabled the Germans to prevent 4 Para from reaching the high ground from which they would have dominated Arnhem. At divisional headquarters the commander was still unaccounted for, so at about midday Brigadier Hicks took temporary command. 2 Para inflicted heavy casualties on a German unit heading for the bridge, but the pressure was increasing, and both 1 Para and 2nd South Staffordshire (part of 1st Airlanding Brigade) tried but failed to reach the bridge. The British 1st Airborne Division was now split into three: 2 Para at the northern end of the bridge; a group on the western edge of Arnhem; and the third group west of Osterbeeck. Meanwhile, the relief force, 30th Corps, was held up by some very heavy opposition.

On D+2 (September 19) the Germans systematically attacked 2 Para, although the battalion's presence prevented the 10th SS Panzer Division from using the bridge as it

rushed to oppose the U.S. landings at Nijmegen. Meanwhile, ongoing communications problems plagued the operation, while many resupply drops were falling straight into German hands. This tragic situation arose partly because ground markers could not be seen by the low-flying aircraft, but also because information on DZ changes was taking 18 hours to arrive at the dispatching airfields.

At 7:30 A.M. on D+3 (September 20) Major General Urquart rejoined his division HQ and sent another force to relieve 2 Para, but to no avail. There were two supply drops, but most fell into enemy hands.

Early on D+4 (September 21) 2 Para was overrun, with virtually all men either killed or captured. To the west, the remainder of the division was squeezed ever tighter, its position increasingly desperate. The Polish parachute brigade was delivered to the DZ south of the river by 53 C-47s and once on the ground Major General Sosabowski reorganized the 750 men into two weak battalions. But these were unable to reach the northern bridgehead, since it was impossible to use the ferry. On a brighter note, 30th Corps was now sufficiently close for its artillery to give supporting fire to the beleaguered paratroopers. The Guards Armored Division was held up in its attempted break-through along the nine-mile road from Nijmegen to Arnhem and, since it was poor tank country, the corps commander put the 43rd Infantry Division in the lead, although the changeover cost several hours.

Just after dawn on D+5 (September 22) an armored car squadron from 30th Corps reached the Polish brigade at Driel, while the 214th Infantry Brigade (43rd Infantry Division) attacked the strongly held village of Elst, but also sent a battalion around a flank, which joined the Polish brigade that evening. Bad weather prevented resupply and at 8:20 P.M. the commander of the 2nd British Army gave permission for 1st Airborne to withdraw.

On D+6 (September 23) the position of the paratroops was even worse, although a resupply drop from the U.K. did take place. The 214th Infantry Brigade fought throughout the day in Elst but, although the 130th Infantry Brigade (43rd Infantry Division) had established itself in Driel, they were unable to ferry a battalion across the river, since the crossing was dominated by fire by German units.

Left: Men of the 1st Battalion, 180th Infantry Regiment, advance through a German town, March 27, 1945. An elderly German woman, seemingly oblivious of the soldiers, looks with despair at the ruined shops and houses, but the German army had inflicted far worse damage during its rampages across Europe in the previous five years.

On D+7 (September 24) all plans to take the Arnhem bridge were canceled and the 214th Infantry Brigade continued in its efforts to clear the strong German opposition in Elst. The 130th Infantry Brigade again tried to get a battalion across the river, this time in rubber boats, but the current carried them well downstream of the paratroops' narrow perimeter. By now the paratroops were out of food and very short of ammunition. D+8 (September 25) was the final day and the Allied withdrawal took place that night, with heavy supporting fire from 30th Corps artillery. In all, 6,400 men were killed or captured, while 2,398 escaped.

This disaster was certainly not due to a lack of courage on the ground or in the air, and five Victoria Crosses were awarded, four to soldiers and one to an airman, Flight Lieutenant David Lord, captain of a C-47 supply plane. On September 19 Lord's C-47 was hit twice in the starboard wing by antiaircraft fire on the approach and the engine was set ablaze. Lord came down to 900 ft. as ordered, holding the blazing aircraft steady while the containers were thrown out. Despite the dispatchers' best efforts, two of the containers remained and David Lord, determined to complete his mission, went around again. His damaged aircraft, now blazing furiously, crossed the DZ for the second time at 500 ft. under constant fire. The two containers finally dropped, and Lord steadied the aircraft for the crew to jump, but the starboard wing suddenly collapsed and the aircraft crashed, killing all except one man, who was thrown clear and survived.

Arnhem was one of history's great "might-have-beens." Had it succeeded the 21st Army Group would have swept through northern Germany, the war could have ended in 1944, and the Western Allies could have entered Berlin before the Soviets. That, however, was not to be.

## THE END IN EUROPE

The final German offensive was also late. It was timed for mid-November, but it was not until December that the 5th and 6th SS Panzer Armies could be reequipped, with the result that the attack could not be launched until December 16. The plan, a revival of old memories, was to attack from assembly areas in the Eifel hills northwest through the Ardennes and across the Meuse with the object of taking Antwerp, so separating the northern wing of Eisenhower's forces into two parts and cutting both off from their new supply base, after which the northern segment would be eliminated. It was far too ambitious for the forces available, and doomed from the start, but it gave the British and Americans an unpleasant shock. Surprise was complete, but the defense put up by the American troops (notably by the 101st Airborne Division at Bastogne) was obstinate, the British 2nd Army redeployed promptly to establish a line along the Meuse, and swift and aggressive reaction by the U.S. formations south of the salient created by the offensive soon threw the Panzers back on the defensive. The Germans were never a soft touch, and it took the Americans a month's hard fighting and some 75,000 casualties to clean up the situation, but in the end all that had been achieved by this last of Hitler's military inspirations was a further, fatal reduction of his armored mobile troops.

Left: Two weary soldiers of the 110th Regiment, U.S. Infantry, December 19, 1944; Private Adam Davis (left) and T/5 Milford Sellars. Their battalion was overrun by the Germans and from the looks on their faces they know that they were lucky to have survived.

Above: Soldiers of a U.S. Army engineer battalion receive the news that Germany has, at long last, been defeated.

Previous pages: Soldiers of the 55th Armored Infantry Battalion and tanks of the 22nd Tank Battalion advance through the German town of Wernberg in the final days of the war in Europe.

aim of the Allies, firmly adhered to by Eisenhower in the spirit of the Yalta agreements, was to meet on the Elbe, crushing all resistance between them. The Red Army led off on January 12, and the caption attached to the operational sketch in Guderian's memoirs is sufficient comment: "The Catastrophe."

In February the British 21st Army Group and the U.S. 8th Army broke into the Siegfried Line and were finally poised along the Rhine after very heavy fighting in the Reichswald and

The Ardennes offensive was the last unpredictable and therefore militarily interesting operation of the war in Europe, the last flicker of mobility and maneuver, and the last of the blitzkrieg. The operations of 1945 were uniformly dull and depressing, savoring as they did of an execution prolonged only by the struggles of the victim. The German army was methodically destroyed by opponents with apparently limitless resources. The astonishing fact is that the resistance it offered lasted four long months. Some idea of what it took in the way of punishment can only be given by figures. On the first day of the operation to clear the Reichswald, which was only the preliminary to their final crossing of the Rhine, the British used 1,050 guns and fired 6,000 tons of ammunition. Hostile batteries received some 1,000 rounds apiece and 50 guns were knocked out.

For their final offensive directed on Berlin, the Russians brought forward seven million rounds of artillery ammunition and assembled 68 infantry divisions, 3,155 tanks and self-propelled guns, and 42,000 guns and mortars, these last being at a density of 250 per kilometer of front at the point of main effort. When the advance was held up by minor resistance on the Seelow ridge barring the way to Berlin, Zhukov simply threw in two tank armies.

An account of the final battles can be little more than a catalog of dates and offensives. The

the Hurtgen forest, eliminating some 18 German divisions. They then forced a passage over the Rhine covered by more massive bombardments and the last airborne attack of the war, after which the British turned north and east, the Americans cleared the Ruhr, and their 1st Army cut another eastward swathe farther south.

If the German resistance in the west was dour and determined, in the east it was fanatical. It was not until April 25 that the 1st Belorussian and 1st Ukrainian Fronts linked up to the west of Berlin. On the same day the Red Army and the U.S. Army met at Torgau on the Elbe. Hitler committed suicide on the 30th, Berlin surrendered on May 2, and on May 7 Colonel General Alfred Jodl signed the instrument of unconditional surrender at Eisenhower's headquarters in Rheims.

The end of the war in Europe and the final destruction of Hitler's war machine took place officially at one minute past 11:00 A.M., Central European Time, May 8, 1945.

Left: A U.S. Army Sherman drives through a German town, watched by a crowd of bemused civilians. For the Germans, life was now going to be very different, with no Nazis and under the rule of the Allied powers.

*Chapter 2*

# THE WAR
# AT SEA

GERMANY'S U-BOATS BEGAN THE WAR AT SEA with the cowardly sinking of the liner *Athenia,* and went on to score many more victories. The Allies struck their first real blow at the Battle of the River Plate, and during the Battle for Norway, before Britain's Royal Navy and other ships had to rescue defeated and disheartened troops from the mainland of Europe. Standing virtually alone, Britain fought the first stages of the Battle of the Atlantic against packs of U-boats intent on stopping convoys carrying vital supplies. In the Mediterranean in 1940 and 1941 the British traded blows with the German and Italian fleets. In the Atlantic through 1942, despite the entry of America into the war, the Allies' convoys continued to suffer from attacks by Germany's submarines and land-based aircraft, although British small ship action at the end of the year provided some hope for the future. The Battle of the Atlantic entered a third and decisive phase during 1943, and technological advances aided the Allies in the battle against the U-boats. At a great cost in men and ships, determined efforts in the Mediterranean saved Malta and contributed mightily to the Allies' victory at El Alamein and the landing of forces in North Africa, Sicily, Italy, and the south of France. Germany's surface challenge to the Allies' naval power virtually came to an end with the sinking of the capital ships *Scharnhorst* and *Tirpitz.*

Right: The epitome of German naval power, the mighty *Bismarck,* widely acknowledged as one of the finest battleships ever built. Here she is in a Norwegian fjord about to set out on her one and only operational cruise, in which she sank the British battlecruiser HMS *Hood* but was herself overcome by the sheer scale of British naval power.

Below: The German U-boat U-47 returns in triumph to her base in Kiel, having penetrated the British naval base at Scapa Flow and sunk the battleship HMS *Royal Oak* with the loss of 833 lives, October 14, 1939. The commanding officer, Günther Prien, stands at the forward end of the bridge, wearing the traditional white-topped cap.

When Britain and France declared war on Germany on September 3, 1939, to honor their promise to go to the aid of Poland if it were attacked, they were too unprepared and ill-equipped to launch any offensive action. By standing on the defensive, therefore, they hoped to gain the time necessary to remedy defects and make good at least some of the deficiencies.

The consequent lack of activity on land and in the air during the fall and winter led to references to the "phony war"—or, in Winston Churchill's less contemptuous phrase, the "Twilight War." It was far from either at sea, however, where, on the first day the British ocean liner, the *Athenia*, became the first of 41 merchant ships to be destroyed in that month, being torpedoed without warning and sunk by the German submarine U-30. In the same month, too, the Royal Navy suffered its first loss of a major warship, the aircraft carrier HMS *Courageous*, unwisely deployed on antisubmarine patrol in the Western Approaches, where she was torpedoed by U-29. Three days earlier

the carrier HMS *Ark Royal* had narrowly escaped the same fate. Although a limited convoy system had been initiated, the old lesson had still to be fully relearned: that it was by escorting the convoys, and not by patrolling the sea lanes, that would allow the submarine attack to be defeated.

One of the vessels that went to the aid of *Courageous* was the destroyer HMS *Kelly*, which, together with its commanding officer, Captain Lord Louis Mountbatten, came to epitomize the fighting spirit of Britain's navy. In the

first eight months of the war *Kelly* steamed thousands of miles, protecting convoys and hunting both U-boats and powerful surface raiders. Like all destroyers she was overworked but she suffered more than most, being torpedoed and mined by the enemy as well as being damaged by heavy seas and collisions.

Another demonstration that the war at sea was far from phony was provided by U 47, commanded by Günther Prien, who skillfully penetrated the unfinished ship barrier of an entrance to Scapa Flow, the Royal Navy's main operational anchorage off the north coast of Scotland. Prien attacked on October 14 and sunk the battleship HMS *Royal Oak* with the loss of no fewer than 833 of her crew.

Mines also took a heavy toll, including magnetic types dropped from planes, which were first encountered on September 16. An important victim was the new cruiser HMS *Belfast*, which suffered a broken back when mined in the Firth of Forth in October. Then on December 4 the Home Fleet flagship HMS *Nelson* was damaged by a magnetic mine off Loch Ewe, where the fleet had transferred its base while the defenses of Scapa Flow were being perfected following Prien's attack.

HMS *Rawalpindi* was a former P&O liner that had been requisitioned by the Admiralty on the outbreak of war and converted into an armed merchant cruiser (AMC). This meant that she had eight 6 in. guns installed, together with magazines and extra communications, but she

Above: A prewar assembly of Type VIIA U boats of the 2nd Flotille. The device with a serrated edge on the bow of U-34 was intended to cut antisubmarine nets, but proved to be of little value and was discontinued.

had none of the armor plating and internal design of a warship. On November 23, 1939, *Rawalpindi* was deployed as part of the Northern Patrol, covering the gap between Iceland and the Faeroe Islands, when her lookouts spotted the ultramodern German battle cruisers, *Gneisenau* and *Scharnhorst*, each armed with eight 11 in. guns, which were making the German surface fleet's first tentative sortie into the Atlantic. In the finest traditions of the Royal Navy, *Rawalpindi's* captain headed straight for the enemy, but it took just fourteen minutes for the *Scharnhorst* to reduce her audacious attacker to a blazing hulk. *Rawalpindi* lost 238 out of a complement of 276, but the two battle cruisers then steered for home, abandoning their mission of penetrating deep into the Atlantic.

Further afield, British merchant ships were falling one by one into the hands of the pocket battleship, *Admiral Graf Spee*, which, with her sister ship, *Deutschland* (soon to be renamed *Lützow*), had been secretly sailed before the war began, to the South and North Atlantic, respectively. The *Deutschland* captured one ship and sank another, but was largely neutralized by the convoy system and then, with the added complication of engine problems, she was recalled to Germany.

The *Graf Spee*, on the other hand, had been finding easy pickings and by December 7 she had sunk nine ships totaling 50,000 tons and had managed to evade several hunting groups formed by the British and French navies to run her to earth. But the time approached for her to return home to Germany and Captain Langsdorff, her greatly respected commanding officer, decided to attack the merchant shipping off the mouth of the River Plate. Just as he arrived, at precisely 6:08 A.M. on December 13, 1939—a calm, blue summer day with maximum visibility—he was intercepted by a British squadron composed of the battle cruiser HMS *Exeter* and the light cruisers *Achilles* of the Royal New Zealand Navy and *Ajax*, flagship of Commodore Henry Harwood.

In the ensuing running fight *Exeter* engaged from one side and the two light cruisers from the other. The *Graf Spee*, aided by the surface warning radar with which she was equipped, quickly found the *Exeter's* range and within 35 minutes had put her out of effective action. The German ship had, however, also suffered damage and

casualties from both the *Exeter's* 8 in. guns and the light cruisers' 5.9 in. guns. By 7:30 A.M. Langsdorff had decided to set a course for the neutral Uruguayan port of Montevideo for repairs. The *Ajax* and *Achilles* followed *Graf Spee* until she entered harbor and then waited, just outside the limits of Uruguayan waters, to see what would happen next.

### A SCUTTLING AND A SUICIDE

During the next few days the British conducted a series of diplomatic maneuvers intended to delay the *Graf Spee's* departure until more and heavier warships could be assembled to engage her when she tried to break out into the open ocean. Langsdorff was misled into believing that the assembly had actually taken place and he concluded that internment or scuttling were the

Left: The British cruiser HMS *Exeter* lying in Port Stanley in the Falkland Islands, showing the damage inflicted by the *Graf Spee* during the Battle of the River Plate. The local repairs were very temporary and she had to return to England for a full refit.

only choices open to him. He chose the latter and on the evening of December 17 the *Graf Spee* steamed slowly out of harbor, manned only by a skeleton crew and when even these last few men had been taken off, she was blown up in the estuary. All her crew then made for Buones Aires, where they were interned. Langsdorff, a man of the greatest integrity, ensured that his crew were as safe and as comfortable as possible in the circumstances and then shot himself. The British people, engaged in what seemed to many to be a phony war, hailed this skirmish off the River Plate as a sensational success, although history suggests that it was less significant than seemed the case at the time.

## THE INVASION OF NORWAY

Meanwhile, plans were being made both by the Allies and by Germany to widen the scope of the war by carrying hostilities to Scandinavia. The British and French initially intended to go to the aid of Finland, which had been brutally invaded by Russia. When Finland capitulated, however, the plans were adapted to meet a new strategic requirement, the need to halt the traffic in Swedish iron ore, which was exported to Germany via the Norwegian port of Narvik. Allied planners decided to achieve this by laying mines along a portion of the route through Norwegian waters, while simultaneously an

expedition was prepared to forestall a possible German retaliatory attempt to seize the Norwegian ports.

The Allied plan was an badly-conceived, amateur affair. The military force allocated was neither equipped nor trained for the rigors of the Arctic climate of north Norway and it was naively believed that the troops would be welcomed by the Norwegians. Also, it was planned that the expedition would be devoid of any significant air support other than a handful of low-performance naval aircraft. On April 7, 1940, however, the day before the first move of the Allied plan was made, it was preempted by the launching of a German plan, long prepared, to seize all the principal Norwegian ports.

For this, almost the entire German surface fleet was employed, divided into six groups, and if they were to avoid interception by the superior force of the British Home Fleet, secrecy was essential. Group I comprised of ten destroyers carrying 2,000 troops to capture Narvik, supported by the *Gneisenau* (flagship of Vice Admiral Lütjens) and *Scharnhorst*, which were to make a diversionary cruise in the Arctic after escorting the destroyers to Vestfiord. Group II, composed of the heavy cruiser *Hipper* and four destroyers carrying 1,700 troops, was to start out in company with Group I, but then divert to occupy Trondheim. These two groups sailed early on April 7 and the secrecy upon which the

Right: The British/French expedition to hold Norway was a complete failure. Here, a fleet anchorage at Harstad, Norway, is protected by a land-based 40 mm antiaircraft detachment of the Royal Artillery, May 14, 1940. The ship on the left wears a special "dazzle" paint scheme, which was intended to confuse enemy gun crews.

German plan relied was broken by the aerial detection of the two groups soon after they sailed. Fortunately for the Germans, however, British hesitation, followed by faulty deployment of the Home Fleet, prevented interception of either Groups I or II, or even of Group III, which was centered on the light cruisers *Köln* and *Königsberg* and was heading for Bergen.

There was, however, one fortuitous encounter on April 8. HMS *Glowworm*, one of the destroyers escorting the battle cruiser *Renown*, had fallen behind in order to search for a man who had been swept overboard. The *Glowworm* was attempting to rejoin her group when, at first light on the 8th, she sighted and engaged two German destroyers of the *Hipper*'s screen. Then the cruiser loomed out of the prevailing haze at short range and severely damaged the *Glowworm* but not before the latter was able to radio her enemy report. Then, unable to escape the destroyers, she was steered to launch her torpedoes and, when those were avoided, to charge suicidally into her overpowering opponent. This despairing effort before she blew up and sank caused considerable damage to the *Hipper*, though not enough to put her out of action. A posthumous Victoria Cross was awarded to Lieutenant Commander Roope of the *Glowworm* in acknowledgment of his gallantry.

In response to the destroyer's report, the Home Fleet commander detached part of his force to try to catch the *Hipper*, but in vain, and at dawn on the 8th the six German invasion groups arrived unhindered at their objectives. Besides the three groups mentioned above, there was Group IV for Kristiansand centered on the light cruiser *Karlsruhe*, a small Group VI for Egersund to occupy the cable station there, and Group V, composed of the heavy cruiser *Blücher*, the pocket battleship *Lützow* (formerly the *Deutschland*), the light cruiser *Emden*, and some smaller craft, carrying 2,000 troops for the occupation of Oslo.

The last of these groups was the only one to meet any determined and effective opposition, suffering the loss of the *Blücher* to the guns and torpedoes of the shore defenses of Oslofiord. Nevertheless, by noon the Norwegian capital was in German hands, as were all the other principal ports.

Far to the north, Admiral Lütjens had parted company with the destroyers of Group I off Vestfiord on the previous evening as planned, and had taken the *Gneisenau* and *Scharnhorst* northward in a mounting northerly gale. At dawn on the 8th he was surprised by the *Renown* and, having suffered considerable damage from three 15 in. hits on his flagship, he fled northward at high speed, accepting further damage from the huge seas into which his ships were forced to escape. The *Renown*, always a

Below: The German battlecruiser *Gneisenau* in 1938. She was armed with nine 11 in. guns in three triple turrets. Her main armored belt can be seen by the bulge in the side of the hull and the absence of portholes. She is carrying two spotter floatplanes: a Heinkel He-116 forward and an Arado Ar-95 aft.

Right: German destroyer *Friedrich Eckoldt* (Z-16) photographed off the Norwegian coast from the cruiser *Admiral Hipper*, April 9, 1940. The *Friedrich Eckoldt* was launched in March 1937 and after a very active war was sunk by HMS *Sheffield* during the attack on Convoy JW.51B, December 31, 1942.

Previous pages: Germany's light cruiser *Leipzig* was launched in 1929 and carried an armament of nine 6 in. guns. Power was provided by an unusual combination of steam-driven outer shafts and a diesel-driven central shaft. She served throughout the war and was scuttled, filled with poison gas shells, in December 1946.

lucky ship, had received two hits that did little damage.

Other surface forces of the Home Fleet, having failed to intercept any of the German groups on their way to their objectives, now found themselves driven away from the Norwegian coast by the lack of fighter cover against attacks by German high-level bombers and dive-bombers, which were now able to operate from captured Norwegian airfields. In spite of considerable expenditure of the limited antiaircraft ammunition, the battleship *Rodney* was hit and damaged and the destroyer *Gurkha* was sunk. British submarines, however, were operating in the Kattegat and Skagerrak and took a steady toll of enemy supply ships; and, of even greater importance, on the evening of the 8th, HMS *Truant* intercepted and sank the cruiser *Karlsruhe* as she was returning home from Kristiansand.

Now that the Home Fleet was properly deployed, the German warships' return voyage was proving to be their moment of greatest peril, although low visibility and wild weather enabled *Gneisenau, Scharnhorst, Hipper,* and *Köln* to evade all the searchers and get safely home. But at Bergen, the *Königsberg,* damaged by the Norwegian shore defenses, was attacked early on the 10th by naval dive-bombers from

Katston air station on Orkney and sunk at her berth, the first major warship ever to be sunk during hostilities by air attack. Late on that same day *Lützow,* returning from Oslo to Kiel, was torpedoed by the submarine *Sunfish* and so badly damaged that she was to be out of action for a year.

### A BRAVE DESTROYER ATTACK

The German navy was thus paying a painful price for their treacherous rape of neutral Norway. And at snow-covered Narvik the ten German destroyers had to delay their departure because of the tankers from which they were to refuel, even though they knew that the danger of being trapped increased with every hour that passed. But, unknown to the Germans, since noon on the 9th four destroyers of the British Second Flotilla (Captain Warburton-Lee)—HMS *Hardy, Hotspur, Havock,* and *Hunter*—had been steering up the Vestfjord with orders to proceed to Narvik to sink or capture the single German ship that was believed to have arrived there.

While seeking further information from the pilot station inside the fjord, Warburton-Lee was joined by HMS *Hostile,* the fifth ship of his flotilla, and he now learned that at least six

Left: The German cruiser *Admiral Hipper*, seen on a prewar cruise. She was the nameship of a class of five laid down in the 1930s, but only three were completed, the other two being reconstructed as aircraft carriers, but never finished. *Hipper* operated mainly in northern waters during the war and was broken up in 1948–49.

German warships larger than his own were at Narvik. These were by no means insuperable odds and relying upon the effect of surprise, he signaled his intention of attacking at dawn. Thus, as the curtain of snowfall and mist parted at dawn, Warburton-Lee saw three German destroyers anchored off of Narvik, with two more alongside the tanker, still refueling.

The first indication that the Germans were under attack was the explosion of a torpedo, that wrecked the *Wilhelm Heidkamp*, flagship of Commodore Bonte, who was killed. Two more German destroyers were also sunk by torpedoes, while the *Diether von Roeder* and *Hans Lüdemann* were heavily damaged by gunfire, and a number of merchant ships in the harbor were sunk at their moorings. This action occupied the best part of an hour, after which Captain Warburton-Lee turned to retire seaward with his flotilla.

Unknown to the British, the remaining German ships were berthed in inlets off the main fjord, and these now arrived on the scene to take the British force between two fires. The *Hardy* was quickly shattered and set on fire, her captain killed, and the ship herself beached in a sinking condition. The *Hunter* was next to be crippled and sunk, while the *Hotspur* was severely damaged. In reply, two of the new

arrivals had taken considerable damage from the British gunfire and fortunately the other German destroyers were too short of fuel to chase the *Hotspur* as she limped away, covered by the *Havock* and *Hostile*, which escaped serious damage. Thus for the loss of the *Hardy* and *Hunter* and the crippling of the *Hotspur*, all but four of the German flotilla had been either destroyed or so damaged as greatly to reduce their battle worthiness.

## AIR ATTACKS TAKE THEIR TOLL

Warburton-Lee's incisive leadership compared very favorably with the uninspired and vacillating behavior of some other British commanders in the area, as a result of which it was not until the afternoon of the 13th that a force of nine destroyers and the battleship HMS *Warspite* moved into the Narvik fjord. In the interval the German destroyers had been given time to make repairs and the action that followed was by no means the one-sided affair it might otherwise have been. The entire German force was destroyed, it is true; but in reply the destroyers *Punjabi*, *Cossack*, and *Eskimo* were seriously damaged. Further delays in following up with a military landing force were now also to give the German occupying troops, who had fled into the hills, time to regain their morale before returning. The capture of Narvik was thus to be delayed for six weeks.

Elsewhere, British and French naval units had been engaged in landing and supporting two military expeditions at Namsos and Aandalsnes, which were north and south, respectively, of Trondheim. These were two arms of a pincer movement that was aimed at the recapture of Trondheim, one of the most important ports in the country. Both the warships and transports were repeatedly bombed during the landings, and the air attacks continued throughout subsequent daylight hours as the warships lay in the little harbors to give antiaircraft gun support to the troops. Most suffered damage but, incredi-

bly, only one of those stationary targets, the sloop HMS *Bittern*, became a total loss.

Without air support and exposed to unhindered dive-bombing attacks by German Stukas based on nearby airfields, the military expeditions were doomed from the start and only some two weeks after the landings it was decided to reembark them by night between April 30 and May 2. This operation was brilliantly carried out and casualties among the ships engaged were avoided until the morning of May 2. Then, however, the full fury of the disappointed Luftwaffe descended upon the destroyers carrying the rearguard of the Namsos force. Nearly two hours of continuous attacks achieved nothing, but then a hit was at last obtained on the

Right: The German fleet at sea in August 1938. In the lead is *Gneisenau*, followed by *Admiral Graf Spee*, *Admiral Scheer*, and *Deutschland*, with unidentifiable cruisers in the distance. The German navy expended considerable resources on its surface fleet, but it is questionable whether the relatively poor results in World War II justified the effort.

French destroyer *Bison*, which caught fire and had to be abandoned. Then the British *Afridi*, which had picked up many of the French crew, was herself caught by three Stukas and also sent to the bottom.

## HEROISM AVERTS A TRAGEDY

All of Norway, with the exception of the extreme northern reaches of the country, had now been abandoned by the Allies and when the Germans launched their great offensive into France and Belgium on May 10 it soon became clear that the Allies' resources were far too meager to retain even this small foothold. On April 28 British, French, and Polish troops at last captured Narvik, but it had already been decided to evacuate the whole of Norway. Once again the British navy found itself committed to the disheartening experience of a withdrawal of the army. A series of convoys of fast troopships or slow supply transports was organized beginning on June 4.

Although the convoys were given close escorts, a certain complacency, bred perhaps by the absence of any surface threat from the German navy, coupled with a paucity of resources available to the commander in chief of Home Fleet at the time, led to a lack of any adequate heavy covering force. So that when the *Scharnhorst, Gneisenau,* and *Hipper* and four destroyers arrived on the convoy route on the night of June 7, there were all the elements of impending tragedy.

During the forenoon of the 8th the German squadron intercepted a tanker and its trawler

Above: British battleship HMS *Warspite* was launched in 1913 and served throughout World War I. She underwent a major reconstruction in 1934–37 and was still armed with eight 15 in. guns, but all internal fittings and secondary armament were thoroughly updated. She is seen here during the British operation to take Madagascar from the Vichy French. In the background is the Dutch cruiser HMNIS *Heemskerck.*

Right: Gun crew training on a *flakvierling* (quadruple antiaircraft mount) aboard the cruiser *Prinz Eugen* in Brest harbor, with battlecruisers *Gneisenau* and *Scharnhorst* just visible in the background. These three ships posed a major threat to the British and great efforts were expended in trying to sink them.

escort and an unescorted empty troopship, which were all sunk. The *Hipper* and the destroyers, short of fuel, were now ordered away to Trondheim, but the two battle cruisers remained in position to intercept a troop convoy believed to be carrying 10,000 troops, an encounter that would inevitably have resulted in heavy loss of life had it taken place. But instead, at 3:45 P.M. that afternoon the carrier HMS *Glorious*, escorted by the destroyers *Ardent* and *Acasta*, loomed up over the horizon.

*Glorious* had been employed during the closing period of the Narvik campaign in transporting RAF Gladiator and Hurricane fighters to operate from Norwegian airfields. This was done, but when the time came for evacuation the pilots appealed to be allowed to land their planes on board rather than destroy them, even though none of them had ever landed on a deck before and their aircraft were not fitted with arrester hooks. This was agreed and performed with great skill—and without a single loss. The unfortunate consequence was that the flightdeck was so crowded that operations by the carrier's own aircraft were impossible and she was caught by surprise with steam only for moderate speed available. *Glorious* was quickly overwhelmed by the Germans' 11 in. guns and at 5:40 P.M. she sank.

Having tried and failed to screen the carrier with smoke, the two destroyers then steamed gallantly for the enemy in order to attack with torpedoes. *Ardent's* attack failed and she was quickly torn apart and sunk, but *Acasta* did succeed in hitting the *Scharnhorst* aft, the explosion killing 48 of her crew, putting her after turret out of action and flooding two of her engine rooms, reducing her speed to 20 knots. In her attack, *Acasta*, too, was sunk, but the German admiral shaped course for Trondheim with both ships. The threat to the Allied troop convoys had been thus dramatically removed by a deed of gallantry, by two tiny destroyers attacking two mighty battle cruisers, an operational success far beyond what could have been expected of them.

So ended a campaign notable on the German side for the ruthless efficiency of the forcible occupation of a neutral country and the bold acceptance of a calculated risk of disaster to a fleet in the face of greatly superior force. On the Allied side, there were some notable small actions, but overall there was an amateurish

lack of understanding of the effect of airpower upon an amphibious expedition and the failure—mainly due to vacillation in the higher echelons of command—to use the seapower available to make an enemy pay the full price for his aggression.

Meanwhile, the phony war had ended in a blazing German attack as Hitler's Panzers rolled across France and Belgium, driving most of the British Army and a portion of the French into a coastal bridgehead at Dunkirk by May 26. There, every available destroyer of the Royal Navy (for the most part veterans of World War I brought out of reserve), a few French and Polish destroyers, and a swarm of civilian craft ranging from cross-Channel passenger boats to motorboats, gathered to evacuate them.

British destroyers had been already engaged since the beginning of the German blitzkrieg in evacuating the Netherlands government and royal family and carrying out demolition of Dutch port facilities, and in bringing refugees home through Ostend and taking reinforcements to the British troops holding Calais and Boulogne. The price was three destroyers sunk and others damaged by German dive-bombers. Now, between May 26 and June 4, when the

"miracle" of Dunkirk came to an end, six British destroyers and three French, and eight personnel ships were sunk, a further 19 British destroyers and nine personnel ships put out of action, but, of greater importance, well over 300,000 British and Allied troops had been brought off. It is, however, interesting to speculate how much of this could have been achieved, and at what cost, if so many German ships had not been lost or damaged during the Norway campaign.

## THE COST OF GERMANY'S GAMBLE

Dunkirk was the largest and most spectacular evacuation of Allied troops in the great withdrawal from continental Europe, but there were a number of others. One, sadly, was a failure when the rescue of the 51st Highland Division, cut off under French command at St. Valeryen-Caux, was frustrated by the descent of fog at the crucial moment. Others were much more successful, although their fame has been far eclipsed by that of Dunkirk. These included: Le Havre—11,059 British troops; Cherbourg—30,630; St. Malo—21,474; Brest—32,584; St. Nazaire and Nantes—57,175; La Pallice—2,303 British and more than 4,000 Poles; Bordeaux and

Bayonne—more than 15,000 Poles. In total, including the figures for Dunkirk, a total of 368,491 British and 189,541 Allied troops were brought away to resume the fight at a later date.

## BATTLE IN THE ATLANTIC

Unlike in the early days of World War I the need for merchant ships to be gathered in convoys was accepted by the Allies in September 1939 and they were soon operating a regular cycle across the Atlantic, the outward-bound being given a close escort to points about 100 miles west of Ireland, where they were dispersed. The escorts then picked up a homeward-bound convoy that, having assembled at Halifax, Nova Scotia, would have had to that point the escort of an armed merchant cruiser or perhaps a solitary sloop.

The number of escort vessels available was ludicrously inadequate until the large building program of Flower-class corvettes, put in hand in July and August of 1939, could begin to bear fruit; furthermore, too many destroyers were employed fruitlessly patrolling the empty ocean wastes. Nevertheless, the system was largely effective in giving the ships in convoy at least

Above: Arado Ar196 floatplane on the catapult aboard the battlecruiser *Gneisenau*. The aircraft was launched from the zero-length catapult and on completion of its mission landed near its parent ship and taxied alongside until it could be picked up by one of the two cranes seen in the background. The three guns are 11 in. caliber, which was a light weapon for a ship of the size and sophistication of *Gneisenau*.

Right: British troops crowded on the beaches of Dunkirk, awaiting evacuation, with the burning port in the distance. The naval side of this operation was masterly, making the maximum use of a wide variety of resources, ranging from warships to various civilian motor yachts and even some dinghies.

some protection during the first nine months of the war against the handful of U-boats that could be kept on patrol. The system, however, was not complete. Ships capable of over 15 knots or less than nine sailed alone and it was these that the submarines naturally preferred to attack, sinking 102 of them by the end of 1939. There was a lull even in this activity when all U-boats were recalled in March 1940 to take part in the invasion of Norway.

At the end of March 1940 the disguised merchant commerce raider *Atlantis* sailed from Germany. This vessel was the first of seven to operate in the distant oceans between this time and the end of 1941. *Atlantis* was the most successful commerce raider, accounting for 22 ships of 145,697 tons before she was caught and sunk in November 1941.

Another, *Pinguin*, sank 17 freighters and 11 whalers, for a total of 136,551 tons before she, too, was disposed of. The remainder were much less successful, though one of them, *Kormoran*, was intercepted by the Australian cruiser HMAS *Sydney* on November 19, 1941, and in an extraordinary engagement, both were sunk.

These commerce raiders were a considerable nuisance and tied up a considerable British naval force involved in hunting for them. The commerce raiders, however, never constituted such a mortal threat as did the U-boats at the height of their campaign.

## DEADLY "WOLF PACKS" FORM

The conclusion of the Norwegian Campaign released the German U-boat fleet to prey again upon Allied shipping in the North Atlantic. But a far more significant development—which was as unexpected to the Germans as to the British— came when the collapse of France enabled the German U-boat commander, Karl Dönitz, to establish new bases on France's Atlantic coast. This enabled the U-boats to establish patrol areas much further out into the Atlantic and to maintain a much larger proportion of their total number at sea. The rate of production of new U-boats was also increasing, while the number of British and Canadian escorts available to combat them was so reduced by the casualties during the withdrawal from Europe that convoys were often sailed under the illusory protection of a single destroyer or sloop. Nor could Coastal Command of the RAF obtain what they

Above: HMCS *Trillium*, a Canadian-operated Flower-class corvette. The design of these small antisubmarine warships was based on a prewar whaleboat. They were small, had insufficient range, and were uncomfortable for their crews, but proved effective in the early years of the Battle of the Atlantic against the German U-boats.

Left: A convoy changes course on its zigzag progress across the Atlantic. The merchant ships were under the overall command of a commodore of the Royal Naval Reserve who was a retired officer of either the Royal Navy or the Merchant Navy. The merchant seamen on such convoys showed great courage in the face of the ever-present danger of a possible U-boat attack.

considered a fair share of the long-range aircraft they needed to fulfill their dual function of reconnaissance for the Home Fleet and convoy escort. As for their ability to play an offensive role, not until 1941 were they to develop an effective airborne depth charge.

At the same time the Luftwaffe was brought into the campaign by the establishment of a squadron of four-engined, long-range Focke-Wulf Condor aircraft at Bordeaux, whose missions were to reconnoiter for the U-boats as well as to attack ships with bombs. As the summer wore on, the U-boats roamed ever further westward to attack ships from outward-bound convoys after they had dispersed and escorting had to be extended to 17 degrees west. But it was on the more valuable homeward-bound, deep-laden convoys that the U-boat attack was mainly

Right: U-boats being mass-produced at a shipyard in Germany. The *Kriegsmarine* devoted great energy and resources to building its U-boat fleet, which in its turn caused huge damage to Allied shipping and required the Allies to devote huge resources of men, ships, and equipment to defeating them.

Previous pages: The crew of U-48 loads a torpedo at their base in Kiel. It has to be maneuvered into the angled frame, which will then guide it down inside the boat. Once there, it will have to be manhandled into a storage rack. This was a difficult, arduous, and potentially dangerous task for submarine crews in every navy.

concentrated; and a new tactic of massed attack by groups of submarines—which came to be known as "wolf packs"—was developed.

Aided by the German ability to decipher British naval signals, these groups of six or more surfaced U-boats were spread across the expected track of a convoy. The first to sight it signaled the necessary information by high-frequency wireless to U-boat headquarters, from where it was rebroadcast to the other U-boats, who steered to intercept toward dusk.

The Germans had discovered two fatal flaws in the British submarine detection capabilities of opposing surface warships. The first was that their Asdic equipment (later to be better known by its American name, sonar) could not detect a surfaced submarine; the second that the conning tower of a surfaced U-boat was almost invisible by night from the bridge of an escort. These problems would be solved several years later when radar came into widespread use, but all that was available in the early days was the famous "Mark One Eyeball"; in other words, the skill of the lookouts, aided, perhaps, by star shells. Attacking by night, therefore, the U-boats could evade the sparsely spread convoy-screen to loose their torpedoes at close range at the target of massed merchant ships. One or two of their most skillful commanders—such as the top-scoring "ace," Otto Kretschmer of U-99—took advantage of this to the extent of penetrating between the convoy columns, where they could pick off their victims at their leisure.

### ACES SLAUGHTER A SLOW CONVOY

Using these methods, U-boats made a number of successful attacks and got away unscathed. In October 1940 they achieved results amounting to massacre on two homeward-bound convoys. The first of these was the slow convoy SC.7, which originally consisted of 34 ships, although four of these subsequently became separated in bad weather (three of these then met the fate of most such stragglers and were torpedoed). The lone escort was the old, 14-knot sloop HMS *Scarborough*, although when the convoy reached longitude 21° 30' west on October 16, she was reinforced by another sloop, HMS *Fowey*, and the corvette HMS *Bluebell*. There, too, the convoy was detected by a U-boat and Dönitz's headquarters directed a wolf pack, which included U-99 and U-100, onto it.

In preliminary attacks by single U-boats during the next two nights, two merchant ships were sunk and a third crippled, all by torpedoes. On the third night, October 18, the wolf pack moved in and, in spite of the addition of two more escorts, sank 15 ships and damaged another; they themselves suffered no loss or damage from the overwhelmed escorts, which were fully occupied picking up survivors. By the morning of the 19th the remnants of SC.7 were nearing the North Channel and their tormentors drew off; those that had any torpedoes left were diverted to the fast (10 knot) convoy HX.79, which had been located and reported by Günther Prien, hero of Scapa Flow, in U-47.

The escort of HX.79 was numerically large, consisting of two destroyers, a minesweeper, four corvettes, and three trawlers, but they were hastily assembled and most of them were newly

Above: A burning tanker. The ship will soon explode, covering the sea with burning oil and leaving her crew with very little prospect of survival.

Below: Watchmen aboard a U-boat. Diesel-electric submarines had to travel on the surface to recharge batteries, but it was essential that lookouts spot any approaching ship or aircraft, so that the captain could order a rapid dive to escape detection.

Right: The battleship *Bismarck* practices refueling from the cruiser *Prinz Eugen* in the Baltic in 1940, in preparation for their ill-fated Atlantic operation. When German ships replenished at sea, they always used the slow and clumsy astern method shown here, not the much more efficient abeam method used by the U.S. and British navies.

commissioned and manned by inexperienced crews. The result was that they were swamped by the massed attack that developed during the night of October 19 and by daylight 12 ships had been sunk and two more damaged. Not one U-boat had been attacked in reply.

The massacre of these two convoys was a painful shock to the British Defence Committee, which found itself forced to release a number of destroyers from other duties to join the escort force, which was promptly rewarded by the destruction of three U-boats. Meanwhile, in September the prime minister had negotiated the transfer of 50 older destroyers from the reserve of the U.S. Navy and these would in due course become available. Nevertheless, the problem of combating night attacks by surfaced U-boats remained insoluble and it was fortunate that, with fewer than 30 operational U-boats in commission, pack operations like those in October were followed by a lull until early December, when four U-boats sank 11 ships from convoy HX.80, including the armed merchant cruiser HMS *Forfar*.

### A NEW AND POWERFUL MENACE

Meanwhile, a new threat to Allied shipping was being posed by the German surface fleet. On November 5 the pocket battleship *Admiral Scheer*, which had passed undetected through the Denmark Strait into the Atlantic, intercepted Convoy HX.84. The convoy's solitary escort,

the armed merchant cruiser HMS *Jervis Bay*, ordered the convoy to disperse immediately and then steamed straight for the enemy in the finest traditions of the Royal Navy. The outcome of such an unequal fight was inevitable and the *Jervis Bay* was duly sent to the bottom, but the very gallant defiance of Captain Fegen and his crew imposed sufficient delay for the convoy to scatter so widely that Admiral Scheer could find and sink only five of its 37 ships.

Scheer then made for the South Atlantic and Indian Ocean, where over the next five months he accounted for 11 more independently sailing ships before returning to Germany. Surface raiders such as these could not risk attacking escorted convoys, since they dared not incur major damage when far from dockyard support. Thus, the cruiser *Admiral Hipper* similarly broke out into the Atlantic on December 7 and,

later that month, encountered a troop convoy, but she was driven off by the cruiser escort and forced to make for Brest for repairs. Emerging again in February, she was fortunate to find an unescorted convoy from which she sank seven ships before ending her brief cruise.

On February 4, 1941, a potentially much more serious threat developed when the powerful battle cruisers *Scharnhorst* and *Gneisenau* also broke out into the Atlantic. But they, too, sheered away from two convoys as soon as they saw a single veteran battleship escort. Their only successes came when they got among ships recently dispersed from outward-bound convoys—five ships on February 22, sixteen on March 15–16. They returned to Brest, where they awaited the planned sortie of the splendid new battleship *Bismarck* and the heavy cruiser *Prinz Eugen*. Together, these four modern and

Left: The German surface fleet at a prewar review in Kiel harbor. The nearest ship is *Admiral Graf Spee*, with *Deutschland* astern. Note the wings of the catapult-launched Heinkel He-60 reconnaissance aircraft.

powerful ships were expected to form a deadly combination that would devastate the transatlantic traffic that was so vital to Britain's survival. But this would not be until May and, while waiting, the battle cruisers became the object of repeated bomb and torpedo attacks by aircraft of the RAF, which inflicted damage on both, while RAF aircraft and the minelayer HMS *Abdiel* laid mines in the bay and river mouth. Meanwhile it was the U-boat force, now increasing in numbers, that kept up the attack.

### THE "HAPPY TIME" ENDS IN DEATH

The British, too, were gradually increasing their strength, and both the quality of their ships and the training of their men were beginning to improve markedly. Regular groups were being organized, the crews of individual escorts were becoming experienced, radio-telephone communication between escorts greatly improved cohesion, and a primitive radar set, adapted from the airborne set (ASV) with a fixed aerial was being fitted in escort destroyers—it had very limited performance, but was far better than nothing. Another device intended to remove the cloak of darkness during night attacks was the "Snowflake" illuminating rocket, which was provided to merchant ships and escorts, but it

was not a success and was soon withdrawn.

When the wolf pack, containing the experienced aces Kretschmer, Prien, and Schepke, was concentrated in March against convoys south of Iceland, they discovered that the happy time they had been enjoying was over. Prien's U-47 was surprised on the surface and hunted to destruction by the destroyer HMS *Wolverine*, then U-70 was sunk by the corvettes *Camellia* and *Arbutus*. And in the same week, first U-100 was rammed and sunk by HMS *Vanoc* and then *Kretschmer* and his crew were captured when U-99 was sunk by HMS *Walker*.

The shock of this disastrous week led the U-boat command to shift their boats yet further westward, where they were immediately successful when a convoy whose escort had not yet arrived was intercepted and ten ships were sunk out of 22. The British Admiralty responded by basing aircraft and ships in Iceland, which enabled them to escort convoys between 35 and 18 degrees west. Then, from May 1941 onward, the ever-increasing Royal Canadian Navy began to provide ever-stronger escorts between the Canadian coast and 35 degrees west.

May 1941 also included a major new development in the sea war when, for five days, the whole convoy system became threatened with dislocation and disruption by the 42,000-ton

Below: HMS *Hood* at speed. She was a very handsome ship and appeared to be very powerful, mounting a heavy main armament of eight 15 in. guns; she was also very fast. But all this was achieved at the expense of armored protection, which was poor and contributed significantly to her loss in the fight with the German battleship *Bismarck*.

battleship *Bismarck* and the heavy cruiser *Prince Eugen*, which broke out through the Denmark Strait. The German ships were intercepted on May 24 by the British battle cruiser HMS *Hood* (42,100 tons) and the brand-new battleship, HMS *Prince of Wales* (36,750 tons). In a very brief but violent engagement the *Hood* was sunk with great loss of life, while *Prince of Wales* was seriously damaged and forced to return to base. Then, having survived the attack by a handful of torpedo planes from the carrier HMS *Victorious*, they shook off the shadowing cruisers and disappeared from British view. But *Bismarck* had not escaped unscathed and damage from hits by the *Prince of Wales*'s 14 in. guns and the consequent loss of a thousand tons of oil fuel forced the fleet commander, Admiral Günther Lütjens, to order her to cut short her patrol and make for Brest for repairs. The British lost *Bismarck* for 32 agonizing hours, but then she was relocated by an aircraft of Coastal Command and she was first damaged by a torpedo from a Swordfish aircraft from the *Ark Royal* and finally overwhelmed and sunk by the guns and torpedoes of the Home Fleet.

The main threat to Atlantic shipping now reverted to the U-boats and the battle spread ever wider. The Allies at last were able to provide continuous escorts across the Atlantic, so

U-boat concentrations were shifted to new areas, searching for weak links in the chain, and from time to time painful losses were inflicted when a convoy with a weak or inexperienced escort was intercepted. But many convoys were getting through without loss. The U-boat strength was increasing; at the end of August there were 198 in commission, with 80 operational, and there were not many lost that summer; but their achievements also decreased.

In September 1941, however, the U-boat chief, Admiral Dönitz, found the new soft spot he had been looking for, in this case the western section of the convoy route where inexperienced ships of the Royal Canadian Navy formed the escort and Convoy SC.42, for example, lost 16 of the 65 ships with which it started. Dönitz prepared to take advantage of this, but before he could do so, he was ordered by Hitler to send U-boats to the Mediterranean and by late November the entire force of operational U-boats was either in that sea or in the approaches to the Straits of Gibraltar. The British were thus given a welcome respite to replace the weak link in the transatlantic chain.

## AIR POWER TO THE RESCUE

The convoy route between Gibraltar and the U.K. had for long been a favorite target for the four-engined Focke-Wulf Condors, and the first attempt to combat these aircraft were merchant ships equipped with a catapult for a Hurricane fighter. These were, quite literally, one-shot weapons, because the pilot had to bail out on

Above: *Bismarck* photographed from the cruiser *Prinz Eugen* during the action against the British ships *Hood* and *Prince of Wales* in the early hours of May 24, 1941. The German ships sank the British battlecruiser *Hood* and seriously damaged the *Prince of Wales*, which was forced to return to port for repairs.

Left: One of the four twin turrets carried by HMS *Hood*. Each mounted two of the massive 15 in., 42-caliber guns seen here, which fired a 2,048 lb. projectile to a maximum range of 35,550 yards.

Above: Two British aircraft carriers, early in the war, with a Fairey Swordfish torpedo aircraft overhead. Ahead is HMS *Ark Royal*, which, after many successes, was sunk by a single torpedo from U-81 on November 14, 1941, but as she took some time to sink, only one life was lost. The second carrier is HMS *Argus*, one of the first carriers in the world, which was built on the hull of the unfinished Italian liner *Conte Rosso* and completed in September 1918.

completion of his mission and hope that he would be picked up, and they achieved moderate success. The next development was the first escort carrier, HMS *Audacity*, which was equipped to operate six U.S.–supplied Grumman Martlet fighters; but in the event her aircraft were to demonstrate that not only were they effective against the Condors, but they were also of great value in combating U-boats, even though they carried no antisubmarine weapons.

In December 1941 *Audacity* was attached to the 36th Escort Group, commanded by the redoubtable Commander F. J. Walker, who was to become the most successful U-boat killer of the war. He was a dedicated specialist in the art of U-boat hunting and he had trained his group of two sloops and seven corvettes both carefully and thoroughly, but it was strengthened by the addition of three destroyers as well as the *Audacity* to escort the homeward-bound convoy HG.76, which left Gibraltar on December 14, 1941. In a running fight extending from the night of the 16th, when the first of a U-boat pack arrived on the scene, until the morning of the 22nd, when Dönitz called the survivors off, four U-boats were sunk and only two ships of the convoy torpedoed. The

*Audacity*, whose aircraft had played an important part in the destruction of the submarines as well as shooting down two of the Condors and driving off several others, was torpedoed and sunk, as was the former American destroyer HMS *Stanley*. But, despite these painful losses, the action was judged by both sides to be a notable victory for the escorts, and a combination of new skills, improved equipment, and a new confidence was inspiring them. Indeed, the stage seemed set for a decision in the Battle of the Atlantic during 1942, but it was not to be, because on December 7, 1941, Germany declared war on the United States. A whole new complex of trade routes from the Caribbean to Canada, hitherto the neutral U.S. Security Zone, which had been forbidden · to Dönitz's sea wolves, was thrown open to devastating attack. Until these routes were made secure, the U-boats would continue to wreak havoc.

## FLUCTUATING FORTUNES IN THE MEDITERRANEAN

It was a basic tenet of Anglo-French strategy from the outbreak of war in 1939 that the French would be responsible for the control of the western half of the Mediterranean. But, when Italy entered the war on Germany's side on June 11, 1940, followed shortly afterward by the collapse of France, this strategy was in ruins and the Royal Navy found itself alone in facing the modern and well-equipped Italian navy. The British Mediterranean Fleet, commanded by Admiral Sir Andrew Cunningham, was based in the Egyptian port of Alexandria. It consisted of four old battleships, of which only one, HMS *Warspite*, had been modernized, six light cruisers, 20 destroyers, and the elderly aircraft carrier HMS *Eagle*. Such a force could not hope to more than hold its own in the eastern half of the Mediterranean, in the face of Italian strength of three old, but very skillfully modernized battleships, seven modern heavy and 11 light cruisers, as well as more than 100 submarines. (It is generally overlooked that on the outbreak of war, the Italians had by far the largest submarine fleet in the world.)

The British hastily assembled a fleet, designated Force H, at Gibraltar on June 28, comprising the battle cruiser *Hood*, flagship of Admiral Sir James Somerville, two old and slow battleships, one aircraft carrier, *Ark Royal*, two light cruisers, and 11 destroyers. Sadly, the first duty put upon it was that of persuading the French fleet at Mers-el-Kebir to demilitarize itself so that it could not be taken over by the Germans. But the French admiral refused, leaving the British no option but to put it out of action by bombardment—a tragic event that took place on July 3.

The basic situation, which was to persist for the next two years and ten months, involved the rival naval and air forces fighting around two main convoy routes. These were the 2,000-mile east-west Gibraltar-Malta-Alexandria route of the British convoys and the 500-mile north-south Italy–North Africa route of the Axis convoys supplying their armies in Libya.

The first major clash in this long campaign occurred on July 9 when a greatly superior Italian fleet fled after their flagship had received just one hit from the *Warspite's* 15 in. guns at extreme range. But, for the next four days the British fleet was subjected to repeated massed air attacks by high-level bombers. These attacks failed to achieve concrete results, but it was clear that British air strength would have to be greatly increased if the British fleet was to operate in the central basin with any confidence.

As a result, the new carrier, HMS *Illustrious*, operating 12 Fulmar two-seater fighters and 22 Swordfish torpedo-reconnaissance planes, was sent out to the Mediterranean on September 1, together with the modernized and radar-equipped battleship, HMS *Valiant*, and two

Left: British battleship HMS *Warspite* sailing from Portsmouth, January 5, 1938, having just completed a rebuild, which included the new large, boxlike bridge structure.

small antiaircraft cruisers. In the previous month, too, an old aircraft carrier, HMS *Argus*, had flown off 12 Hurricane fighters to Malta from a position south of Sardinia to join the three old Gladiator biplane fighters and the nine Swordfish that had been the island's total air strength until then. This was the first of a long series of deliveries of fighters by carriers over the next two and a half years, which was to play a decisive part in Malta's successful defense.

### A BRAVE AND DECISIVE RAID

The air support provided by *Illustrious* was not particularly strong, but the fleet commander, Admiral Cunningham, sought opportunities to

bring the Italian fleet to action while covering convoy operations, which included supply convoys to Greece that had been invaded by the Italians in October. But although the Italian admiral, Campioni, had by now been reinforced by the fast and powerful new battleships *Vittorio Veneto* and *Littorio*, he was under strict orders to follow the strategy of not accepting battle without an important ulterior object.

Realizing that the Italians were avoiding battle, Cunningham decided to attack them in their lair. During the night of November 11, 1940, a force of 21 Swordfish from the *Illustrious* raided the Italian fleet at Taranto, putting the *Littorio*, *Caio Duilio*, and *Conte di Cavour* out of action—the first two for five and

Right: Aerial photograph of Taranto harbor after the raid by British carrier-borne aircraft on the night of November 11, 1940. Note the burning ships and the Trento-class cruiser (top, center) spreading fuel oil. This daring and very successful attack by twenty-one Swordfish aircraft was studied by most contemporary navies and, in particular, by the Imperial Japanese Navy.

Previous pages: Despite the formidable firepower of warships, it was naval aviation that assumed an increasingly vital role in the war at sea.

six months, respectively, and the third permanently. This daring attack meant that Italian ability to dispute the control of the central Mediterranean was temporarily at an end. This became only too evident when their fleet refused action with Force H, by now reduced to *Renown, Ark Royal*, two cruisers, and five destroyers, when they were covering a convoy to Malta at the end of November, while Cunningham's fleet, simultaneously covering a convoy from Alexandria, did not even consider itself to be under threat at all. The attack on Taranto, where a carrier force devastated an enemy fleet lying at anchor in its own base, was the first such air attack in history, and, as will be seen, the Japanese learned the lesson well.

Taking advantage of the improved situation, the British ran another convoy in January 1941 from Gibraltar for Malta and Greece, which was covered by Force H, while a second major convoy was dispatched simultaneously from Alexandria under cover of the Mediterranean Fleet. This improved situation for the British was not to last too long, however, as the Germans had already decided to go to the aid of their ally by deploying *Fliegerkorps X* to the Mediterranean Theater; this comprised some 300 aircraft of all types, including Junkers Ju 87 Stuka dive-bombers, which had received special training in attacks on shipping. Thus, when the Mediterranean Fleet moved into the Sicilian Narrows, this formidable force suddenly appeared and concentrated its attacks upon the carrier, *Illustrious*; the attack was virtually unopposed, even by the carrier's handful of low-performance Fulmar fighters, as these were caught off-guard. The carrier was hit by seven bombs, but, fortunately for the British, her armored flight deck, a design feature of all modern Royal Navy carriers, saved her from destruction. However, she was forced to go first to Malta, where she survived further prolonged attacks, before escaping to Alexandria and thence to the U.S. for proper repairs. Other attacks by *Fliegerkorps X* sank the cruiser HMS *Southampton*, while her sister ship, HMS *Gloucester*, was badly damaged.

## HEAVY ITALIAN LOSSES

When the fleet retired from the area, *Fliegerkorps X* and Italian bombers turned their full attention to Malta in their first serious

attempt to neutralize the island. This they failed to do and RAF Wellington bombers from the island's airfields continued to retaliate against their Sicilian bases, while the naval Swordfish torpedo bombers took a steady toll from the Libya-bound convoys. Furthermore, a submarine base was set up on Malta and, starting in February 1941, Axis convoys carrying *Afrika Korps* troops and equipment to Tripoli were regularly attacked, an early victim being the Italian light cruiser *Armando Diaz*, sunk by the British submarine HMS *Upright*.

On March 27, the Italian navy finally

Above: HMS *Renown*, a battlecruiser that was completed in World War I and rebuilt in the 1930s. Just visible is the line of the degaussing cable, which completely surrounded the hull and was electrically charged to give protection against magnetic mines.

Left: IIMS *Illustrious*, completed in 1940, with a Fairey Swordfish about to take off. Note the plume of smoke forward, which indicated the direction of the wind, and the radio masts that have been lowered to avoid interference with flying. The guns in the circular turrets are 4.5 in. caliber; sixteen were mounted in eight twin turrets. The destroyer astern is on "plane guard" duties, ready to pick up any survivors from a crash.

Above: The flight deck of HMS *Formidable* as a squadron of Fairey Albacore torpedo bombers prepares to launch. Note the arrester wires crossing the deck in the lowered position.

responded to the impatient urging of their German ally and sent their fleet to sea to intercept supply ships running between Egypt and Greece. The Italian force comprised the battleship *Vittorio Veneto* (Admiral Angelo Iachino), six cruisers with 8 in. guns, two cruisers with 6 in. guns, and accompanying destroyers, and it was located and reported by an RAF Sunderland flying boat south of Messina the following morning (March 28). This early report enabled Admiral Cunningham in the battleship *Warspite*, accompanied by two more battleships, *Barham* and *Valiant*, and the carrier *Formidable* (which had been sent to replace the *Illustrious*), to sail from Alexandria that evening.

Cunningham steered for a rendezvous at dawn off Gavdo Island with a squadron of four cruisers that had been operating in the Aegean. The two fleets met at the Battle of Matapan, in which *Vittorio Veneto* and the cruiser *Pola* were both damaged by torpedoes launched by the Swordfish aircraft from *Formidable*. Pola was immobilized, so two more cruisers, *Zara* and *Fiume*, were sent to stand by her, but all three cruisers were found and sunk by the British, together with two of their escorting destroyers.

The pendulum of fortune now began to swing toward the Axis as Rommel started his successful offensive in Libya, where the British army, depleted through the dispatch of aid to

Mediterranean Fleet was forced to turn its whole attention to the evacuation of the army from Greece. A total of 50,732 troops were safely embarked, but it was at a cost of four troopships and two destroyers that were sunk by dive-bombers.

The fleet was next called upon, in conjunction with Force H, to cover the passage through the Mediterranean of the "Tiger" convoy, which was carrying desperately needed tank reinforcements to General Wavell's army in Egypt, while at the same time supplies for beleaguered Malta were to be run through from Alexandria. Somewhat to British surprise, the operation was a considerable success, not least because the Italian surface fleet did not venture to intervene. There were air attacks on Force H and the convoy to the west of Malta, but these were successfully driven off by the *Ark Royal*'s little force of Fulmars, until they came under the umbrella of Beaufighters, specially deployed on Malta for this operation. One transport was lost through being mined in the Skerki Channel and another was slightly damaged. Beyond Malta and through the channel between Crete and Cyrenaica, the *Formidable*'s Fulmars were similarly successful and on May 12, some 238 tanks and 43 crated Hurricanes were safely delivered at Alexandria.

### DESTRUCTION OF A FLEET

There was little time or incentive for celebration of this success, however, because the British government had decided that the island of Crete was to be held. The air strength available to defend Crete was some half-dozen Hurricanes

Below: A Fairey Fulmar fighter comes in to land. Note the raised arrester wires on the deck, the lowered flaps and arrester hook on the aircraft, and the landing control officer. This man was always an experienced pilot and gave the pilot continuous signals during his final approach to ensure a good and safe landing.

Greece, was soon in full retreat, while in Greece the German 12th Army crossed the frontier from Bulgaria and was overcoming all resistance. Malta's offensive air strength had been reduced by *Fliegerkorps X*'s assaults to a handful of Swordfish, although reinforcements in the shape of 82 Hurricanes flown off to the island from the *Ark Royal* in March, April, and May prevented its complete neutralization. However, the British submarines continued to operate and a division of four destroyers based on the island succeeded in intercepting and annihilating a convoy of five transports and its escort of three Italian destroyers during the night of April 13.

During the last week in April, the British

and twelve obsolete Gladiators, opposed to which were the German *Fliegerkorps VIII* plus part of *Fliegerkorps X*, together with *Fliegerkorps XI* of parachute and airborne troop carriers. Thus, when the German attack began in earnest on May 20, the British fighter defenses had already been virtually eliminated during softening-up attacks.

It was clear from the start that naval participation in the defense of the island would involve heavy losses and so it proved. The total cost to the fleet was three cruisers and six destroyers sunk, among the latter being the gallant *Kelly* and her sister, *Kashmir*, which were set upon by two dozen Ju 87s on the morning of May 23, while two battleships, the only aircraft carrier, two cruisers, and two destroyers were damaged beyond local repair, and three cruisers and six destroyers less seriously damaged.

The main strategic consequence of the loss of Crete was the acquisition by the Luftwaffe of the island's airfields, from where they could attack British ships passing between Egypt and Malta, as a result of which the route earned the grim title of "Bomb Alley." Since the arrival of

*Fliegerkorps X* in Sicily and the consequent cessation of supply convoys for Malta from the west, the island had been kept going in austere conditions by the dispatch of single ships, notably the naval commissioned supply ship, HMS *Breconshire*, which made numerous trips from Egypt. Now, however, resupply became increasingly difficult and as a stopgap the larger types of submarines of the Alexandria flotilla were pressed into service, bringing aviation spirit, kerosene, medical stores, and other urgent supplies, although using submarines as transports has never been a satisfactory solution.

On the other hand, *Fliegerkorps VIII* and part of *Fliegerkorps X* were transferred to the German Eastern Front for the attack on the Soviet Union, which Hitler launched on June 22, leaving the remainder of *Fliegerkorps X* to cover the whole eastern Mediterranean. The neutralization of Malta was left to the Italian air force, which proved to be a task they were incapable of fulfilling, so the island's air offensive capability was able to recover and to complement the aggressive activities of the Valetta-based 10th Submarine Flotilla.

Below: HMS *Kelly*, a K-class flotilla leader, passes a message to another destroyer by line. This famous ship was launched in 1938 and was commanded by Captain Lord Louis Mountbatten. After numerous adventures in various campaigns, she was sunk by bombing in the eastern Mediterranean, May 23, 1941.

Above: HMS *Snapper*, a Shark-class submarine, is cheered as she returns from a patrol in Norwegian waters.

## BRITISH SUBMARINES STRIKE BACK

The submarines had, indeed, been performing brilliantly throughout the year, the most successful of an impressive team being HMS *Upholder*, whose captain, Lieutenant Commander M. D. Wanklyn, was to earn the Victoria Cross following a successful attack to sink the strongly escorted troopship *Conte Rosso*. In September he sank two other big, escorted liners carrying troops to Libya, the *Oceania* and *Neptunia*; while yet another, the *Esperia*, fell victim to Lieutenant A. R. Hezlet's HMS *Unique*. These were, however, only the highlights of one part of the campaign of steady attrition of Italian shipping on the Libyan convoy route.

With the relaxation of the air assault on Malta, two squadrons of Blenheim bombers were also deployed to the island. These aircraft gallantly bombed at masthead height by daylight at a fearful casualty rate, while the naval Swordfish took up the attack by night. Thus, the pendulum of fortune swung back again in favor of Britain.

By July, however, the problem of keeping Malta supplied had become acute. It was decided to send a convoy from the west—

Operation Substance—to be fought through at all costs; so six store ships left Gibraltar on the 21st. They were covered by Force H—*Renown* (Admiral Somerville), *Nelson, Ark Royal*, the cruiser *Hermione*, and six destroyers—as far as the Sicilian Narrows, where a close escort took over for the final run to Malta, comprising three cruisers, the fast minelayer HMS *Manxman*, and 11 destroyers. Opposition to this force was confined to aircraft of the Italian air force, which succeeded in sinking the destroyer HMS *Fearless* and torpedoing the cruiser HMS *Manchester*, although the latter was able to get back to Gibraltar. They also torpedoed and damaged one of the transports, but the remainder got through to make Malta viable for the next two months.

The lack of enterprise by the Italian surface fleet was shown up by the very gallant attack on Valetta's Grand Harbor at dawn on July 26, 1941, by the Italian special forces unit *Decima*. Using a combination of explosive motorboats and human torpedoes, they penetrated as far as a bridge at the entrance to the harbor before being detected. The losses were very heavy and the plan was flawed, but there was no doubting the courage of the participants.

Right: Two Italian "frogmen" aboard their human torpedo. The very brave crews of these craft, despite the terrible handling qualities of the weapons, carried out some very daring raids against British targets and scored some notable successes.

By September it had again become urgent to resupply Malta, so Operation Halberd, which was similar to the earlier Operation Substance, was mounted. On this occasion the Italian fleet did put to sea to pose a threat but Admiral Iachino, bound by orders not to join action unless he had a clear superiority of strength, kept his distance. A succession of aerial torpedo attacks was beaten off by the *Ark Royal*'s fighters and the guns of the escort, though one Italian aircraft attacking in the moonlight did manage to sink one of the nine supply ships. The remaining eight did, however, reach Malta safely and the island was now stocked and victualled until the following spring.

This success was followed by the arrival at Malta on October 21, 1941, of Force K—the cruisers *Aurora* and *Penelope*, accompanied by two destroyers. During the night of November 8, they intercepted an Italian convoy of seven merchant ships escorted by two cruisers and ten destroyers. The British destroyed all the merchantmen, together with one of the escorting destroyers, without any loss to themselves.

Once again, however, the swing of the pendulum toward British success was being reversed and gathered speed toward disastrous setbacks. Hitler had been dismayed by the defeats being suffered by his Italian ally at sea, so he ordered Dönitz to deploy some of his U-boats from the Atlantic to the Mediterranean. Dönitz protested strongly, but was overruled and six U-boats were sent to the Mediterranean in September, followed by another four in October and they quickly achieved two resounding successes. The first, on November 13, was when *Ark Royal* was returning from a quick delivery to Malta and was torpedoed and sunk by U-81 off Gibraltar, fortunately with the loss of only one life. Twelve days later, at the other end of the Mediterranean, U-331 attacked the fleet as it returned from a sweep and with three torpedoes blew up the battleship *Barham* in a cataclysmic explosion. At the same time, again at Hitler's orders, *Fliegerkorps II* was moving to Sicilian airfields to take up once again the task of neutralizing Malta and by the end of the year the renewed *blitz* was well under way.

There were, however, two British successes, which went some way to offsetting these disasters. In the first of these, a force of four Allied destroyers—three British, *Sikh*, *Maori*, and *Legion*, and the Dutch *Isaac Sweers*—managed to intercept the Italian cruisers *Da Barbiano* and *Di Giussano* off Cape Bon; both of these cruisers were sunk while the Allied force was unscathed. At the same time, the Italian battleship *Vittorio Veneto* was torpedoed by the British submarine HMS *Urge* and put out of action for several months.

## BRITAIN'S SQUADRON OF TWO

But for the remainder of 1941, the way was downhill for the Mediterranean Fleet. Rear Admiral Sir Philip Vian's flagship, the cruiser HMS *Galatea*, was torpedoed and sunk off Alexandria by U-557, reducing his squadron to two cruisers. However, when it became necessary to send *Breconshire* to Malta with urgent supplies of oil fuel for Force K, an escort was assembled consisting of Vian's two cruisers and eight destroyers, plus *Aurora* and *Penelope* and four destroyers from Malta. When this British force encountered the Italian fleet, composed of three battleships, *Littorio*, *Andrea Doria*, and *Giulio Cesare*, escorted by two heavy cruisers and ten destroyers, on December 17, it was the Italians who blinked first and turned away under threat of a torpedo attack by Vian's ever-aggressive destroyers. This was, however, quickly followed by disaster when the cruisers, *Neptune*, *Aurora*, and *Penelope*, and a number of destroyers entered an enemy minefield in the dark. *Neptune* was lost with all hands, while the destroyer *Kandahar*, was so badly damaged that she had to be scuttled, and *Aurora* and *Penelope* were both damaged and put out of action. By any standard, it was a calamity.

Then, to add to the British woes, three Italian chariots (human torpedoes) were trans-ported to the Egyptian coast by the submarine *Scire*, from where they penetrated Alexandria harbor and attached their charges undetected to the battleships *Queen Elizabeth* and *Valiant*. This well-executed feat resulted in both ships sinking to the shallow harbor bottom. Thus, in a few disastrous days, Cunningham's fleet had been reduced, apart from destroyers, to three light cruisers and an old antiaircraft cruiser, HMS *Carlisle* in Alexandria, and the light cruiser HMS *Ajax* at Malta.

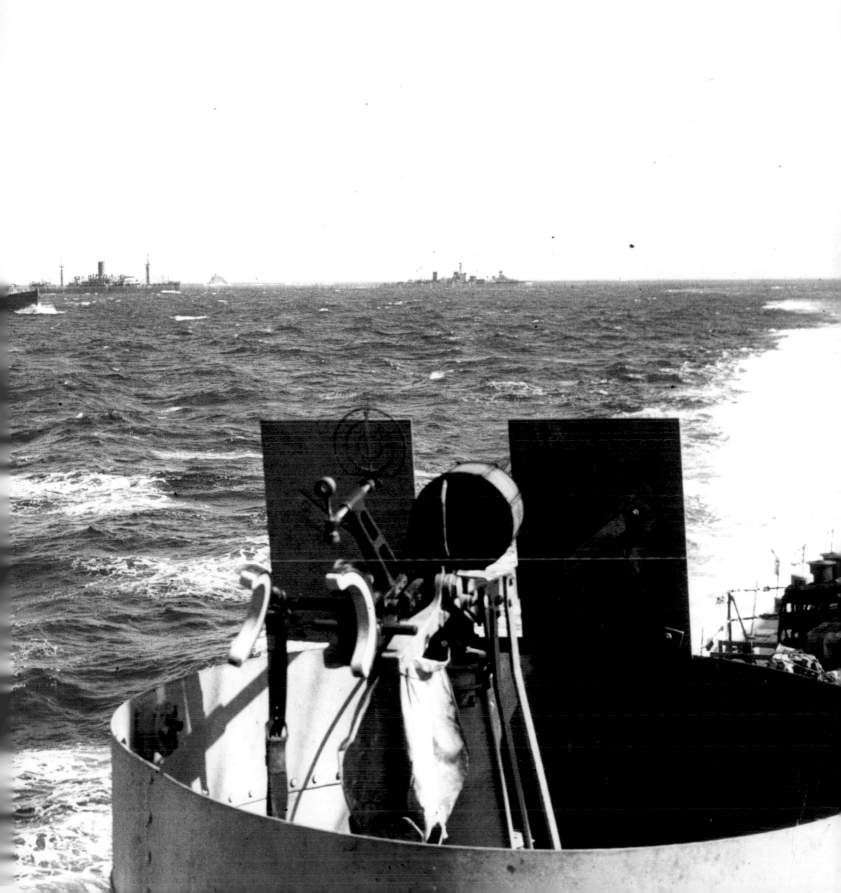

In the last days of 1941, Rommel's army was driven out of Cyrenaica by the British 8th Army, which meant that the airfields in Cyrenaica could be used by the Royal Air Force to provide fighter cover for supply ships sailing between Egypt and Malta. But the time was coming when this would no longer be the case and the 8th Army would be driven back yet again, the airfields would be lost, British seapower in the Mediterranean would reach its nadir, and the time of Malta's greatest suffering would then come.

### ACTION IN ARCTIC WATERS

Despite its protestations of neutrality, the United States had been giving the Allies actual aid—although not openly admitted—in the defense of shipping in the Atlantic. In July 1941 American troops relieved the British garrison in Iceland and at about the same time Allied ships were permitted to join convoys sailing between the U.S. and Iceland under protection of the U.S. Navy. Then, on September 1, 1941, the U.S. Navy began taking a share in escorting transatlantic convoys in the western half of the ocean on the grounds that they contained ships for Iceland. When, three days later, the destroyer USS *Greer* hunted and was, in turn, attacked unsuccessfully by a U-boat, an undeclared state of local war between the U.S. and Germany had begun. This led to the USS *Kearney* being torpedoed and severely damaged with a number of casualties on October 15 and fourteen days later the USS *Reuben James*, escorting convoy HX.156, was sunk, with 115 of her crew lost.

Despite this state of affairs, Hitler remained anxious to avoid a full-scale war with the United States and he would not allow German U-boats to operate against the ships thronging the sea routes between the Caribbean and New York. But, when Germany declared war on the U.S. on December 9, 1941, Admiral Dönitz immediately saw the great opportunity being presented and he was allowed at first to divert only five Type IX long-range, 1,000-ton U-boats from the Mediterranean, but this number was later increased and maintained between 12 and 18 by the use of "milch-cow" submarines to supply fuel, stores, and torpedoes. It was astonishing that the United States' authorities, who had been given complete access to British experience to date, took no steps toward the preparation of a convoy system on their coastal routes, enabling the U-boats to inflict a holocaust on their ships for the next six months.

Not until May did the Americans bestir themselves to organize a convoy system along their coasts. Losses there began to fall dramatically, but the U-boats simply transferred to the Gulf of Mexico and the Caribbean, where they continued their massacre until a convoy system was extended to that area in July. This brought the second "Happy Time" for the U-boats to an end and the focus of the Battle of the Atlantic swung back to mid-ocean—and this time it was to be decisive.

### *SCHARNHORST* BREAKS OUT

On February 12, 1942, the *Scharnhorst*, *Gneisenau*, and *Prinz Eugen*, escorted by six destroyers, sailed from Brest, where they had been sheltering for many months, and boldly dashed through the English Channel under the umbrella of a swarm of Luftwaffe fighters from French and Dutch airfields. Due to a variety of British errors and shortcomings—and despite

Previous pages: A British convoy en route to Malta, with a Dido-class antiaircraft cruiser in the center of the picture. These Mediterranean convoys were extremely hazardous, with threats from Axis submarines and land-based aircraft, with the ever-present possibility that the powerful Italian surface fleet would also put to sea. But the lifeline to Malta had to be kept open, so the convoys had to continue.

various standing patrols designed to prevent such a thing happening—the German squadron reached the Straits of Dover before any action was taken to try to stop them. The first of these was a "forlorn hope" in the shape of six slow Swordfish torpedo-planes, which was pressed home with great gallantry and earned its leader, Lieutenant Commander Eugene Esmonde, a posthumous Victoria Cross. Another abortive attempt was made by the squadron of veteran World War I destroyers based on Harwich. The only consolation for the British was that both German battle cruisers were mined off the Dutch coast and the *Gneisenau* was never to go to sea again.

Meanwhile, in the Atlantic, U-boat strength had reached a new high level and was increasing yet further. By July there were 140 operational boats at sea and wolf packs of as many as 20 could be assembled, improving the chances of, first, intercepting convoys and then, secondly, of swamping their defenses. The Germans also understood the significance in the mid-Atlantic gap, which was not covered by Allied aircraft and tried to take full advantage of it.

Above: A U-boat on patrol off New London, Connecticut, late 1941 to early 1942. During this period, lax U.S. control of merchant shipping off the East Coast enabled the U-boats to sink many targets.

Left: A Flower-class corvette hurries about its business in northern waters. The entire forepart of the ship is covered in ice, which will add considerably to its weight. Conditions in these ships were hard at the best of times, but even worse in Arctic conditions such as these.

Above: HMS *Lookout*, an L-class destroyer, built by Scott's on the Clyde and launched November 4, 1940. She carries an armament of six 4.7 in. guns in three twin turrets, four 21 in. torpedo tubes, and a quad 2 lb. pom-pom abaft the stack. Some L-class ships had another quad torpedo mounting, but in this ship that has been replaced by a single 4 in. gun in an open, high-angle mounting.

On the other hand, the forces available for convoy escort had not only increased numerically, but the equipment and training were also very much improved. New equipment included 10-centimeter, shipborne radar, which could detect a surfaced U-boat at a range of several miles; shipborne High Frequency Direction Finders (HF/DF or "huff-duff"), which could pinpoint a U-boat radio transmitter with great accuracy; and much-improved depth charges. The developments were not just in sensors and weaponry, but also in tactical methodology, and in such matters as sending tankers with the convoy to refuel the escorts, and rescue ships to relieve the escorts from the need to stand by sinking ships and thus enable them to concentrate on attacking the U-boats. Also, aircraft, both land- and carrier-based, were carrying better sensors and more effective weapons over ever-increasing ranges. Not least important was that the group commanders, ships' captains and crews, and the aircrews were now not only very experienced, but were beginning to feel that they were winning, all of which combined to make them very dangerous opponents indeed.

### THE ARCTIC CONVOYS BEGIN

While all this had been going on in the Atlantic and Caribbean, a new convoy route had been growing in importance, through the Arctic to

Left: The battlecruisers *Scharnhorst* and *Gneisenau*, the cruiser *Prinz Eugen*, and a number of destroyers and E-boats returning from Brest to Germany by the most direct route straight up the English Channel. The operation took the British completely by surprise and efforts to stop the German ships were weak and uncoordinated.

Above: The convoys to and from Russia became much more hazardous from March 1942 onward, when the Germans deployed battleship *Tirpitz*, a cruiser, and a number of U-boats to Norway, as well as additional aircraft. Attacks on the convoys increased, as here, where two Tribal-class destroyers are engaged: HMS *Eskimo*, in the foreground, and HMS *Ashanti*, hidden behind the spray of a very near miss.

Archangel or Murmansk. The first convoy sailed on August 22, 1941, less than two months after Russia had become a reluctant ally of Britain through Hitler's treacherous attack. The first 11 convoys suffered only trifling losses and it was not until March 1942 that a serious threat developed as a result of the deployment to northern Norway of the battleship *Tirpitz* and the heavy cruiser, *Admiral Scheer*, together with eight U-boats, and a number of Luftwaffe bomber squadrons.

On March 6, 1942, the *Tirpitz* and three destroyers narrowly missed intercepting, first, the outward-bound convoy PQ.12 and, second, the homeward QP.8.[1] In her turn, the battleship was located and unsuccessfully attacked by torpedo planes from the carrier, HMS *Victorious*, a narrow escape that led to a ban on *Tirpitz*'s employment against the convoys. But U-boats, destroyers, torpedo planes, and bombers steadily increased their attacks, as a result of which convoy PQ.13 lost five of its 19 ships. The German destroyer Z-26 was sunk by the escort, but in reply the destroyer *Eclipse* was damaged, while the cruiser HMS *Trinidad* was hit by one of her own torpedoes that

malfunctioned in the bitter cold. Despite the damage, she managed to reach Murmansk only to be sunk by air attack two months later on her way back to England.

A surface action developed around QP.11, homeward bound at the beginning of May. First, the covering cruiser, HMS *Edinburgh*, was torpedoed and so badly crippled that she had to turn back for Murmansk, barely under control, screened by the destroyers *Forester* and *Foresight*. This left just four elderly destroyers to defend the convoy against three powerful German Z-class destroyers that intercepted it on May 1; but the escort leader, Commander M. Richmond, deployed his very limited resources with great skill and boldness, forcing the Germans to keep their distance until they eventually gave up and steered for easier prey. Their new target was the now limping *Edinburgh* and in a series of confused fights the *Hermann Schoemann* was sunk by the cruiser, but both the British destroyers were also damaged. Then a German torpedo at the end of its run hit the Edinburgh, finally immobilizing her and she had to be scuttled. The Germans then withdrew.

and they assembled considerable forces to achieve this. The air component comprised: 103 Junkers Ju 88 bombers, 30 Ju 87 dive-bombers, 15 Heinkel He 115 torpedo seaplanes, 42 He 111 torpedo bombers, and 74 reconnaissance aircraft of various types. The sea component was also impressive: 10 U-boats and 14 surface ships—1 battleship (*Tirpitz*), 3 heavy cruisers (*Lützow, Admiral Scheer,* and *Admiral Hipper*), and 10 destroyers.

PQ.17's escort comprised of three central elements. The close escort, under Commander J. E. Broome in the old destroyer HMS *Keppel*, was numerically impressive, but they were

[1]Convoys were designated by letters indicating their start point and destination, followed by a unique number. Thus, convoys "PQ" were from Iceland to Murmansk, and "QP" from Murmansk to Iceland, while PQ.17 was the seventeenth to follow that particular route.

Below: Officers stand at the rail of British Southampton-class cruiser HMS *Sheffield* as they escort a Mediterranean convoy through the Sicilian channel. Guns above their heads are 6 in. caliber, of which these ships carried twelve, in four triple turrets.

## CONVOY PQ.17 SAILS TO DESTRUCTION

The handling and fate of Convoy PQ.17 has been argued over for the past sixty years, and it will remain a controversial issue for many decades to come. On May 3, 1942, newly arrived Heinkel He 111s carried out their first torpedo attack against Convoy PQ.15, in which they sank three ships. The attack on the next convoy, PQ.16, was again mainly by aircraft that sank six ships, although another was sunk by a U-boat. The further running of Arctic convoys during the summer period of continuous daylight had become what Admiral Sir Dudley Pound, First Sea Lord, described as "an unsound operation with the dice loaded against us in every direction." Nevertheless, Churchill and Roosevelt decided that, for political reasons, they needed to be seen to aid their hard-pressed Russian ally, so the convoys were to continue. Thus, on June 27, 1942, Convoy PQ.17, comprising 34 freighters and tankers, the majority American, sailed from Iceland.

At the same time, the German High Command decided that an all-out effort by air and naval forces should be made to destroy it

merely old destroyers, corvettes, minesweepers, trawlers, or little antiaircraft ships. Such a force could not be expected to do more on its own than delay the German surface squadron if it attacked. Next came a supporting escort of two British and two American cruisers under Rear Admiral Louis Hamilton in HMS *London*, whose orders were not to commit his force too far into the Barents Sea. Finally, there was a covering squadron, centered on two battleships (one British, one American) and the aircraft carrier *Victorious*, which hovered distantly, far to the west.

Between the evenings of July 2 and July 4, Broome's close escorts defeated every effort of the U-boats to get at their convoy, and they kept the casualties from air attack down to three ships lost and one damaged, for which they exacted a stiff toll of aircraft shot down. But when the Admiralty learned that *Tirpitz* had arrived in Altenfiord and was obviously awaiting its chance to attack PQ.17, they ordered that the cruiser squadron was to withdraw and that the ships of the convoy were to scatter. Up until then the convoy had been compact and well-defended, but these fateful signals delivered it piecemeal and defenseless into the hands of the U-boats and aircraft. No fewer than 21 ships were sunk during the next five days, and while *Tirpitz, Scheer, Hipper*, and seven destroyers put

Right: The scene on the flight deck of HMS *Victorious* on the evening of May 24, 1941, during the action against the *Bismarck*. A squadron of Fairey Swordfish awaits the order to take off; when they did, these antiquated, desperately slow biplanes inflicted damage that eventually brought the mighty battleship to bay.

to sea on the afternoon of July 5, they returned to harbor the same day because there were no remaining targets for them. The massacre of PQ.17 was both a major naval disaster and a stain upon the reputation and honor of the Royal Navy, and what happened and why has remained controversial from that day to this.

## SPECIAL LUFTWAFFE EFFORT FOR CONVOY PQ.18

The next convoy, PQ.18, was run in September, and once again there was to be no support by a battle squadron or aircraft carriers inside the Barents Sea. Instead, the Admiralty assumed—correctly—that the Germans would not risk their few remaining large surface units to a powerful torpedo threat, so a strong "Fighting Destroyer Escort" of no fewer than 16 destroyers was provided. The close escort of antisubmarine vessels was reinforced by the antiaircraft cruiser HMS *Scylla*, two converted antiaircraft ships, and—significantly—the escort

carrier HMS *Avenger*, operating three antisubmarine Swordfish and 12 Hurricane Mk I fighters, with her personal escort of two destroyers.

As with PQ.17 there was a "Cruiser Covering Force" of three cruisers and a "Distant Covering Force" centering on the battleships HMS *Anson* and *Duke of York*. In the event, the Germans did not send their surface ships against PQ.18, so neither of these forces played any significant part. Instead, the German air force in northern Norway, comprising more than 220 bombers and torpedo planes, and the U-boat arm were enjoined to make a special effort.

In response to these instructions the U-boats succeeded in sinking three of the convoy, but lost three of their own number in the process. The massed air attacks began on September 13 and were initially rather more effective.

The guns of the escorts took a certain toll of the first swarm of torpedo planes as they sped in low over the water. *Avenger*, however, whose crews were as yet inexperienced in convoy

Above: HMS *Duke of York* fires a broadside from her 14 in. guns while steaming at speed. She mounted ten 14 in./45 Mark VII guns in two quad and one twin turret, the guns firing a 1,590 lb. projectile to a maximum range of 38,500 yards at the maximum elevation of forty degrees. Two of the turrets each mounted four guns and proved to be somewhat cramped. *Duke of York* took part in the action against *Scharnhorst* and survived the war, being broken up in 1957.

Above: During the Battle of the Barents Sea on December 31, 1942, when the Germans attacked convoy JW.51B, the covering force was commanded by Rear Admiral Robert Burnett, who flew his flag in the cruiser HMS *Sheffield*. In this post-battle scene, *Sheffield* lies off Murmansk, with the minesweeper HMS *Seagull* alongside.

Previous pages: Just as seizing the French Atlantic ports gave U-boats direct access to the Atlantic, so possession of the Norwegian coast enabled German units to shelter in the fjords and threaten the Allied traffic to and from the Soviet Union. Thus, Allied commanders always had to take into account the possibility of a German surface battle group sallying forth, as here, to rampage among the convoys.

defense, deployed all her fighters against a number of Ju 88 bombers and had none left to deal with the torpedo bombers.

The surviving majority of the torpedo planes, therefore, were able to launch scores of torpedoes at close range to sink eight ships. The British, however, profited from this experience and learned the lessons quickly, as a result of which later German attacks found the Hurricanes ready for them and the antiaircraft ships deployed where they could bring their guns most effectively into action. The Germans suffered heavy losses and the second and subsequent attacks were not pressed home with great vigor, as a result of which PQ.18 lost only two more ships, while some forty German aircraft were shot down.

The majority of the escorts then transferred to the homeward-bound convoy, QP.14, which was attacked only by U-boats. But, in the absence of the *Avenger* and her Fleet Air Arm Fairey Swordfish, and in water conditions that made the Asdic ineffective, the U-boats succeeded in sinking the destroyer HMS *Somali*, the minesweeper HMS *Leda*, and also four merchant ships.

## THE BIGGEST CONVOY YET

PQ.18 was the last of the summer convoys to Russia, chiefly because escorts could not be spared from the more vital operation to be launched in the fall—Operation Torch, the Anglo-American landings in North Africa. This was in itself the greatest convoy operation ever mounted up to that time and it was surprisingly uneventful. The many troop and supply convoys that set out during October 1942 from the United States or the United Kingdom completed their Atlantic voyages undisturbed and almost totally unseen by the enemy.

This was largely due to the fact that the U-boats were fully occupied attacking trade convoys, mainly across the northern Atlantic, but also on the route between Sierra Leone and the U.K. Several of the former suffered heavy losses in September and October, while in the south, ten U-boats were concentrated against the northbound SL.125, from which 13 ships were sunk in seven days.

Dönitz was taken completely by surprise by the Torch landings and a hasty redeployment resulted only in the loss of seven U-boats in one

week, for meager successes against the heavily protected convoys. Then, against his earnest protests, he was ordered to send more boats to the Mediterranean and the approaches to Gibraltar. Thus the heavy loss rate among transatlantic shipping in November had been sharply cut by the end of the year, aided by the seasonal tempestuous weather. Nevertheless, the U-boats were employing, in the words of an Admiralty report, "a bolder and more reckless strategy" and it was clear that 1943 would be the crucial year in the U-boat war.

## THE BATTLE OF THE BARENTS SEA

Meanwhile, on the last day of 1942, and far away from the Torch landings, the German surface fleet was to suffer a moral defeat, which was to have fatal consequences for it. The Arctic convoys to the Soviet Union had been resumed in December. The first was left undisturbed by the German surface warfare squadron, comprising *Admiral Hipper*, *Lützow*, and six destroyers, which had assembled in Altenfiord, and the Allied ships arrived at Murmansk unscathed. But German Admiral Schniewind,

commanding in the north, was determined that this should not happen to the next convoy to Murmansk, which, from the reports of shadowing U-boats, would be off the North Cape early on December 31. Thus, the squadron sailed late on the 30th, commanded by Admiral Kummetz, aiming to intercept at dawn the following morning.

The convoy, JW.51B, had started with 16 merchantmen, but by the time it approached North Cape two stragglers had been left behind during a fierce gale with driving snow. The close escort comprised five destroyers, two corvettes, two trawlers, and a minesweeper, and was commanded by Captain R. St. V. Sherbrooke, while some 30 miles to the north at dawn on the 1st was Rear Admiral Burnett's covering force of two cruisers, HMS *Sheffield* and *Jamaica*.

The German admiral knew of the close escort that, at least in theory, posed little threat to his cruisers since Captain Sherbrooke's small command consisted of only four O-class destroyers, each armed with four puny 4 in. guns, and the old destroyer HMS *Achates*. However, his corvettes and trawlers would be

Above: HMS *Sheffield* at sea in May 1944. *Sheffield* and her four sisters originally mounted four triple 6 in. turrets, as seen here, but in 1944–45 one was removed from the survivors (*Southampton* was lost in 1941) to make space and weight available for additional antiaircraft weapons.

of absolutely no use in a surface engagement and, in any case, one was escorting one of the stragglers and the minesweeper HMS *Bramble* was looking for the other. Kummetz had no knowledge of the cruisers to the north, although experience of previous British tactics should have suggested to him that there would be some heavier ships in the offing. Thus, Kummetz assumed that the situation was one in which his squadron would be able to brush aside the meager opposition of the close escort and massacre the convoy. As the Arctic night slowly gave way to a musty grayness interspersed with the black of drifting snow storms, the interception was duly made at 8:20 A.M. on the 31st.

First on the scene were *Hipper* and three destroyers and for the next three hours they were held off by the threat of torpedo attack by Sherbrooke's little ships, which, as Royal Navy destroyers were trained to do, acted very aggressively. During that time, *Achates* screened the convoy with smoke, but was fatally damaged,

eventually to sink, while the little *Bramble*, returning from her search, was blown out of the water. The escort commander's ship, *Onslow*, was heavily damaged, but the convoy was unharmed. Sherbrooke had radioed for assistance and *Sheffield* and *Jamaica* arrived at 11:30 A.M., immediately damaging *Hipper*, which immediately retired, while one of her destroyers was sunk.

The second German group, comprising *Lützow* and three destroyers, arrived according to plan at the far side of the convoy at 10:45 A.M., but her captain seems to have been too timid to risk an attack until the weather cleared at 11:40 A.M., by which time his admiral was calling for a general withdrawal, which he obeyed, having achieved nothing.

This was a futile performance by the German commanders, although part of the blame lay with Hitler, whose injunctions against taking any risks with the surface fleet certainly had some influence on the events. Such considerations had no effect on Hitler, however,

Below: HMS *Onslow*, one of the five destroyers that took part in the Battle of the Barents Sea. Royal Navy destroyer captains were trained to act aggressively at all times, giving them a tactical impact greater than the small size of their ships or their relatively weak armament warranted. On the right is HMS *Ashanti*, one of the larger Tribal-class destroyers.

who ordered Grand Admiral Raeder to decommission all the big warships. Raeder objected and resigned, to be replaced by Dönitz, and the war at sea now revolved mainly around the activities of his U-boats.

## DECISION IN THE ATLANTIC

The year 1943 opened with operations in the North Atlantic proceeding at a modest tempo as each side in the battle girded itself for a decisive encounter. As long before as August 1942 Dönitz had written in his diary that "difficulties which confront us in the conduct of the war can only lead, in the normal course of events, to high, and indeed intolerable losses." The fact was that Allied scientists were winning the technical war, particularly in the introduction of short wave radar and shipborne H/F D/F, about neither of which the Germans were aware. German scientists had not been able to provide their U-boats with radar of their own. The "Metox" search receiver being fitted in U-boats

to detect enemy radar transmissions was designed for the earlier 1.5-meter wavelength and was useless against the very much higher frequency (10-centimeter wavelength) sets now being fitted in escorting ships and aircraft. Urgent measures to improve the U-boats' equipment were being carried out, such as a torpedo to home acoustically onto the noise of a ship's propellers, a "schnorchel" breathing tube to enable batteries to be recharged while submerged, and new U-boat designs with a very high submerged speed. But none of these would emerge in time to affect the decision in the Battle of the Atlantic.

On the Allied side, much-improved technical equipment was being provided. The escort commanders and their crews were becoming more and more expert as a result of experience combined with the very thorough training now being provided. In addition, the number of escorts available had at last become adequate. This had

Above: German type VIIC U-boat on patrol in Arctic waters. The gun on the foredeck is a naval 88 mm/45 weapon, but was totally unrelated to the German army's famous 88-mm gun. In fact, the two weapons could not even use the same ammunition.

come about partly as a result of operational research under the leadership of Professor P. M. S. Blackett (later Lord Blackett), which was able to demonstrate statistically that by increasing the size of convoys open to attack at any one time, losses could be enormously reduced.

Fewer convoys meant either larger surface escorts or a surplus of escorts, and initially the latter was accepted and converted into groups that could reinforce the regular escort of a convoy under threat. Some of these groups were centered on escort carriers that, having been first used in the North African landings to provide fighter cover until Air Force squadrons could get themselves established ashore, were now given the employment for which they had been designed. The first to operate in the Atlantic had been USS *Bogue* in March, but by the end of that month HMS *Biter* had become the center of a British Support Group shepherding convoys through the "Black Gap."

Furthermore, the fewer convoys could more easily be given continuous escort by the shore-based VLR (very long range) Liberator antisubmarine aircraft. Professor Blackett had forecast that, with continuous air escort, a 64 percent reduction of losses in convoys could be expected. This, and his calculations to show how much more useful results an aircraft could achieve on escort duty compared to bombing operations over Germany, resulted in the number of such aircraft allocated to the Coastal Command being raised from 10 to 40, allowing about 13 to be operational at any one time.

Another factor giving the defense improved prospects was the remarkable accuracy with which the tracking team in the Admiralty was able to plot the positions of U-boats from the various intelligence sources available to them by this time. Convoys could and often were able to successfully divert away from the patrol lines spread to catch them.

So it was that Allied prospects in the Battle of the Atlantic at the beginning of March 1943 were brighter than ever. Yet it was in that month that three homeward-bound convoys suffered such appalling losses, with the U-boats concerned apparently remaining unscathed, that, in the Admiralty, despairing voices were raised to cast doubt upon the convoy system. The first of these convoys, SC.121, was disorganized by mountainous seas with snow, followed by fog as

the winds took off. Seventeen U-boats that pursued through the storm picked off stragglers and then pressed on to get among the main body of the convoy and sink a total of 13 ships without loss to themselves.

That an efficient escort could beat off such an attack was, in the same week, demonstrated by the escort of HX.228, where the mixed British, Free French, and Polish Group, led by Commander A. A. Tait in the destroyer HMS *Harvester*, kept losses down to four of the convoy while destroying two U-boats and seriously damaging several others. Unfortunately, *Harvester* was immobilized after ramming a U-boat and was immediately torpedoed and sunk.

But when the next convoy, HX.229, was set upon ten days later, again in the Black Gap, by no fewer than 38 U-boats, the escort was overwhelmed and 13 ships were sent to the bottom in the first two days. The same wolf pack then attacked SC.122, from which eight ships were sunk. Not until Liberators from Iceland were

Left: U-848, a type IXD-2 long-range boat, under attack by U.S. Navy Liberators from nearby Ascension Island, November 3, 1943. Note the crewmen vainly trying to take cover on the conning tower. The beleaguered U-boat fought off its attackers for two days, but was eventually sunk. Only one survivor was found, but he was delirious and died two days later.

able to join the escort was one U-boat destroyed. Although Dönitz wrote that "nearly all the other boats suffered from depth charges or bombs and two were severely damaged," this was not known by the crews of the surface warships.

Although the total of 34 ships lost out of three convoys was calamitous, it had to be seen in conjunction with the several other convoys that, at around this time, got safely through to their destinations.

## THE CLIMAX OF THE BATTLE

Toward the end of March a lull occurred in the battle around the convoys. This was partly owing to the succession of storms of hurricane force, which swept the routes and partly owing to the necessity for those U-boats that were not in need of repair to return to base for replenishment and rearmament. Fresh boats from Germany and from the Biscay bases streamed forth to take their places—no fewer than 98 during April. But to Dönitz's chagrin they had, according to his war diary, "meager success, achieved generally at the cost of heavy losses." In fact, during the last week in April five U-boats were destroyed around the convoys and many others damaged for an almost negligible loss of merchant ships. A supreme effort by a concentration of the huge number of U-boats on patrol was organized.

Their target was the small, slow, outward-bound Convoy ONS.5 of 40 ships escorted by Group B7, led by Commander Peter Gretton, one of the most successful and best-trained groups, comprising the old destroyer HMS *Duncan* (Gretton's own ship), another old destroyer, HMS *Vidette*, the frigate HMS *Tay*, and four corvettes. After a week of appalling weather the gathering of elderly freighters had battled their way through mountainous seas to a position south of Iceland on April 28, where it was intercepted and reported by the first of the swarm of U-boats spread in waiting for it. That night the wolves began to close in; but though they made repeated efforts to penetrate the screen, they were detected by radar every time and driven off. Only one U-boat, waiting submerged ahead of the convoy, managed to sink one ship on the next morning and escape.

Below: The unmistakable silhouettes of British World War II destroyers. In this case, they are HMS *Kipling* (foreground) and HMS *Kimberley*. The latter survived the war, to be broken up in 1949. In 1941, *Kipling* was part of Mountbatten's 5th Destroyer Flotilla and rescued the survivors from HMS *Kelly* (including Mountbatten) and *Kashmir* when they were both sunk on May 23, 1941. *Kipling* took part in many actions, including sinking U-75 (December 22, 1941), but was herself sunk off the North African coast by Junkers Ju-88 bombers on May 11, 1942; 221 survived, twenty-nine were lost.

The foul weather then returned in full fury and over the next five days the convoy became disorganized. A support group of five destroyers had joined in the interval but, due to the appalling weather, three of them, as well as the *Duncan*, were unable to refuel from the escort tanker, and by May 3 had been forced to return to harbor. That left Lieutenant Commander R. E. Sherwood, RNR, aboard *Tay* as Senior Officer of the Escort. During daylight on the 4th a number of U-boats were sighted and chased, including one that was sunk by a flying boat of the RCAF. The U-boat attack, however, started after dark and lasted throughout the next day, during which time eleven ships were sunk, although one U-boat was depth-charged to destruction by the corvette HMS *Pink* during the 5th, a rate of exchange that seemed to foretell the annihilation of the convoy.

## OFFENSIVE FROM OUT OF THE FOG

But at dusk that day the convoy slipped under the shroud of dense fog, which often followed in the wake of an Atlantic cyclone. The advantage of invisibility was suddenly transferred to the radar-equipped defenders: through the night that followed, the groping U-boats were surprised repeatedly. The corvette *Loosestrife*, the destroyers *Vidette* and *Oribi*, and the frigate *Pelican* each sank a U-boat, while not one ship of the convoy was touched and at daybreak the defeated wolf packs were called off. The final grim score was that 12 merchantmen had been lost, but against this five U-boats had been destroyed by surface escorts and two more by associated air patrols, while another two, pounding through stormy seas, had collided and gone to the bottom. This was recognized by Dönitz as a clear defeat for the U-boats.

This convoy battle has been generally recognized as the grand climax and the moment of decision in the Battle of the Atlantic. U-boats gathered again, assembled around many subsequent convoys, but knowledge of these losses of their comrades and of the many narrow escapes from destruction of the survivors seems to have eroded the morale of the U-boat commanders. Even when not prevented from reaching attacking positions by the ubiquitous escort planes, either the shore-based Liberators or the carrier planes, they now shrank from closing into the attack. Those which did were pounced upon

and sunk or severely damaged before they could achieve anything.

During May 1943 the U-boat fleet suffered appalling losses, with 41 failing to return, of which 25 were sunk by convoy escorts, sea or air, including one in which Dönitz's son was serving. Such losses could not be sustained and the German navy withdrew the survivors from the North Atlantic.

### DÖNITZ'S COSTLY TACTICAL ERROR

Six of the sunk U-boats had been destroyed on passage to and from their bases by aircraft on Biscay patrol, which came about as a result of a costly tactical mistake by Dönitz. Up until now, the Bay of Biscay air patrols had not

Above: The scene aboard U-582, a type VIIC, as she reenters Brest, August 11, 1942. She had attacked the U.S. merchant ship *Stella Lykes* (6,801 tons) southwest of Freetown on July 27, 1942, and when her victim refused to sink, men were sent aboard to place demolition charges, giving them the opportunity to purloin the Stars and Stripes. U-582 was sunk on her next patrol by the U.S. Navy PBY *Catalina*, November 10, 1942, with the loss of all forty-six aboard.

Above: An Allied merchant ship lies abandoned and sinking in the North Atlantic. Germany tried desperately hard to cut the maritime lifeline between the British Isles and the rest of the world, particularly North America, but failed. Many thousands of merchant seamen were killed or drowned in the process, and many also had harrowing voyages in life rafts before being rescued.

Previous pages: The aft gun control tower (GCT) aboard a British Town-class cruiser. The canvas cover has been lowered and the gun control officer, a sublieutenant of the Royal Navy Volunteer Reserve, is searching for a target. The spindle on the left side of the GCT is one arm of the optical range finder.

been particularly profitable, accounting for only an average of one U-boat a month at a cost in flying hours some 25 times greater than that required for each kill by aircraft operating around the convoys. But the situation changed dramatically when, unknown to the Germans, Allied aircraft began to be fitted with a 10-centimeter radar.

The U-boats' Metox device was supposed to detect enemy radar transmissions, but when evidence came to hand that it was failing to do so, Dönitz ordered his U-boats to dive by night and surface long enough to charge batteries by day, diving if attacked. When this led to four losses during the first half of May, Dönitz ordered his commanders to stay on the surface and fight it out with the aircraft. This was a disastrous policy, which cost 27 U-boats between then and the end of July, when the earlier tactics were resumed and sinkings reverted to the one-a-month average.

From May to September 1943, operating in the South Atlantic, the Gibraltar approaches and the Arctic, the U-boats sank just nine ships in convoy at a cost of 33 of their own number sunk by the escorts. From June 1943 onward, the number of merchant ships emerging from

Allied shipyards greatly exceeded the losses from all causes, while U-boats led an increasingly harried existence, with an average life expectancy of a mere 1.5 patrols before being destroyed. As time went on it was no longer only in the vicinity of convoys that they were in dire peril. Increasingly, their movements were effectively tracked and they fell victims to hunting groups, such as that led by Captain Walker, which accounted for six U-boats in a single patrol in February 1944, or to groups centered on escort carriers, the majority American, which had a rich harvest of them between March and July of that year.

By September 1943 the new German acoustic homing torpedo was in production and the U-boats returned with renewed hope to the North Atlantic, but after only a brief success with the new weapon they were again totally defeated.

In 1944, U-boats began to be fitted with the *schnorchel* breathing tube, which was to give them greater immunity from air attack and enable them to operate in coastal waters of the British Isles. But this did not affect the issue and their loss rate remained agonizing, particularly when they were deployed against the Allied

Left: A torpedo is loaded aboard a type VIIC in preparation for the next operational patrol. Note that the gun has been turned away to port, to make space for the crew and the deck frame.

Below: U-175, a type IXC, sinking 400 miles North of the Azores, April 17, 1942. She had been depth-charged during the night by USCG cutter *Spencer* and was forced to the surface soon after dawn. The U-boat crew fired a few shots, killing one of *Spencer*'s crew, and then abandoned ship; thirteen died and forty-one were rescued.

invasion forces in the English Channel. Nor did the new, fast U-boats under development become operational before the end of the war.

With a discipline and courage that their enemies were forced to admire, U-boat crews continued to operate widely spread over the oceans to the last, tying down vast forces of the Allies. As Dönitz put it in his memoirs: "We came again and again to the same conclusion: the U-boat campaign must be continued with the forces available. Losses, which bear no relation to the success achieved, must be accepted, bitter though they were."

## THE ALLIES' ENIGMA TRIUMPH

One of the Allies' greatest victories took place not in physical combat, but in the ether, with the interception of German radio traffic. This was not, in itself, difficult, but when combined with the astonishing feat of breaking the Enigma codes it became a battle-winner. The *Kriegsmarine* used several different methods of encrypting message traffic, but the most important involved the Enigma machine. This device, which was about the size of a small suitcase, was marketed commercially by its inventor, a Dr.

Scherbius of Berlin, from 1923 onward and in 1926 the German navy became the first military service to procure it. The Navy was followed by other services and by the mid-1930s there were several different models in use with all the German armed services as well as with a number

of civil organizations. The Kriegsmarine model was designated Enigma M (Marine), of which the essentially similar models M1, M2, and M3 were in service in 1939.

Enigma was an off-line encryption system; that is to say, it did not itself transmit. Indeed, it did not even act as a typewriter to produce hard copy in the form of either a typewritten page or tape. Instead, it had a keyboard and when a key was pressed a complicated electrical circuit was completed, which lit a lamp giving an alternative letter, which could be any other letter of the alphabet, but never the original letter itself. Although the entire operation could be performed by one man, there were normally two: one sat behind the machine and typed the mes-

sage, while the second observed the lamps, wrote down the letters as they lit up, and then transmitted the encrypted message using the Morse key. At the distant end the situation was reversed, with the Morse operator passing the incoming (encrypted) message to the Enigma team, one of whom typed the encoded message one letter at a time, while the second wrote down the clear message as the lamps lit up.

All stations needing to talk to each other had to use the same settings, which was achieved by a document known as the *Schlüssel M*. Each key covered a calendar month and changes were made daily at 12:00 P.M. German Standard Time, although more frequent changes could be implemented on receipt of a code word. When a U-boat sailed it was given enough of these keys to cover its anticipated voyage (plus a reserve). These keys were top-secret and were issued on a very carefully controlled basis. Complications arose if U-boats stayed on patrol longer than expected (for example, having been refueled or when sailing to and from the Indian Ocean) and they ran out of Enigma keys. In such cases they had to rendezvous with another boat to obtain the keys necessary for use during their return.

Messages containing particularly sensitive information were double-encrypted and the first words revealed to the operator starting the normal decoding process were "officer only." This meant that aboard the U-boat the radio operator had to hand the message to the

**Right above:** The three rotors from an Enigma machine assembled on the axle. Each rotor had twenty-six contacts on each side, which were connected internally in a random order. Each station held eight of these rotors, numbered I to VIII; those with the same number had the same internal wiring. The knurled flanges extended outside the casing to enable the operator to set each rotor using the letters that were visible through a window, done according to the daily key.

**Right below:** A complete three-rotor Enigma machine. The operator set up the machine by aligning the rotors (see picture above) and connecting pairs of sockets on the plug board (on face of machine) using cords, which are not shown here for clarity. He then keyed the message into the machine, one letter at a time, and read off the letter that was lit up on the lapboard (between keyboard and rotors). One element, thought to enhance security, was that no letter could ever be coded as itself, but this proved to be one of the crucial elements in breaking the codes at Bletchley Park in England.

communications officer who, in privacy, decrypted the second crypt. There was also a system for "officer-to-officer" conversations known as *Funkschlüsselgespräch* (coded radio conversation), which involved three participants at each end: the officer and two operators. The officer dictated his remarks, which were typed by the Enigma operator and then transmitted by the Morse operator—letter by letter—as the lights lit up. At the receiving end the Enigma operator typed the message onto the Enigma as

it was received, with the other operator writing out the clear-text message as the lamps lit up and passing the text to his officer. The method was slow and cumbersome and gave several clear "signatures" to Allied listeners, and it was seldom used.

The Germans were aware of a possibility that Enigma might be broken, although they considered this to be very remote; nevertheless, they took several steps to improve the system. From 1939–42 the Kriegsmarine divided its

Left: The tower of a surrendered type IXC/40 U-boat. The tall pole on the left is the *schnorchel* tube, which lay in a well on the foredeck when not in use and was then raised by an electric motor. The *schnorchels* enabled U-boats to recharge their batteries while traveling submerged, and initially made it more difficult for the Allies to find them. But the head had to be exposed above the water and the Allies quickly developed radar sets that could detect them.

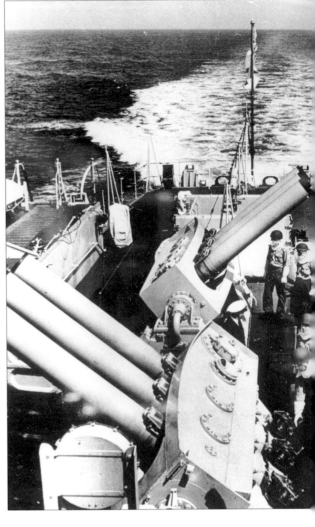

Above: A hinged *schnorchel* tube lying in its well on the foredeck.

Above right: Limbo mortars, which were mounted on the quarterdeck and lobbed depth bombs over the ship's superstructure to explode in a predetermined pattern and at a depth set according to the particular engagement. Weapons such as these were all part of the antisubmarine armory built up by the Allied navies, and which totally defeated the U-boats.

Enigma users into three communities, each of which used the same settings for its Enigmas. The first was for all warships (including U-boats) on the high seas, designated *Ausserheimische Gewässer* (foreign waters), and also as *Hydra*. The second was *Heimische Gewässer* (home waters), also known simply as *Heimisch*. The third was used by shipyards, and was known as *Werft*. However, there were a large number of non–U-boat users on both *Hydra* and *Heimisch*, and Dönitz obtained authority for an exclusive U-boat setting, designated *Triton*, whose introduction on February 1, 1942, coincided with introduction of the new Enigma M4 machine. This was a new version with a fourth rotor, which greatly complicated the decoders' problems; for example, the number of possible starting positions were increased from 263 to 264.

## GERMAN SUSPICIONS

One of the earliest incidents arousing German suspicions about the Allies accessing Enigma naval codes took place on the night of September 27, 1941, when three boats were ordered to rendezvous at Tarafal Bay, San Antao Island, in the Portuguese Cape Verde Islands, a particularly remote spot that had never been used before. Several messages were required to set up such an unplanned rendezvous, which were duly intercepted and decrypted by the British Ultra organization and, as a result, the British decided to attack. Thus, at about midnight on September 27, the British River-class submarine HMS *Clyde*, met the three U-boats in Talafera Bay and in a confused melee U-67 was damaged while attempting to ram the British submarine. In the end, all four boats survived and escaped from each other. In reviewing the incident, Dönitz found it hard to believe that *Clyde*'s arrival had been by chance and convinced himself that the British were reading Enigma. As a result, he ordered an immediate change of all keys to be followed by an investigation by Vice Admiral Maertens, Chief of Naval Communications. Maertens' report concluded that such a thing was impossible.

In another incident on January 12, 1943, U-459, a Type XIV tanker, was instructed by radio to rendezvous with an Italian submarine at a spot 300 miles east of St. Paul's Rock. When U-459 arrived, however, it found a number of Allied destroyers carrying out ASW searches and the captain concluded that they must have been fully aware of the time and place of the rendezvous. He reported this conclusion to Dönitz, who initiated a further review of cryptographic security. Once again the conclusion was that the Allies could not possibly have broken the codes, not least because the four-wheeled Enigma had recently been introduced. These conclusions were reinforced by information obtained by the *Beobachtungs-Dienst* (radio interception and decrypting agency), which suggested that the Allies' use of airborne radar was somehow to blame. Another complication was that in 1942 the Germans had captured a French resistance worker who was accused of transmitting the time and rough destination of all U-boat sailings, which suggested that espionage—always a popular scapegoat—might be to blame.

Yet another incident, this time in the Far East, reawakened suspicions in 1944. Two German tankers, *Charlotte Schliemann* and *Brake*, were operating in the southern Indian Ocean, refueling U-boats going to and returning from the German bases in Malaya. *Charlotte Schliemann* disappeared without explanation on February 11, 1944, while the ex-Italian submarine UIT-22 was sunk on March 11 en route to a rendezvous with *Brake*. That tanker was then sunk on the following day by a British destroyer, an event that was observed and reported to U-boat headquarters by U-168. The Germans were alarmed to lose two tankers and a U-boat in the same remote and deserted area, all within 50 miles of their respective rendezvous, and in such a short space of time. So, the chief of naval communications carried out yet another investigation, in the course of which he discovered that UIT-24, which had been scheduled to replenish from Brake a few days after the first three, had sent some signals from a position south of Mauritius. The usual suspects—compromise of the U-boat codes and treason—were once again

Above: HMS *Petard*, the only Allied warship to sink a submarine of each enemy navy: U-559 (Germany), October 30, 1942; *Uarsciek* (Italy), December 15, 1942; and I-27 (Japan), February 14, 1944. Most important of these was U-559, which was forced to the surface, whereupon the crew abandoned ship and were rescued. The U-boat remained on the surface while two Britons, Lieutenant Fasson and Able Seaman Grozier, went inside and retrieved codebooks that proved invaluable in breaking Enigma's codes. These very courageous men were trying to obtain yet more when the U-boat suddenly sank, taking them to their deaths.

Right: A British signaler sends a message by an Aldis lamp while his comrade notes down the other ship's reply. Such traditional means of communication between ships were slow, but in an age where radio communications were increasingly vulnerable to hostile interception, were very secure. Lamp communications were largely replaced by VHF and UHF radios for ship-to-ship communications toward the end of the war, but remain of value to this day.

examined, as was the possibility of interception of radio traffic to Japan, but nothing could be established and, as had happened after the previous investigations, the matter was left there.

Great efforts were made to eliminate all possible sources of leaks, such fears even extending to the naval communications staff in the Admiralty in Berlin. Thus, on September 9, 1941, a new system was introduced in which map squares were encoded using a simple code (which was to be changed at irregular intervals) before the message was passed to the cypher office, in order to conceal the positions even from the otherwise highly trusted communications staff.

In fact, apart from a break of several months in 1943, the Allies were indeed reading Enigma. In combination with other technological advances such as DF and airborne radar, this enabled them either to find many U-boats and destroy them, or to reroute convoys in order to avoid them, which made a very significant difference to the war at sea.

### VICTORY IN THE MEDITERRANEAN

The safe passage of three supply ships from Alexandria to Malta in a convoy covered by the meager remnant of the Mediterranean Fleet—Rear Admiral Vian's four light cruisers—in the second half of January 1942, was made possible by the British possession of the Cyrenaican airfields, from where fighter cover could be sup-

plied over the whole route. It was to be Malta's last substantial relief for many months; and in the meantime the island was suffering the most devastating of the several air assaults she endured, as *Fliegerkorps II*'s count of raids rose in January to 262, opposed by Hurricanes whose number had fallen to 11 by the middle of February.

This blitz was reducing Malta's offensive capabilities, aerial and submarine, to negligible proportions, and even the submarine base had to be closed down at the end of April. The British naval objective was now confined to attempting to keep Malta supplied. Force H, deprived of the *Ark Royal's* air support, could no longer bring in convoys from the west. It was able, however, to cover the old carriers *Eagle* and *Argus* when they sortied on three occasions during March to fly off a total of 45 Spitfires for the first time to the island. A first attempt to run a convoy from Alexandria in mid-February resulted in two of the three escorted transports being sunk by air attack in "Bomb Alley" between Crete and Cyrenaica; the third was damaged and sent into Tobruk. A further convoy of three fast merchantmen and the supply ship HMS *Breconshire* set out on March 20 with a close escort of the cruiser *Carlisle* and seven destroyers, which was covered by Vian's three cruisers, *Cleopatra* (flagship), *Dido*, and *Euryalus*, and four more destroyers. From Malta the cruiser HMS *Penelope* and a destroyer came out to meet them. Although bold and brilliant tactics by Vian's force fended off a much superior Italian squadron under Admiral Iachino in the Gulf of Sirte to allow two of the freighters and Breconshire to reach Malta, German dive-bombers sank the latter before she could be unloaded and only 5,000 tons from the remainder were saved.

## AXIS CONSIDERS MALTA DEFEATED

The enemy's bomber sorties against Malta during April totaled 9,599 with 6,700 tons of bombs. In spite of further deliveries of Spitfires flown in from the American carrier, USS *Wasp*, the dockyards became untenable and the submarine base had to be closed down. Italian convoys were crossing the Mediterranean virtually unscathed. The Axis commander in chief, Field Marshal Kesselring, reported Malta

neutralized and transferred much of his air force to Libya.

Even as he was doing so, however, Malta's ability to survive was being restored by the arrival of a further 60 Spitfires from USS *Wasp* and HMS *Eagle* on May 9, which brought about a dramatic transformation in the aerial situation. The worst of Malta's ordeal by bomb had passed but the problem of supplying her remained critical. It was decided that a convoy must be attempted in June—simultaneously from east and west on this occasion.

The convoy from Alexandria (Operation Vigorous), 11 freighters escorted by all that was left of the Mediterranean Fleet under the tactical command of Rear Admiral Vian, was set upon by a swarm of German dive-bombers. Two freighters had been sunk and another two had been sent back to harbor, when, on the evening

Below: German aerial photograph of Malta's Grand Harbor under attack in 1942. The Axis air forces expended great efforts on attacking this small Mediterranean island and the British defenses were always very hard-pressed. Nevertheless, the British armed forces managed to hold on while the civilian population endured great hardships with such fortitude that they were collectively awarded the George Cross on the personal initiative of King George VI.

of June 14, it became clear that if it continued on its existing course the convoy would inevitably encounter the Italian battle fleet in full force at daybreak. While efforts to halt the latter were made by submarines, by torpedo planes from Malta and by torpedo planes and high bombing American Liberators from Egypt, the convoy marched and countermarched indecisively, being attacked after dark by German E-boats, which sank the destroyer *Hasty* and damaged the cruiser *Newcastle*. The air attacks failed to deter the Italian fleet, although the cruiser *Trento* was torpedoed and

immobilized, later to be sunk by the submarine HMS *Umbra*. With antiaircraft ammunition running low, the convoy was ordered to retire. During its return journey it suffered the loss of the cruiser *Hermione*, torpedoed by U-205, and of the destroyers *Nestor* and *Airedale* to dive-bomber attacks.

Meanwhile, Convoy Harpoon was coming from the west, five freighters and a tanker. Westward of the Narrows a handful of Sea Hurricanes and Fulmars in the old *Eagle* were able to keep the achievements of enemy air attacks from Sardinia and Sicily down to one

Right: A Short Sunderland flying boat patrol above an Atlantic convoy. Based on the prewar Empire passenger flying boat, the Sunderland proved a great success, having a long range, good offensive capability, and, as discovered by numerous German aircraft that got within range, a robust defensive system.

Previous pages: HMS *Indomitable* with a Fairey Albacore flying overhead and four Hawker Sea Hurricanes on the flight deck. Originally intended to be the fourth ship of the Illustrious class, her design was changed during construction to enable her to accommodate twelve more aircraft, but at the cost of less armor on the hangar sides. She was hit by bombs and torpedoes, but survived the war to be broken up in 1955.

freighter sunk and the cruiser *Liverpool* damaged. However, the covering force had then to retire, leaving only the little cruiser *Cairo* (Captain C. C. Hardy) and nine destroyers to escort onward to Malta.

## Convoy to prevent starvation

At dawn the next morning an Italian force of two cruisers and five destroyers came on the scene. While Captain Hardy's escort was coping with this threat, Stuka dive-bombers attacked unopposed to sink another freighter and disable

the tanker. The simultaneous attack by air and sea sank two more freighters, the tanker and the destroyer HMS *Bedouin*. Fortunately the Italian admiral failed to follow up his advantages and the last two freighters reached Malta with 15,000 tons of cargo to keep the garrison and civil population meagerly fed for another two months. Although British fortunes elsewhere were reaching their lowest ebb with Rommel's armies at El Alamein only 160 miles from Alexandria—causing the British commander in chief, Admiral Harwood, to evacuate the base and disperse his fleet between Haifa, Port Said, and Beirut—Malta was rising from the ashes. A renewed attempt to neutralize it by air attack was defeated by the strong force of Spitfires now based there, the submarine base was reopened and once again Rommel's supplies became scanty and unreliable.

On the other hand, by August the island was facing early starvation unless a proportion at least of the convoy, Operation Pedestal, which passed Gibraltar on the 10th, could be fought through. The convoy comprised a number of freighters and the tanker *Ohio*. On this occasion the task force escorting it as far as the Narrows was to be particularly powerful, with HMS

Above: A photograph, taken from HMS *Victorious*, of HMS *Indomitable* followed by HMS *Eagle* in the Mediterranean in 1943. Sea Hurricane fighters can be seen aboard *Victorious* and *Eagle*, while aboard *Indomitable* are Sea Hurricanes (in front of bridge), two Grumman Martlets (on flight deck), and four Albacore torpedo bombers (three on flight deck, one airborne).

*Nelson* (flagship of Vice Admiral E. N. Syfret) and *Rodney*, two new carriers, *Victorious* and *Indomitable*, and the old *Eagle*, three cruisers, three aircraft carriers, and 24 destroyers. As usual, most of these went no further than the Narrows, after which only the three cruisers and 12 destroyers remained as escort.

In opposition the Axis powers put out their maximum effort. German submarines met the force on the 11th, sinking *Eagle*. That evening and throughout the next day massed air attacks were kept up from Sardinia and Sicily. The majority were beaten off, but one freighter was sunk, *Indomitable's* flight deck was put out of action, and the destroyer *Foresight* was torpedoed. Italian submarines encountered on the 12th achieved nothing, the submarine *Cobalto* being destroyed and the *Ern* damaged.

## OHIO'S EPIC STRUGGLE

Admiral Syfret's covering force had to turn back at nightfall when the convoy reached the entrance of the Skerki Channel, which coincided with a concerted attack by Italian submarines, dive-bombers, and torpedo planes. The antiaircraft cruiser, HMS *Cairo*, and two freighters were sunk, the heavy cruisers *Nigeria* and *Kenya* were torpedoed and damaged, and so too was the all-important tanker, *Ohio*. But, stopped and

on fire, *Ohio* now began an epic struggle against repeated air attacks and mounting damage, which was to get her finally to Malta under tow and in a sinking condition.

Then, about midnight, Italian E-boats took up the attack. The cruiser *Manchester* was torpedoed and immobilized, and despite heroic labors by her crew, she had to be abandoned and scuttled the following day. Four freighters were sunk and a fifth, the *Rochester Castle*, was torpedoed but was kept going. Dawn on August 13 discovered her leading the undamaged *Waimarama* and *Melbourne Star*, followed at a little distance by the *Ohio*, which was now making 16 knots, and finally Convoy Commodore Venables' flagship, *Port Chalmers*, and the *Dorset*. One other damaged ship, the *Brisbane Star*, was on her own, following a different route, hugging the Tunisian coast.

The convoy's ordeal was far from over, even though it was now coming within range of Spitfire air cover from Malta. Dive-bombers blew up the *Waimarama*, while the *Dorset* was first crippled and then sunk. *Ohio*, the favorite target for every attack, was damaged yet again and efforts began to get her in tow of a destroyer, but early in the afternoon she had to be temporarily abandoned, to await darkness and further help in the shape of minesweepers, which arrived from Malta. While they struggled,

Below: A British Hunt-class destroyer in the Atlantic, equivalent in size and role to the U.S. Navy's destroyer-escorts (DEs); it was built in four models. The Type 1 (twenty-three built) was designed to mount six 4 in. guns, which had to be reduced to four after serious stability problems were encountered, plus one quadruple 2 lb. pom-pom. The Type 2 (thirty-three built) were generally similar but with a 30 in. larger beam, restoring stability and enabling the original armament of six 4 in. guns to be mounted. The Type 3 (twenty-eight built) had one twin 4 in. mount removed and replaced by two torpedo tubes. The Type 4, while of a similar size to the others, was built to a Thornycroft design, with a very long forecastle deck, a design feature copied in most British postwar frigate designs.

between intermittent air attacks, to get her under way, the *Port Chalmers*, *Rochester Castle*, and *Melbourne Star* were receiving well-deserved heroes' welcomes as they entered the Grand Harbor.

*Ohio* had to suffer yet another day of painful progress, but, as the distance from Malta decreased and the Spitfire effort grew, the air attacks petered out. Then, early on the 15th, the tanker finally reached harbor, shortly after the enterprising *Brisbane Star*. It had been an epic battle and, yet again, the civilian crews of the merchant ships showed that they were every bit as courageous as the sailors aboard the warships.

There had been a grievous loss of ships and lives, but Malta had been given a new lease of life that, in the event, was to prove just sufficient to save her. Ironically, even this costly success would have eluded the British had the Italian navy intervened, but an interservice disagreement meant that the Italian air force failed to

Above: The flight deck of USS *Santee* (CVE-29) en route to the landings in North Africa. One of the Sangamon-class escort carriers, *Santee* had originally been the oiler *Seakay* (AO-29) and even after conversion she retained a replenishment capability. Her air wing comprised thirty-one aircraft and on this occasion her flight deck is lined with Douglas SBD-3 Dauntless dive-bombers. Note the very small bridge island to starboard.

Left: HMS *Clare*, formerly USS *Abel P. Upshur* (DD-193), was one of fifty elderly destroyers that were handed over to the Royal Navy in 1940 as part of a deal brokered by Roosevelt and Churchill.

provide air cover for the six cruisers assembled for the purpose and the operation was canceled. To make matters worse for the hapless Italians, the ships were intercepted as they returned to harbor by the submarine HMS *Unbroken*, and the heavy cruiser *Bolzano* and the light cruiser *Attendolo* were both torpedoed and put out of action for the rest of the war.

## THE NAVY WINS A TANK BATTLE

The steady attrition of Rommel's supplies now continued from Malta's airfields and submarine base, as well as from the Egyptian airfields and the submarine base at Haifa in British-administered Palestine. The relative situation of the German and British armies facing one another across the Alamein line was thus that the former's supplies of every category were

shrinking critically whereas the latter, their 14,000 miles of supply route around the Cape of Good Hope made secure by Allied seapower, needed only time to build up an overwhelming superiority. Realizing this, Rommel, his health breaking down under the frustrations of his situation, was forced to launch an early offensive on the night of August 30.

In the Battle of Alam el Halfa that followed, the early exhaustion of fuel reserves for Rommel's armor played an important part in his defeat. And so the stalemate on land set in, while at sea the October German casualty rate of ships sunk or damaged en route to Libya increased to 40 percent. On the British side, equipment and supplies arrived in a steady stream, so that by the time of Alamein, General Montgomery had an advantage of five tanks for every two possessed by Rommel, and, of equal

Below: A beach in French Morocco, as U.S. troops land for the first time on African soil. The strategic sea move of vast numbers of men and equipment from bases in the United States and United Kingdom was an outstanding success and took both the Germans and the Vichy French completely by surprise, but the actual landings and the subsequent land campaign was not so effective. Lessons were learned, however, and errors were corrected before the next landings in Sicily.

importance, the British also had huge stockpiles of ammunition and fuel. Thus, seapower provided Montgomery with the favorable odds he demanded before opening the Battle of El Alamein on October 23, 1942.

As the Axis armies in North Africa were driven westward, the Cyrenaican airfields once again fell into British hands, enabling a replenishment convoy to be run through to Malta, arriving on November 20 without loss to the transports. The island's ordeal was at last over.

Meanwhile, the greatest convoy operation in history up to that time had been in progress since October 2, when the first convoy of Operation Torch, the Anglo-American invasion of French North Africa, had sailed from the Clyde for Gibraltar. Between that date and November 8, when simultaneous landings were made by American forces in French Morocco and Oran and by a mixed Anglo-American force at Algiers, no fewer than 16 large convoys from the United States and Britain made their way unmolested, partly because many of Dönitz's U-boats had been concentrated upon a trade convoy from Sierra Leone.

Even when the invasion fleets for Oran and Algiers were reported in the Straits of Gibraltar, the German Naval Staff did not guess their destination, having been completely outwitted in the intelligence game, as they were subsequently to admit. Not until the 8th did any air attack upon the Allied convoys develop and it was the 11th before Hitler gave orders for a German army to be transported to Tunisia.

## SACRIFICIAL GALLANTRY

In this first, very large-scale amphibious assault mounted by the Allies there were bound to be miscalculations and mishaps, but in general the landings were successful. The most difficult and dangerous were the triple landings on the surf-pounded Moroccan coast where, apart from the natural hazards, the French coastal defenses and naval forces, including the battleship *Jean Bart* and the heavy cruiser *Primaguet*, were on the alert. Faulty landfalls on the flat, featureless coastline and the heavy surf combined to cause much confusion and the loss of a high proportion of the landing craft. Fortunately, no opposition was encountered at the beaches or the confusion would have inevitably led to disaster.

The French navy, reacting with sacrificial gallantry to the superior naval force opposing it, had the *Primaguet* and two destroyer leaders driven ashore heavily damaged, four destroyers and seven submarines sunk, and the *Jean Bart* and a number of smaller ships damaged by gunfire. On the 10th, U-boats made a belated appearance and sank four Allied transports and damaged a destroyer and a tanker. All this counterattack activity did not, however, affect the issue and French resistance on shore ceased at midnight on November 10 on orders from

Top: Allied warships provided artillery support during amphibious operations, although sometimes the enemy hit back. Here a shell has landed on a turret of a U.S. Navy cruiser.

Above: Lieutenant Ray Kellogg was in charge of fast patrol boats operating along the North African coast.

Above: Following the Torch landings, cruiser USS *Savannah* (CL-42) lies at anchor in an Algiers roadstead, while further inshore ships burn as a result of the senseless Vichy French resistance, which caused casualties in a situation where Allied success was inevitable.

their commander in chief, Admiral Darlan.

At Algiers and Oran the landings were made on beaches along the coast on either side of the two ports, and these were also subject to some confusion and delay. But, it was during the operations to force the harbors from seaward before the facilities were destroyed that the worst casualties were suffered. At Algiers the old British destroyers, HMS *Broke* and *Malcolm*, were carrying three companies of U.S. infantry and tried unsuccessfully in the dark to find the harbor entrance. They came under fire from the forts, with *Malcolm* being hit and forced to withdraw, while *Broke* finally forced her way through the boom after daybreak and landed her soldiers. But, accumulating shell damage forced her to put to sea, where she foundered the next day in heavy weather.

At Oran the two lightly armed and very vulnerable ex–American Coast Guard cutters, HMS *Walney* and *Hartland*, broke the boom, but were met by overwhelming fire from the French defenders, which destroyed the ships and killed or wounded most of their crews. To add to the bitter wounds inflicted on each other by former Allies, French warships put to sea to engage the naval covering forces "for the honor of the flag." During the two days

before Oran finally capitulated, these forces lost one flotilla leader, three destroyers, a corvette, six submarines, three armed trawlers, and five minesweepers; it seemed a particularly senseless sacrifice.

## SURPRISE LANDING IN SICILY

With Force K, made up of British cruisers and destroyers, now operating out of Malta and a similar Force Q based on Algiers, the central Mediterranean passed under Allied sea and air domination from the end of November. In spite of dogged courage by Italian seamen in continuing to run supply convoys through to Tunisia and Tripolitania in the face of daunting losses, the Axis forces were doomed to defeat. The surrender came at the beginning of May 1943, but there was to be no miracle of Dunkirk for them; very few escaped, but a quarter of a million prisoners fell into Allied hands.

Meanwhile, at the Casablanca Conference in January 1943, it had been decided that the next Allied objective should be Sicily. Once again a complicated organization of convoys started from widely separated points—in this case Egypt, Tunisia, Algiers, Oran, and Great Britain—organized into an Eastern Task Force

(mainly British and Canadian, commanded by Vice Admiral Sir Bertram Ramsay, RN), and a Western Task Force (mainly American, under Vice Admiral H. K. Hewitt, U.S. Navy). These came together on July 10 to land on the beaches on either side of Cape Passero, Sicily's southern tip. The task forces arrived virtually unscathed, having lost only four ships out of this huge armada to U-boats, and achieved complete surprise, followed by rapid success. By August 17 the whole of Sicily was in Allied hands.

Naval losses by the Allies in assaulting the coast of the strongly held island in the face of powerful land-based air forces and numerous submarines were inevitable, but they were less than could have been expected. Submarine attack accounted for four merchant ships and two LSTs (landing ships, tank) sunk, and two cruisers and three merchantmen damaged. In reply, three German and nine Italian U-boats were destroyed. Axis air attacks sank seven transports, two LSTs, a destroyer, and a minesweeper, and damaged the carrier HMS *Indomitable*, a monitor, two destroyers, as well as a number of transports and landing craft.

On September 3, 1943, the Allied armies crossed the Straits of Messina under cover of a massive bombardment by the 15 in. guns of the

British monitors HMS *Abercrombie*, *Roberts*, and *Erebus*, and the smaller guns of two cruisers, six destroyers, and two gunboats as well as the British 8th Army's own artillery. As the armies began their advance up the Italian peninsula, plans were made for a classic employment of seapower in landing an army far behind the enemy's line. The position chosen was the Gulf of Salerno, from where it was intended to capture the vital port of Naples. Salerno was just within extreme range of air cover by fighters from Sicily, but at that distance those aircraft could remain over the battle area only for only a few minutes. It was decided, therefore, to include in the mainly British naval covering force a squadron under Vice Admiral Sir Philip Vian of five escort carriers operating Seafires, naval adaptations of Spitfires, which would reinforce the air cover until a landing ground on shore could be secured. These ships in turn were to be given fighter cover from the carriers *Illustrious* and *Formidable* of Force II operating further to seaward.

## SINKING BY GUIDED BOMB

D-day for the landing was September 9, but as the assault convoys were approaching on the

Above: British battleship HMS *Nelson*, at Gibraltar on July 4, 1943, immediately prior to departure to take part in the landings on Sicily. (Sister ship HMS *Rodney* is in the distance, left.) *Nelson* and *Rodney* were both completed in 1927 and were armed with nine 16 in. guns in three triple turrets. In an unusual arrangement, which was not repeated in subsequent classes, all three turrets were mounted forward, with the superstructure aft. Both ships survived the war and were scrapped in 1948.

Right: The cruiser HMS *Mauritius*, providing naval gunfire support for the British Fifth Army, ashore in Italy. With forward observers collocated with the troops to call down fire missions and then signal corrections, and a good communications link, ships could provide quick and accurate fire. *Mauritius*'s 6 in. Mark XXIII guns had a maximum range of 25,500 yards.

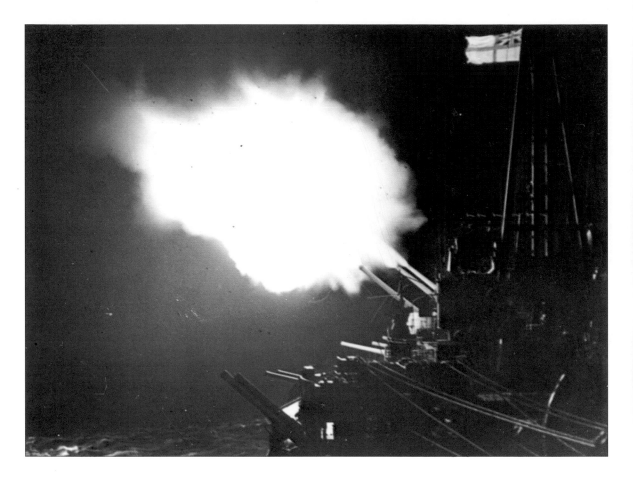

Previous pages: British battleship HMS *Nelson*. Almost every navy entered World War II with battleships in their fleet and most continued to build such ships during the war. But as the war progressed it became clear that, huge and impressive as they were, the battleship's day was done and that the aircraft carrier was the favored ship.

evening of the 8th, news of the Italian capitulation was broadcast. On the following morning the main body of the Italian fleet, consisting of the battleships *Roma*, *Vittorio Veneto*, and *Italia* (formerly *Littorio*), accompanied by six cruisers and eight destroyers, sailed from La Spezia to surrender. Not surprisingly, the Germans were furious and a squadron of Luftwaffe bombers, armed with a brand-new weapon, the FX-1400 stand-off guided bomb, attacked the Italian fleet, sinking the *Roma*. The remainder duly arrived at Malta, where they were joined on the following day by the rest of the Italian fleet—a triumphant moment for Admiral Sir Andrew Cunningham who, after an interval during which he had been the Allied Naval Commander of the Expeditionary Force for Operation Torch, had resumed his earlier title of Commander in Chief Mediterranean, but now he was under the supreme command of General Eisenhower.

The assault convoys reached their objectives at Salerno on time, having met little opposition en route, but on this occasion tactical surprise was not achieved. As a result, there was some stiff fighting ashore with disaster at some points being only narrowly averted, mainly due to timely and accurate gunfire support from the battleships HMS *Valiant* and *Warspite*, cruisers USS *Savannah* and *Philadelphia*, the 15 in. monitors, and numerous destroyers.

Capture of the airfield was delayed, so the fighter cover from the escort carriers, which had been intended only for D-day, was maintained until the 12th when the surviving Seafires were flown ashore to a landing strip that had been prepared at Paestum. There they continued to operate until the 15th when the airfield at Montecorvino was finally overrun by the advancing Allied troops. By the 17th the assault phase was over and on October 1 the Allies entered Naples.

During the Salerno operations casualties among major naval units were restricted to the destroyer USS *Rowan*, sunk by a motor torpedo boat, while USS *Savannah* and HMS *Warspite* and *Uganda* were hit by FX–guided bombs and put out of action. Considering the great strategic success achieved, such losses were far from insupportable.

### HEAVY LOSSES TO AIR ATTACK

The next occasion on which the Allies' naval superiority was put to strategic use in support of the land campaign in Italy was putting the Allied

VI Corps ashore at Anzio on January 22, 1944. The transport and landing of the troops with their tanks and artillery achieved complete surprise and by the end of D-Day some 36,000 men with 3,600 vehicles were ashore, together with a large quantity of stores; casualties were trifling. Had the troops exploited this success and moved inland rapidly, they could have advanced to the Alban Hills overlooking Rome and thereby cut the supply route of the German 10th Army and perhaps even occupied the capital itself. Instead there was hesitation and delay, during which the Germans, always masters at redeploying troops to meet a crisis, were able to deploy forces sufficient to pin the Allied forces down in their beachhead for four months.

During all that time, the naval supporting forces and the supply ships were exposed to intensive air attack, including glider bombs and torpedoes, to E-boat and U-boat attack, and to the gunfire of enemy artillery on shore. Glider bombs sank the British light cruiser HMS *Spartan* and the destroyer *Inglefield*, both with heavy loss of life, as well as two transports,

Left: The Italian battleship *Roma* was one of the Italian warships en route to Malta to surrender when they were attacked by a formation of fifteen Dornier Do-217 bombers equipped with FX-1400 glide bombs. These 10.8-ft. long missiles had four small wings, tail controls, a radio to receive guidance signals from the launch aircraft, and a 661 lb. warhead. *Roma* was hit by two glider bombs, one of which penetrated the forward magazine, which exploded and the ship broke in two and sank, with the loss of 1,352 lives.

Below: USS *Philadelphia* (CL-41) opens fire in support of ground troops engaged in Operation Anvil/Dragoon, August 15, 1944.

Above: Destroyer USS *Gleaves* (DD-423) during the invasion of southern France. In the middle distance is the British cruiser HMS *Dido*.

Below: The night of August 17, 1944, as Allied warships off St. Tropez fire antiaircraft guns at German bombers.

and damaged the destroyer HMS *Jervis*. Her sister ship, HMS *Janus*, was sunk by a torpedo plane, the USS *Mayo* was mined, and the cruiser *Penelope* and two of the LSTs were sunk by U-boats.

The next and final major naval operation of the war in the Mediterranean was the invasion of the south of France on August 15, 1944. Designated Operation Anvil/Dragoon, it was mounted under the overall command of Vice Admiral H. K. Hewitt, U.S.N. An Anglo–American–Free French Naval Task Force

was to land Lieutenant General A. M. Patch's 7th U.S. Army, consisting of U.S. VI Corps and the Free French II Corps (General de Lattre de Tassigny) on a number of beaches on the Riviera extending from the Baie de Cavalaire to Calanque d'Anthéor. A provisional airborne division carried out a parachute landing in conjunction with the amphibious forces.

Naval support of the landings was provided by five battleships—three U.S., one British, and one French—and three U.S. heavy cruisers, as well as the usual destroyers and gunboats for close-in gun support. Aerial cover was supplied by fighters from nine escort carriers: five British under Rear Admiral Tom Troubridge and four U.S. under Rear Admiral Durgin.

Thorough training and exhaustive rehearsals ensured the faultless execution of the assault. By the end of D-Day, 56,390 troops and 8,240 vehicles had been landed and the Germans were in full retreat. Toulon and Marseilles surrendered on August 28, 1944.

This was the last full-scale naval operation of the war in the Mediterranean, although many more minor ones were to engage Allied naval forces in the Adriatic and the Aegean as scattered German garrisons fought stubbornly against their inevitable ejection from the islands.

## THE END OF GERMAN NAVAL POWER

In the Arctic, the approach of the fall equinox of 1943 brought with it the prospect of short, gray, stormy days and long, dark nights, so the Western Allies made plans to restart the Murmansk convoys, carrying desperately needed war supplies to the Soviet armies. But, to avoid any repetition of the debacle of PQ.17, it was essential that the immensely powerful battleship *Tirpitz* should be eliminated.

The RAF had made several attempts to achieve this in 1942, but without success. Then, in October of that year, a gallant attempt was made using "human torpedoes" (also known as "chariots") to damage her as she lay refitting at Trondheim. These were transported across the North Sea lashed under the bottom of a Norwegian fishing boat commanded by Lief Larson, the famous resistance fighter, but the mission did not succeed.

In March 1943 *Tirpitz* rejoined *Scharnhorst* and *Lützow* in Kaafjord near the North Cape and she lay there throughout the summer apart from one brief sortie. This involved both *Tirpitz* and *Scharnhorst* and the two ships went to Spitzbergen, where they used their huge guns to destroy the wooden huts of the Norwegian weather reporting station. It was scarcely one of the most glorious episodes in naval history.

Meanwhile, in a remote Scottish loch, a little band of men were being trained to operate the new midget submarines, which were given the cover name of "X" craft. Each had a crew of three and were fitted with detachable side panniers, carrying a two-ton charge of high explosive, which would be laid on the bottom underneath their moored target.

Six of these craft were towed across the Norwegian Sea by three submarines. Two were lost on passage, while another broke down, leaving X-5, X-6, and X-7 to press on up the 50 miles of fjord to the battleship's anchorage. Two of the craft, X-6 (Lieutenant Donald Cameron) and X-7 (Lieutenant Godfrey Place) are known to have evaded the patrols and penetrated the net defenses, and it is possible that X-5 (Lieutenant Henty-Creer) may have done so as well. Thus, at least four and possibly six charges were placed under *Tirpitz* and the resulting explosions caused heavy damage to the ship. *Tirpitz* was out of action throughout the coming winter and, with *Lützow* back in Germany for a refit, only *Scharnhorst* and six destroyers

Left: British midget submarine X-25. These tiny craft, which were developed specifically to deal with the German battleship *Tirpitz*, displaced 29.7 tons submerged and had a crew of four. They carried two side containers, each holding 4,000 pounds of explosives. Once in position beneath the target, the clockwork delay systems were set (the maximum was six hours), the containers jettisoned, and the submarine and its crew then escaped.

Right: Destroyers tightly encircling the three major units, *Scharnhorst*, *Gneisenau*, and *Prinz Eugen*, all intent on returning to Germany through the English Channel. The German surface fleet consumed vast resources in men and materiel, and certainly caused the British a number of problems, but it is questionable whether those resources could not have been better deployed elsewhere.

Right: The British battleship HMS *Duke of York*. Note the secondary armament, which comprised of sixteen 5.25 in. guns in eight high-angle mountings.

remained effective in the north. The way was clear for the Allies to resume their convoys.

## MASTERY OVER THE U-BOATS

Through November and the first half of December 1943 the Allies' ships ran almost unmolested, even by U-boats. The mastery established by the escorts over the U-boats left the surface ships as the only means of attacking the convoys during the dark midwinter months. On Christmas Day, therefore, accompanied by five destroyers, *Scharnhorst*, flying the flag of Rear Admiral Bey, left Altenfiord and steered north into the wild westerly gale that was tormenting the men of Convoy JW.55B and its escorts in the Barents Sea.

Bey's plan, in accordance with the strict instructions given him, was for the battle cruiser to annihilate the convoy with her powerful armament, but if any heavy enemy ships came on the scene, *Scharnhorst* would retire at once, leaving the destroyers to fight a rear-guard action. Nevertheless, from Dönitz, now head of the German navy, had come signaled exhortations "to exploit tactical situations with skill

and daring and not end the battle with half a victory." The Grand Admiral assured Bey of his "faith in your spirit of attack."

Bey signaled that, because of the heavy weather prevailing, his destroyers would have little fighting value and asked if the operation should proceed. The High Command was torn with indecision, which was finally brought to an end by Dönitz's decree that only the man on the spot could decide. The German squadron drove on into the Arctic night, but Bey's signals, intercepted by Allied direction-finding stations, had alerted the commander in chief of Home Fleet, Admiral Sir Bruce Fraser, who was hovering 200 miles to the west in his flagship, the battleship HMS *Duke of York*, accompanied by the cruiser HMS *Jamaica* and four destroyers. Fraser steered at once to cut the Germans off from their base. He had previously followed a hunch that the convoy might be threatened and so had ordered four destroyers of the escort of the homeward-bound convoy RA.55A to reinforce the escort of JW.55B. Another force, which was approaching the convoy from the east, was Vice Admiral Bob Burnett's squadron of three cruisers, HMS *Belfast* (flagship), *Norfolk*, and *Sheffield*.

Bey was aware of none of this owing to the grounding of all reconnaissance aircraft. It was still dark when, at 9:30 A.M., without any warning from *Scharnhorst's* two radar sets, Bey found his ship illuminated by star shells bursting overhead. They had come from *Belfast* to the east and were followed by salvos of 8 in. shells, one of which burst against the

Below: Victory smiles from Admiral Sir Bruce Fraser (fifth from left) and some of the commanding officers who had taken part with him in the action against the German battlecruiser *Scharnhorst.* They are on the quarterdeck of Admiral Fraser's flagship, HMS *Duke of York.*

*Scharnhorst's* foretop, wrecking her forward radar, and another on her forecastle.

Unable to see his enemy, Bey increased to full speed and swung away to the south. Had he at once given up and steered for his base, he could have gotten clean away, but as he drew out of range he decided to use his superior speed in the heavy sea to circle around to east of the British cruisers, hoping to achieve a new thrust at the convoy. A breakdown in communications with his destroyers at this time caused them to get so far detached that they were to play no further part in the events that followed. Meanwhile, Burnett, now in company with four British destroyers, sensed Bey's intentions and steered to intercept him again—and at 12:05 P.M. the *Belfast's* radar detected *Scharnhorst* approaching from the east. As the guns on either side roared out, Bey finally gave up hope of breaking through to the convoy and at his best speed shaped course for base.

He was too late. Fraser's squadron could now intercept him, aided by the information coming from Burnett's cruisers. And at 4:15 P.M. radar contact was established at 23 miles. At 4:50 P.M. *Scharnhorst*, all unaware of the trap,

was illuminated by star shells from the *Belfast*. At the same moment the *Duke of York's* 14 in. guns opened fire, obtaining a hit abreast the battle cruiser's foremost turret almost at once. A minute later another plunged on to her quarter deck. The *Scharnhorst* fled eastward, the *Duke of York* careering along in chase, but making no more hits and unable to match the *Scharnhorst's* speed. At 5:15 P.M. the two pairs of British destroyers were sent on at their best speed to attack with torpedoes, but in the heavy following sea they gained very slowly. Then, suddenly, the situation was changed completely as a 14 in. shell hit and penetrated the German battle cruiser, causing her speed to fall off rapidly. By 6:40 P.M. the destroyers were exchanging gunfire with her—and soon afterward, as she swung around, apparently turning at bay, they attacked in pairs, firing a total of 28 torpedoes, scoring probably four hits.

At the same time *Scharnhorst* was being battered to a wreck by the guns of the *Duke of York* and *Jamaica* from one direction and of the *Belfast* from another. Then the *Duke of York's* guns fell silent as *Belfast* and *Jamaica* closed to fire torpedoes, obtaining two more

Right: The hulk of the German battleship *Tirpitz* lies capsized, her career at an end. Simply by lying in a Norwegian fjord, this powerful battleship posed an ever-present threat to Allied convoys moving between Iceland and Scotland and the Soviet Union. All this meant that every convoy had to have a strong escort in case she came out, and also that the British expended considerable energy in trying to sink her. She was attacked by midget submarines, Royal Navy Barracuda aircraft, and finally by RAF Lancasters, which dropped the huge Tallboy bombs that finally disposed of her.

hits and being followed by four destroyers, which delivered the *coup-de-grâce* with six more. At 7:45 P.M. a heavy underwater explosion was heard and the disappearance of the glowing center of a smoke cloud marked the end of the *Scharnhorst*.

## SAD END FOR *TIRPITZ*

The repairs to *Tirpitz* were completed in March 1944, but she was promptly put out of action again by a carrier-borne air attack. This took place on April 3, with a striking force of 42 Fairey Barracuda dive-bombers taking off at dawn from the flight decks of the carriers, HMS *Victorious* and *Furious*. They were escorted by a swarm of fighters—Grumman Wildcats and Hellcats, and Vought Corsairs—which took off from the escort carriers HMS *Emperor, Fencer, Pursuer,* and *Searcher.*

They covered the 120 miles to the target at wave-top level to avoid radar detection and as a result achieved complete surprise. They scored 14 hits with their bombs, putting *Tirpitz* out of action yet again and inflicting damage from which she never fully recovered. She was eventually moored at Troms—to act as a coastal defense battery—but was finally destroyed by the RAF's famous 617 Squadron dropping 12,000-pound Tallboy bombs.

The remaining major German surface units—the cruisers *Prinz Eugen* and *Hipper*, the light cruisers *Nürnberg* and *Leipzig*, and the armored ships *Lützow* and *Scheer*—had by this time been deployed in the Baltic, where, until the end of the war, they were providing support to the German armies as they withdrew in front of the Soviet onslaught. Meanwhile, the Arctic convoys continued to run until the end of the war, menaced during the midwinter months by U-boats only.

These U-boats were equipped with the *schnorchel* and the acoustic torpedo. They were deployed in the inshore approaches to Murmansk, where they were more difficult to counter than in the open sea.

The U-boats caused a number of losses among the escorts, but only very few of the merchantmen suffered. When increasing hours of daylight enabled the German air force to join the U-boat effort, their bombers had no success and were made to pay heavily by fighters from the escort carriers.

Above: U.S. Navy landing ships, tank (LST) loading for D-Day at an English port. The mighty battleships, hard-working carriers and cruisers, and dashing destroyers basked in the limelight in the naval war, but without the thousands of plodding, unglamorous amphibious landing ships and craft the armies would never have gotten to France or hopped from one Pacific island to another.

## THE NORMANDY LANDINGS

One last, great naval enterprise remained to the Allies in the war—the landings on France's northern coast on June 6, 1944. This involved the delivery over the beaches of Normandy of five divisions—two American, two British, and one Canadian—as well as follow-up troops and supplies. This was to be the biggest convoy operation and the biggest amphibious assault in history and some idea of the scale can be gauged from the statistics, with the initial landings employing 1,213 warships, together with 4,126 landing ships and craft of 23 different types.

## BOMBARDMENT SURPRISE

Two Naval Task Forces were formed (see box on page 203). General Eisenhower was in supreme command of the whole Allied Expeditionary Force and under him were the supreme naval commander, Admiral Sir Bertram Ramsay, and the land force commander, General Sir Bernard Montgomery. Due to the narrowness of the English Channel—and unlike previous amphibious operations in this war—it was possible to

Below: The naval task force organization. The crossing of the channel and successfully landing two huge armies and all their supporting weapons and logistic supplies was one of the greatest feats in military history and a masterpiece of intricate planning.

| NAVAL TASK FORCE | COMMANDER | TROOPS | LANDING AREA | BEACH NAMES |
|---|---|---|---|---|
| Western | Rear Admiral A. G. Kirk, U.S.N. | U.S. 1st Army | Varreville | Utah |
| | | | St. Laurent | Omaha |
| Eastern | Rear Admiral Sir Philip Vian, RN | British 2nd Army | Asnelles | Gold |
| | | | Courseulles | Juno |
| | | | Ouistreham | Sword |

provide entirely land-based air cover by 171 squadrons of fighters, which achieved absolute air supremacy long before D-Day.

The five assault forces embarked in their landing craft and ships at various ports between Plymouth and Newhaven, on Britain's south coast, and sailed in time to converge during the night of June 5 on a junction area south of the Isle of Wight, known as "Piccadilly Circus." From there they turned south to follow the ten channels, one for each of the groups into which the assault forces were organized, which had already been swept and marked by the minesweepers. Time for touchdown of the first assault craft (H-hour) depended upon the time at which the beach obstacles became uncovered to allow the clearance teams to get to work on them. It was, therefore, 6:30 A.M. in the American sector, 7:30 A.M. in the British.

The naval shore bombardment opened at 5:30 A.M. and so well had the time and place of the assault been kept hidden from the Germans that this shattering hail of shells was the first intimation they received of it. The scale of the bombardment was huge and involved:

- Five battleships: 3 U.S. (*Arkansas*, *Nevada*, and *Texas*) and 2 British (*Warspite*, *Ramillies*).
- 21 cruisers: 2 U.S., 14 British, 2 Dutch, 2 French, 1 Polish.
- 58 destroyers: 17 U.S., 33 British, 2 Canadian, 1 Free French, 3 Norwegian, 2 Polish.

At four of the beaches—Utah, Juno, Gold, and Sword—the landings were brilliantly successful. At Omaha, however, the combination of rough sea conditions, a lowering position too far out for the assault landing craft, and a failure of the amphibious tanks, led to great confusion, much delay, and a cruelly high casualty list. Nevertheless, by the end of D-Day the so-called impregnable defenses of Hitler's *Festung Europa* (Fortress Europe) had been well and truly breached. By the end of the day, a grand total of 132,715 Allied soldiers had been put ashore and were advancing inland, at the comparatively low cost of some 6,000 American and 4,300 British casualties.

Getting these assault troops ashore was one thing, and what was next required was to consolidate the bridgehead, and then to expand the assault into a full-scale invasion, which required an immense and constant flow of reinforcements, supplies, vehicles, and ammunition. This started with the "follow-up" troop convoys from the Thames, Plymouth, Falmouth, and Harwich, and with the "buildup" convoys from the Bristol Channel and the Thames. Until proper ports were captured and put into operation, two artificial harbors, known as "Mulberries," were established, the arms of which reached out about half a mile from the shore to an outer breakwater three and a half miles long, composed of concrete caissons towed across the Channel and sunk in position. Inside this enclosed area were floating jetties, connected by floating piers to the shore, at which coasters, barges, and LSTs could unload. Three other smaller areas were enclosed by sunken blockships to form shelters for small craft close inshore; these were known as "Gooseberries."

The construction of these artificial harbors proceeded smoothly and within a week the two Mulberries were working at a capacity worthy of regular ports. The chief hazard to the transports and their escorts were the German mines. Initially, these were the magnetic and acoustic types, which had various types of delayed-action fuses, partially defeating the efforts of the minesweepers, and enabling them to claim a number of victims. Later, the Allies also encountered the newly developed "oyster" mines, which were strewn in large numbers by enemy aircraft and were actuated by the increase in water pressure as a ship passed over them.

The Luftwaffe did not make its first appearance until the night of June 7 and in the course of the following days it had some success with Dornier Do 217 aircraft launching glider bombs. The overwhelming Allied air power, however, kept the enemy's efforts contained within negligible proportions.

## SMALL CRAFT ACTION BY NIGHT

So depleted were the resources of the German navy by this time that the only surface units available were three large Z-class destroyers—ZH1, Z24, and Z32—plus the large torpedo boat T24. These left Brest for Cherbourg on the night of June 6 and were intercepted west of Cherbourg during the night of June 8 by a mixed flotilla of British, Canadian, and Polish destroyers. After a confused battle, ZH1 and Z32 were sunk, while the other two, both badly damaged, limped back to Brest.

The E-boats from Le Havre came into action at dawn on D-Day and sank the Norwegian destroyer, *Svenner*. Thereafter, they were out almost nightly, being met by Allied motor gun-boats (MGBs), which prevented them having much success as they tried to get at the convoys making for the invasion anchorage. On June 14 a raid by 325 Lancaster bombers on Le Havre destroyed 14 of these E-boats, as well as 40 other small craft and the next night the port facilities at Boulogne were destroyed as well.

But there was a much greater danger to the Allied invasion than all the enemy's efforts: the sailor's traditional enemy—the sea. At midnight on June 18 there began a summer storm of extraordinary severity, which blew from the northeast until the 22nd. It demolished the Mulberry off the American beaches and nearly succeeded in doing the same to the other one, as well as the Gooseberries and piers. More than 800 craft of all types were stranded between June 16 and 19 as compared to 64 lost to enemy action and 30 by stress of weather during the first six critical days of the assault. The whole great military enterprise came very close to foundering through the interruption of supplies, and before the normal flow was resumed on the 22nd it had become necessary to ration ammunition among the troops ashore.

In spite of the aerial pounding given to Le Havre, the Germans transported more E-boats there by rail and they now began to threaten the eastern flank of the invasion anchorage with these and with the ingenious, unorthodox weapons they had devised. These included one- and two-man human torpedoes, as well as conventional torpedoes, which were set to be launched well outside the anchorage and once inside it to circle until they hit something. They also used explosive motorboats, derived from those used by the Italians in the Mediterranean. Some of these achieved a few minor successes at first, but they were soon countered by the Support Squadron Eastern Flank, which was specially formed to deal with them.

Finally, there were some 36 U-boats in Brest on D-Day, of which only about half were fitted with the new *schnorchel* tubes. Fifteen boats were immediately ordered up the Channel to attack the invasion convoys. But they found the approaches patrolled by surface escort groups and by such dense around-the-clock air patrols

that the non-*schnorchel* boats could not cross the area without surfacing and as soon as they did so they were immediately detected and attacked. So effective were the Allied defenses that in the first three days five U-boats were sunk and a further seven were so badly damaged that they had to return to base. A further eight were sunk by escorts or aircraft before the end of June. The U-boats finally abandoned efforts to operate in the Channel on August 23, by which time they had sunk three escorts and one empty troopship, and damaged four supply ships, a paltry return for the loss of 13 U-boats.

U-boats based in Norway and Germany continued to operate in small numbers in the Atlantic, in the coastal waters of Britain, and in the approaches to Murmansk, but they never became more than a harassment.

The only area where the German navy managed to achieve anything at all was in the Baltic, where they managed to rescue many thousands of German troops and civilians either threatened or cut off by the advance of the Red Army. The figures are extraordinary: it is estimated that over one million civilians and at least four Army divisions were brought out of Kurland alone, with more being rescued from Gdynia (Gdansk), Königsberg, Pillau, and Kolberg in March and April of 1945.

By then, as on the land and in the air, the Third Reich's naval power was at an end, and once again the German people had to begin to pick up the pieces.

Above: In June 1944, British motor gun boats (MGBs) return just after dawn from an E-boat patrol off the French port of Cherbourg. This was part of the vast naval effort to protect the amphibious shipping concentrated off the invasion beaches and carrying men, equipment, and supplies across the channel.

# Chapter 3

# THE WAR
# IN THE AIR

IN SEPTEMBER 1939 A NEW WORD ENTERED THE LANGUAGES of the world—
blitzkrieg. Its meaning was "lightning war," war carried out with a
frightening and deadly efficiency combining fast-moving ground attacks
with a furious air assault. This first campaign of World War II resulted in
the conquest and occupation of half of Europe and the creation of a
spectacular, yet not entirely deserved, reputation for the Luftwaffe that
was to have enormous repercussions in the ensuing conflict. In the
summer of 1940, Britain's fighter pilots, the "Few" immortalized by
Churchill's oratory, were the victors in the first air battle fought
independently of a ground offensive, inflicting the first defeat upon the
Nazis. Against enormous odds they only just managed to pull off one of
the greatest feats in military history. A year into the war, the established
conventions were totally abandoned and strategic bombing began in
earnest as both sides pursued their indiscriminate assault on civilian and
military targets, before precision bombing attacks were achieved.
Germany's abundant fighters tore Allied bombing raids to shreds until
the Allies introduced superlative long-range fighter escorts, while each of
the combatant major powers also built effective maritime aircraft, and
also developed transport aircraft and tactics that could
fly airborne soldiers into battle.

Right: Early production Vickers Wellington Mark I bombers on their way to France on July 7, 1939, to demonstrate
RAF air strength at the last French national celebration on July 14. Just a few weeks later, war broke out and most
of the aircraft in this formation were lost in the early months of operations.

Below: The Henschel Hs-123 dive-bomber entered service in 1936 and proved very effective in the Polish campaign in 1939. It also served with great success on the Eastern Front; indeed, it was so effective and reliable that it was almost placed back in production in 1943.

The first Blitzkrieg (lightning war) campaign of World War II saw the destruction of Poland's armed forces by the German *Wehrmacht* (armed forces) in just four weeks—September 1–28, 1939. This campaign seemed to prove that the German Panzer divisions were invincible on the ground and that the Luftwaffe was invincible in the air. In reality, neither was true. In particular, the vaunted cooperation between the Luftwaffe and the ground forces, supposedly rehearsed and perfected in the Spanish civil war, proved to be a technique still in process of evolution during the Polish campaign, with much still had to be learned. Similarly, although the Polish campaign was claimed to be the Luftwaffe's first victory—and superficially it did look impressive—the successes did, in fact, conceal some long-term and very

serious shortcomings in the German air force.

Geography favored Germany in her invasion of Poland: the frontier of the Reich curved around western Poland like an open hand poised to snatch and the two army groups entrusted with the invasion took full advantage of this fact, advancing into Poland on converging lines. Each army group had its own air cover in the shape of a *Luftflotte* (air fleet): Luftflotte 1

under Kesselring in the north and Luftflotte 4 under Löhr in the southwest. As with the army, the Luftwaffe's deployment was based on the gamble that the French would not attack in the West in support of Poland, since not even Hitler's Germany would have been able to fight an all-out, two-front war in September 1939.

In Poland the Luftwaffe enjoyed a marked superiority in numbers, with more bombers than its enemy and more fighters to protect them. The German level bombers—Heinkel He 111s and Dornier Do 17s—were medium bombers with adequate ranges for the missions they would have to fly; their weaknesses in defensive armament would not be revealed as long as the fighters gave them proper protection. The dive-bombers—the Junkers Ju 87 *Sturzkampfflugzeug* or Stukas—and ground-attack aircraft—Henschel Hs 123s—proved capable of delivering very accurate pinpoint attacks in support of the ground forces. On the other side, Poland's best fighter was the PZL P. 11, but it was obsolescent, with an open cockpit and high, strutted wing, and was totally out-classed by the Messerschmitt Me 109, while even the long-range, two-seater Me 110 heavy fighters or *zerstörer* (destroyer), in which Göring had such great—and totally misplaced—pride, could hold their own against them.

The Luftwaffe's initial mission was to gain undisputed control of the air as soon as possible. However, this plan went awry at the outset of the campaign, and a week of improvisation was needed before it became apparent that

Above: The Luftwaffe's Dornier Do-17 took part in many of the early German campaigns. The Do-17 left front-line use in 1942, but was still in service as a glider-tug in 1945.

large-scale Polish bomber reprisals were not going to materialize.

## FOG, FAILURE, AND ANTICLIMAX

On the morning of September 1, fog forced the cancellation of Operation Seaside—Göring's grandiose plan for a massed initial strike against Warsaw—and the rest of the day was one of failure and anticlimax for the Luftwaffe. Ju 87 Stukas were dispatched to prevent the Poles from blowing the vital Vistula bridge at Dirschau, in the "Polish Corridor," which ran between Pomerania and East Prussia. Their target was the demolition-point, which had been carefully identified by reconnaissance, but although the Stukas hit their target, the Poles still managed to blow the bridge.

Half the Stuka Gruppen (wings) in Löhr's air fleet were assigned to bombing airfields far behind the Polish lines, and the only effective ground-support mission flown on the southern sector on September 1 was by one Gruppe of Hs 123 biplanes, which were armed with two machine guns and lightweight incendiary bombs. Kesselring's bombers hammered the known Polish airfields but the anticipated total destruction of the Polish air force did not take place, which proved to be one of the biggest failures of the campaign. Instead, the Polish fighter pilots and bomber crews were actually thrown more off-balance by the speed of the German advance on land, which overran their forward Polish airfields, rather than by events in the air.

As soon as concentrations of Polish troops were identified, they were broken up by Stuka attacks and then, as the shaken Poles conceded defeat in the western provinces of the country and began to pull back to the Vistula for a rally in the east, the Stukas switched to road and rail keypoints in the path of the retreat. There were, of course, mistakes, most notably at the expense of forward troops who were bombed by their own side on several occasions in the confusion of battle—a tragic by-product of modem war which has never been eliminated, even in the 21st century, as events in the Second Gulf War have shown.

Another example of battlefield confusion was on September 8, when Stukas took out bridges across the Vistula at Gora Kalwarja. Their mission was to block the Polish line of retreat across the river, but instead they destroyed the bridges before the tanks of 1st

Panzer Division could dash across and the air force was, therefore, instrumental in causing a halt in the advance, while engineers were brought forward to throw a new bridge across.

## THE POLES RECOIL

The finest hour for the Ju 87s and Hs 123s came during the crisis of the campaign: the Battle of the Bzura. Battered, disintegrating, but still formidable in numbers, the Polish Poznan Army was falling back on Warsaw when, on the night of September 9–10, General Kutrzeba seized the opportunity of launching it across the River Bzura, at the flank of the German 8th Army. The German thrust at Warsaw was thrown out of gear by this menace, and the German 8th and 10th Armies were forced to wheel to their left to contain the harassing Polish attacks, while the Luftwaffe used both Stukas and Henschels to strike at the Polish bridgeheads across the Bzura.

The Henschels tackled the Piatek/Bielawy bridgehead, while the Stukas struck at Lowicz and Sochaczew, and the level bombers also joined in to deal with the crisis. After 48 hours of fierce fighting, the Poles were forced back across the Bzura in the face of these incessant Luftwaffe attacks. Then the troops of 8th Army reinforced the Germans' left flank, sealing the Poles into a massive pocket around Kutno, where they held out until September 19.

Once the crisis on the Bzura had been weathered, the Germans sealed off Warsaw and drove their "outer pincers" into eastern Poland to sweep up the surviving Polish forces in the field. Five more days passed before the Polish High Command realized that the campaign was lost.

On the 17th, under terms secretly agreed at the time of the German–Soviet Non-Aggression Pact of August 23, 1939, the Red Army rolled into eastern Poland. On that day the surviving Polish aircrews were ordered to fly their machines across the frontier and seek asylum in Romania; a number also managed to escape to be interned in Latvia. Up until the 16th, the Poles had continued to throw sporadic bombing attacks against the advancing Germans, but the Russian invasion was the end. Once Red Army and Wehrmacht forces made contact in the Brest-Litovsk area, the last bastions of Polish resistance were the trapped pockets to the west and in Warsaw, the capital, which were determined to hold out to the last.

What happened at Warsaw was a result of that steely determination. Warsaw was not an "open city" as understood by international law: it contained troops and guns, an armed garrison, which not only refused to surrender but also barricaded and fortified all approaches. The intensive air bombardment of September 25 was ordered by Hitler, although it was not carried out by the full strength of Luftwaffe strike air-

craft, because the great redeployment for the expected campaign in the West had already begun. On the 25th, however, Warsaw was savaged by 400 bombers, dive-bombers, and ground-attack aircraft, all making repeated sorties. Large areas of the city were reduced to blazing ruins and the garrison commander opened surrender negotiations on the following day. With the formal capitulation of the shattered capital on the 28th, the Polish campaign came to its end.

The Polish air force lost 333 aircraft in the campaign, 82 of them bombers, and before the final collapse some 116 aircraft of all types got out to Romania, where they were interned. But they had inflicted much heavier losses on the Luftwaffe than was appreciated at the time, total German aircraft losses of all types coming to 285 aircraft. Of these, 67 were single-engined fighters, 12 twin-engined fighters, 108 bombers and 97 other types. In addition, the Luftwaffe had to strike 279 severely damaged aircraft from its strength, making a total loss of 564 aircraft in a 28-day campaign.

## SCANDINAVIA'S TURN

The German occupation of Denmark and Norway in April 1940 revealed another potent weapon in the Luftwaffe's armory—airborne forces.[1] It also proved the deadly effect of the Ju 87 Stuka when employed against shipping, and showed—for those willing to see it—the suicidal results of sending warships into waters dominated by enemy aircraft when it was impossible to give the ships their own air cover.

The German plan was that Denmark would be tackled by a combination of the army pouncing across the frontier with no declaration of war, while paratroops would secure key airfields and bridges. The invasion of Norway, which would follow, was a more complex problem, in which the Navy would land troops at Narvik, Trondheim, Bergen, Kristiansand, and Oslo, while airborne troops would take the vital airfields at Stavanger and Fornebu.

The majority of the initial landings on the morning of April 9, 1940, went well, apart from the attempt to seize Oslo and Fornebu airfield. In the Drobak Narrows of Oslofiord the

[1]Unlike the American and British forces, where airborne troops were part of the army, in the German Wehrmacht they were part of the air force.

Left: Heinkel He-111 medium bomber dropping bombs on Polish targets. Normal bomb load was eight 250 kg bombs or a larger number of smaller bombs carried internally, as here, but an alternative was one 2,000 kg bomb externally plus one 500 kg bomb internally.

180 B    He 111

Above: The original He-111s had a conventional stepped windscreen, but the He-111P introduced the smooth, fully integrated nose shape, which has remained a characteristic of the aircraft ever since.

Norwegian defenders were not taken in as the German warships approached and opened fire, sinking the new German cruiser *Blücher* and forcing the other warships and transports to retire. Meanwhile, the lumbering Junkers Ju 52 transports carrying the paratroops to Fornebu were forced to turn back by the bad weather.

By now, the Norwegians in the Oslo/Fornebu region were thoroughly alerted; their handful of obsolescent Gloster Gladiator biplane fighters had time to take to the air and engage the Me 110s sent to patrol over Fornebu in support of the paratroop landing. In fact, it was an Me 110 squadron—*1./ZG 76*—that finally tipped the scales at Fornebu, when its commander remained too long over Fornebu, waiting for the Ju 52s to arrive and coping easily with the gallant attacks of the Norwegian Gladiator pilots. Suddenly realizing that his Me 110s were down to their last dregs of fuel, he made the audacious decision to land his fighters on Fornebu and try to gain a foothold. As a result, five Me 110s landed on the enemy airfield and managed to hold it until the Ju 52s returned with the paratroops—a piece of military impudence that retrieved a near-disastrous situation for the Germans. Meanwhile, the five surviving

Norwegian Gladiators were ordered to divert and land on frozen lakes to the north and west of Oslo, but only one managed it successfully; thus, by the second day of the campaign, the Luftwaffe possessed total air superiority over southern Norway.

### AIR SUPERIORITY IS DECISIVE

This air superiority enabled the German expeditionary force in Norway to consolidate its hold on the south of the country and begin its drive to the north to join up with the forces that had landed from the sea. Thus, when the British finally landed in Norway at Namsos and Aandalsnes in an effort to restore the situation, they had to do so in the teeth of Luftwaffe air power, which smashed remorselessly at their bases and supply ships, and harassed the movements of their troops ashore. The Allies pushed down the Gudbrandsdal Valley as far as Lillehammer before falling back on Aandalsnes, but by April 26 the situation had become so hopeless in the two burning bases that the decision was made to withdraw from central Norway and concentrate on taking and holding Narvik, the one sector where the Allied countermeasures had met with a degree of success. The Luftwaffe made desperate efforts to reinforce General Dietl's Alpine troops which had been pushed out of Narvik, but the Allies continued to advance against them and it seemed that Dietl's men must either surrender or cross into Sweden and accept internment. But this small Allied success was more than canceled out by the fiasco in Belgium and the evacuation from Dunkirk, which was taking place at the same time, and the British and French troops in far-off Norway had to pull out from Narvik in the first week of June.

The Norwegian campaign saw the first successful airborne invasion and one of the earliest airlift of supplies in military history. It was an easy battle for the Luftwaffe; the worst threat to the German fighters were the Norwegian Gladiators, but these were all eliminated in the first 48 hours. In addition, the successes of the

Left: The pilot of a Luftwaffe Heinkel He-111H, the main operational variant during the Battle of Britain. Of the 500 that were in service, 246 were lost, but the type inflicted a great deal of damage on British targets.

Stuka against the Allied bases and, in particular against the shipping at Namsos and Aandalsnes, showed it to be a deadly and terrifying weapon, but it was not appreciated at the time that such effectiveness was totally dependent upon a particular set of circumstances.

## SWEEP INTO THE LOW COUNTRIES

In 1914 the German *Schlieffen* plan, the masterplan for the defeat of France, had respected Dutch neutrality and accepted the risk that the German violation of Belgian neutrality might provoke Allied countermoves—which it most certainly did. The result had been four years of static trench warfare in the West and ultimate defeat. Twenty-five years later Hitler resolved to reduce both the Netherlands and Belgium as the prelude to the decisive Battle of France, although it was obvious that the decisive victory could not be won there. Speed would be of the essence, not least because of the ease with which the Low Countries could be flooded and converted into morasses of water obstacles.

Denmark and Norway had been the first to feel the impact of German airborne troops, but those had been relatively small-scale affairs, and it was now intended that the Netherlands and Belgium would be the first theaters of World War II where those airborne forces would win decisive victories. Thus, the killer punch against the Netherlands would be spearheaded by para-

troops taking the airfields around The Hague, to prevent them being used as advanced bases by the Allied air forces, and also arresting the Queen and the Dutch Government. Meanwhile, other airborne forces would seize the Maas bridges at Rotterdam and hold them until the ground forces, driving northwest from Breda, could join up.

The attack was supported by two air fleets: Kesselring's Luftflotte 2 covered the operations of Army Group B (Bock) in the Netherlands and Belgium, while Sperrle's Luftflotte 3 supported von Rundstedt's Army Group A on the central sector. Between them these two Luftflotten numbered 1,120 level bombers (Do 17s, He 111s, and Ju 88s), 358 dive-bombers (nearly all Ju 87 Stukas), 1,264 fighters (Me 109s and Me 110s), and 648 reconnaissance aircraft (Fieseler Fi 56s, Hs 126s, and He 46s). In addition, there were 475 Ju 52 transports and 45 DFS gliders.

The Dutch air force was negligible in comparison with the might of Luftflotte 2, being equipped with just nine Fokker T. V medium bombers and ten single-engine Fokker C. X reconnaissance bombers. Their best fighter, the Fokker D. XXI, was simply no match for the German Me 109—and, in any event, there were only 29 of them in an operational status. There were 23 modern Fokker G. I. twin-boom heavy fighters/ground attack machines, and the Royal Dutch Navy could contribute 11 Fokker T. VIII-W reconnaissance and torpedo-bomber float-

Left: Heinkel He-46c in the Luftwaffe's prewar markings. This was a two-seat army cooperation and reconnaissance aircraft; note the vertical rods above the wing to support a horizontal radio antenna for communications with ground troops. It entered service in 1936 and, although quickly replaced by more modern types, remained in service until 1944 on the Eastern Front.

planes. This pitiful weakness in air power was the direct result of four decades of determined neutrality and parsimony in defense spending.

## FIASCOS AND FORCED-LANDINGS

In consequence, the Luftwaffe encountered little or no resistance in the air during the attack on the Netherlands, although it ran into plenty on the ground. The airborne attack on the airfields around The Hague—at Ypenburg, Ockenburg, and Valkenburg—was a fiasco, worse even than the initial setback at Oslo during the Norwegian campaign. The German transport aircraft were generally foiled by the volume of flak sent up from the Dutch airfields and by the various ground obstacles strewn over the most obvious landing approaches; as a result, the Ju 52s were forced to use The Hague autoroute or crash-land on the coastal dunes. If they managed this, spirited resistance flung the German airborne troops off The Hague airfields.

Left: The Dornier Do-17 was originally designed as a high-speed passenger and mail transport aircraft. The aircraft, however, was never suitable for the role as it was extremely difficult for passengers to enter the separate cabins in front of and behind the wing. The prototypes were placed in storage after testing but were rediscovered by a Lufthansa test pilot who quickly realized their military potential after a flight test.

Right: The small and ungainly Fieseler Fi-156 Storch (stork) was an exceptionally useful aircraft, used for staff transport/liaison, ambulance, reconnaissance, and rescue missions. It had excellent short take-off and landing capabilities, and was particularly popular with senior officers such as Rommel who could use it to visit units very near the front line.

Above far right: A combat formation of Heinkel He-111 bombers. The He-111 was the main bomber type in use during the Battle of Britain and was subsequently used in large numbers on the Eastern Front.

Below far right: The He-111 was too small for a tail gunner, but the dorsal and ventral positions gave reasonable coverage of the rear quadrant. Early in the war defensive armament comprised three 7.9 mm MG15 machine guns, one each in the nose, dorsal, and ventral positions, but this was later increased to one 20 mm cannon, one 0.5 in. MG, and up to seven MG15s.

At Rotterdam, one group of Germans were flown in aboard 12 Heinkel He 59 seaplanes and managed to capture the vital Willems bridge across the Maas, while paratroops were taking the city's Waalhaven airfield in the teeth of desperate resistance from the Dutch Queen's Grenadiers. Prompt Dutch countermeasures sealed off the tenuous German hold on the Maas crossing, through which they had hoped to break the resistance of Rotterdam, and the German foothold in the city was reduced to a small bridgehead, which was under constant counterattack.

The Germans' next plan was to blow out the Dutch hold on the northern bank of the Maas by a mass bombing attack, which went ahead, even though the city's surrender was actually being negotiated at the time. An attempt to contact the bombers to call it off failed and some 57 He 111s of *Kampfgeschwader* (bomber group) 54 dropped 97 tons of high-explosive bombs into the designated triangular target area on the north bank of the Maas. The resulting fires gutted the heart of Old Rotterdam in a tragic accident, but one which, nevertheless, finally cracked the Dutch will to resist. Accepting the inevitable, the Netherlands surrendered on May 15.

So, the Netherlands fell in just five days and once again the Luftwaffe's airborne forces had been in the forefront of the battle, although they had taken a severe mauling. Out of the total of 430 Ju 52 transports allotted to the Dutch land-

ings, two-thirds were either destroyed or so badly damaged that they were beyond repair. The going had been hardest around The Hague, where German losses stood at an astonishing 90 percent. It has often been pointed out that the losses suffered by the German navy during the Norwegian campaign were a decisive factor on limiting German hopes for an invasion of Britain. But, the huge losses in the German airborne arm in the Netherlands were no less important and they could not be made good in a mere three to four months.

## EPIC AT EBEN-EMAEL

In May 1940, Belgium's Albert Canal was reputed to be one of the best antitank obstacles in western Europe; the waterway was wide, the banks were steep-sided, the area was studded with pillbox defenses, and at the most crucial point it was anchored by Fort Eban Emael. This fortress, completed in the 1930s, was supposed to be as tough a proposition to standard attack as anything the much-vaunted, French-built Maginot Line had to offer. Despite all this, the Germans took Eben-Emael in a matter of hours in a daring attack, which wrote a new chapter in the brief history of gliderborne warfare.

Eben-Emael was in fact only one of four targets earmarked by the Germans for the surprise cracking of the Albert Canal line. Four "special attack detachments," all of them glider-borne, had been trained under conditions of the strictest secrecy for the mission, the other three being assigned to bridges over the Canal at Vroenhaven, Verdzewelt, and Kanne. But it was the Eben-Emael attack in May 1940 that won the attention of the world.

The German glider force delivered a group of specially equipped assault engineers to the outer carapace of the fort—men equipped with the newly invented hollow-charge explosive for cracking armored cupolas and blinding observation-domes. Acting with great energy and enormous daring these 55 men overcame the much larger Belgian garrison in a short period, despite the assault commander having to return to base because of a malfunctioning towing aircraft.[2] It was the first successful use of glider-borne troops in World War II. Once again "Auntie Ju," as the Germans called the

---

[2]In a pre-operation briefing, Hitler told the young Lieutenant Witzig to contact him direct if he needed any help. On returning to base Witzig was told that there was no replacement aircraft available. He promptly telephoned Hitler in person and a new towing aircraft appeared within the hour!

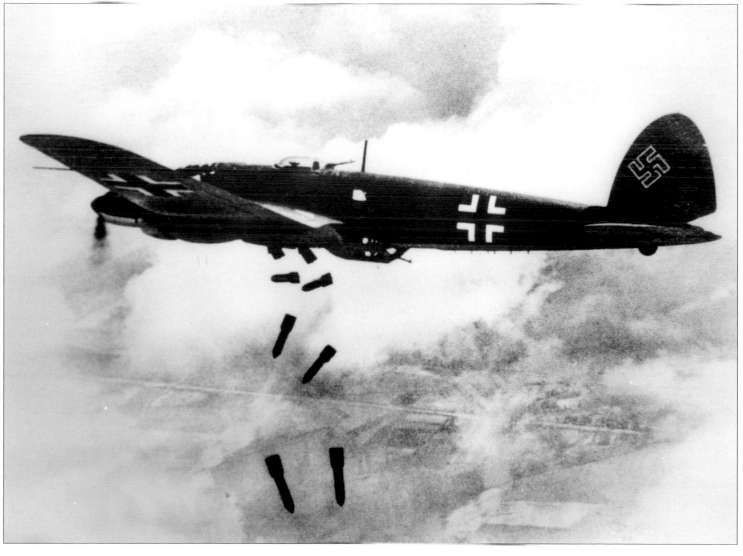

hardworking Junkers Ju 52 transport, proved its worth, delivering the gliders (each of which could take up to ten soldiers) to their targets. These troops overcame the main Belgian defense-line along the Albert Canal, and they opened the way to Brussels, at the very heart of Belgium, for the orthodox ground forces.

### OUTNUMBERED AND OUT-THOUGHT

But the main German assault was the central drive by Army Group A through Belgium and Luxembourg to the Meuse, breaking through the Albert line at Sedan and driving westward to reach the Channel in ten days. Here the Luftwaffe showed its virtuosity as a tactical group, while the Allied air forces suffered from outnumbered and inferior aircraft—and the permanent loss of the initiative in the first 24 hours of the campaign.

The French contributed the majority of the Allied fighters: 278 Morane-Saulnier M.S. 406, 36 Dewoitine D.520s (a modern design that had just begun to arrive at the front), 140 Bloch MB. 151/152 fighters, and 98 Curtiss Hawk 75s (the latter purchased from the United States just before the outbreak of war). The British fielded some 40 Hurricanes and 20 Gladiators (the two British Gladiator squadrons were on the point of receiving their new Hurricanes when the offensive opened). The Belgian air force also operated a handful of Hurricanes.

In bombers, the Allies were hopelessly out-classed. The best of the modern French bombers (LeO 451s, Breguet 693 AB-2s, and Amiot 350s) had only just begun to enter service and were flung into the battle in driblets. Of the British bomber squadrons in France, the Fairey Battle light bomber was a death trap when faced by modern fighters and the excellent German flak, while the Bristol Blenheim, although an infinitely better machine, still needed the protection of fighters. Nor were all the losses in the air, and at least one Blenheim squadron (No. 114) was wiped out on the ground by a Do 17 strike on the morning of the 11th, before it had managed to fly a single mission.

From the outset of the campaign the Allied bombers were frittered away on fruitless missions that were carried out with great gallantry but at an appalling cost. The deadliest targets of the first ten days were the German-held bridges across the Albert Canal. Here British bomber pilots of World War II won their first Victoria Crosses—posthumously. German fighter opposition was not the only headache for the Allied pilots, and the highly mobile and very effective German antiaircraft guns could be in position within minutes; in fact, the guns accounted for most of the victims shot down while attacking the Albert Canal bridges.

Nor were the Allies given the opportunity to operate from secure bases. The scorching pace of the German advance kept the Allied squadrons retreating from one hastily improvised airfield to another, and once again, the Ju

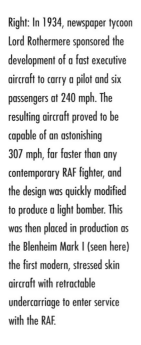

Right: In 1934, newspaper tycoon Lord Rothermere sponsored the development of a fast executive aircraft to carry a pilot and six passengers at 240 mph. The resulting aircraft proved to be capable of an astonishing 307 mph, far faster than any contemporary RAF fighter, and the design was quickly modified to produce a light bomber. This was then placed in production as the Blenheim Mark I (seen here) the first modern, stressed skin aircraft with retractable undercarriage to enter service with the RAF.

87 Stukas were key weapons in the German offensive. The all-important crossing of the Meuse on May 13 was spearheaded by a Stuka strike at the French-held bank, which was so minutely timed that the first German troops across were actually landing while clumps of mud thrown up by the Stuka bombs were still returning to earth.

## SETBACK FOR THE LUFTWAFFE

Once the great Allied retreat had begun, the German fighters and Stukas took on another role, keeping the roads behind the Allied front clogged with terror-stricken floods of refugees, while Do 17 reconnaissance aircraft spied out Allied troop concentrations as soon as they were formed. But the Luftwaffe's successes in this initial, fluid stage of the battle for the West were noticeably curtailed when the advance on the ground ran out of steam. On May 24, von Rundstedt's need to rest the Panzer units approaching Dunkirk along the coast was endorsed by Hitler, the motive being that the German tank forces must be conserved for the decisive attack on central and southern France.

The initial mobile phase was over; and in the last act at Dunkirk, the lion's share of the action was passed to the Luftwaffe, which undertook an impossible task with very mixed results. Göring, an eternal optimist, assured Hitler that his precious Luftwaffe could easily cope with the smashing of the Dunkirk pocket, but, neither for

Above: Hermann Göring was a fighter ace in World War I and an early supporter of Adolf Hitler. He went on to play a major role in the creation and development of the Luftwaffe and is seen here in his uniform as Reichsmarschall, inspecting Luftwaffe unit in 1942.

Left: Elated pilots gather around their leader after a successful mission; France 1940. Note that this Messerschmitt Bf-109 has a yellow engine cowling, which was a very practical measure necessary for instant identification in the confusion of a dogfight.

Above: Hawker Hurricane IIB. Developed from the fighter-bomber Hurricanes (sometimes known as "Hurribombers") initially carried 250 lb. bombs (as seen here) but later either 500 lb. bombs, eight rockets, drop tanks, or 40 mm cannon could also be carried.

Right: Messerschmitt Bf-109E-3 in France during the Battle of Britain already has 69 combat victories marked on its rudder. In the background Göring addresses the men of the squadron.

the first nor last time in this war, his subordinates knew perfectly well that they had been given a job beyond their resources. However, Göring's lofty status in the Nazi hierarchy and his unassailable personal influence with Hitler meant that there was nothing they could do about it.

Adverse weather and dense smoke over the target area meant that during the nine days of the Dunkirk evacuation, which lasted from May 26 to June 4, the Luftwaffe was only able to launch effective attacks over a period of 60 hours, less than three days. German bombers—particularly the Ju 87s—managed to sink seven French destroyers and torpedo-boats, six British destroyers, five large passenger ships and a quarter of the myriad "little ships" flung into the evacuation by the British. But, despite these undoubted successes, the Luftwaffe failed to prevent some 338,000 troops soldiers from getting away, the British, Belgian, and some of the French to England, although a proportion of the French made their way to ports further along the coast

Spirited patrolling by the British fighter squadrons in southern England cost the Luftwaffe 156 aircraft, which was 50 more than the RAF's own losses during the fight and the most punishing "round" fought by the Luftwaffe since the opening of the offensive on May 10. To take one example, on May 27, the day of the first heavy Luftwaffe attack on Dunkirk, *Fliegerkorps II* lost 23 aircraft, which exceeded the combined total of the previous ten days.

## THE BATTLE OF BRITAIN

The Battle of Britain was not the first encounter for which the Wehrmacht, the three German armed forces, had never planned: Denmark and Norway claim that honor. But the Wehrmacht had certainly never been given the right tools for the job of crossing the Channel and conquering Britain. There was a small nucleus of a battle fleet of excellent modern warships, but it was not due to reach its planned strength until 1994 and had suffered heavy losses in April and May 1940; but, regardless of that, it had neither an invasion fleet nor the doctrine and training for conducting a major opposed landing. Nor did the Luftwaffe have any long-range heavy bombers, while its airborne troops had suffered

heavy losses in the earlier campaigns. Additionally, Hitler was reluctant to invade Britain, but when Churchill refused to be what he called "reasonable" and give up, he decided that he had no other choice.

After France capitulated, a whole month went by until Directive 16 ("Sea Lion"), ordering preparations for an invasion to begin, was signed on July 16. From the start the onus was placed on the Luftwaffe. The German army claimed that it was ready to go, but the German navy could not guarantee to protect the invasion fleet from determined British attacks. It was essential, therefore, that the Luftwaffe destroy all opposition from the air and guarantee the total command of the skies during—and after—the crossing, which meant destroying RAF Fighter Command in a battle fought on German terms.

On the British side, Air Chief Marshal Sir Hugh Dowding had managed to keep Fighter Command alive by refusing to allow his fighter squadrons to be frittered away in the Battle of France. He knew that his No. 11 Group, in southeast England—"invasion corner"—must inevitably bear the brunt of the fighting and that the chain of radar stations along the south and east coasts would be absolutely invaluable for advance information of approaching German air formations. His vestigial reserves in the north and west must be doled out to 11 Group as sparingly as possible. Fighter production from the factories was increasing at an encouraging rate, but the RAF was dwarfed by the Luftwaffe's

Above: Heinkel 111 over the Isle of Dogs, London, during the Battle of Britain. This hard-fought battle was the first significant setback suffered by the Luftwaffe.

Above: The Supermarine Spitfire was the descendant of the race-winning Schneider Trophy seaplanes. It was first flown in March 1936.

Previous pages: A pair of Hurricanes take off from Gravesend on August 15, 1940. This squadron was one of a number of units of the Royal Auxiliary Air Force, which flew with great distinction alongside their regular counterparts throughout the battle.

numbers, and Dowding knew that incessant attacks on the southern fighter bases and the radar chain could destroy Fighter Command within a week.

In a long-term battle of attrition, the RAF's chances of victory were negligible but the British had an immense advantage—they were fighting on their home ground. If their pilots got shot down they would not be captured but could be flying again within hours. The British also had the obvious advantage in endurance, whereas the best weapon in the Luftwaffe's armory—the Messerschmitt Me 109 fighter—had an operational endurance over southern England of 20 to 30 minutes, at best.

## LUFTWAFFE OBJECTIVES

The Battle of Britain was the first—and only—large-scale and "pure" air battle of World War II. Dowding's objective was simple: to maintain Fighter Command as an active threat. The Luftwaffe commanders—Kesselring (Luftflotte 2), Sperrle (Luftflotte 3), and Stumpff (Luftflotte 5)—had a multitude of somewhat hazy objectives, which prevented them from marking down the destruction of Fighter Command as

the crux of the battle. These objectives included the interdiction of British shipping traffic in the Channel, the bombing of radar and fighter stations, and—due to Hitler's interference—the bombing of London. The last was ostensibly Germany's "response" to a small-scale British raid on Berlin, but in reality it was intended to crack the British will to resist.

The Battle of Britain opened in earnest in the month of July, with the three Luftflotten attacking coastal convoys, ports, and fighter bases in the southeast. These attacks were met head-on by the RAF and were roughly handled, but the pressure on Fighter Command was intense from the start and never let up. To take just one example, as early as July 10, No. 54 Squadron (Spitfires), based at Hornchurch, could put up only eight aircraft and 13 pilots—a loss of ten aircraft in 48 hours. Only the constant rotation of battle-weary squadrons by Dowding and Air Vice Marshal Park (commander of the all-important No. 11 Group), plus the much increased production of aircraft under the dynamic impetus of Lord Beaverbrook, Churchill's Minister of Aircraft Production, enabled Fighter Command to continue the battle without bleeding to death.

In August the three Luftflotten at last put out their full strength. Infuriated by the lack of progress, Göring ordered that there should be a new offensive, to be heralded by a smashing and concentrated blow—to which he gave the codename Adlertag (day of the eagles)—although this took over a fortnight to materialize.

Adlertag was finally scheduled for August 13, and was to be preceded by pinpoint raids to "blind" the British radar stations on the 12th. Some radar stations were indeed put off the air on that day, but only for a few hours and then they were back in operation again. Adlertag itself proved to be a sorry anticlimax, going off at half-cock in the morning, when coordination between the German fighters and bombers was bad, while the afternoon raids failed to saturate the British defenses. The greatest flaw in the German plan lay in faulty intelligence and even if every identified airfield had been attacked according to plan, none of them was, in fact, vital to Fighter Command's deployment pattern.

August 15 was the first and only time that the three Luftflotten attacked together. It was also the heaviest single day's fighting of the entire battle, with the Luftwaffe flying over 2,000

sorties and the RAF 974. Luftflotte 5, having the longest distance to fly, came off the worst, suffering losses of just under 20 percent, after which it played no further large-scale part in the battle, leaving it to Luftflotten 2 and 3 to keep up the pressure in the days which followed the battles of the 15th. August 18 in particular stands out as a definite landmark in the defeat of the dreaded Stuka. The eight Stuka Gruppen had lost 39 out of 281 aircraft in the first two weeks of August and on the 18th they lost another 17 and had to be pulled out of the battle.

Göring intervened in the battle on the 19th, appointing new (and younger) fighter commanders—Galland, Trautloft, Mölders, Lützow— all operational airmen and proven aces. He insisted that the Me 109s must stick closer to the bombers—which only restricted the German fighters still more. Göring also refused to accept the proven weaknesses of the Me 110 and Ju 87, not to mention those of the much-vaunted "wonder bomber," the Ju 88. The Ju 88's main asset had been considered its speed, but that (and its weak defensive armament) could not stand up to the much faster eight-gun Spitfires and Hurricanes. A four-day comparative lull ensued—and then the crisis of the battle opened

for RAF Fighter Command, with massive attacks concentrating, at last, on the vital airfields of Kent, Surrey, and Sussex. By September 7, Fighter Command was on the brink of defeat, but was then saved when the Luftwaffe switched its tactics to mass daylight attacks on London.

London had been marked out as a major target since the night of August 24–25, when some German bombs intending to attack the

Above: A Kette (flight) of Messerschmitt Bf-110E-1s fighter-bombers of squadron II/SKG-210.

Below: Luftwaffe ace Adolf Galland (left) meeting Hermann Göring in France, 1940.

Thameshaven oil tanks—a "correct" military target according to the conventions upon which Hitler himself was still insisting—missed the target and scattered their bombs over London's dockland. Churchill immediately ordered the bombing of Berlin in retaliation, to which Hitler responded by vowing to raze Britain's cities, starting with London.

## MASS RAIDS BROKEN UP

Like the German invasion itself, everything now turned on the survival of RAF Fighter Command and for as long as the target was London the vital airfields could operate again. By September 14 Fighter Command was back on its feet with a vengeance. The mass daylight raids on London on Sunday, September 15, were broken up by the British fighter attacks—with interceptions by more than 300 Spitfires and Hurricanes in 20 minutes. The speed with which the formations were broken up on the 15th also proved that the morale of the German bomber pilots, not unnaturally, was beginning to falter.

The Luftwaffe, in switching from the airfields to London, had squandered another week, but it might still have won the battle. What mattered was that by nightfall on September 15, Fighter Command was still very much alive—with only Dowding, Churchill and a few of their closest collaborators knowing just how near the Command was to breaking point. However, the equally exhausted Germans felt they were making no progress and this, together with the impressive damage being done by RAF Bomber Command to the German invasion barges across the Channel, caused Hitler to postpone Operation Sea Lion indefinitely on September 17 and to order the dispersal of the invasion fleet. The bombing of London and other major British cities—which the British always referred to as the Blitz—was approaching the close of its second week and would rage on throughout the winter of 1940–41. But the continuing raids were largely devoid of military significance, since Britain's survival had been secured in the critical days of September 1940.

Fighter Command's ordeal in the first two weeks of September is conclusive proof that the Luftwaffe should have won the Battle of Britain. August was a month that the Germans squandered, and as far as the invasion of Britain was concerned they could not afford to do so. Bad

Right: A Heinkel He-111 heads through typical English haze across a country town en route to London in 1940. This picture makes it clear just how low these bombers flew in such operations, even with enemy antiaircraft guns waiting for them.

intelligence was partly to blame: it took until the end of August before Fighter Command's defenses were sounded out. The Luftwaffe's commanders completely underestimated the British rate of fighter production—in 1940 it was twice as high as that of Germany. And, finally, Göring and his subordinates were hopelessly off the mark in failing to use a systematic approach to their problem, constantly changing the main objectives to be attacked. All these failures worked to the advantage of the British.

Fighter Command's mainstay in the Battle of Britain was the Hurricane, as far as numbers were concerned, but this aircraft was slightly inferior to the Me 109 and soon came to be earmarked for attacks on the bomber streams. The German fighters—including the Me 110 "destroyers"—had the benefit of cannon armament, enabling their pilots to land damaging hits at longer ranges than were available to the Spitfires and Hurricanes with their octuple batteries of machine guns. However, crippled by their endurance limitation and by the close support tactics forced on them by Göring, the Me 109s could not defend the bombers, all of which had revealed grave deficiencies in their defensive armament.

## DEFIANT TOO EASILY DEFIED

But RAF Fighter Command was also found to have some weak cards in its hand, notably the

Boulton Paul Defiant, a two-seat fighter with a rear turret. This had shown considerable promise during the skirmishing over Dunkirk, but over the English skies it proved to be easy meat for the Luftwaffe's fighters and had to be withdrawn from the fight at the end of August after the almost complete destruction of No. 264 Squadron. Like the German Me 110, the Defiant was the product of fallacious thinking between the wars, and whereas the German

machine was too large and slow for a day fighter, the smaller British two-seater had no forward firing armament.

The Me 109 was slightly faster than the Spitfire, but of greater significance was the superior German system of fuel injection, which enabled Me 109 pilots to get out of trouble by half-rolling into a steep dive. The Rolls-Royce Merlin which powered the Spitfires and the Hurricanes during the battle had a floating

Above: The result of bombing. One house has been totally demolished by a direct hit, leaving a gap in the row, with debris all over the street, and a London Transport double-decker bus thrown into the front of the house next door by the blast of the explosion.

Left: The Bolton Paul Defiant, with its rear-mounted quadruple turret seemed like a good idea, but was an absolute failure in its designed role as a day fighter. One of its greatest weaknesses was that it had no forward firing guns, all firepower being concentrated in the turret. These crews are from the 264 Squadron, the first to operate the type, which suffered great losses, first in France and then in the Battle of Britain.

229

carburetor and the "negative G" caused by a sudden dive caused the engine to cut. When the British were able to make their first evaluation tests on a captured Me 109, another advantage of the German machine was revealed: the rudder pedals were placed some 6 in. higher in the Me 109, making it harder for the blood to sink to the pilot's feet during a sharp pull-out, and therefore harder for him to "black out" because of the centrifugal drain of blood from the brain. On the other hand, the clumsier cockpit design of the Me 109 gave its pilots inferior visibility to that enjoyed by the RAF pilots. The Me 109 was even smaller than the trim Spitfire and its cockpit was found to be uncomfortably cramped when examined by the British.

As far as tactics were concerned, the Germans had the advantage of greater experience when the Battle of Britain opened. The more far-sighted British fighter leaders were quick to abandon the neat, geometrical patrolling formations and attack patterns laid down in the prewar years and adopt the more flexible method of the Germans. This became known as the "finger-four": a basic unit of four aircraft, with each leader protected by his wing-man.

A major controversy was caused by the "wing theory": the coordinated use of entire squadrons in combat which the British tried with indifferent results during the battle. Championed by the commander of No. 12 Group, Air Vice Marshal Leigh-Mallory, and by the forthright, "legless" pilot Douglas Bader, the idea was tried with Bader's Duxford Wing of five squadrons. None of the top commanders in the Luftwaffe was sacked for their shortcomings in the Battle, but in Britain Dowding and Park, who were the real victors, were shabbily treated and removed to unimportant commands. On the other hand, Leigh-Mallory eclipsed Dowding and eventually rose to the command of the Allied Expeditionary Force in 1944.

## THE BOMBING OFFENSIVE

Caution and restraint were the initial watchwords when the bomber war opened in September 1939. While the Wehrmacht was engaged in smashing Poland, neither the Allies (Britain and France) nor Germany sought to escalate the war by opening an all-out bombing offensive. The Allies sought to localize and confine the conflict, while Hitler hoped that a settlement could be reached with the Allies once Poland was out of the way. Thus, for nearly a full year the bombing campaign was conducted

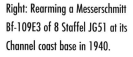

Right: Rearming a Messerschmitt Bf-109E3 of 8 Staffel JG51 at its Channel coast base in 1940.

Left: At the start of the Battle of Britain, the basic British formation consisted of a section of three aircraft in a tight "Vee." A squadron normally cruised in two flights, each of two sections, a total of twelve aircraft. It was not ideal for a number of reasons, primarily because it was far too rigid, and the Luftwaffe's four-ship Schwarm proved greatly superior.

Left: Some of the pilots of 242 Hurricane Squadron at Duxford in 1940. Fourth from right is the commanding officer, Squadron Leader Douglas Bader, who lost both legs in a flying accident in 1931, was invalided out of the RAF in 1933, and argued his way back to full flying duties in 1939. He shot down 23 enemy aircraft; but on August 9, 1941, he shot down two Bf 109s over France, but collided with a third. He parachuted to safety but his metal legs were damaged. The Germans invited the RAF to send an aircraft with a spare pair of legs, an operation that was accomplished with complete correctness on both sides.

231

Above: A formation of Bristol Blenheim Mark IVs of No. 139 Squadron, RAF. One of these 139 Squadron aircraft flew the first RAF operational patrol of World War II.

under what can best be described as a mixture of strict military decorum and voluntary restraint. Nor could politicians overlook the fact that for twenty years, fear of the bomber had been a nightmare. The dread of mass air raids showering bombs filled with either poison gas or high explosive on civilian populations was reinforced by numerous movies and books. Then, this feeling of approaching doom had seemed to be borne out by the German air raid on Guernica during the Spanish civil war.

But, quite apart from such political and strategic considerations, there were technical and financial problems, although these were carefully hidden from public view. In Germany, for example, the desire to mass-produce as many offensive aircraft in the shortest time possible led to the adoption of tested and proven twin-engined bomber aircraft types, to the exclusion of the four-engined bomber.

However, even the experts could not always agree. For example, Germany's General Wever, Luftwaffe Chief of Staff until his death in an air crash in 1936, had championed the cause of a long-range heavy bomber program. But he was blocked by the Luftwaffe's Quartermaster General, General Udet, by the Secretary of State for Air, General Milch, and by Göring himself, all of whom were knowledgeable and experienced airmen. In Britain the brilliant aircraft designer Barnes Wallis, the brains behind the

R-100 airship and the Wellesley and Wellington bombers, presented his plan in 1939 for a "Victory Bomber" that could carry a 10-ton bomb against strategic targets, but his idea was "pooh-poohed" as science fiction.

Thus, in 1939 neither Germany nor the British and French were equipped to wage a strategic bomber offensive; the very idea was anathema to politicians and the public alike. As a result, military targets were the only objectives to be considered, but there was the greatest confusion as to what they might be. For both sides, however, one target was clear-cut right from the start—warships and their bases. Even so, British and German bomber crews were under the strictest orders not to bomb even these naval bases unless the enemy ships were there, for fear of inflicting civilian loss of life and provoking reprisals.

The aircraft of RAF Bomber Command in 1939 consisted of the Handley Page Hampden, the Bristol Blenheim, the Vickers Wellington, and the Armstrong Whitworth Whitley—all of them twin-engined, with bomb loads up to 4,500 lb., apart from the Whitley with its maximum of 7,000 lb., and all with inadequate defensive armament. Their average maximum range with light bomb loads was approximately 1,340 miles. Considerable confusion was caused to British antiaircraft gunners by the fact that the Hampden and Blenheim both bore some

superficial resemblances to the German Do 17 and Ju 88 respectively.

### A LESSON IN DESTRUCTION

The Blenheims and Hampdens opened Bomber Command's war with strikes against German warships in the Schillig Roads, the pocket-battleship *Admiral Scheer* being the main target.

It was an innocuous debut, but the British were learning from scratch—everything from taking off with a full load of bombs and fuel, to finding the target in bad weather and coping with enemy flak. A more expensive lesson was to come on December 18, 1939, when 22 Wellingtons flying in close formation flew over Wilhelmshaven and the Heligoland Bight in perfect, cloudless fighter weather—and without any

Above: The Armstrong Whitworth Whitley entered service in 1937 and was one of several twin-engined bombers equipping the RAF when war broke out. A total of 1,814 were produced and the type ceased to serve in Bomber Command in 1942, although a few remained in other roles until 1943. This No. 78 Squadron aircraft was painted black for the night bombing role, a practice that was soon found to be unnecessary.

Left: A 4,000 lb. bomb is delivered to a waiting Vickers Wellington Mark IC of No. 419 Squadron. The Wellington was designed by Barnes Wallis, the inventor of the Dambuster bomb and was built using his geodetic structure, which gave it exceptional strength. Indeed, many RAF aircrew owed their safe return in a damaged Wellington to the amazing ideas of Barnes Wallis.

Above: The Welsh city of Swansea was raided on three successive nights in February 1941. Municipal buildings, churches, schools, and shops were demolished; this is the gutted ruin of a large department store.

Previous pages: A Bristol Beaufort torpedo bomber of 217 Squadron RAF, in Coastal Command's 1940-pattern camouflage (it later changed to blue/white). Derived from the Blenheim, the four-man Beaufort had more powerful engines and carried either a single 18-in. torpedo semi-recessed into the bomb-bay or 2,000 lb. of bombs. Typical armament was four 0.303 in. machine guns: one fixed forward, one in a remote-controlled chin blister and two in the dorsal turret. A very successful design, it served in the Australian and British air forces.

fighter protection of their own. It had been believed that the massed firepower of such bombers in formation would keep off fighter opposition, but it quickly became apparent that the Wellington was extremely vulnerable to beam attacks. Ten Wellingtons were shot down during the sweep and another three were written off in crash-landings back in Britain. The losses suffered by this daytime "Battle of Heligoland Bight" were instrumental in Bomber Command's switch to night operations, upon which it concentrated for the rest of the war.

In this early, cautious period of mutual antishipping strikes the Luftwaffe did no better than the RAF. Prime targets for the Germans were the capital ships of the British Home Fleet, most notably the battleships HMS *Rodney* and *Nelson*, the world-famous battle-cruiser HMS *Hood*, and the aircraft carrier HMS *Ark Royal*. Thus, when the British Home Fleet was sighted on a North Sea sweep on September 26, nine He 111s and four Ju 88s were immediately sent out to attack. *Hood* was hit by a dud; *Ark Royal* was narrowly missed by a dive-bombing Ju 88, whose pilot claimed a possible hit. The German propaganda machine promptly claimed that *Ark Royal* had been sunk and the subsequent embarrassment when the ship was shown to be very much still in business drove the blameless German pilot to the verge of suicide.

Later, on October 16, the Luftwaffe attacked the Home Fleet base at Rosyth in the Firth of Forth in Scotland. The *Hood* was there but was not attacked, but the cruisers Edinburgh and the Southampton were slightly damaged. The following day, four Ju 88s attacked Scapa Flow, the great British naval anchorage in the Orkneys, but they managed to damage only the battleship HMS *Iron Duke*, an elderly veteran of the Battle of Jutland in 1916, and now being used as a training and depot ship—scarcely a prime target.

## BOMBER MYTHS DISPELLED

Thus the opening weeks of World War II dispelled many prewar myths about the potency of the bomber. Antishipping attacks needed pinpoint accuracy, but as the Ju 87 Stuka attacks demonstrated during the Norwegian campaign of April 1940, the dive-bomber could be highly effective in this role—given the right conditions. One of those conditions was air supremacy, since the Stukas were extremely vulnerable to fighter attack. Another problem, which faced both the Luftwaffe and the RAF, was that far too many of their bombs were

failing to explode, due primarily to faulty fuses and detonators.[3]

But the story of strategic bombing in World War II really began in the summer of 1940, when both sides abandoned their concern for civilian life. The Luftwaffe, for example, found that even the heaviest raids they were capable of mounting could not bring about the total destruction of the so-called "military targets," the most obvious examples in the early phases of the Battle of Britain being port installations, aircraft factories, radar stations, and fighter airfields. Thus, both the commanders of the Luftwaffe and of RAF Bomber Command entered a new phase in their campaign, trying to create an offensive strategy out of the deliberate bombing of civilian populations.

Therefore, throughout most of 1940 Bomber Command's objectives were constantly changing. In April the British bombers were sent to mine the canals of Denmark and the waters of the Kattegat to cut off the German footholds in Norway—a technique that naturally proved ineffective against the German air-lift. During the Battle of France they attacked industrial targets in the Ruhr and oil tanks at Hamburg—

which had little effect on the fighting—and also made what were termed "billiard-shot" attacks, by trying to place delayed action bombs into railway tunnels, in an attempt to slow the German advance.

## BERLIN IS BOMBED

Then came Churchill's order to bomb Berlin in retaliation for the German bombs that had been dropped on London. The long distance to Berlin inevitably reduced bomb-loads to the lightest, but the initial morale effect was striking, not least because Göring had promised that no British bomber could ever get to Berlin. But the mood of the Berliners was soon turned to hatred and a desire for vengeance by Goebbels' very efficient propaganda machine, and the loathing of the "cowardly Allied *terrorflieger*," once implanted, was never quenched throughout the war. Further, despite the increasingly severe damage from first RAF and then RAF and USAAF bombers, the German civilian population held

[3] This was also the period when the German U-boats were having major problems with faulty torpedoes, and the U.S. Navy was to suffer similar problems in 1941–42.

Below left: The remains of a Heinkel He-111 that crashed near Fordinbridge in Hampshire, England, demolishing the right half of the house in the background as it came in. Two determined airman, the one on the right with bayonet fixed and rifle cocked, stand guard.

Below: Dorsal turret on a Luftwaffe bomber, armed with Rhoinmotall Borsig MG-131 13 mm heavy machine gun.

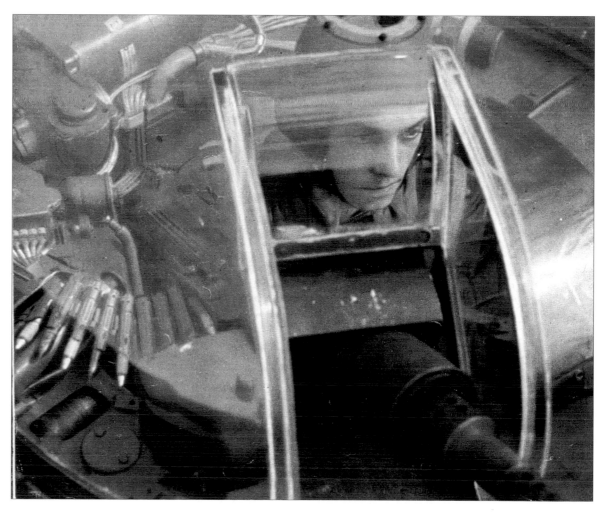

Above: The scene from a Bristol
Blenheim as it hauls away from
the target on August 12, 1941.
The target of this very low-level
raid was the Fortuna power
station that provided power for
the German city of Cologne.

as firm under Allied bombing as did the British under the Blitz.

Hitler's reaction was to order the razing of every major British city, but this was easier said than done. Anyone could find and hit London—it covered a huge area and England's biggest river coiled its way right through it. But, for targets deeper inland, electronic devices had to be used, such as overlapping Lorenz radio beams, which told the pilot when he was on course, and the intersecting *Knickebein* and *X-Gerät* beams, which crossed above the target and signaled an automatic bomb release as the bomber hit the intersection point. The specially-trained Kampfgruppe 100 used the X-Gerät guidance system on the night of November 14, 1940, when 449 bombers from Luftflotten 2 and 3 savaged Coventry. But the rapid British discovery that both these German systems could be jammed or, even better, distorted so that the bombers dropped their loads on empty fields, did much to negate the threat for the time being. These events were actually of even greater significance than appeared at the time, since they were the first escalations in the electronic war, as the scientists and engineers on both sides sought to develop ever newer "black boxes" that would aid their troops and frustrate the enemy.

The British had to swallow an unpalatable home truth in mid-1941, when the great German invasion of Soviet Russia gave convincing proof that Germany's industrial capacity had not only been totally underestimated, but also that all of Bomber Command raids carried out against German industrial targets so far had been useless. Further, the attempts to cripple the communications system of the Ruhr valley had failed completely. Closer investigations showed that the bomber crews, for all their bravery and determination, were simply not hitting their targets, while Luftwaffe General Kammhuber's nightfighter network, controlled by radar, was beginning to make itself felt. There was, however, a brighter side, particularly as the big new bombers were entering service in increasing numbers, including the Short Stirling and Handley Page Halifax, with maximum bomb loads of 14,000 lb. and 13,000 lb., respectively. The twin-engined Avro Manchester suffered from repeated engine trouble, but a four-engined version, developed as an experiment, led to the four-engined Lancaster, the most successful British bomber of the war.

For Bomber Command, the course of the war still produced weakening distractions from what was seen as its *raison d'etre*—the attack on

Germany. Thus, in 1940 the Command was required to bomb the assemblies of invasion barges in German-held Channel ports, while in 1941 it was required to carry out repeated attacks on the German battlecruisers, the *Scharnhorst* and the *Gneisenau* sheltering in Brest, and posing a constant threat to Allied shipping in the Atlantic.

## HARRIS'S WAR ON WILL

The year 1942 was an important turning-point for Bomber Command, when, on February 22, Air Marshal Sir Arthur Harris took charge. He was convinced—although he was never able to prove it—that bombing could have an absolutely decisive effect on the conflict by destroying Germany's ability to wage war and her will to do so. Churchill backed him enthusiastically.

At the same time, Harris had absorbed the lesson that greater accuracy was needed and that electronic aids were the answer. Three new British devices were eventually found to provide satisfactory answers: Gee, which gave navigators the benefit of a radio grid for pinpointing their position; Oboe, which gave an exact pinpoint guide for bombing or target marking

accurately, and H2S, which provided a radar map of the ground over which the aircraft was passing. These new devices enabled bombers to fly in denser formations—known as "bomber streams"—and also considerably reduced the time the spent over the target area, although time was also needed for commanders, staffs, and aircrew to acquire experience in using them. Another process that Harris backed was target marking; the birth of the "Pathfinder" force, which flew ahead of the main bomber stream and marked the target with colored flares. Some tragic errors were made during the learning process, most notably when target markers missed Saarbrücken and by mistake illuminated the small town of Saarlouis instead, which resulted in its elimination.

Nevertheless, Harris's obsession with the psychological effect of mass bombing led to the first "thousand-bomber raid" which took place on the night of May 30–31, 1942, when a total of 1,046 aircraft headed for Cologne. It killed 469 civilians and rendered 45,000 of them homeless, but it did not bring about the abrupt termination of the war, as Harris had hoped, nor did it seriously effect Cologne's industrial output. To reach the "magic figure" of 1,000 had

Above: An apparently tranquil scene as an Avro Lancaster Mark III cruises above the clouds. Hidden inside the aircraft, however, is a very large number of bombs (the normal load was 14,000 lb.) while defensive armament comprised six 0.303 in. Browning machine guns (two in the nose turret, four in the tail turret), plus two 0.5 in. in the dorsal turret.

required not only the total strength of Bomber Command, but also all suitable bombers from Coastal Command, as well as 367 aircraft from training and conversion units. British losses for the night were 43 aircraft, or 3.6 percent of the total. Nor did the "thousand raid" disrupt the German fighter defenses, as had also been hoped. A dispassionate analysis shows that the Cologne raid proved yet again that Bomber Command could not deliver knock-out blows, although it was an ominous warning of what the Germans could expect in the future. It was also a major tonic for the British people, because it showed that after the devastating German attacks of 1940–41, the RAF was now "hitting back" and giving the German people a taste of the same medicine.

Throughout 1942 the RAF also made a number of experiments with daytime raids on specially selected targets and by October a total of 45 such attacks had been launched. Favorite targets for the Lancasters in these raids were the U-boat yards at Danzig, Gdynia, and Lübeck, which were along the Baltic coast and which were at ranges impossible to cover before the advent of the Lancaster. The loss levels among the bomber crews in these daylight raids were, high, however. For example, in the low-level precision raid against the M.A.N. works at Augsburg on April 17, 1942, seven of the twelve aircraft involved were lost. The target was undoubtedly important—it was the prime source of the diesel-engines for the German navy's U-boats—and the factory was so badly damaged that it did not resume full production for six months, but a 58 percent loss rate would be unsustainable for Bomber Command.

## THE DAM BUSTERS' RAID, MAY 17, 1943

One of the most spectacular precision bombing attacks of the war, the Dam Busters' raid, was a major success, both because the dams were breached, as intended, and because it showed that tightly controlled, precision attacks were feasible. The Ruhr dams had long been listed by the Air Ministry and the Bomber Command as vital to the German war effort, since they controlled the reservoirs that supplied the industrial region of the Ruhr with much of its water and electricity. The problem, however, was how to actually carry out the attack and the solution came from a brilliant scientist,

Barnes Wallis, and while his "bouncing" bombs were being constructed and tested, specially selected pilots and aircrew were brought together by RAF Bomber Command to form a new unit, 617 Squadron.

Harris was somewhat skeptical about the intended operation, but the project went ahead and the new squadron was formed under the command of one of the great operational airmen of the war, Wing Commander Guy Gibson. Although he was only 24 years old at the time, the much-decorated Gibson was one of Bomber Command's most experienced pilots, a meticulous planner and a natural leader of men. He was a firm and forthright disciplinarian who exercised tight control over his unit, but invariably led from the front, placed himself at the point of greatest danger, and never asked his men to do anything he was not prepared to do himself.

The 133 aircrew of 617 Squadron had one thing in common: they had all been specially selected by Gibson as men who possessed the "right stuff" for the operation. Among their number were 29 Canadians, 12 Australians, 2 New Zealanders, and an American Flight Lieutenant Joe McCarthy. The training that followed involved a punishing routine of low-level flying

Right: One of the most famous bomber pilots of the war, Wing Commander Guy Gibson, DSO*, DFC* leads his crew into their Lancaster bomber for the Dambuster's raid. They are (from left): Trevor-Roper (rear gunner), Pulford (engineer), Deering (front gunner), Spafford bomb-aimer), Hutchison (wireless operator), Gibson (pilot), and Taerum (navigator). Deering and Taerum were Canadians, Spafford was Australian, and the remainder were British. Of these seven young men, all returned safely from this raid, but not one of them survived the war.

Far right: Gibson and fellow aircrew from 617 Squadron with his beloved black labrador. The dog was run over and killed just before the raid, causing Gibson considerable grief.

and bombing exercises, with precision being of the essence. The target was still a secret, even from Gibson, although he had been informed by Wallis that the attack would be made over water at a height of 150 ft.—a figure later revised down to 60 ft.—and the bombs had to be released at precisely 1,275 ft. from the target.

This raised many problems, including how to judge the height over water and the exact distance from the target on the bombing run. The first was solved by fitting two spotlights on the underside of each Lancaster, one on the nose, the other on the rear fuselage. These were mounted at an angle such that their beams coincided on the surface of the water when the aircraft was at the correct height. To solve the other problem— how to judge the point of release—the bomb aimer was given a simple V-shaped wooden device with two nails at the ends of its arms, and when these coincided with the towers at either end of the dam, the bomb was dropped.

Meanwhile, Barnes Wallis and his team were working frantically to perfect the design of the bomb and between May 11 and 14, the aircraft of 617 Squadron used full-sized practice bombs to attack canvas towers on the promenade at Reculver on the north coast of the county of Kent.

At last, on the May 15, Guy Gibson was told that the attack—code named Operation Chastise— would be mounted on the night of the following day, Sunday May 16. Six dams had been chosen as targets and Gibson was to lead the main contingent, consisting of three formations of three aircraft, to attack the Möhne dam, then the Eder, and, if any bombs were still left, the Sorpe. The second wave of five aircraft, flying singly, would attack the Sorpe. The final five aircraft were to fly as a reserve, taking off two hours after the first wave, to be directed against any of the main targets or three other dams, the Lister, Diemel, and Ennepe. To evade German air defenses, the Lancasters were to fly at under 500 ft. for the entire mission.

Above: The Dambusters bomb (covername Upkeep) was dropped from a modified Lancaster at an altitude of 60 ft. Upkeep was cylindrical in shape and was given 500 rpm backspin to ensure that when it hit the dam wall, it would remain in contact with the face as it sank to a depth of 30 ft. where it exploded

Above: Taken on the morning of May 17, 1943, this picture shows the huge damage caused to Germany's Möhne dam by Barnes Wallis's extraordinary bouncing bomb. Barnes Wallis had designed Upkeep with his normal mathematical precision and the result shows that his calculation were right on.

Led by Gibson, the first wave took off from Scampton just after 2030 and as they flew across the Ruhr at tree-top height a power cable accounted for one of his Lancasters. On arrival over the first target—the Möhne dam—Gibson commenced the first attack shortly after midnight. Flying through heavy antiaircraft fire, he dropped his bomb slightly off target; it burst on the reservoir bank just to the left of the huge dam and he was followed in by the second Lancaster, which got its bomb marginally off too late; it overshot the dam but wrecked the power station beyond. Badly damaged by flak, the crippled Lancaster flew on for another three miles before exploding in a sheet of flame; its pilot, Flight Lieutenant Hopgood, had predicted that he would not survive the mission.

The third bomb missed the dam, but the fourth hit and then the fifth actually caused the breach, and a huge volume of water began to cascade through the dam into the valley beyond. To Gibson, circling over the target, the floodwaters released by the bomb looked like "stirred porridge" in the moonlight and he transmitted the codeword for success, named after his beloved black labrador, which had tragically been run over earlier in the day.[4]

Gibson then led the remaining three aircraft with bombs to the Eder, while the others headed for home. At the Eder, which was shrouded in early morning mist, the first two bombs failed to break the dam, but the third punched a gaping hole in it. A tidal wave of water poured through, eventually engulfing an area of 250 square miles. Elated, the crews turned away, but two more Lancasters were lost on the homeward leg.

The second wave, attacking the Sorpe, hit early trouble when two Lancasters were forced to turn back. Another was shot down by flak and a fourth crashed after hitting a power cable. Only one Lancaster, *T for Tommy*, piloted by the American, McCarthy, reached the dam. In contrast to the other dams, which were masonry structures and had been attacked with the bouncing bombs at right angles, the Sorpe had sloping earth sides, which meant that McCarthy had to fly lengthways along the crest and drop his mines directly on top of it. The approach was so difficult that McCarthy made ten runs before releasing his bomb, which struck the top of the dam, but, as he flew away, McCarthy realized that he had failed to breach it.

This left the reserve group, two of whose aircraft had been shot down on the outward flight, while a third had been forced to turn back. Of the remaining two, one attacked the Sorpe, but, like McCarthy, could do no more than dent the top of the dam. The other Lancaster attacked one of the secondary targets, the Ennepe, again without success. It was the last aircraft to arrive back at Scampton, at 0615.

Harris and Barnes Wallis were there for the debriefing. In all, eight of Gibson's nineteen Lancasters had been lost on the operation, two of them on the return leg of the raid, and fifty-six men failed to return, of whom only three survived as prisoners of war. Guy Gibson was immediately awarded a Victoria Cross and many of his men were decorated. The Dam Busters' raid quickly assumed legendary status, and at the time gave an enormous psychological boost to the British morale.

There is no doubt that the attack had been brilliantly conceived and heroically executed. It caused loss of life and had a major impact on industrial production, although this was somewhat shorter-lived than had been anticipated by the British planners. However, it is important to remember that when the plans were being made, all British analysis indicated that these were very worthwhile targets, and once Barnes Wallis had produced the technical means to achieve it, the only thing to do was to put it to the test.

## TWO GREAT AIRCRAFT

One of the greatest nuisance weapons with which the RAF plagued the Luftwaffe was the de Havilland Mosquito, which started its career as a low-cost private experiment that was ignored by RAF top brass. Powered by twin Merlins, it had a maximum speed of nearly 400 mph and in one version it was armed with four 20 mm cannon and four machine guns, which made it a formidable fighter. In its unarmed bomber version the Mosquito could eventually carry up to 4,000 lb. of bombs. It was the ideal intruder for daytime reconnaissance, easily outpacing intercepting fighters, and when fitted with the "Oboe" navigation pin-pointer it was used to

[4]Gibson was able to exercise such close control over the aircraft in his squadron because all 617 aircraft were fitted with the (then) brand-new VHF radios, their first operational use.

Left: On their return from the raid, Gibson's crew are debriefed by an intelligence officer (seated, left). To his left and around the table are Spafford, Taerum (with hat), and Trevor-Roper (nearest camera on right). Partly hidden on right are Pulford and Deering. Meanwhile, the commanders can only stand behind and listen: Air Chief Marshal Sir Arthur Harris (left), the famous commander in chief of Bomber Command, and Air Vice Marshal the Hon. R.A. Cochrane (right), commanding No. 5 Group, to which 617 Squadron belonged.

put down the initial marker flares for the incoming night bomber streams.

The Lancaster became Bomber Command's best heavy bomber. With a crew of seven it had a maximum range of 1,660 miles and usually carried 14,000 lb. of bombs. As just described, modified Lancasters carried Barnes Wallis's "bouncing bomb," while in 1944 and 1945 the massive "Tallboy" (12,000 lb.) and "Grand Slam" (22,000 lb.) bombs—also products of Wallis's ever fertile mind—appeared and were dropped by Lancasters. Outsize, streamlined projectiles that passed the speed of sound as they dropped, Tallboy and Grand Slam were designed to penetrate deep below the surface on impact and destroy their target by the "earthquake effect." In fact, as Wallis had promised, near-misses proved as good—indeed, sometimes

better than—direct hits. He was proved right by the shattered span of the Bielefeld Viaduct in 1945, while other targets shattered by his bombs were the U-boat pens and the sites for Hitler's V-1 and V-3 secret weapons.[5]

## THE BOMBING CAMPAIGN

Although these special operations took place from time to time, the bulk of Bomber Command was reserved for the Battle of Germany. Guided to their targets by the colored flares of the preceding Mosquitoes and other "Pathfinder" aircraft, RAF Bomber Command's aircraft carried the war home to Germany with clusters of incendiaries and 4,000 lb. high explosive bombs—the proportion of the incendiaries depending on the estimated inflammable nature of the town being attacked.

The American B-17, which had been designed from the outset for daylight missions, concentrated much more having defensive armament than did the Lancaster, carrying up to thirteen 0.5 in. caliber heavy machine guns. It had a crew of ten and maximum range of 1,850 miles and it was confidently expected that, when massed in formation, the B-17s would be able to put up an impenetrable barrage of defensive fire. This was proved disastrously fallacious on August 17, 1943, when Schweinfurt and Regensburg were attacked. The targets were vital, being the heart of the German ballbearing industry, but the day was a disaster for the B-17s; of the 363 B-17s that set out, only 315 arrived at the targets, and total losses for the day came to 60 shot down plus over 100 damaged. This loss rate worked out at 19 percent of the

raiding force—an unprecedented score. Nor was this first raid on Schweinfurt unique; between October 8 and October 14, 1943, Bremen, Marienburg, Danzig, Münster, and Schweinfurt were attacked in daytime for an overall loss of 148 aircraft.

The main reasons for these losses were the German fighters. During the first Schweinfurt raid, for example, the Luftwaffe sent up approximately 300 fighters during the day, while the only fighter escort that the Allies could provide covered a shallow arc barely extending to the Paris-Cologne area. As a result, these deep-penetration raids were doomed to murderous losses until the long-range P-47 Thunderbolt and P-51 Mustang escort fighters came into operational service in sufficient numbers in 1944.

The Allied reaction to the losses was to switch the focal point of the bombing offensive to the German aircraft factories, which had some effect, In the winter of 1943–44, however, the German war industry, under the brilliant

Above: USAAF B-17s flew in tight, multilayered formations to maximize firepower against fighters. One consequence was that bombs occasionally fell onto an aircraft immediately below. The results were catastrophic because the bomb did not need to explode—its kinetic energy was sufficient to tear off a wing or a tailplane. Whether the crew managed to escape then depended on whether the pilot could hold the aircraft steady.

Far left: Two B-17Gs showing the camouflage and natural finish sported by 8th Air Force bombers.

[5]V-1 was a pulse-jet powered cruise missile known to the British as the "doodle-bug." V-3 was a multibarreled very long range gun.

Above: A formation of five P-51 Mustang long-range fighters, taken in early 1944; farthest away is a single P-51B, the remainder are P-51Ds. They belong to 361st Fighter Group of 8th Air Force and are operating out of Bottisham, a wartime airfield east of Cambridge in central England.

leadership of *Reichsminister* Albert Speer, was effectively dispersed. Also, superhuman efforts on the production lines increased German fighter production to record levels; thus, in February 1944, 905 Me 109s and 209 Focke-Wulf Fw 190s were turned out, but in June these figures had increased to 1,603 and 689, respectively. Thus, despite all the Allied attacks, total fighter production for 1944 reached 25,285 aircraft—by far the best figure for any year of the war. But there was another side to the coin, and between January and April 1944 the Luftwaffe lost over 1,000 pilots, which, unlike their aircraft, could not be assembled in a factory. So, by the summer of 1944, the Luftwaffe's main problem was trained manpower and soon another would be added—fuel.

### INSOLENT CHANNEL DASH

From its inception in the spring of 1940, Allied bomber chiefs were regularly forced to switch the objectives of their bombing offensive. By the spring of 1944, a few isolated tactical successes had been won but the overall balance showed very little practical reward for the thousands of tons of bombs that had been dropped. The

Battle of the Atlantic had brought about the bombing of U-boat factories and pens. The unwelcome presence of *Scharnhorst* and *Gneisenau* in Brest had concentrated Bomber Command's attentions upon that port for nearly a year, and still the ships had been able to steam almost insolently home to Germany through the Channel. Harris's carpet bombing of German cities had by no means caused German morale to shatter. Renewed mass attacks on strategic targets in daylight for accuracy had been hideously mauled by the Luftwaffe fighters, and subsequent attempts to destroy the Luftwaffe had also failed.

But beginning in May 1944, the vital fuel stocks of the Reich were singled out for destruction. Targets long planned were now hit again and again: synthetic oil and petrol plants in Germany at Brüx, Böhlen, Leuna, and Zwickau; the great Rumanian oil wells at Ploesti—the latter hammered 20 times in six weeks. At the end of May, Ploesti, with its former monthly output of 47,000 tons, was put out of business for two months. Luftwaffe fuel reserves, so painfully amassed, vanished. By September 1944 the Luftwaffe was down to one-fifth of its minimum requirements: 30,000 tons. And it was at this

point that the collapse of German industry, so long averted by Speer's efforts, began in earnest.

Long before the catastrophic effects of the Allied fuel offensive were felt in depth by the Luftwaffe, the bombing offensive in the West had become integrated with the invasion of Europe. Preinvasion bombing was vitally important. The idea was to seal off the whole area behind the Normandy battlefield by wrecking the road and rail centers through which the Wehrmacht could rush reinforcements to the invasion sector, and this was effectively done. But the whole vexed question of tactical bombing raises the constant problem of air/ground liaison. This had already been shown at Monte Cassino in January 1944, when the generals insisted that the Abbey be destroyed. This the bombers emphatically achieved, but at a sad cost to the front-line troops in the area. The same happened in Normandy in July, when American bombers laid down an "explosive carpet" along the break-out line. It must be concluded that the most effective work done on the Western Front between D Day and the end of the war was that of the fighter-bombers with their rockets, not the level-bombing formations.

As the Allied front crawled eastward to the frontier of the Reich and finally closed up to the Rhine, the British and American strategic bombing program continued to hammer at the German cities. On the night of February 13, the area bombing of Dresden began—the most deadly raid of the war in the West and the casualties are still impossible to compute. And still Berlin remained a top-priority target. The raids went on without respite until the morning of April 21, 1945, when the U.S. 8th Air Force launched the 363rd Berlin raid of the war—the very morning that the first Russian shells fell on the German capital.

## WAS IT ALL WORTH IT?

What did the Allied bombing achieve? For years it was the only way in which the war could be carried home to the German people, and this undoubtedly was of the highest importance to Allied morale. It failed to ruin that of the Germans. By the time that the bombing finally managed to grind German war production to a standstill, the Eastern and Western Fronts were closing in on the German homeland anyway. With special weapons and training, immense damage was done to special targets—the *Tirpitz*,

Above: The awesome nature of Allied airpower was clearly shown when the northwards advance up Italy was held up by German positions around the monastery of Monte Cassino. To clear the way, the Allied air forces demolished both the monastery on the hill and the town below. This is the scene on March 15, 1944, as clouds of black smoke billow down the hillside from the monastery, while the houses in the town collapse under the weight of the attack.

the dams, the U-boat pens—but never on a large scale. But it is certain that the continuation of the mass raids was instrumental in whittling down the Luftwaffe's reserve of trained pilots. It is equally certain that had the German aircraft industry been able to deliver jets such as the Me 262 earlier, the Luftwaffe might have caused the Allies to severely restrict the bomber offensive.

Another effect of the bombing war was the immense progress made in radar and navigational aids. By 1944 bombers were relying almost exclusively on instruments to get to their targets by night—so much so that one Luftwaffe officer advocated the suspension of the Berlin blackout in order to illuminate the bombers more clearly. As the tank man's war was governed by the race to find a bigger gun to beat the enemy's thicker armor, so the bomber's war depended on the need to develop interference-proof electronic devices while continuing to jam those of the enemy.

Hamstrung by the rejection of a heavy bomber construction program, the Luftwaffe's bomber arm dwindled rapidly after 1943, but it still showed that it was fully capable of mounting a devastating strike. In June 1944, American bombers flew to Soviet Russia to operate from Poltava and Mogilev airfields on their first "shuttle bombing" raids against Germany. Tracked to its destination by a Heinkel He 177, the American bomber force was attacked on its airfields by 200 German bombers on the night of June 22. A flight of 600 miles was involved and total surprise was achieved. Not a German aircraft was lost, but 43 B-17s and 15 Mustangs were destroyed on the ground, together with 300,000 gallons of fuel. It was a daring and effective raid; but its effects were immediately overshadowed by the great Soviet summer offensive, which opened the following day and eventually drove the Wehrmacht back to the Vistula. If one seeks to compare the comparative effects of air and ground warfare, a cynic might well use this example as a symbol. Bombs can destroy. But only troops can occupy ground.

## THE FIGHTER WAR

After the failure to break RAF Fighter Command in the Battle of Britain (September 1940) and the German invasion of Soviet Russia (June 1941), the Luftwaffe in the West assumed the strategic defensive for the remainder of the war. The fighter war in the European Theater of Operations (ETO) now became an inevitable extension of the Allied bombing offensive. The British, and later American, attempts to break Germany's ability to make war turned on whether or not the German fighter arm could inflict unacceptable losses on the Allied day and night bomber streams. It was a defensive battle that the Luftwaffe had to win and it certainly could have done so; indeed, it came within an ace of victory. But although the Luftwaffe had superb fighters and a generous cross-section of the best fighter pilots in the world, it also had Hitler and Göring, whose ignorant meddling in the work of their professional subordinates effectively prevented their air force from retaining command of the skies over western and central Europe.

Göring publicly ridiculed the figures of American bomber production as faked. As soon as the big Allied raids started hitting the cities of

Below: A Lancaster over Hamburg in January 1943. The aircraft is silhoutted against a background of fire and flak that form a strange pattern against the night sky.

the Reich, Hitler reacted by ordering more bombers for retaliation, rather than more fighters to shoot down the Allied bombers. General Adolf Galland, the fighter ace promoted to the command of the German fighter arm, had fought in the Battle of Britain and to him and the other seasoned Luftwaffe fighter commanders it was a nightmare to know that the reasons for the German defeat in the skies over Britain had not been learned where it mattered—at the top—and that Germany was bidding fair to lose in its own skies for the same reasons. Galland described the Luftwaffe's deployment in Soviet Russia, the Reich, the West, the Mediterranean and North Africa, as like a blanket that was not big enough—stretching it in one place would only tear it in another. But as far as Hitler was concerned, fighters were defensive weapons, and in his personal brand of military philosophy defensive battles were not to be considered—all

that mattered was being aggressive and taking the fight to the enemy.

In 1941 the German fighter arm was given a significant injection of power with the entry into service of the improved Messerschmitt fighter— the Me 109F and the new Focke-Wulf 190. The Me 109F was more streamlined and faster than its predecessor, the Me 109E, and its cannon had a higher rate of fire. The Fw 190 was even more hard-hitting because it was armed with four 20 mm cannon and two machine guns. Its maximum speed of 395 mph at 17,000 ft. was complemented by superb maneuverability. The Fw 190 gave its British opposite number, the Spitfire V, a very hard time indeed in 1941, and only the hurried introduction of the Spitfire IX began to restore the balance. Indeed, in many ways the appearance of the Fw 190 was comparable to the World War I "Fokker Scourge" of 1915.

Left: Sixty years after the Battle of Britain, preserved examples of the old rivals, a Spitfire and a Bf-109, pose for the camera. Such World War II aircraft are now highly valued and are maintained, as are these two, in pristine condition.

Right: A Focke-Wulf Fw-190A-3 is refuelled between missions. Development of this outstanding fighter was kept a complete secret from the Allies, so its first appearance in combat in 1941 came as a very nasty surprise. Then, in June 1942 a German pilot landed by mistake at a British airfield and detailed technical examination and test flights showed that it was even better than had been thought, with a powerful armament, very strong construction, and excellent maneuverability, while its cockpit and hood design gave the pilot excellent vision in all directions.

## GALLAND'S FIGHTER UMBRELLA

The Me 109F and Fw 190 played a leading role in one of the greatest operational victories won by the Luftwaffe in World War II—the escape of the *Scharnhorst*, *Gneisenau*, and *Prinz Eugen* from the French Atlantic port of Brest through the English Channel to Germany in February 1942. Galland commanded the air side, upon which the success of the operation depended. He called up every available fighter along the Atlantic coastline for the job of guaranteeing constant orbiting cover throughout daylight hours and at all levels. The result of this masterly plan was that the battle squadron was able to run the Straits of Dover and enter home waters in safety—at least from the air—and, thanks to Galland's air umbrella, neither a bomb nor a torpedo hit the ships, although both *Scharnhorst* and *Gneisenau* ran on to mines. One extraordinary feature of the day was that when lumbering Swordfish biplanes tried to torpedo the ships, the Fw 190s were so fast that their pilots had to lower their wheels and flaps in order to get their speed down in order to attack. But such successes were peripheral—and, in reality, while the "Channel Dash" was an operational success, and caused the British great embarrassment, it was a strategic defeat for the Germans because the surface fleet never again posed a threat in the Atlantic, and Allied bombers no longer had to bomb Brest.

By the summer of 1941, General Kammhuber's night-fighters had proved that the chain of radar stations, each controlling the interception of a single fighter, was very good when dealing with isolated raiders. Further, while the early German night-fighters were not new types, the Me 110 finally found a role for itself in night operations, and the ubiquitous Ju 88 also proved very suited to the nocturnal combat. These fighters were fitted with Lichtenstein airborne radar from August 1941 onwards, which increased their scores and night-fighter aces began to appear: Streib, Lent, Schnaufer, the Prince of Lippe-Weissenfeld, and others.

The Allied bombing offensive became an even greater threat to Germany in 1942 with the first American B-17 raids from British bases. As the latter got into their stride, it became clear that Germany could expect nothing less than round-the-clock bombing—the Americans by day and the British by night.

Kammhuber's system was severely tested by the first mass raids of 1942. The problem was that by restricting the fighter to its ground-control radar zone it was prevented from operating in the bomber stream itself. But the beginning of the end was signaled in the last week of June 1943 with the repeated fire raids on Hamburg, the first "firestorm" raids of the war. German radar was blinded by a new British device consisting of clusters of metal foil strips, known as "Window," which were cut to the same wavelength as the German radar sets, thus cluttering the screens with false contacts. The shock of the Hamburg raids triggered off frantic orders—for more fighters.

The German air defenses were constantly trying out new tactics, one of these being *Wilde*

*Sau* (Wild Boar), which was born of the Allied radar jamming. This involved single-engined fighters roving at will without radar, intercepting by visual contact, but, by special arrangement, the German AA fire was kept below a certain level and once the raiders dropped their markers the action would start. There were some initial successes with the system, but these were soon reversed, and faced by heavy and mounting losses the technique was dropped in March 1944.

## DEADLY "SLANTING MUSIC"

More German night successes were due to the improved Lichtenstein SN-2 radar and the use of *Schräge Musik* (slanting music). The latter consisted of two cannon mounted inside the fighter's fuselage, but firing obliquely upwards, thus enabling the fighter to attack by closing in from behind and below. The SN-2/*Schräge Musik* combination inflicted startling new losses on Bomber Command during the winter of 1943–44 and set back Harris's plan to "wreck Berlin from end to end." The combination enabled German night-fighters to hack down 78 out of 823 bombers during the attack on Leipzig (February 1920, 1944) and in the biggest night battle of the war, which took place over Nuremberg on the night of March 30–31, 1944, it destroyed 95 out of 795 RAF Lancasters and Halifaxes involved in the raid.

But the dominant problem for the Germans was the mass formations of B-17 Flying Fortresses which came by day. It was not merely a question of putting up enough fighters to cope with the massed fire-power of the American formations but of the fire-power needed to knock

Above: One of the most unenviable positions in a World War II bomber was that of the rear gunner. He was physically separated from the rest of the crew, in a cold and lonely position, and, as shown with this Short Stirling, was a particular target for enemy attacks.

down the giant bombers. The Luftwaffe tried everything it could think of: head-on attacks, dive-bombing, rocket attacks with 21 cm missiles. And—on Hitler's personal orders—experiments were even made with mounting onto the Me 410 heavy fighter 50 mm cannon that were normally carried in armored cars,[6] but the pulverizing recoil of such a large gun led to the abandonment of the project.

The rocket experiment, however, was not so hare-brained as first thought and led to the 50 mm R4M rockets, which proved to be devastatingly successful, but arrived too late to make any difference. They were, in fact, part and parcel of the sad story of the Messerschmitt Me 262: the revolutionary jet fighter that could and should have denied the Allies the control of the skies over Europe in 1943.

### THE FIRST JET FIGHTER

Experiments with jet-propulsion were not a German preserve: revolutionary gas-turbine engines were developed virtually simultaneously—but in complete isolation from each other—by the British as well as the Germans. However, the first prototype of a successful combat jet was certainly the German Me 262, which flew in July 1942. General Galland flew the aircraft in May 1943, but Hitler did not see it fly until November 1943, and when he did, his immediate reaction was that "here at last is our Blitz bomber!" As a result, he insisted that the air-

craft be developed as a bomber and refused even to consider any further development as a fighter until it was far too late. The final variant of the Me 262 was capable of firing salvoes of R4M rockets, and was a deadly operational reality by the end of the war—but it should have entered service two years earlier.

Other desperate Luftwaffe fighter attempts to beat the swarms of Allied bombers included the Me 163, the only rocket-powered fighter in history to see service. Armed with cannon and rocket missiles it could climb to 39,370 ft. in 3 minutes 25 seconds—but its powered endurance was a mere 8 minutes. An even more desperate venture was the Heinkel He 162 *Salamander*—the so-called "People's Fighter." This was designed for mass operations by pilots from the *Hitlerjugend* (Hitler youth) and was constructed of lightweight nonstrategic materials. It was powered by a dorsally mounted turbojet, which gave a maximum speed of 522 mph at 19,680 ft. and was armed with two cannons. The trouble with the People's Fighter was that it was so tricky to fly that it required the most experienced pilots, rather than enthusiastic but untrained amateurs from the *Hitlerjugend*, and by 1945, when the aircraft was declared "operational," experienced Luftwaffe pilots were very few indeed.

Those day fighter pilots who had survived—justly termed Experten—were flying the 109G and 109K, the latest marks of the time-tested Messerschmitt fighter, or its stable mate was the

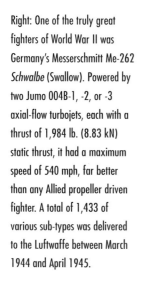

superb Focke-Wulf 190. The latter had been developed into the excellent Ta 152, a "long nose" version with a maximum speed of 468 mph at 34,500 ft. and an armament of one 30 mm and four 20 mm cannon. The best piston-engined night fighter was the Heinkel He 219 *Uhu*, but only 294 of this type had been produced by the time that Germany surrendered.

## TEARDROPS AND TANKBUSTERS

The Spitfire, like its opposite number the Me 109, remained in front-line service throughout the war. Later versions, still powered by the Merlin, included the Mark V, introduced in 1941–42, the Mark IX, which appeared in 1942 and remained in front-line service until the end of the war, and the belated Mark VIII that entered service in 1943, with most being sent overseas to the Mediterranean and Burma fronts. The Mark XIV was the first to be powered by the new Rolls-Royce Griffon engine, and later examples of this series also had the advantages of the cut-down rear fuselage and "teardrop" cockpit hood. The last versions of this remarkable aircraft were the Marks 21 and 22, but these were just too late to see war service.

Several versions of a navalized variant, the Seafire, were produced for service aboard aircraft carriers of the Fleet Air Arm.

The Hurricane, too, served on and became a major item of British Lend-Lease, with many being supplied to the Soviet Air Force. The Mark IIB had twelve wing machine guns, while the IIC had four 20 mm cannon. The IIID was a modification carrying a pair of 40 mm cannon under the wings and did sterling service in North Africa as a "tankbuster" proving yet again what a splendid gun platform this aircraft was.

Unlike the Luftwaffe, the RAF did not get itself hamstrung in its fighter development. Early experiments with heavy, twin-engined fighters produced the splendid Bristol Beaufighter, with its murderous armament of four 20 mm cannon and six wing machine guns and a maximum speed of 321 mph. The Beaufighter was then successfully developed into an antishipping strike aircraft, carrying rockets or a torpedo. From the Hawker stable a new

---

[6]The Me 410 was a sad story and showed how the Germans sometimes persisted with something which was clearly a failure. In this case, the original Me 110 was a disaster and was succeeded by the Me 210. This ended up to be a failure, so the Me 410 was developed, which was also a failure.

Above: The Messerschmitt Me-163 fighter was powered by a Walther rocket motor and was capable of 597 mph at 39,000 ft. It took off on a wheeled trolley that was then jettisoned, and landed on a retractable skid. This was a daring and innovative design, but as dangerous to the pilot as to the enemy—the fuel was volatile and prone to spontaneous combustion; if the trolley was released too early it bounced back to hit the underside of the aircraft; and if the pilot survived all that plus the hazards of combat, landing was the most dangerous of all.

Above: The Hawker Hurricane was a strong, sturdy fighter with a good performance for its time. Until well into 1941, it was the most numerous fighter in RAF service, and it bore the brunt of the fighting during the Battle of Britain, but its reputation has always been overshadowed by that of the more graceful and charismatic Spitfire.

concept of heavy, single-seat interceptor fighter emerged. First came the Typhoon, which was dogged by engine trouble, but finally developed into a superb low-level, ground-attack aircraft. That was followed by the Hawker Tempest, which was fitted with the specially designed "Hawker High Speed Wing" and armed with four Hispano Mark V cannon. The Tempest's very high speed (432 mph at 18,400 ft.) and hitting-power enabled it to take on the best of the 1944–45 German fighters, even the jet-propelled Me 262.

The Americans were swift to push ahead with long-range fighters. The first of these to see service was the Lockheed P-38 Lightning, a distinctive twin-engined, twin-boomed aircraft that proved to be prone to technical troubles in

the air over Europe but which served with distinction in the Pacific Theater. The massive Republic P-47 Thunderbolt had a wing span of 40 ft. 9 in. and a loaded weight of 13,360 lb. and, with a 200-gallon drop-tank, a range of 1,125 miles; it was the first successful long-range fighter to escort the B-17s.

But the best American fighter of the European war was undoubtedly the North American P-51 Mustang, the result of close cooperation between Britain and the U.S. The excellent Mustang airframe married to the Rolls-Royce Merlin engine produced, at last, a fighter which could escort bombers deep into Germany and as far as Berlin itself. Escort tactics had to be learned the hard way, since at first the Allied fighters tended to stick too close to the

bombers thus restricting their maneuver-ability and making it easier for the German fighters to engage and defeat them. Later, however, the escorts learned to stay much further away from their charges, and this enabled them to engage German interceptors much more effectively.

## OTHER FIGHTERS

Other American fighters also did invaluable service in the European Theater. The Curtiss P-36 was exported to France just before it fell and quantities were then passed to the RAF, which employed them as the Mohawk IV in the Mediterranean and Far East. The Curtiss P-40, America's land-based fighter mainstay in 1940–41, also served with the British Desert Air Force as the Tomahawk, while the more advanced P-40E became the Kittyhawk in British service. The RAF also experimented with the Bell P-39 Airacobra, a remarkable design in which the engine was positioned behind the cockpit, driving the airscrew by a 10-foot shaft passing beneath the pilot's legs. This design was not very popular with the RAF, but the Soviet Air Force was particularly enthusiastic, being given no fewer than 4,773 by the United States.

The Soviet air force needed time to recover from the terrible first weeks of the German invasion of June 1941, which virtually wiped out the front-line strength of the Red Air Force. The principal Soviet fighter at that time was still the stubby little Polikarpov I-16, which had earned the nickname "Rata" in the Spanish civil war. But, as with the Red Army and the T-34 tank,

Below: Lockheed P-38J Lightning of 364th Fighter Wing, identified by "N2" on tail boom as belonging to 383rd Squadron based at Honington, England. The 364th arrived in the European Theater on February 8, 1944, and flew its first operational mission on March 2, and flew P-38s until August, when they were replaced by P-51 Mustangs. During the time that it was on combat status (March 2, 1944, to May 6, 1945) the group accounted for 455 enemy planes destroyed, 24 probably destroyed, and 282 damaged.

much better designs were in an advance stage of development, the first of these was the Yakovlev Yak-1, which had been rushed into large-scale service at the end of 1939. The Yak-1 resembled the British Hurricane, but had an armament of one 20 mm cannon and two 12.7 mm machine guns. In the following year the Yak-1 was supplemented by the LaGG-3 and Mikoyan-Gurevich MiG-3, then from 1943 onwards the Yak-9, the La-5, Yak-3, and the La-7.

The main emphasis until 1943 was on mass-production and none of the early "second generation" Soviet fighters was the equal of the best German fighters on the Eastern Front, but their numbers increasingly dwarfed those of the Luftwaffe as the campaign progressed. The odds were as heavily stacked against the German pilots in Russia as against those tackling the Flying Fortress bomber streams in the West—frequently with as few as ten German fighters pitted against 300 Soviet. Subsequently, however, it was not just a matter of numbers and the later Soviet fighters, particularly the La-7 and Yak-3 were equal to, if not better than, the best the Germans had, and from then on the Soviets did not look back.

### FOR WANT OF A CANNON—THE ITALIAN STORY

In the interwar years the Schneider Trophy led to the rapid development of high-speed seaplane racers and this, in turn, led to major developments in land-based fighter designs, such as the British Spitfire. Italy, too, had been a top contender in the Schneider trophy, but, unlike the British designer of the Spitfire, R. J. Mitchell, who was able to use a succession of excellent Rolls-Royce engines, Italy's Mario Castoldi was hampered by the lack of similar high-power engines. Thus, his Macchi C.200, designed in 1937, was the best Italian fighter at the outbreak of war, but it had only a medium-powered Fiat radial engine. In addition, its armament of two fuselage-mounted 12.7-mm machine guns was extremely light. The Fiat G 50 and the Reggiane Re 2000 which followed had excellent maneuverability, although this fell off abruptly above 15,000 feet, but still had very light armament.

By far the best Italian fighter of the war was the Macchi C.202 Folgore, which appeared in 1942. This had the advantage of having a well-developed engine, the German-designed Daimler-Benz DB 601, which was built under

license by Alfa Romeo. But again, the C.202 was impaired by its light machine gun armament. Better Italian designs were in the pipeline by the time the country dropped out of the war in 1943, most notably the Regianne Re 2001, the Re 2005, and the Macchi C.205 *Veltro*, although production of all three was hampered by dwindling supplies of German engines.

### THE SUPERIORITY OF THE CANNON

Italy was the last major power to accept that the vastly superior hitting power of the cannon was

Right: The Italian Macchi C.202 Folgore was essentially the C.200 Saetta reengined with the 1,175 hp Alfa Romeo RA1000, an Italian-built version of the Daimler-Benz DB 601A-1; it also had a completely enclosed cockpit. The C.202 had good performance and about 1,500 were delivered to the Italian Air Force between July 1941 and mid-1943, before production switched to the C.205 with the yet more powerful 1,400 hp Fiat RA1050 (DB 605A-1).

indispensable to modern fighter combat. The RAF had seen some stormy debates leading to the introduction of cannon as a modification of the original eight-gun batteries of wing-mounted machine guns, but once introduced, the cannon proved its worth a hundred times over. Also, apart from its value in air-to-air combat, the cannon gave the fighter an additional role in ground-attack, using its highly lethal explosive shells. The massed cones of 0.5 in. machine gun fire thrown out by the B-17 formations were justly dreaded by the German fighter arm, but the smaller caliber of the British 0.303 in. Browning machine guns gave much less trouble

to the Me 110s and Ju 88s of the German night-fighter arm. However, in both cases cannon-fire—and later rockets—were indispensable in attacking such defenses.

## CAB RANKS AND SUICIDE

In the final resort, any aircraft can carry bombs and the concept of the fighter-bomber enjoyed a checkered history in World War II. Hitler's obsession with retaliatory bombing imposed impossible tasks on the German fighters operating over Britain. On the other hand, dive-bombing attacks on Flying Fortress formations, pioneered

Far right: Hawker Typhoon Mark 1b fighter bomber. The "Tiffy's" early career was troubled by the unreliability of the Sabre engine and generally poor performance. The faults were overcome, resulting in a first-class machine, capable of catching any propeller-powered Luftwaffe fighter. It was well armed with four 20 mm cannon and eight rockets, and capable of destroying anything that moved on the ground. Some 3,300 were delivered, all but the first 300 having the clear-view canopy shown here.

Below: This Heinkel He-111 bomber returned to base despite some 50 hits from British 0.303 in. machine guns. Hurricanes and Spitfires were armed with eight of these rifle-caliber weapons, but despite the volume and high rate of fire the actual damage inflicted by each round was relatively small. Heavier weapons such as 0.5 in. and 20 mm cannon had a slower rate of fire but stood a greater chance of destroying the target.

by Leutnant Heinz Knocke, obtained some results, at least initially. The Hurricane II, a ground-attack development of the basic fighter, was very successful, earning itself the nickname of the "Hurribomber," while among the twin-engined types, first the Beaufighter and then the Mosquito proved to be "naturals" in the fighter-bomber role. The advent of effective air-to-ground rockets added more punch to the fighter-bomber and a salvo from a Beaufighter could, quite literally, blow a ship out of the water. Similarly, the effectiveness of the rocket-firing Typhoon made it the aircraft most feared by the German army, especially in the bloody fighting for Normandy where "cab ranks" of fighter bombers, stacked up over the battlefield, made it virtual suicide for any German vehicle to move by day in good flying weather.

But the Allies did not always have things entirely their own way. On January 1, 1945, the Luftwaffe mounted its last great fighter offensive of the war. On that day massed fighter ground-strafing sweeps wiped out whole groups of Allied aircraft on their airfields—nearly 300 in all. For a week, the RAF's 122nd Wing had to carry on the fighter war in northwest Europe virtually single-handed. Nor was Hitler's insistence that the Me 262 must operate as a bomber totally misguided, and low-level attacks by bomb-carrying Me 262s remained a headache on the Western Front right down to the end of the war. Traveling fast and low, they made it almost impossible for Allied radar screens to pick them up, but Tempest pilots evolved a technique called

"rat-catching" in which they sent a brace of Tempests to known Me 262 bases to catch the German jets as they landed. There were some limited successes, but the dense flak that screened every German airfield used by jets made these forays very dangerous and unprofitable. By May 1945 Allied aircraft operating in the European skies enjoyed speed and hitting-power which would have been inconceivable five years before, but it was still found that even the fastest and most heavily armed

fighter was still not immune to well-directed barrages of defensive fire from the ground.

## AERIAL COMMAND OF THE SEAS

Until the early years of the 20th century, warships could roam the oceans virtually at will with only the opposing navy to worry about. But then there appeared the submarine, whose threat to surface ships was greatly under-rated until 1914, when it became a major consideration in any deployment. Then, starting from the end of World War I, came a new threat—from the air.

During World War II this was of particular importance in the European Theater, where the role of coastal and maritime aviation became of paramount importance to the Allies. It was, however, paid much less attention by Germany, which, in its attempts to strangle Britain's supply lifeline across the Atlantic, totally failed to bring the modern resources of air power to bear. One of the main reasons for this was the ad hoc way

Above: Douglas A-20 Havoc light bombers bombing over France in early 1944.

Previous pages: Bristol Beaufighter TF.X (Torpedo-Fighter Mark 10) of the RAF's No. 455 Squadron. It was armed with four forward-firing 20 mm cannon, plus a flexible 0.303 in. Vickers K gun for the observer and could carry either one torpedo, or eight rockets, or two 1,000 lb. bombs. A total of 5,564 Beaufighters were built in England and another 364 in. Australia, and the type remained in service until 1960.

"everything that flies belongs to me." Only once in World War II did the Luftwaffe and the German navy work closely together and that was during the Channel Dash of February 1942—a venture that was pressed forward on Hitler's insistence.

The Luftwaffe's technical experience could have given Admiral Raeder a German fleet air arm by 1939 but for Göring's jealousy and pig-headedness. And a measure of common sense tempered by generosity could have given Admiral Dönitz better long-range reconnais-

in which Germany's new military might was developed from 1933 onwards, when the allocation of money and resources for development depended as much (perhaps sometimes even more) upon the personalities of the leaders of the Reich and their influence with Hitler than any considerations of strategy or tactics. The results of this were serious enough for the bomber arm of the Luftwaffe, but the situation was even more glaring as far as naval/air liaison was concerned.

Despite the splendid new warships built for Germany after Hitler's accession to power in 1933, the need for a powerful modern naval air arm as an adjunct to the activities of the fleet was never accepted. Göring, who had been a genuinely talented fighter pilot in World War I, developed a paranoid obsession with his private aerial empire and his watchwords were that

sance for the U-boats in the Atlantic, which, while it might still not have won the Battle of the Atlantic for Germany, would at least have made the Allied victory much more difficult to achieve. As it was, the U-boat packs were often vectored onto their targets by the relatively small number of far-flying Condors available. More such aircraft would probably have meant much worse Allied shipping losses.

It was not that the Luftwaffe had failed to acquire the machines. There was the Heinkel He 115 twin-engined floatplane, a sound torpedo-bomber; the Blohm & Voss Bv 138 with a range of 2,670 miles, and the Dornier Do 18 and Do 24 flying boats. The Ju 87 dive-bomber, the Ju 88, and the Heinkel He 111 also proved excellent antishipping aircraft. But it cannot be denied that the basic weakness was a long-range bomber. The Luftwaffe sought a stopgap in the form of the converted Focke-Wulf Fw 200 Condor, an elegant four-engined airliner. Heavily armed with a 20 mm cannon in a dorsal turret plus five machine guns, the Condor could carry up to 4,620 lb. of bombs, and had a

Below: The pilot heaves his Blohm & Voss Bv 138A-01 off the sea. This first model to reach service status suffered from a number of problems and only 25 were built before production switched to the improved Bv 138B.

maximum range of 3,950 miles. A Condor squadron was formed in 1940 for reconnaissance work and strike duties over the British naval approaches and was subsequently raised to *Geschwader* (Group) status. But, only 263 Condors of all versions were ever built and so urgent was the need, their crews had to go to the factory to collect their new machines as they crawled off the production line.

## A SPECIAL NAVAL COMMAND

Condors took part in bombing raids on England in 1940, most notably in the Blitz on Liverpool and Birkenhead in August. Antishipping operations got under way with a spectacular start when the 42,000-ton liner *Empress of Britain* was sunk off the northwest coast of Ireland on October 26, 1940. Then, in March 1941 a special naval command, *Fliegerführer Atlantik* (air commander, Atlantic), was established to coordinate all antishipping operations by the Luftwaffe, and

air operations against Britain's Atlantic convoys at last got under way.

The sight and sound of a Condor shadowing a convoy from well out of reach of their AA guns was somewhat demoralizing for the men in the ships below, who knew that the pilot was calling up more aircraft in order to attack them. The first British response was CAM (Catapult Aircraft Merchantmen) ships, which could launch a Hurricane against enemy airborne raiders. Popularly known as "Hurricats," these aircraft could only be launched when the threat was deemed to be very serious, since there was nowhere for the pilot to land and he thus had to bale out at the end of his mission and hope to be picked up after descending by parachute. Despite the limitations of such a "one-shot" weapon, the CAM ships soon proved their worth and by the fall of 1941 the Condors were reduced to reconnaissance duties, radioing back information and leaving the attack to U-boats. The CAM ships were succeeded by escort carriers and in December 1941 a succession of Condors homed

Below: Dornier Do-24T-1 serving with a Seenotstaffel (sea-service squadron) in 1943. This was a particularly rugged flying boat, with a very strong hull, and was able to operate in sea states that would have defeated other types. It was very successful as a rescue aircraft and saved many downed airmen's lives.

Left: Focke-Wulf Fw 200C-3/U2 Condor maritime patrol aircraft. Based on an airliner, it was originally developed for a military role to meet a Japanese requirement, but when these could not be delivered they were diverted to the Luftwaffe. An early mission involved patrols over the Atlantic and for many Allied convoys a Condor circling out of range of the ships' guns was a prelude to a U-boat attack. Later, Condors conducted antishipping strikes, particularly against Allied convoys crossing the Bay of Biscay.

six U-boats onto Convoy HG.76, but the action cost them a total of six Condors, which were shot down by Fleet Air Arm Martlet fighters (British-flown Grumman F4Fs) from the new escort-carrier HMS Audacity.

The situation in the Atlantic became increasingly depressing for the Germans, but in early 1942 they woke up to the fact that, apart from convoys between the British Isles and North America and the Middle/Far East, the Allies were also sailing convoys to Soviet Russia around the North Cape with what amounted to total immunity. As a result, General Stumpff's Luftflotte 5, which had had only a very quiet

Above: The CAM (Catapult Aircraft Merchant) was a merchant ship with a catapult on the foredeck from which a fighter was launched, sometimes a Fulmar but more often a Sea Hurricane IA. There were 35 CAM conversions with a pool of 200 Sea Hurricanes in Britain and 100 in Canada. Between May 1941 and August 1943, CAM ships made 170 round trips, but only eight aircraft were launched, resulting in six kills, for the loss of one RAF pilot. On completion of the mission, pilots had to parachute into the sea. This is Empire Tide; note the radar antennas on the foremast.

role since its ignominious defeat in the Battle of Britain, suddenly found itself in the front line once again, since it was in a position to launch heavy air strikes against convoys that had little or no fighter defenses.

Luftflotte 5 was hastily reinforced and soon included the only bomber unit that had specialized in torpedo-work—Kampfgruppe (KG) 26, the *Löwen Geschwader*, equipped with torpedo-carrying He 111s. The Russian convoys soon felt the results, starting with Convoy PQ.15 in May 1942. The attacks were preceded by shadowing by Blohm & Voss Bv 138 flying-boats, followed by Ju 88 dive-bombing attacks and then torpedo attacks by the He 111s. Convoy PQ.16 came in for the same treatment during its passage (May 22–30), but the real slaughter was reserved for PQ.17. This convoy was scattered because the British Admiralty was unable to pinpoint the whereabouts of the German battleship *Tirpitz* and assumed that she had put to sea to attack the convoy. No such danger actually existed, but the scattered ships of the convoy were left totally defenseless. Between them, U-boats and the aircraft of Luftflotte 5 sank 21 out of the 34 ships in the convoy.

## GOLDEN COMB BARES ITS TEETH

The next convoy, PQ.18, sailed in September and it had an escort-carrier, HMS *Avenger*. The

same pattern was repeated, with spotting and shadowing by a Bv 138 being followed by torpedo and bombing attacks. This time the German pilots used the *Goldene Kamme* (Golden Comb) technique, in which a formation of 30 Ju 88s and 55 He 111s approached in line-abreast, with all aircraft dropping their two torpedoes simultaneously. Despite the fact that, to avoid a repetition of the PQ.17 disaster, PQ.18 had been given the strongest escort ever provided for a convoy to Soviet Russia, 13 out of its 40 ships were sunk on passage.

These attacks finally convinced the British Admiralty that the PQ convoys could not continue in their existing form and when they resumed they were sailed in two parts, in order to disrupt the attackers. Then, the convoys were discontinued entirely in the summer of 1943 and when they resumed again at the end of 1943, Luftflotte 5 was a shadow of its former self, because the demands of the other fronts since Stalingrad, coupled with the loss of Tunis and increased demands in Italy, meant that the Far North had been bled of many of its resources.

One flicker of hope for the prospects of efficient long-range naval operations reposed in the Junkers Ju 290, which was intended to be the replacement for the Condor. Like the Condor, the Ju 290 was a development of a civilian airliner, but it was the nearest the

Germans ever got to producing a long-range heavy bomber, apart from the disastrous Heinkel He 177 *Greif*. Only a limited number of Ju 290s were ever completed and these were soon taken off antishipping operations, being confined thereafter to reconnaissance and patrol duties.

Inter-service rivalry, as well as the belated recognition of the strategic meaning of an unanticipated war against Britain in 1939, deprived the Luftwaffe of any major and continuing success on the Atlantic sea lanes. It did have more triumphs against the Russian convoys, attacks against which were carried out by orthodox, medium-range aircraft operating in the absence of efficient Allied fighter cover, but eventually that campaign, too, was ultimately unsuccessful.

The other theater in which the Luftwaffe achieved considerable success in antishipping operations was the Mediterranean. During the May 1941 battle for Crete the British land forces were strongly supported by Admiral Cunningham's Mediterranean Fleet. Apart from the handful of Allied aircraft defending Malta, however, the Luftwaffe had the skies over the Mediterranean virtually to itself and it amassed a formidable concentration of aircraft on the airfields of southern Greece, organized into eight bomber and five fighter

*Gruppen*. By June 1, 1941, when the British finally completed the evacuation of Crete and had left the island to the decimated German paratroop units, these German aircraft had sunk three cruisers and six destroyers, while two battleships, the carrier *Formidable*, two cruisers, and two destroyers had been so badly damaged that they could not be repaired in the British Mediterranean dockyards. Thus, for the time being, German air power had neutralized the British Mediterranean Fleet.

Above: The Focke-Wulf Fw 189A-2 Uhu (eagle owl) reconnaissance aircraft was a major success, being rugged, reliable, very agile, and particularly pleasant to fly.

Below: Designed as a catapult-launched spotter aircraft for warships, the Heinkel He 60 was also used by Luftwaffe coastal reconnaissance units.

Above: Messerschmitt Bf 100D-1 of North Africa–based ZG26. Much was expected of this long-range, twin-engined, two-man Zerstörer (destroyer), but its performance was never better than ordinary and it was easily outfought by most single-engined fighters, such as the Hurricane and Spitfire.

## MALTA STRIKES BACK

As was to happen time and again, however, the opportunity for the Germans to exploit success in one area was effectively canceled out by the demands of other fronts. The impending German invasion of Soviet Russia, which was to be launched on June 22, required that half the Luftwaffe strength in the Mediterranean had to be withdrawn to take part in what was seen as a higher priority operation. One immediate result of this was that Malta got an inevitable reprieve and the British on the island immediately began to strike back at the Axis convoy routes using destroyers, submarines, and antishipping aircraft, which were so effective that by November 1941, the Axis loss rate on sending supplies to Rommel in North Africa was as high as 60 percent.

The effectiveness of the British air offensive against the Axis depended largely on the up-and-down fortunes of the desert war. When the British held the airfields of Cyrenaica, they could throw in Blenheims, Beaufighters, Douglas Bostons, and Wellingtons against the Axis convoy routes; when Rommel stood on the Egyptian frontier, Malta alone had to carry on the offensive. Realizing this, in the first quarter of 1942 Axis air forces made furious attempts to neutralize Malta, as a prelude to the conquest of the island. By May the Luftwaffe had virtually accomplished this task, flying nonstop raids from the airfields of Sicily, which were only 60 miles away from the island. Last-minute deliveries of Spitfires retained a vestige of fighter defense for the island, which was then given another reprieve, paradoxically enough by Rommel's defeat of the 8th Army at Gazala and his invasion of Egypt. The conquest of Malta was shelved and, when it was finally recognized that Rommel had been fought to a standstill, however temporarily, at Alamein, Malta had

## FAILURE AND A LUCKY STRIKE

The Beauforts and Beaufighters stationed in the United Kingdom had mixed successes. They failed completely to score even one hit when the *Scharnhorst* and *Gneisenau* dashed through the English Channel in February 1942, although this was the fault of the staff planners and not of the squadrons themselves. Eight months earlier, No. 42 Squadron, flying Beauforts, had been sent out for a night strike against the pocket-battleship *Lützow*, which was known to be returning to Germany down the Norwegian coast. A solitary Beaufort got lost, but then found its target by accident and launched a lone attack. To the aircrew's surprise there was no AA fire from the *Lützow* and one hit on the target put her in dry dock at Kiel, although it did not knock her out of the war.[7] Individual hunting (known as "Rover" missions) by torpedo bombers was tried but losses were heavy.

One of the most daring Beaufort strikes of the war took place in December 1941, after RAF photo-reconnaissance had found that the battlecruiser *Gneisenau* had been moved out into the open waters of Brest harbor, offering a slim chance of a torpedo attack. Flight

[7] It was later believed that the crew aboard the warship might have mistaken the Beaufort for a Junkers Ju 88, both aircraft being twin-engined and bearing a vague resemblance to each other.

Below: Messerschmitt Bf 109E-4Trop of JG 26 awaiting a mission at a North African airbase. Luftwaffe pilots built up impressive scores with such aircraft, but against ageing aircraft such as the Hurricane and P-40 Kittihawk.

once again received just enough reinforcements to hold on.

By the end of August 1942 Malta was on the offensive again, the main weapons in the strikes against the Axis convoy routes being Bristol Beaufort torpedo-bombers escorted by Beaufighters. The Beaufort, like the Beaufighter itself, owed much to the basic Blenheim design and was the standard RAF torpedo-bomber from December 1939 until it was replaced in the torpedo role by the Beaufighter in 1943. These air strikes, through August and September, meant that Rommel had no margin whatsoever as far as fuel reserves were concerned, and were, therefore, instrumental in helping Montgomery beat off the last German offensive into Egypt at Alam Halfa at the end of September. Indeed, it was a Beaufort that torpedoed "Rommel's last tanker"—the *Proserpina*—whose load of fuel might possibly have given his army some crucial help at Alamein.

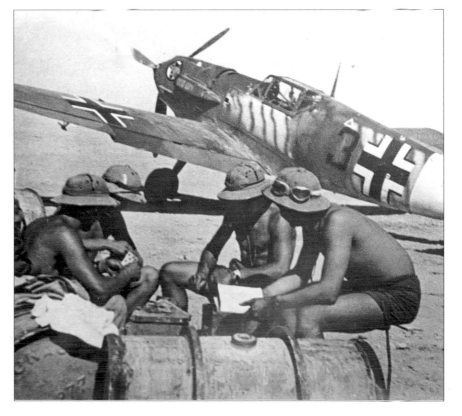

Above: The land-based Bristol Beaufighter proved a great success against naval targets.

Previous pages: Junkers Ju-52 transports flying across the Mediterranean to Tunisia, February 1943. The workhorse of the Luftwaffe's transport fleet, the three-engined Ju-52 could accommodate 18 passengers or, with seats removed, a considerable quantity of freight; both troops and stores could be dropped by parachute or air-landed.

Lieutenant K. Campbell pressed home his attack and wrecked *Gneisenau's* starboard propeller shaft, but was shot down and killed by the withering flak from the German battlecruiser and the harbor defenses.

As far as the British Fleet Air Arm was concerned the outstanding torpedo aircraft of the war was the antiquated Fairey Swordfish, a three-seater torpedo bomber with a maximum speed—without a torpedo!—of 138 mph. The Swordfish first distinguished itself on the night of November 11, 1940, in the famous torpedo attack on the Italian battle fleet in Taranto harbor, where the Italian battleships *Littorio, Conte di Cavour,* and *Caio Duilio* were all sunk or beached, swinging the naval balance in the Mediterranean decidedly in favor of the British. The Taranto raid made history—it was the first time that aircraft proved decisively that air power had rendered the traditional might of the battlefleet helpless without constant air cover.

Swordfish from the carrier *Victorious* put the first British torpedo into the battleship *Bismarck* in May 1941, while others from *Ark Royal* later succeeded in jamming the German ship's rudder, thus ensuring that she would be brought to action by the battleships of the British Home Fleet.

The Swordfish's most tragic operation was the hurried and ill-fated Fleet Air Arm strike against *Scharnhorst* and *Gneisenau* during the "Channel Dash," when all six aircraft attacking were shot down by the swarming German fighter escorts, without scoring a single hit. But even this failure, however heroic, did not hasten the

demise of the Swordfish as an operational aircraft.

A successor, the Fairey Albacore, was indeed mooted and produced, but the Albacore did not in fact replace the Swordfish, which continued to serve with the Fleet Air Arm. The final chapter in the extraordinary story of the Swordfish came in 1943 when it was pressed into service as an antisubmarine weapon, firing salvoes of underwing rockets at U-boats caught on the surface. The Swordfish is quite rightly given a proud place in the annals of the Royal Navy, but the sad fact is that it was the outcome of an inefficient and ineffective procurement system and its very courageous crews really deserved something far better.

Britain's major long-range naval reconnaissance aircraft of World War II was the Short Sunderland flying-boat. In the same way as the Fw 200 Condor, the Sunderland was descended from a civilian design, in this case the Short Empire passenger flying-boat of the 1930s and much of the Empire configuration was retained in the military design. It was a big machine, with a span of 112 ft. and a length of

84 ft., and had two decks containing crew's quarters, sleeping berths, an officers' wardroom, a workshop, and the galley.

Most of the Sunderland's facilities were very welcome on the long ocean patrols that the Sunderland flew, its normal range being 2,980 miles. The Sunderland could carry up to 2,000 lb. of bombs or depth-charges and its long range automatically made it a vital weapon in the struggle against the U-boats. It carried a crew of thirteen and bristled with defensive armament: two 0.50 in. and up to twelve 0.303 in. machine guns. This defensive capability impressed itself strongly on its Luftwaffe opponents, who dubbed the Sunderland *Fliegendes Stachelschwein* (the "flying porcupine"). The Sunderland, which entered service in five different marks, continued in production up to October 1945, with over 700 being built.

### THE LONG-RANGE "CAT"

The other key Allied flying-boat of the war was equally as famous: the American Consolidated PBY Catalina, whose most important quality was its enormous range—its two Pratt & Whitney Twin Wasp radial engines and good

Above: Deck parties aboard HMS Illustrious fold the wings of a Fairey Firefly 1 on its return from an attack on Japanese positions (note the southeast Asia command roundels on the wings). The British retained manual wing-folding longer than the U.S. Navy, which may have been cheaper and lighter, but, as shown here, was very manpower intensive.

Left: The Fairey Swordfish was a carrier-based torpedo bomber and this example is seen overflying the aircraft carrier, HMS *Ark Royal*. These antiquated appearing biplanes achieved many successes with the Fleet Air Arm, but it is difficult to avoid the conclusion that their crews deserved something better and that the technology to provide it was readily available.

fuel capacity giving it a reach of some 3,100 miles. The PBY first flew in 1935. In May 1941 it was a Catalina that located and shadowed the *Bismarck* after the sinking of the *Hood*, without which the German battleship would almost certainly have escaped in safety to France. Catalinas were used in all theaters of the war by the American and British services, most of them serving with the U.S. Navy, which received an overall total of 2,026 (the RAF received some 650). A substantial number were also flown by

the Soviet Naval Air Arm, most of them being a license-built version known as the GST, but 138 improved PBN-1s were also supplied to Soviet Russia in 1943–44 under Lend-Lease.

### ENTER THE WALRUS

Another British aircraft came from the same company, Supermarine, as the Spitfire, but whereas the fighter was supremely elegant the Walrus was an ungainly looking biplane with a

### THE HELL-SHIP IS STOPPED

In the early stages of the war at sea, much valuable work was done by two lesser-known aircraft. The first of these was the Avro Anson, known throughout the RAF as "Faithful Annie," which first entered service in 1936 and was not phased out until the 1960s. The Anson was a twin-engined, shore-based maritime reconnaissance aircraft, defended by two machine guns, one forward-firing, the other in a dorsal turret. This model stayed in first-line service until 1942 and then soldiered on as a trainer. Total British production (which ended in May 1952) reached 8,138 machines (plus an additional 2,882 built in Canada) and the Anson became a familiar sight in the early war years shepherding coastal convoys around the British Isles.

The Anson was incredibly airworthy, as was proved by the case of two Australian Ansons, one of which crashed bodily on top of the other during an airborne collision. The crews baled out, but the pilot of the upper machine found that his controls were still answering and managed to make a belly-landing with the aircraft still locked together.

Another maritime patrol workhorse—and a real boon to the RAF—was the Lockheed Hudson, a twin-engined design originally produced in the United States to British specifications. Some 800 Hudsons were purchased directly for the RAF while a further 1,170 or so were supplied under Lend-Lease. It was a Hudson that located the "hell-ship" *Altmark* in February 1940. *Altmark* had been the supply-ship to the pocket-battleship *Graf Spee* in the South Atlantic and, the warship having been scuttled off Montevideo, it was trying to return to Germany, still carrying British Merchant Navy prisoners-of-war taken from its various prizes by *Graf Spee*. The Hudson's report led to *Altmark* being intercepted by a British destroyer, which then boarded it in neutral Norwegian waters and reclaimed the prisoners, whose triumphant return to England gave a considerable boost to national morale.

A Coastal Command Hudson was also the first aircraft to sink a U-boat with rockets, in May 1943. The Hudson had a crew of five and a maximum range of 2,800 miles; later versions could carry up to 1,400 lb. of bombs. During

pusher engine. The Walrus entered service with the Fleet Air Arm in 1936 and was the first amphibious aircraft to be catapulted from a warship. It then became the standard spotter plane carried by British battleships and cruisers and large numbers were also used as air/sea rescue machines. During the PQ.17 fiasco on the Russian run, the British warship escort withdrew so precipitately that a Walrus making a scheduled patrol was left behind, although its crew was rescued and survived the ordeal.

Left: The Consolidated PBY Catalina was built in greater numbers than any other flying-boat before or since and was widely used by the U.S. Navy, RAF, and RCAF during the war to provide very long-range maritime patrol. One of these aircraft serving with 209 Squadron of the RAF's Coastal Command, with a British pilot and American copilot, found the *Bismarck* at 1030 A.M. on May 26, 1941, during the great chase and ensured that its position was radioed to the British fleet.

Above: The nearest the Germans got to an in-service aircraft carrier were catapult-launched seaplanes operating from the larger warships, such as this Arado Ar 196 aboard the battlecruiser, *Gneisenau*. It had excellent characteristics, both in the air and on the water, and while most Ar 196s had twin floats, a small number of Ar 196Bs with only a single central float were also built. Large numbers of Ar 196s also operated from coastal bases.

the later war years the Hudson served on air/sea rescue, training, and troop transport duties.

Mention must also be made of an Italian design that proved to be a very effective land-based torpedo-bomber during the campaign in the Mediterranean: the Savoia-Marchetti S.M.79 *Sparviero*. It hardly looked the part—being a hunchbacked tri-motor design dating back to mid-1930s—but by the time of Italy's entry into the war it was the standard bomber of the *Regia Aeronautica*. The S.M.79H was developed specifically for the torpedo-bombing role and it did much damage to the Malta convoys. It had a crew of four and had a maximum speed of 270 mph and a range of 1,243 miles. It could carry up to 2,750 lb. of bombs or two torpedoes.

## THE ALLIED DEBT TO HITLER AND MUSSOLINI

The obvious requirements of coastal and carrier-borne aircraft are range, endurance, hitting-power, and, last but not least, a modicum of comfort for the crews committed to hours of weary patrolling over the sea. It was not surprising that the leading naval powers of World War II—Britain, the United States and Japan—all produced excellent examples. But it was also significant that Germany and Italy both had a basic misconception of naval strategy and thus failed to understand the importance of air power and the aircraft carrier in modern naval warfare. One consequence was that the aircraft they used, with the honorable exception of the Italian S.M.79, proved woefully inadequate.

Thus, it is no exaggeration to say that the Allies owed a great deal to both Hitler and Göring, for their repeated interference and the very low priority they gave to their naval and staffs' building plans. One example is that an adequate long-range German maritime patrol aircraft force could not only have almost certainly saved the *Bismarck*, but would also have transformed the course of the commerce war in the Atlantic. Moreover, even a limited carrier-building program could have sent *Scharnhorst, Gneisenau,* and *Bismarck* (let alone the powerful pocket-battleships) out on to the high seas with their own carrier protection, to wreak havoc among Allied convoys. As it was, only one German aircraft carrier—*Graf Zeppelin*—was launched, and the "stop-go" policy which then dogged her progress

meant that she was never completed.

Mussolini's navy fared even worse, for excessive reliance was placed on land-based aircraft operating from Italy, which enjoyed a commanding and central position in the Mediterranean. When, at long last, Mussolini ordered the liners *Roma* and *Augustus* to be converted into carriers, it was already far too late. By the time of the Italian armistice in September 1943, the *Roma* (rechristened *Aquila*) was almost ready for her sea trials, but had not received any aircraft, while work on the *Augustus* had only gotten as far as removal of her liner superstructure.

## FLYING TO FIGHT

The military dream of the sudden, surprising and decisive attack was made a reality by the interwar development of aircraft, parachutes, and gliders. This new and daring method of attack was widely used during World War II and, inevitably, lessons had to be learned from

Below: Only five Dornier Do-26D-0 were procured for the Luftwaffe and these served from August 1939 to late 1940. They were powered by four Junkers JuMo 205D diesel engines, which were located back-to-back, with the unusual feature that the rear engines were raised 10 degrees for takeoff to keep the propellers clear of the spray from the hull.

Above: The Ju-52, "Tante Ju" (aunty Junkers) to its German aircrew, supported the army and air force from the ice and snow of Norway and Russia to the sand and heat of the North African desert. It was rugged and reliable, but extremely vulnerable to enemy air attack, its own defenses of one or two machine guns being no more than a token gesture. Here, Ju-52s bring fuel and personnel to a Bf 110 forward base somewhere in the desert.

the heavy casualties of the early combined operations before any airborne forces could be unleashed against their objectives with any kind of certainty of success. But these early efforts paved the way for some spectacular military operations in which aircraft and aircrew played a key role.

Three principal methods of airlifting troops into action were developed in World War II: by parachute, by direct airlift in transports, and by glider. The evolution of the aircraft between two world wars had seen extensive experimentation with airborne troops by all major powers, which bore fruit between 1939 and 1945.

The first country to use airborne troops in World War II was Germany. The *Fallschirmjäger* (paratroops) were the responsibility of the Luftwaffe, whose workhorse for this type of operations was the Junkers Ju 52/3m, which despite its antiquated appearance served throughout the war. Some 3,000 machines were built, and operated by a two- or three-man crew, they could carry up to eighteen troops or some 10,000 lb. of cargo. They were employed during the Norwegian campaign, but, as described earlier, it was the glider-borne troops who hit the headlines in May 1940 with their amazing assault on Fort Eban-Emael in Belgium. They used the standard German troop-carrying glider of World War II, the DFS 230, which could carry ten fully armed soldiers. These gliders were also used during the hazardous landing on Crete in May 1941, in North Africa, and in September 1943 during the daring rescue of Mussolini by the German airborne commandos from his prison in an Italian mountain-top hideaway.

Soviet Russia was the first country in the world to comprehend fully the potential of airborne and parachute troops, as they demonstrated to the world on maneuvers near Kiev in 1937. The country went on to organize at least eight airborne brigades, although these specially trained units were actually used only once in the role conceived for them. This was in fall 1943 when, owing to poor navigation by their transport crews and the unexpected arrival of a German mechanized division, the operation turned into a bloody fiasco and there were no further large-scale Soviet airborne activities until the Soviet invasion of Japanese-held Manchuria, which took place one week after the first nuclear

bomb had been dropped on Japan.

The Japanese also used paratroops, both in the invasion of the Dutch East Indies in 1942 and three years later, in attempts to reinforce the Philippines against the American invaders.

But, by far the most extensive use of airborne troops was made by Britain and the United States in the liberation of Europe, between 1943 and 1945, the first large-scale Allied airborne attack taking place during the assault on Sicily—Operation Husky—in July 1943. This was the first bi-national invasion that the Allies attempted, and was shared by the British 8th Army and the American 7th Army. In the British sector the airborne attack was a

Below: U.S. Army paratroops help each other with final preparations before emplaning for the flight to an operational jump during the invasion of Sicily. Their transport is the ubiquitous Douglas C-47 Dakota.

Above: German mountain troops of the Alpine Division deplane from a Junkers Ju-52 at Maleme airfield on the island of Crete.

Right: Paratroopers of the U.S. Army's 82nd Airborne Division load a Jeep into a Waco CG-4A glider in preparation for the invasion of Sicily. Some 12,400 were built and they could carry 15 fully-armed troops or up to 5,210 lb. of cargo

Previous pages: Douglas C-47 parked on a temporary strip in Sicily, July 1943, under the protection of a 40 mm antiaircraft gun and its crew. As the war progressed it became increasingly important to establish such forward airheads to enable men, equipment, and supplies to be brought in and casualties to be evacuated.

regiments blocked the approaches to Rome against all comers for over four months, was their finest hour.

For the decisive assault on the Normandy coast in June 1944 the British and Americans used airborne forces to secure the west and east flanks of the beach-head: the American 101st and 82nd Divisions for Utah Beach in the west

tragedy. It was made by 134 gliders towed by American-flown Douglas C-47s. On D-Day, July 10, the airborne force (the British 1st Airborne Division) had to contend with strong winds, made worse by the faulty navigation of their tugs, and as a result the gliders were released too far out to sea. Consequently, nearly fifty of them came down in the sea, drowning their troops, while most of the others landed way off target; only twelve reached the correct landing-zone. Only 73 officers and men reached their objective—a key bridge on the Syracuse road—and by the time the British 5th Division had fought its way through to them the airborne troops were down to a mere 19 men.

## SPECIALISTS IN DECISIVE ROLES

Nor did the American glider force supporting the 7th Army fare much better, being scattered over a wide area of southeastern Sicily, their main contribution being to add to the demoralization of the Italian forces on the invasion sector. Apart from everything else, this tragic muddle led to more attention being paid to the navigational proficiency of airborne transport crews. During the battle for Sicily, and later on in Italy as well, German airborne troops were encountered. Although after Crete they did not operate in their correct role, these specially picked men were formidable ground troops, holding on to defensive positions in apparently impossible situations. The battle of Cassino, where a couple of battered German parachute and the British 6th Airborne Division for Sword Beach in the east. Both airborne assaults used a mixture of paratroops and glider-borne troops. The Americans favored the Waco CG-4A glider, which carried 15 fully laden troops, while the British used the Airspeed Horsa and General Aircraft Hamilcar. The latter was very large and could carry either a light 7-ton tank, or two Bren-gun carriers, or two scout cars, or a mobile Bofors gun. Tugs for these gliders ranged from C-47s for the Americans to Stirlings, Halifaxes, and Albemarles for the British.

The D-Day airborne landings were perilous. They were made at night and the Allied air forces commander, Leigh-Mallory, had warned Eisenhower that losses of 80 percent to tugs and

Right: En route to Normandy in June 1944, a Handley Page Halifax tows a British General Aircraft Hamilcar glider.

Below: Airspeed Horsa gliders used in the D-Day landings scattered about a landing zone near Ranville in Normandy. After landing, the tail was detached to enable the cargo to be rapidly unloaded.

gliders might be expected. Scanty AA fire, excellent radar jamming, and evasive tactics combined to avoid anything like this loss figure, but the drops were far from accurate. Only one-sixth of the U.S. 101st Division was in position by dawn on June 6, the result largely of scatter caused by evasive tactics. Nevertheless, the sluggish German response plus the gallantry and dash of the troops going into action ensured that the objectives had been secured by the time the seaborne assault force arrived.

The next major Allied airborne operation was a brilliant success—but strategically unnecessary. It was the spearhead of the invasion of southern France, originally intended to be synchronized with the Normandy landings, then delayed by the slow pace of the Italian campaign plus the need to concentrate tugs and gliders for the Normandy assault, and finally launched in August 1944 on the insistence of the Americans and Russians. Operation Dragoon, as the invasion of southern France was code named, was largely a paratroop affair, carried out by 396 aircraft in nine relays and preceded by special pathfinders. It was the most successful Allied airborne operation to date, with 60 percent of the paratroops landing on or nearby their dropping-zones. But it was largely a sledge-hammer to crack a nut, for after the heavy losses suffered in Normandy it was no part of the Wehrmacht's plan to fight for the south of France.

Below: Close air support of ground troops became an increasingly important mission for the air forces, although not all pilots were regarded with such a spectacular result as this, where a German ammunition truck has been blown up by an attacking P-47 Thunderbolt.

Above: C-47s of the USAAF's 9th troop Carrier Command carry paratroops toward their drop zone in the Netherlands, September 17, 1944.

## ARNHEM AND THE RHINE

The most daring airborne undertaking of the war was Montgomery's Operation Market Garden, which has already been described in the section "War On Land." After that setback there followed an exhilarating two weeks of nonstop advance to the line of the Elbe, halted only by the pressures of grand strategy and international politics that stopped the American 9th Army from pushing right on to Berlin itself. This decision meant that the daring plan to attempt a *coup de main*, establishing the Allies in Berlin itself, was never put into effect.

This would have been the crowning operation in "Eclipse," the code name for the final defeat of Germany. The plan was drawn up by General Gavin, whose U.S. 82nd Airborne Division had taken Nijmegen in the Arnhem campaign, and General Taylor, commander of the U.S. 101st Division. The main targets in Berlin were the airfields: Tempelhof for 82nd

Division and Gatow for 101st. Desperate resistance was only to be expected and the assault force was huge: the initial plan called for 3,000 fighters for close escort, 1,500 transport aircraft, over 1,000 gliders, and 20,000-odd paratroops—a much larger force than that which had landed in Normandy on the morning of D-Day.

Between Paderborn and Berlin itself, twenty-two objective lines had been marked out for the 9th Army's advance on Berlin. By April 15 the Americans were across the Elbe—Objective Gold—and were building up a bridge-head before they pushed on to Objective Silver and beyond that to Silk, Satin, Daisy, Pansy, Jug, and then, finally, Goal: the airfields on the out-skirts of Berlin. However, on April 15, 1945, General Simpson heard—much to his astonishment and disappointment—that he was to go no further than the Elbe. Berlin was to be left to the Russians—and the most sensational air-borne attack plan of World War II was thus returned to the files.

Left: Consolidated B-24 Liberator bombers have been pressed into service to make a supply drop to the troops in the ground, September 18, 1944. As far as the eye can see the ground is covered with Waco CG-4 gliders.

# WAR
# IN THE
# PACIFIC

# Chapter 4

# THE WAR AT SEA

AT THE OUTBREAK OF WAR IN THE PACIFIC, the Japanese held all the advantages. Britain's naval presence did not amount to much and America's Pacific Fleet was outnumbered in every type of ship and aircraft by the Japanese, who possessed the largest carrier-based air force in the world. The Japanese believed they had to win quickly, and they struck a crippling opening blow at Pearl Harbor. But the Americans hit back, first in the Coral Sea and then at Midway, gaining parity with the Japanese. They then went onto the offensive and throughout 1943 the sea battle raged from Alaska to Australia, with carriers and other heavy units of both fleets involved in many sharp and bloody confrontations. In 1944 Japan lost four million tons of ships, the bulk to submarine attack, leaving it unable to maintain civil life, far less effectively wage a war. Japan was losing on the ground and in the air, while America and its allies established bases from which to launch the last part of its drive on Japan itself. The Japanese navy was all but finished off in a massive and decisive battle in Leyte Gulf, but the Allies had to suffer the onslaught of the fanatical, suicidal kamikazes. With Japan's oil shortage becoming increasingly crucial during 1944, and America continuing to achieve submarine successes against merchant and navy shipping, the Allies' island-hopping offensive and the drive overland toward Japan were able to continue relentlessly. The atomic bomb finally forced Japan's surrender, appropriately signed on the battleship *Missouri* in September 1945.

Right: The U.S./Japanese naval battles in the Pacific were among the largest and most violent naval engagements in history. This is the Battle of Santa Cruz, October 16, 1942, as the U.S. naval task force peppers the skies with antiaircraft fire against attacking Japanese aircraft.

Previous pages: Far more telling than the victory ceremonies in Tokyo, these two U.S. paratroopers look out over the Philippines after landing on Corregidor on February 16, 1945.

In July 1941 the Japanese took control of Indo-China from the colonial power, France, which had been beaten a year earlier by Germany, and was thus in no position to resist. But the Americans, British, and Dutch responded by halting all trade with Japan. This was a particularly telling measure since Japan was heavily dependent on overseas supplies, particularly oil, which came from the Dutch East Indies (present-day Indonesia). This meant that she would soon be brought to her knees unless Japan complied with President Roosevelt's demand that it withdraw not only from the French colonies but from China as well. Diplomatic maneuvering that summer and fall led nowhere and, at least in the Japanese view, all that was left was war. That came on December 8, which, on the eastern side of the International Date Line, was December 7.

The U.S. Pacific Fleet had been moved in the spring of 1940 from its bases on the California coast to Pearl Harbor in the hope that it would deter the Japanese from attacking the western colonies in Asia. But by late 1941 the Pacific Fleet had been so reduced by the needs of the war in the Atlantic (even though the United States was not actually a belligerent) that it was in all respects inferior to the Japanese Combined Fleet.

Under the grandiose title U.S. Asiatic Fleet, the Americans had long maintained a small naval force in the Far East. In December 1941 this "fleet," based on Manila, consisted of three cruisers, 13 old destroyers, and 32 sea-based patrol planes. There were also 23 new submarines, which represented about half the country's total strength in modern boats of that type, and six old ones. After two years of war else-

*Below: This Japanese model of Pearl Harbor is not a planning model for the attack, but was constructed after the attack for use in a motion picture.*

where, Great Britain had few warships left in East Asian waters, only three elderly cruisers and seven destroyers; the cruisers and five destroyers were based in Singapore, the other two destroyers in Hong Kong. There were no aircraft carriers, no battleships, and no submarines. The third of the navies, the Dutch, had three cruisers, seven destroyers, and 13 submarines, but although most were of relatively modern construction, their designs were somewhat dated.

The U.S. Navy was inexperienced with war. It had developed skill in daylight gunnery and tactics, and had developed naval aviation highly. But it was not very good at night fighting, submarine warfare, or antisubmarine warfare, and was only just starting to develop an expertise in amphibious warfare. Aboard ship, the big guns were good, but not the light weapons, and the torpedoes were seriously ineffective, although nobody knew that yet. The ships were good, as were the aircraft, and in both cases there were even better ones on the way.

The British were adept at surface action both by day and by night and, with two years of hard experience, particularly good at antisubmarine warfare. Their submariners were also a potent force, but the British had no important experience, or any doctrine, of amphibious warfare and, while their carrier aviators were brave and skilled, their aircraft were distinctly second-rate. The ships of the Royal Navy generally were more seaworthy but less battle worthy than

Above: Japanese warships at sea in the Pacific immediately prior to the attack on Pearl Harbor, December 7, 1941. They were taking up their war positions ready for instant action as soon as they received the order from the commander in chief.

Above: Aichi D3A Val takes off from a Japanese aircraft carrier for the attack on Pearl Harbor. Note the crew lining the deck and cheering the aircraft and its crew on their way.

Right: Japanese map showing the deployment of both their own and enemy forces on the day of the attack on Pearl Harbor.

those of other major navies. Their officers and men had learned how to endure.

The Japanese also knew how to endure. They were very highly motivated, and were generally well-equipped. There were large numbers of ships, which looked powerful, purposeful, and battle worthy, although they were to prove to be much less impressive in action.

The ships' guns were good and the torpedoes were the best in the world, being both very effective and highly reliable. Their naval aircraft were as good as, or better than, any other aircraft in the sky, especially their Zero fighters. Like the British, they were skilled at night fighting and, at first, they were better than anyone in carrier warfare.

In addition to possessing the world's largest carrier-based air force, they also had a large shore-based naval air force. They were the world's most experienced in amphibious warfare, and had a powerful submarine fleet. But they were uninterested in antisubmarine warfare and the protection of shipping. Their merchant marine, on which the weight of their newly acquired empire was to rest, was not big enough for its task and, more important, not valued highly enough by the fighting navy.

The instruments used on either side were rather more modem than were the concepts of most of the admirals wielding them. But the concepts quickly caught up with, and eventually led, the instruments. At first the Japanese admirals were the most advanced conceptually, but the Americans soon outdistanced them.

## ADMIRALS AND POLITICIANS

The strategic insight of Isoroku Yamamoto, commander in chief of the Japanese Combined Fleet, was sound, but the ideas of most of the principal admirals below him were more limited, while the quality of both American and British admirals was generally very good. All three groups, however, had problems with their

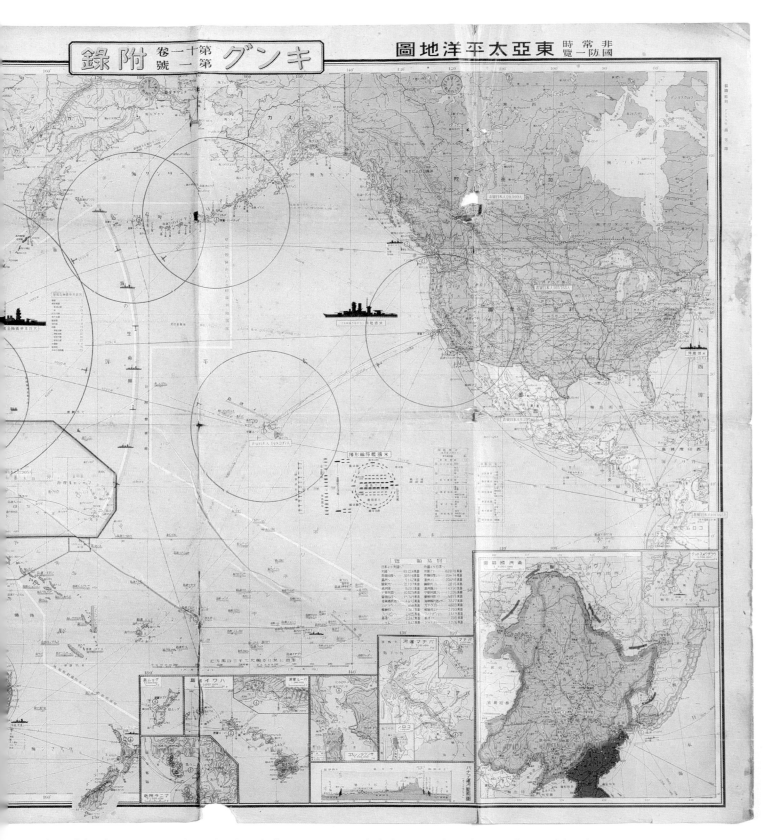

political leaders. Roosevelt and Churchill saw themselves as both strategic thinkers and activists, but their ideas were not always of a quality to match the huge power they possessed to deploy fleets and armies across the globe. The Japanese admirals, on the other hand, had to contend with generals such as Prime Minister Tojo, who were hypnotized by the idea of conflict on the Asian mainland. These men failed to see that the Pacific was the decisive theater.

Admiral Yamamoto felt the need to protect his country's drive to the south from interference by the U.S. Pacific Fleet at Pearl Harbor. He appreciated the industrial might of the United States and feared, correctly, that if Japan did not win within the first 18 months it would not win at all. Indeed, in common with the opposing

just before eight o'clock the first Japanese airplanes attacked the unsuspecting Americans. Purely by chance, not one of the American carriers was at Pearl Harbor, but eight of the Pacific Fleet's nine old battleships were, in addition to a substantial number of cruisers, destroyers, submarines, and auxiliaries. Ashore were thousands of U.S. servicemen, together with hundreds of shore-based aircraft, the majority of which belonged to the U.S. Army Air Corps, the remainder to the U.S. Navy and Marine Corps.

Nagumo lost 55 men and 30 aircraft, but killed over 2,000 American sailors, soldiers, and marines, destroyed 188 aircraft, and sank two old battleships, USS *Arizona* and *Oklahoma*, and an old auxiliary. Over a thousand men were wounded and scores of aircraft damaged. Three other battleships, USS *Nevada*, *California*, and *West Virginia*, were so badly damaged that they

Above: A scene of devastation with, in the foreground, the destroyers *Downes* (DD-375) (left) and *Cassin* (DD-372) (right). These two Mahan-class destroyers were so heavily damaged that their machinery and guns had to be removed and installed in completely new hulls built for that purpose. These new ships were then given the names and numbers of the originals. Astern of them is the battleship, USS *Pennsylvania*, which was relatively lightly damaged and returned to service within weeks.

admirals at Singapore, Pearl Harbor, and Manila, he wished for no war at all, but the decision on that matter was taken at a higher level.

Admiral Yamamoto had an exaggerated opinion of the strength of the U.S. Navy's Pacific Fleet. True, the Americans had six large carriers and a small one, and a seventh large carrier had been commissioned just a few weeks before, but only three of these were in the Pacific. He had six large carriers, too, all in the Pacific, as well as four smaller ones. In every type of ship and aircraft, his fleet outnumbered the Pacific Fleet. Moreover, his ships were nearer their objectives than were the Americans', and his government was motivated both by a common arrogance and a common desperation, while the Americans were divided as to purpose.

Yamamoto sent his six best carriers—*Kaga, Akagi, Hiryu, Soryu, Shokaku,* and *Zuikaku*—with well over 400 aircraft, to attack the American fleet at Pearl Harbor. Most of his cruisers, almost half of his destroyers, and the bulk of his shore-based aircraft took part in the attacks to the south under command of Vice Admiral Kondo.

### THE FIRST DEVASTATING BLOW

When about 200 miles north of Pearl Harbor at dawn on December 8 (December 7, local time), Vice Admiral Nagumo, commander of the Japanese task force, launched his aircraft and

were out of action for a year or more, while dozens of other ships suffered lesser damage.

After this stunning success, Nagumo withdrew and sailed for home, but on the way he detached the carriers *Hiryu* and *Soryu* to help take the island of Wake, whose Marine Corps defenders proved harder to subdue than anticipated. As a result, the island was not taken until December 23, while an American relief task force bumbled about getting refueled 500 miles to the east. In other attacks, Guam and the Gilbert Islands fell on December 10, while the British colony of Hong Kong fell on December 25.

The main attack on the Philippines began with a noon air raid by Kondo's shore-based aircraft of the 11th Air Fleet, which destroyed half of the U.S. Army Air Corps' modern bombers and a third of the fighters on their fields near Manila. The success of this attack, and the superiority of the Zero naval fighter over the U.S. Curtis P-40, meant that the skies over the Philippines were open to Japan. Most of America's Asiatic Fleet cruisers and destroyers had earlier been sent south to join the Dutch at Java and the rest soon followed. The submarines stayed based on Manila, the idea being that they would deploy to frustrate Japanese invasion attempts, but, in the event, it was the submarines that were frustrated, mainly because their torpedoes were virtually useless. Meanwhile Japanese aircraft destroyed the navy yard and dominated Manila Bay by day, so, having accomplished almost nothing, the submarines followed the surface ships to Java.

## JAPANESE LAND UNHINDERED

The Japanese landed on the Philippines over a multitude of beaches, unhindered by either air-

Left: The unforgettable image of USS *Arizona* (BB-39) burning.

Above: British battlecruiser HMS *Repulse* departs the Singapore Naval Base on December 8, 1941. This was to be her final voyage; two days later she was sunk by Japanese bombers, together with the flagship, the battleship, HMS *Prince of Wales*.

Previous pages: A gallant small-boat crew closes on the burning USS *West Virginia* (BB-38) to rescue a sailor struggling in the water.

craft or submarines. The main landing came on December 22 at Lingayen Gulf on Luzon's western coast. General Douglas MacArthur's Filipinos and a few Americans attempted to meet the Japanese at the beaches, but they were brushed aside everywhere and quickly fell back to the Bataan Peninsula at the entrance to Manila Bay. From the beginning the defenders were on short rations and, shortly after, they fell sick. Nonetheless, they held out till April 9, while others on the fortified islands, which commanded the entrance to Manila Bay, lasted till May 6. In March, MacArthur, at the order of President Roosevelt, left the Philippines by motor torpedo boat and bomber. Australia was his destination, where he was first to lead the defense of that continent and then prepare for the recovery of the Philippines.

Meanwhile, an hour or so before the aircraft

attacked Pearl Harbor, amphibious forces of the Imperial Japanese Navy landed men and equipment for General Yamashita's Twenty-Fifth Army on the Malayan peninsula. Landings were made at Khota Bahru, Singora, and Patani, and two thrusts were started, one down either coast, towards the goal of Singapore (which the Japanese called *Shonan*).

Despite the misgivings of the Royal Navy, Prime Minister Churchill had ordered that the new battleship HMS *Prince of Wales* and the 25-year-old battlecruiser HMS *Repulse* should sail to Singapore, accompanied by an aircraft carrier and four destroyers. The force, lacking any air cover, arrived in Singapore just before the Japanese attacked, but very unfortunately the carrier ran aground before she could join them. Following news of the Japanese invasion *Prince of Wales* and *Repulse* sailed in search of the

Japanese troop transports, failed to find them, but were themselves found by the twin-engined bombers of the 11th Air Fleet, which was based at Saigon in Japanese-occupied Indo-China. The 84 aircraft, armed mainly with torpedoes, sank both ships mid-day on December 10 at almost no cost to themselves. The Royal Air Force, already overwhelmed and ignorant of the ships' position or their need for help, got some fighters to the scene after the ships had been sunk.

## A BRAVE EFFORT IN VAIN

Moving down through Malaya, the Japanese continually outflanked the defenders, sometimes using captured boats for this purpose, unhampered either by the RAF's aircraft, which had largely been destroyed, or by the Royal Navy, which had no small fighting ships with which to oppose the aggressors. But the British and Dutch navies did escort reinforcements to Singapore, laden with some 45,000 troops and modern aircraft, but it was all in vain. General Yamashita's troops soon arrived in southern Johore, opposite Singapore Island, and after only a brief pause crossed the strait on February 7, and it fell only eight days later.

Admiral Kondo's task was by no means finished, however, and he also invaded Borneo, where he made the first of seven landings on December 16; Celebes (first landing of three on January 11); and Amboina, on January 31. For the last-named Kondo had the assistance of the

Left: HMS *Exeter* protects a trooping convoy from air attack while passing through the Bangka Straits on what proved to be the last convoy to reach Singapore before it fell. *Exeter*, which had fought so gallantly in the Battle of the River Plate, drove off this particular air raid and survived the loss of Singapore, but was sunk only a few weeks later in the Java Sea.

carriers *Hiryu* and *Soryu*, which had joined him from the Pacific operations. The only effective Allied response was a night torpedo attack by four American destroyers against the invasion ships anchored off Balikpapan, Borneo, on January 24. The destroyers sank four transports and an escort ship, but they did not stop the invasion.

Meanwhile far to the east, Admiral Nagumo with four of his carriers struck at the small British and Australian garrisons at Rabaul, New Britain; Kavieng, New Ireland; and Lae and Salamaua, New Guinea. The preliminary attacks by carrier aircraft were quickly followed by troops who stormed ashore to secure their new holdings.

On February 5, a combined Dutch and American force of cruisers and destroyers under the command of Dutch Rear-Admiral Karel Doorman headed for another Japanese invasion force reported near the southern end of Makassar Strait. Doorman's ships were attacked by 37 twin-engine bombers of the 11th Air Fleet flying from a captured field on Celebes. All three cruisers were damaged, one, USS *Marblehead*, almost fatally, and so Doorman was forced to retire.

Below: A moment of national humiliation as U.S. and Filipino officers advance under the white flag to surrender the garrison on Negros in April 1942. This paralleled the equally unhappy scene on Singapore island where General Percival surrendered the British garrison.

On February 14, the day before Singapore surrendered, the Japanese dropped paratroops on Palembang, the capital of Sumatra. That attack failed. But the next morning Japanese amphibious ships were at the approaches to Palembang. On hearing that an Allied naval force was approaching, the invasion force put about, while aircraft from the light carrier *Ryujo* attacked Rear Admiral Doorman's mixed force of five cruisers and ten destroyers representing four navies.[1] The *Ryujo's* attack sank none of the ships but it was enough to frustrate Doorman's purpose. The invasion

took place on the 16th and soon the whole island was in Japanese hands.

Above: The battle over and the surrender signed, Japanese troops come ashore at Corregidor.

## DARWIN IS ABANDONED

The same day, over a thousand miles to the east a small convoy carrying American and Australian troops from Darwin to Timor came under a fierce but unsuccessful attack by 46 Japanese land-based aircraft. But, because of the known presence of Nagumo's carriers to the north, the convoy was ordered back to Darwin. The day after their return there, Admiral Nagumo attacked with 190 aircraft from four carriers, sinking nearly everything that floated and destroying nearly everything else. What was left of Darwin was abandoned.

While Nagumo's aviators were attacking Darwin, Kondo was landing troops on Bali and the next day on Timor. Nothing could now be done about Timor and Admiral Doorman's attempt in a night action in Badoeng Strait to break up the landing at Bali cost the Dutch a destroyer, without inflicting much harm on the Japanese.

All that now remained for Kondo was to take the main island of Java, so he sent Rear Admiral Ozawa in from the west (56 transports)

[1] U.S. Navy, British Royal Navy, Royal Netherlands Navy, and Royal Australian Navy.

307

Right: Vice Admiral Kondo Nobutake was commander in chief of the Southern Fleet in 1941–42; his units were involved in the sinking of HMS *Prince of Wales* and *Repulse* (December 10, 1941), and in the invasions of Malaya, the Dutch East Indies and the Philippines. Kondo then commanded the 2nd Fleet at the Battles of Midway, Eastern Solomons (August 23–25, 1942), Santa Cruz (October 1942), and Savo Island (November 12–13, 1942). He became a member of Japan's Supreme War Council in May 1945.

and Rear Admiral Nishimura in from the east (41 transports). On the afternoon of February 27, Admiral Doorman sailed to attack Nishimura's transports, and once again he was leading a force of five cruisers and ten destroyers from four navies. The Japanese Navy had four cruisers—*Nachi*, *Haguro*, *Naka*, and *Jintsu*—and 14 destroyers, commanded by Rear Admiral Takagi. In a long action that began in the afternoon and ended after dark the Japanese lost no ships, while the Allies lost the Dutch

light cruisers *De Ruyter* (with Doorman on board) and Java, together with three destroyers.

The other Allied ships, including the severely damaged British heavy cruiser HMS *Exeter*, were ordered to make good their escape, and some went east and others to the west. Four American destroyers went to the east, slid through a shallow strait between Java and Bali, and made their way safely to Australia, but not one of those that went westwards reached safety. The American heavy cruiser USS *Houston* and the Australian light cruiser HMAS *Perth* were heading for the Sunda Strait when they ran into Ozawa's invasion force. They fired until their magazines were empty and then, engaged by the heavy cruisers *Mogami* and *Mikuma*, the light cruiser *Natori*, and ten destroyers, they perished. The next morning *Exeter* and two destroyers were sunk by a combination of gunfire from four Japanese heavy cruisers and aircraft from the carrier, *Ryujo*.

Meantime Nagumo with his carriers and Kondo with a pair of battleships were south of Java, where they caught and sank two American destroyers and an assortment of minor warships, auxiliaries, and merchant ships, all of which had been desperately trying to seek safety in Australia.

## JAPANESE PUSH ON TO RANGOON

While these enormous events were taking place in the waters surrounding the islands of Asia, Japanese troops pushed through Thailand into Burma, reaching the capital, Rangoon, on March 8. Before the end of the month the Andaman and Nicobar Islands in the Bay of Bengal were in Japanese hands and, hampered more by the jungle and the monsoons than by anything else, Japanese ground troops were soon on the border of British India.

Left: The U.S. Navy's senior commanders photographed during their meeting at Pearl Harbor in October 1943, where they mapped out their overall strategy against the Japanese. Admiral Ernest J. King (center) commander in chief U.S. Navy (COMINCH), with Admiral Chester Nimitz (left), commander in chief Pacific Fleet, and Admiral William F. Halsey (right), commander South Pacific Force and South Pacific Area.

Above: In the Indian Ocean, British Admiral Somerville and Japanese Admiral Nagumo sparred with each other, seeking to avoid action except on their own terms. A decisive action was avoided, but when the old carrier HMS *Eagle* was temporarily exposed on April 7, 1942, with none of her own aircraft aboard, Japanese aircraft sprang into action and sank her with just a small cluster of bombs.

Previous pages: Young aviators of the Imperial Japanese Navy are briefed for a mission. For a period of about a year these young men carried all before them, spreading their emperor's rule over an ever-expanding empire. It did not last long.

But the tale of Japanese triumph was still not over and the IJN once again came into the forefront. Admiral Kondo needed to secure the Japanese conquests in the Bay of Bengal and ensure that the seaborne resupply of their forces in Burma would not be disrupted, so he dispatched Nagumo into the Indian Ocean with five large carriers (all the Pearl Harbor ships except the *Kaga*) to attack the British. This Nagumo did with a raid by 180 aircraft on Colombo, Ceylon (now Sri Lanka), on April 5, with a second raid by a similar-sized force on the British naval base at Trincomalee four days later.

On both occasions, the carrier planes brushed aside defending interceptors to enable them to attack ships, port facilities, and airfields. Chance sightings by Japanese scouting aircraft enabled Nagumo's main forces to find and sink the small British carrier HMS *Hermes* (which had no aircraft aboard), the heavy cruisers HMS *Cornwall* and *Dorsetshire*, and a destroyer. Meanwhile Admiral Ozawa with the

carrier *Ryujo*, six cruisers, and four destroyers cruised off India's east coast, sinking 23 merchant ships in five days. The British had some 300 aircraft on Ceylon, but their only response was an attack on Nagumo's fleet by Blenheirn bombers on the 9th, which action achieved no hits and lost five of the nine aircraft taking part.

## BRITAIN'S NAVY WITHDRAWS

Admiral Sir James Somerville, the British commander in chief, Eastern Fleet, had two carriers, HMS *Indomitable* and *Formidable*, which had about 80 aircraft between them. But this was not the whole story, because not only did his fleet have only a quarter the number of aircraft his enemy possessed, but they were also of inferior performance and capability.

Somerville sought opportunities for a night strike against his powerful foe, but the opportunity did not arise. Then, while Nagumo and Ozawa left the Indian Ocean through the

Malacca Strait, never to return, Somerville sent some of his ships to the port of Kalindini[2] on the East African coast to provide protection for ships supplying the Eighth Army in Egypt. He then took his remaining ships to Bombay where he could dominate the Arabian Sea.

On May 5, British forces who had sailed from the United Kingdom, guarded by the carriers *Illustrious* and *Indomitable*, made an amphibious descent upon the huge French island of Madagascar (present day Malagasy Republic) which lies off the southeastern coast of Africa. The island was held by French loyal to Marshal Petain and the British needed to prevent the harbor at Diego Suarez at the northern end of the island from being either handed over to or seized by the Japanese, as had happened in Indochina. The British takeover was completed by May 7, with little loss.

However, in June and July, and before the British could base sufficient antisubmarine forces in the area, Japanese submarines arrived

and sank 20 merchant ships in waters near Madagascar. Having wrought such destruction, the Japanese submarines then departed and naval activity in the Indian Ocean reduced in tempo. In fact, by the end of August, Somerville was down to one carrier, HMS *Illustrious*, and in January 1943 even she was taken from him for use elsewhere. It would not be until late in 1944 that powerful naval forces would reenter that ocean.

## AMERICA STRIKES BACK

The attack on Pearl Harbor led to a desire for revenge on the part of Americans that did not end until Japan lay in ruins in 1945. One of the first consequences, however, was a change in naval leadership, with Admiral Ernest J. King taking control in Washington as both commander in chief, U.S. Fleet, and chief of naval

Above: Part of the Japanese attack force at Pearl Harbor was a number of A-type two-man midget submarines, of which a large number had been built in the 1930s. These were specifically designed to attack defended harbors, but were not particularly successful, as with this example, found abandoned on a beach near Pearl Harbor after the attack.

[2]Kalindini is the port for Mombassa.

operations, and Admiral Chester W. Nimitz doing the same at Pearl Harbor, where he became both commander in chief Pacific Fleet and, soon after, commander in chief Pacific Ocean Area. Thus, Nimitz commanded all Allied forces in the Pacific, except for those in General MacArthur's corner.

Pearl Harbor also permitted the Pacific Fleet to pursue a strategy that, even had there been no attack, would have been the best possible. This was to hold the line between the U.S. West Coast and Hawaii and a thousand miles beyond, to Midway Island, and to maintain communications with Australia. This meant that it was necessary to station strong garrisons in Samoa and the other islands on the route to Australia, but it also meant a tacit acknowledgment that the Philippines and Dutch East Indies were acknowledged as lost, and would not be retaken, at least in the short term.

Meantime, some ships which earlier had been transferred to the Atlantic were recalled to

Right: Having been recovered from the dawn raid on Marcus Island on March 4, 1942, aircraft are refueled and rearmed aboard the carrier USS *Enterprise*. Right forward are five Grumman F4F Wildcat fighters; all other aircraft are Douglas SBD Dauntless dive-bombers. Note the early wartime aircraft roundels with the red circle inside the star, and the slotted divebrakes in the Dauntless's groups.

the Pacific, of which the most important was the carrier USS *Yorktown*. The effect of her arrival on the balance in the Pacific was, however, off-set by the torpedoing of the carrier *Saratoga* by a Japanese submarine in January, which put the latter out of the war for five months. Be that as it may, the flow of modern high-class ships, once from the Pacific into the Atlantic, was now reversed.

Those things done, Nimitz organized raids upon the Japanese-held islands. The first of these, against Wake, had to be called off when the task force's oiler was sunk by a submarine. But then came a series of small successes as Vice Admiral William F. Halsey and Rear Admiral Frank Jack Fletcher with the *Enterprise* and *Yorktown* raided the Marshall Islands, Wake, and Marcus Island. The latter is less than a thousand miles from Tokyo. An attack by Vice Admiral Wilson Brown with the *Lexington* against Rabaul was called off after the Japanese discovered the task force but, when Brown was reinforced by the *Yorktown*, another raid, against Lae and Salamaua, New Guinea, succeeded.

Though they did little damage, these raids had an impact on the most important place possible, the mind of Admiral Yamamoto. When, after their great successes, the Japanese high command were trying to decide what to do next

Yamamoto, concerned about the resurgent Pacific Fleet, persuaded the others that they should move east, toward Hawaii. An air raid on Tokyo in April by sixteen U.S. Army Air Force B-25 bombers launched from the new carrier *Hornet* strengthened Yamamoto's hand. East it would be.

But first there would be a couple of minor ventures to the south. A seaplane base was set up at Tulagi in the southern Solomons and troopships were loaded at Rabaul for an attack on Port Moresby, the main Australian outpost remaining on New Guinea. The Japanese also wanted Tulagi and Port Moresby, not only to screen Rabaul but also to support attacks on the islands that guarded the American supply route to Australia. Thus, on May 3, ships of Vice Admiral Inouye's Fourth Fleet landed troops at Tulagi, while on the 4th troop transports left Rabaul for Port Moresby in a convoy protected by Rear Admiral Goto, who had the light carrier *Shoho* (21 aircraft), four heavy cruisers, and a destroyer. Meanwhile, Vice Admiral Takagi with the carriers, *Shokaku* (63 aircraft) and *Zuikaku* (63 aircraft), sailed from Truk, and entered the Coral Sea from the east.

After its initial failures, U.S. naval intelligence was now becoming very effective and was able to anticipate these Japanese moves, so that there were two carrier task forces on hand to

Above: Task Force 18 combined with Task Force 16 to take the Doolittle raiders to within range of Japan. The combined force centered on the carrier USS *Enterprise* (CV-6), carrying Doolittle and his men, but this picture shows some of the escorts, including, in the foreground, USS *Fanning* (DD-385), a Mahan-class destroyer, launched in 1936, and a sister ship of *Cassin* (DD-372) and *Downes* (DD-375), which had been so badly damaged at Pearl Harbor. Fanning survived a very busy war and was broken up in 1948.

Right: During the Battle of the Coral Sea (May 8, 1942) the carrier USS *Lexington* (CV-2) was being attacked by bombers, which hit her three times, when, at about 11:20 A.M., she was also struck by two torpedoes. The resulting heavy fires and flooding, which caused a list to port, were brought under control. Then there was a sudden explosion, caused by igniting gasoline vapor. This time matters could not be controlled and all crew were brought to the flight deck where, at 5:07 P.M., the order was given to abandon ship. The men took to the warm waters and were quickly rescued by accompanying warships, as shown here. Captain Sherman and his Executive Officer were the last to leave the blazing ship.

meet the Japanese, one commanded by Rear Admiral Fletcher, centered on USS *Yorktown* (72 aircraft), the other by Rear Admiral Fitch, with *Lexington* (71 aircraft). Meanwhile, Halsey, with the *Enterprise* and *Hornet*, was racing down from Pearl Harbor. On May 7 the Americans discovered what they thought was Takagi's force and attacked; they were mistaken, it was only Goto's, but they sank the *Shoho*, all the same. The same morning Takagi's pilots made a similar mistake, and sank an American destroyer and an oiler.

By now, the American and Japanese carrier groups both knew where the other was, and they exchanged blows. The Japanese attack hit *Lexington* and *Yorktown*, while U.S. aircraft hit *Shokaku* but did not find *Zuikaku*, which happened to be hidden by a rainsquall. The opposing carrier forces headed for home and repairs, but not before the *Lexington* sank, a serious blow to the Americans. More importantly Inouye, who had turned around his transports until the issue was cleared up, postponed his invasion of Port Moresby. That summer, an invasion was attempted overland across the Owen Stanley Mountains and was beaten back at the last minute by Australian and American infantry units.

Toward the end of May, the Japanese began to sail for Midway. Their plan was to open the attack with aircraft from Admiral Nagumo's carriers and then, having wiped out the American air defenses and seriously damaged the ground defenses, they would assault the island with 5,000 troops. The naval task force, commanded by Vice Admiral Kondo, comprised the light carrier *Zuiho* (24 aircraft), two battleships, eight heavy cruisers, and twelve troop transports. A secondary attack was planned to strike the American base at Dutch Harbor in the eastern Aleutians from the air and to capture the islands of Kiska and Attu in the west. Central to the force striking Dutch Harbor were the light carriers *Ryujo* (37 aircraft) and *Junyo* (45 aircraft).

Vice Admiral Nagumo departed from his anchorage in the Inland Sea on May 27, with four carriers, two battleships, three cruisers, and

eleven destroyers. The carriers were *Akagi* (54 aircraft), *Kaga* (63), *Hiryu*, (54), and *Soryu* (56), but both *Shokaku*, under repair from her Coral Sea damage, and *Zuikaku*, which was short of pilots, remained in port. Far astern sailed Yamamoto himself in the giant new battleship *Yamato*, accompanied by the small training carrier *Hosho* (eight aircraft), six old battleships, and some cruisers and destroyers. Sixteen submarines were sent on ahead to form a barrier between Midway and the American base at Pearl Harbor.

Admiral Yamamoto believed the American carriers were still in the Coral Sea, but that if this was incorrect and any of them did happen to be at Pearl Harbor and were to race to join the battle, then the submarine patrol line would either deal with them or provide warning of their presence. But, unfortunately for Yamamoto, U.S. naval intelligence had already been able to inform Nimitz of the Japanese commander's plans and timings. As a result, Nimitz's

Below: USS *Lexington* (CV-2) ablaze on the afternoon of May 8, 1942. There was no hope at all of controlling this gasoline-fuelled fire, leaving Captain Sherman no alternative but to abandon the much-loved ship.

Right: Japanese carrier *Kaga* at sea in 1936. Completed in 1928, she was completely rebuilt (1934–35), during which time the hull and flightdeck were lengthened, the air group increased to 90 aircraft, a bridge island installed (there had been none before), and a third elevator added. She was sunk on June 4, 1942, at the Battle of Midway.

ships were no longer in the Coral Sea, while in the Navy Yard at Pearl Harbor, workmen repaired the damage to *Yorktown*; this work was estimated to require ninety days, but was accomplished in just three days. This enabled Admiral Nimitz to move his three carriers, *Yorktown* (75 aircraft), *Enterprise* (79), and *Hornet* (79), to sea and west of the Japanese submarine patrol line before the submarines had actually moved into position. Nimitz also set up his own barrier of twelve U.S. submarines north and west of Midway.

## AN AMERICAN DISASTER

The Americans made contact with the Japanese when a patrol plane spotted some of Kondo's ships 700 miles southwest of Midway on June 3. The next morning Nagumo, who was approaching the island from the northwest, launched 108 aircraft just before dawn while still about 240 miles away. The Americans had about 100 planes on the island but the majority were bombers or patrol planes and almost all were obsolete. Despite warnings that the Japanese

Right: Japanese carrier *Hiryu* successfully maneuvers during the Battle of Midway to avoid hits from U.S. Army Air Corps Boeing B-17 bombers flying at some 20,000 ft. In the event, *Hiryu's* demise was only postponed by 24 hours, as she was sunk by U.S. Navy divebombers the following day, June 5, 1942.

were on their way, the Americans were unable to stop them, and the island and its defending airplanes were devastated. A simultaneous attack on Nagumo's carriers by ten aircraft from Midway resulted in disaster for the Americans; they accomplished nothing and lost seven of their number, while a later attack by shore-based bombers yielded similar results.

The Japanese aircraft returned to their ships and prepared for a second attack on the island when word came to Nagumo from a scout plane that an American carrier was not far away. Nagumo turned his ships north and began to rearm his planes with torpedoes with which to attack the American carrier, in one of the most famous tactical misjudgments in naval history.

Rear Admiral Raymond A. Spruance, who replaced an ailing Halsey in command of the *Enterprise* and *Hornet* task force, launched aircraft shortly after 7:00 A.M., before Nagumo knew of his presence. Some 90 minutes later, Admiral Fletcher in the *Yorktown* did the same. It took Spruance's torpedo planes a while to find the enemy so the *Yorktown*'s planes almost caught up and then, one after the other, the three torpedo squadrons, 41 planes in all, attacked Nagumo's carriers. They bored bravely in

through defending Zeros and antiaircraft fire only to achieve no hits and to lose all but four of their number. No sooner had the torpedo attack on the carriers ended when the dive-bombing attack began. Three squadrons, 50 planes total, attacked, each squadron picking one carrier and destroying *Kaga*, *Akagi*, and *Soryu*.

Admiral Nagumo, his flagship ablaze, was out of the fight, so Rear Admiral Yamaguchi in the *Hiryu* took over and his aircraft attacked *Yorktown*, putting her out of action. Admiral Fletcher, in *Yorktown*, passed control of all U.S. carrier operations to Admiral Spruance, who responded with an attack on the *Hiryu*, which destroyed that ship shortly after the *Hiryu's* pilots had made a second successful attack on the *Yorktown*.

## PARITY IS WON

During the night Yamamoto canceled the Midway operation and withdrew to Japan, but to add to the Japanese woes, two cruisers, *Mogami* and *Mikuma*, collided while attempting to avoid an American submarine. Attacks by shore-based American planes the next day did them little harm, but on June 6, aircraft from the

Below: The sinking of USS *Yorktown* during the Battle of Midway on June 4, 1942.

*Enterprise* and *Hornet* sank the *Mikuma* and inflicted so much further damage to *Mogami* that she was out of the war for two years. Meanwhile, the Japanese submarine I-168 found the *Yorktown* under tow of a minesweeper and sank both the carrier and a destroyer that was alongside.

Far to the north on June 3, pilots from the *Ryujo* and *Junyo* struggled through the fog to hit Dutch Harbor and then tried, without success, to find some American destroyers, which they knew to be nearby. The next day the carrier aircraft made another attack on Dutch Harbor and then, receiving orders from Admiral Yamamoto, sailed south to join the remainder of the Midway fleet, which shortly headed for home. Kiska and Attu were taken without opposition.

And so, while Japan's advances had not been completely halted, the Americans had, in the space of only six months and against enormous odds, fought back from the brink of total

eclipse in the Pacific to win at least parity in the Pacific. It was a splendid achievement.

## ONTO THE OFFENSIVE:
## GUADALCANAL TO THE ADMIRALTY ISLANDS

Admiral King, anxious to take advantage of the American success at Midway, persuaded the rest of the United States joint chiefs of staff that a small offensive should be undertaken in the Pacific. The objectives were a seaplane base at Tulagi in the Solomons and a newly discovered airfield being built on nearby Guadalcanal, the Japanese intention being to provide a shield for the forthcoming overland drive against Port Moresby. For the Allies, however, aircraft flying from these two bases could threaten the Allied supply routes to Australia.

MacArthur and Nimitz each felt he should command the operation, but to MacArthur's chagrin Nimitz was chosen. Under him Vice Admiral Robert L. Ghormley commanded the

Allied forces in the South Pacific, while the expedition itself was commanded by Rear Admiral Frank Jack Fletcher in the carrier *Saratoga*.

On August 7, Rear Admiral Richmond Kelly Turner's amphibious ships began landing 19,000 of Major General Alexander A. Vandegrift's Marines on Tulagi and Guadalcanal. It required a few days of tough fighting to take Tulagi, but although Guadalcanal was easier at first and the unfinished airbase was soon in the hands of the marines and renamed Henderson Field, it was a long time before the marines controlled much

more of the island than the area immediately around the airfield.

On the second day Rear Admiral Fletcher, anxious about fighter plane losses and the fuel state of his destroyers, unexpectedly announced that he was going to withdraw his carriers. While the other Allied leaders were conferring about this aboard Admiral Turner's flagship, Japanese Vice Admiral Mikawa was hastening south from Rabaul with a task force of seven cruisers (*Chokai, Aoba, Kako, Kinugasa, Furataka, Tenryu,* and *Furutaka*), and a destroyer.

Left: USS *San Juan* (CL-54), an Atlanta-class cruiser, at sea in 1942. These small cruisers were intended to work with destroyers. In effect they acted as a destroyer leader and, unusually for cruisers, were equipped with a sonar and carried depth-charges. They mounted sixteen 5 in. guns in eight twin turrets; three forward, three aft, and two in the waist. This picture shows the crew at general quarters and wearing their full antiflash gear, including the masks. Also visible are a quadruple 1.1 in. AA mount, the three after 5 in. mounts, and the depthcharges on the fantail.

In the darkness of the night of August 9, the Japanese pounced on the unsuspecting Allied cruisers near Savo Island, where they were supposed to be guarding Turner's transports and cargo ships. In little more than half an hour, Mikawa's cruisers had mortally wounded four heavy cruisers—the Australian heavy cruiser HMAS *Canberra* and the American USS *Astoria, Quincy,* and *Vincennes*—and severely damaged another, USS *Chicago.* Then, scarcely touched by the return fire, they steamed back north to Rabaul. It was a masterly operation, although somewhat marred on the return leg, when *Kako* was sunk by torpedoes from the old American submarine *S-44.*

## DESPERATE DEFENSIVE FIGHT

Turner, with most of his cruisers sunk and his air cover gone, pulled his cargo ships and transports south to safety. The marines were ashore, but more than half their weapons, food, and supplies were still in the departing ships. For more

than three months they would be hungry, sick, and involved in a desperate defensive fight to hold Henderson Field. Fortunately for the marines the Japanese underestimated their strength and persisted in sending in small-scale attacks, which the marines had little difficulty in dealing with.

From Henderson Field the Americans were able to dominate the local air—and therefore the local sea—by day, but the Japanese cruisers and destroyers, on the other hand, dominated those same waters by night. The Americans had to get reinforcements and supplies to their men on Guadalcanal by daylight, but at nightfall their ships had to leave. The Japanese had to do the same thing but in reverse; i.e., operate in darkness and leave well before dawn. The burden of the Japanese supply effort fell on Rear Admiral Tanaka and his destroyer squadron, who shepherded troop-laden transports and cargo ships through the dangerous waters and, often enough, carried the troops and cargoes themselves. Both sides raced to build up ashore and

Below: USS *Quincy* (CA-39) lies quietly at anchor on August 4, 1942. *Quincy* and her sister ships *Astoria* (CA-34) and *Vincennes* (CA-44) were sunk in the space of just a few minutes on August 9, 1942, during the cruiser engagement off Guadalcanal.

finally, on November 12, the Japanese outnumbered the Americans.

It was these reinforcement efforts, and Japanese naval bombardments of Henderson Field, that led to the fierce sea fights in Ironbottom Sound and the waters nearby. On August 24, Vice Admiral Kondo, covering a small reinforcement run by Tanaka, who had 1,300 troops embarked, clashed in the Battle of the Eastern Solomons with Rear Admiral Fletcher. Admiral Kondo had the *Shokaku* (59 aircraft) and *Zuikaku* (72), both under Vice Admiral Nagumo and, under Rear Admiral Hara, the *Ryujo* (37). Fletcher had the *Saratoga* (88) and *Enterprise* (88). Early in the afternoon the Saratoga launched 38 dive bombers and torpedo planes, which found the *Ryujo*—which Kondo had sent ahead as bait—and sank her just as she was about to launch her aircraft.

Meanwhile, Nagumo launched the squadrons from his two big carriers, which failed to attack the *Saratoga*, their intended target, but got three hits on the *Enterprise*. That

hard-working ship soon had her damage under control. Several more attacks were on their way from the American carriers but they never found Nagumo's ships and accomplished little. Then the two opponents steamed out of flying range and the fight was over. Tanaka's "Tokyo Express," as the Americans called it, did not finish its run that day.

## ACTION IN IRONBOTTOM SOUND

The Japanese navy's intention with its submarines was that they would be used in direct support of the fleet and thus target enemy warships, unlike Germany's Admiral Dönitz, whose boats were always primarily intended for use against merchant shipping. But, in this period, Japanese submarines reached the peak of their success. Thus, on August 31, I-26 torpedoed the carrier USS *Saratoga* and, for the second time, that big carrier was out of the war, this time for three months. Two weeks later the carrier USS *Wasp*, escorting a troop convoy to Guadalcanal,

Below: The American drive across the Pacific inevitably involved a whole series of amphibious landings, each of which was a major undertaking, involving thousands of Marines who had to get ashore and then be supported in a fight against fanatically loyal Japanese, determined to die virtually to the last man.

Above: The scene aboard USS *Saratoga* (CV-3) as the air group returns from the raid on Rabaul. All the aircraft in view are Douglas SBD Dauntless dive-bombers.

was sunk by the I-19, while I-15 hit the battleship USS *North Carolina* and a destroyer; the former was damaged and eventually repaired, but the latter sank.

The next big clash took place when the escorts of an American troop convoy from Noumea, New Caledonia, with 3,000 soldiers aboard and a Japanese convoy from Rabaul with 700 troops embarked, clashed in Ironbottom Sound. This occurred on the night of October 11–12 when the American escort force, under Rear Admiral Scott, met a Japanese force under Rear Admiral Goto, who was acting as convoy escort but was also intent on shelling

destroyers, ceased firing, while, almost simultaneously, Goto believed he was being shot at by another Japanese force and ordered his squadron to reverse course (he was killed almost immediately after issuing this order).

Fire quickly was resumed by the Americans and when it was all over *Furataka* and one destroyer on each side were gone, while the Japanese *Aoba* and American *Boise* were severely damaged. Bombardment plans forgotten, the surviving Japanese hastened north, while, somewhat ironically, both convoys then proceeded to unload their men and supplies without any further disturbance.

Two nights later a pair of fast battleships, *Kongo and Haruna,*[3] commanded by Vice Admiral Kurita, spent an hour and a half bombarding Henderson Field, during which they destroyed 48 U.S. airplanes and most of the defenders' aviation gasoline. The next night the heavy cruisers *Chokai* and *Kinugasa* repeated the bombardment, albeit on a smaller scale. In the morning the marines could see six Japanese transports unloading troops and supplies and sufficient fuel was found to enable the Americans to fly the short distance to the Japanese ships and sink three of them. That night the heavy cruisers *Myoko* and *Maya* shelled Henderson Field. The same day an American supply convoy was sighted by a

[3]Both were built as battlecruisers, being launched in 1912 and 1913, respectively. Both were totally rebuilt as battleships between 1927 and 1932, but they retained the relatively high speed of 26 knots.

the marines ashore. Goto's force (cruisers *Aoba, Kinugasa,* and *Furataka,* and two destroyers) was surprised off Cape Esperance when, just before midnight, Scott's cruisers *San Francisco, Boise, Salt Lake City,* and *Helena* "crossed their T" and opened fire. After a minute Scott, fearing he might be shooting into some of his own

Below: USS *Wasp* (CV-7) lies burning, September 15, 1942. At 2:44 P.M., Japanese submarine I-19 fired four torpedoes at *Wasp,* of which two hit, starting fires that spread rapidly and inexorably. At 3:27 P.M., the captain ordered his men to abandon the ship which was completed at about 4:00 P.M. Then, having ensured that nobody alive remained aboard, Captain Sherman was the last to leave. Some 200 of the crew were lost, but 1,946 were rescued by the accompanying cruisers and destroyers. She sank at 9:00 P.M.

Above: A U.S. convoy off Guadalcanal under air attack. Under the large pall of smoke are (right) the cruiser USS *San Francisco* (CA-38) and (left) a Japanese aircraft, which was hit by antiaircraft fire and then sideswiped the cruiser before crashing into the sea.

Japanese plane and it turned back, but not before Japanese aircraft from the carrier *Zuikaku* arrived and sank a destroyer.

## ANOTHER MAJOR BATTLE

It was now that Vice Admiral William F. Halsey reappeared, after several months' illness, and resumed command in the South Pacific on October 19. His arrival cheered the hard-pressed Americans, although the run of bad fortune did not end immediately, as the very next day Japanese submarine I-176 found an American task force and torpedoed the heavy cruiser USS *Chester*; the damage was so severe that she had to go to the U.S. East Coast for repairs.

On October 23 the Japanese army began a major drive to capture Henderson Field, but after three days of savage fighting they were forced to acknowledge failure. Meanwhile, Marine dive-bombers found the light cruiser *Yura* on her way to bombard Henderson Field and sank her.

Some two hundred miles to the east, a major sea battle was shaping up near the Santa Cruz Islands. One commander in chief, Admiral Yamamoto, was directing affairs from his flagship anchored at Truk, while Halsey was doing the same thing for the Americans from headquarters in Noumea. Each commander knew of

the opposing fleet's presence, but neither knew exactly where the enemy was, nor just how powerful he was. Admiral Halsey's commander at sea, Rear Admiral Kinkaid, was aboard USS *Enterprise* (83 aircraft) screened by the battleship *South Dakota*, two cruisers, and eight destroyers, with a second task force consisting of USS *Hornet* (88 aircraft), screened by four cruisers and six destroyers. Just before dawn on October 26 Kinkaid received a succinct and unambiguous order from Halsey: "Attack—Repeat—Attack."

On the other side, Yamamoto's seagoing commander was Vice Admiral Kondo with a large fleet at his disposal. Directly under Kondo were the carrier *Junyo* (55 aircraft), two battleships, five cruisers, and 14 destroyers. Kondo's main striking force, commanded by Rear Admiral Nagumo, consisted of the carriers *Shokaku* (61), *Zuikaku* (72), and *Zuiho* (24), accompanied by two battleships, five cruisers, and 15 destroyers. In addition, a dozen Japanese submarines were posted about the expected battle area, ready for either scouting or attack duties, as the opportunities arose.

Two American reconnaissance aircraft found *Zuiho*, attacked her, and inflicted two hits, temporarily putting her out of business. Meanwhile, Nagumo's three carriers had already launched a 65-plane strike and—in a bizarre encounter—these Japanese aircraft

Left: USS *Hornet* (CV-8) under air attack during the Battle of Santa Cruz Islands on October 26, 1942. She survived this attack but was sunk a month later.

Below: The battleship, USS *South Dakota* (BB-57) joined the fleet in 1942. She was fitted as a Force Flagship, with an extra level in the conning tower for the admiral and his staff.

329

Above: Admiral William Halsey, commander South Pacific Force and South Pacific Area.

Previous pages: *Argonaut* (SS-166), built as a minelayer but later converted to a transport, returns to Pearl Harbor, August 26, 1942, carrying the U.S. Marines who had carried out the raid on Makin Island.

damage control, *Smith*'s captain put his ship's bow into the high wake of the nearby battleship, *South Dakota*, which extinguished the flames. The *South Dakota* was struck by one bomb, but was also credited with shooting down 26 Japanese aircraft. In further strikes that afternoon, aircraft from *Junyo* scored more torpedo hits on *Hornet*, frustrating American efforts at salvage, and the flaming carrier had to be abandoned. Kinkaid took the remainder of his ships south, while Kondo, having detached his damaged carriers, started to pursue the Americans, but without any further success, although they did come upon and sink the abandoned wreck of the *Hornet*.

The outcome of all this was that USS

passed 73 American planes from the *Hornet* and *Enterprise* going the other way.

When they arrived, the Japanese aircraft did not see *Enterprise*, which was hidden by a rain-squall, so they concentrated on *Hornet*, which was hit time and again by torpedoes and bombs (and a couple of suicide aircraft) that left her dead in the water. At the other end, the Americans did much the same to the *Shokaku*, except that as she had not been hit by torpedoes (or suicide planes). She was badly damaged but could still raise steam.

A second Japanese air strike then found *Enterprise* and hit her with three bombs, while a torpedo plane crashed into the forecastle of the destroyer USS *Smith*, starting a major fire. In a highly ingenious and quick-thinking example of

*Enterprise* was now the only U.S. carrier left in the Pacific and even she was full of bomb holes and with the forward elevator jammed, although fortunately it was in the raised position so the flightdeck could still be used.

Meanwhile, both sides continued to send convoys to Guadalcanal laden with troops and arms, but the Japanese then planned a major operation in which another battleship bombardment of Henderson Field for the night of November 12–13 would provide the cover for Tanaka, whose eleven destroyers would escort an equal number of transports crammed with 13,500 troops and their arms and supplies. The bombardment force, under Vice Admiral Abe, and consisting of the battleships *Hiei* and

*Kirishima*, the light cruiser *Nagara*, and 14 destroyers, had just passed Savo Island at 0141 on November 13 when contact was made with an American force sent out to prevent the bombardment. The American force, under Rear Admiral Daniel J. Callaghan, consisted of a column of five cruisers and eight destroyers—first four destroyers, then the cruisers *Atlanta* (with Rear Admiral Norman Scott embarked), *San Francisco* (Callaghan's flagship), *Portland*, *Helena* and *Juneau*, and finally four more destroyers.

The Americans headed into the midst of the oncoming Japanese formation and action was joined when a Japanese destroyer's searchlight illuminated the *Atlanta*. Many Japanese ships

Left: Japanese carrier *Junyo* photographed in Japanese waters by USS *Mount McKinley* (AGC-7); September 25, 1945. The ship survived the war, despite having been twice severely damaged, and was then sent on several voyages to recover and repatriate Japanese personnel from the Pacific islands they were occupying at the time of the capitulation.

immediately concentrated on the American cruiser, first with gunfire (which killed Admiral Scott among others) then with torpedoes. She went dead in the water only to be struck by two salvoes of 8 in. guns from the *San Francisco*. Realizing her error, *San Francisco* then fired several salvoes into the *Hiei*, while *Kirishima*, in its turn, fired into *San Francisco* with its 14 in. guns, killing Admiral Callaghan and nearly everyone else on the bridge. The *Juneau* was torpedoed, while Portland, also torpedoed and circling without steering control, fired into the *Hiei* with her 8 in. gun at only two miles.

Of the American cruisers, only *Helena* came through unharmed, while of the eight U.S. destroyers, four were sunk and two damaged. On the Japanese side, two of their destroyers were sunk, while *Hiei* and one destroyer were severely damaged. The affair was very violent but short-lived—it lasted no more than 20 minutes from start to finish—and the American ships then retired southward and the Japanese

northward, but there was no bombardment of Henderson Field.

### SEVEN OUT OF ELEVEN ARE SUNK

When dawn came, the crippled ships picked on one another but soon found that saving themselves was a far more pressing matter. The *Portland* and *San Francisco* survived, but *Atlanta* was beyond help and *Juneau*, torpedoed by I-26, blew up with the loss of all but ten of her people. The Japanese battleship, *Hiei*, was attacked all day by carrier-based aircraft from the *Enterprise* and land-based aircraft from Henderson Field, and finally sank early in the evening. Despite all this, that night two Japanese heavy cruisers, *Suzuya* and *Maya*, returned to shell Henderson Field, destroying 18 aircraft.

The next morning, that of the 14th, aircraft from the *Enterprise* and Henderson Field sank one cruiser, *Kinugasa*, and damaged several others. More important than this, however, was the

Below: Two battleships of the four-strong South Dakota–class: USS *Alabama* (BB-60) (nearest camera) and USS *South Dakota* (BB-57), commissioned in August and March 1942, respectively. They are seen here in July 1943, engaged on joint exercises with units of the British Pacific Fleet.

destruction of the oncoming troop transports, which were screened by Tanaka's destroyers and Zeros from the carrier *Hiyo*. The Americans brushed aside these escorts and sank seven of the eleven transports, although the surviving four, plus four destroyers, continued to Guadalcanal, where they beached themselves, enabling some 2,000 troops to go ashore, while the destroyers raced back to safety.

On the night of November 14, Admiral Kondo personally went south, flying his flag aboard the heavy cruiser *Atago*, accompanied by *Kirishima* (battleship), *Takao* (heavy cruiser), *Nagara*, and *Sendai* (light cruisers) and nine destroyers. Their mission was to bombard Henderson Field, but as they were steaming east of Savo Island at 11:16 P.M., *Sendai* and one of the destroyers came under fire from a battleship. Not surprisingly, they made haste to leave such an unequal contest, covering their escape with smoke. A few minutes later *Nagara* and four destroyers engaged four American destroyers, sinking three and severely damaging the fourth.

The U.S. battleships that had chased off *Sendai* and her companion were, in fact, the new USS *Washington* and *South Dakota*, with Rear Admiral Willis A. Lee embarked in the former. The battleships next fired on the *Nagara* force without result, while the Japanese, in turn, fired thirty-four 24in. Long Lance torpedoes at the

Above: Japanese submarine I-8, seen here on April 12, 1939. The Japanese Navy built a number of very large submarines, such as this, fitted for aircraft operations. The hangar was incorporated into the conning tower, which accommodated the collapsible floatplane. To launch, the submarine surfaced, the aircraft was pushed onto the launching ramp (seen here between conning tower and stern), assembled, started, and then launched. The aircraft landed on floats and were recovered by a crane, disassembled, and returned to the hangar. Such scouting aircraft were used in the Pacific and Indian Oceans, but would have been impossible in the Atlantic, where the long time required on the surface would have ensured the submarine's discovery and destruction.

battleships, but also without result. At this point Kondo with *Atago*, *Takao*, *Kirishima*, and two destroyers entered the fight. A Japanese destroyer managed to illuminate *South Dakota*, enabling Kondo's ships to engage her with Long Lance torpedoes and guns; once again the torpedoes missed, but the guns did not and *South Dakota* was seriously damaged. At this point, *Washington* opened fire on *Kirishima* at a mere 8,400-yard range, and in less than seven minutes the Japanese ship, after being hit by nine 16 in. and forty 5 in. shells, was reduced to a flaming wreck. Aside from another unsuccessful torpedo attack—this time by a pair of Tanaka's destroyers that were screening the transports—the battle was over. The *Kirishima* and a damaged Japanese destroyer were scuttled, and as a chas-

tened Kondo retired to the north, his bombardment plans canceled, Lee and the U.S. ships steamed south.

At dawn the only ships that were in sight were the four Japanese transports that had just beached themselves, so U.S. Marine and Army gunners ashore, pilots from the *Enterprise* and Henderson Field, and a destroyer all combined to destroy them where they lay. The Naval Battle of Guadalcanal was over.

## TOKYO EXPRESS IN REVERSE

Thereafter no more Japanese heavy ships approached Guadalcanal, nor did any large reinforcement convoys carrying Japanese soldiers attempt to run the American gauntlet. Indeed,

Right: Diving planesmen aboard USS *Capelin* (SS-289). Young men such as these kept the U.S. submarines at sea for four years in a very aggressive campaign. The submarine force asserted increasing domination over Japanese surface warships and merchant ships, and, in particular, on the maritime supply lines upon which Japan's increasingly vulnerable empire depended.

Left: Japanese destroyer off the Philippine coast under fire from U.S. Navy aircraft. Within months of Pearl Harbor, U.S. forces were taking the war to the Japanese. Incessant and increasingly daring attacks by aircraft and submarines extracted a heavy toll on the manpower and vessels of the Japanese Navy.

Left: Maintaining the garrisons scattered over the Pacific Islands became a logistic nightmare for the Japanese, and the more isolated garrisons sometimes ran out of food altogether. One of the avoidable problems was the intense interservice rivalry between the navy and army, which led to the latter designing and building its own transport submarines; a major waste of valuable resources.

Above: Loading torpedoes aboard the large cruiser submarine USS *Nautilus* (SS-168); December 1942. U.S. Navy torpedoes suffered from major problems in the early months of the war, which resulted in many duds and a great deal of argument before the problem was identified and then solved. Note the 6 in. (152 mm) gun, one of two mounted in these boats, and very large caliber weapons by submarine standards.

Previous pages: Photograph taken through the periscope of USS *Nautilus* as its victim, Japanese destroyer *Yamakaze*, sinks off Tokyo Bay on June 25, 1942.

although the Japanese army wished to hold on to Guadalcanal, the navy no longer did, and the resulting compromise was an attempt to maintain what they had on the island while building new defenses further up the Solomons chain.

The need for maintenance meant more trips by Tanaka's Tokyo Express, but with destroyers only, which would dart in at night, push off supplies in drums for the defenders near Tassafaronga, and be gone long before dawn. The first of these efforts took place on the night of November 30, and just before midnight, Tanaka with eight destroyers was between Savo Island and Guadalcanal and steaming at 12 knots when he was surprised by a superior American force. The U.S. group consisted of the cruisers *Minneapolis*, *New Orleans*, *Pensacola*, *Honolulu*, and *Northampton*, and eight destroyers. They fired first, both with torpedoes and shells, and overwhelmed one of the Japanese destroyers. Surprised but not unprepared, Tanaka responded with his Long Lance torpe-

does and in a few minutes he had sunk the *Northampton*, blown the bows off the *Minneapolis* and *New Orleans*, and severely damaged the *Pensacola*. The Japanese then made it safely back to base after what can only be termed a good night's work on their part; not for nothing had the U.S. Navy given him the nickname "Tenacious Tanaka."

While the Japanese had deliberately chosen to do no more than hold onto their position on Guadalcanal, the Americans managed both to reinforce and relieve the exhausted defenders of Henderson Field. Then, on January 4, the Japanese decided to evacuate the island, and using the Tokyo Express in reverse itself—and totally unbeknown to the Americans—by February 7 the Japanese navy had quietly removed every Japanese soldier still alive. Apart from this very successful evacuation, the Japanese also won the last major round of the Guadalcanal campaign when on January 30 torpedo planes based on New Georgia sank the

cruiser USS *Chicago*, which had just been repaired following the damage sustained at Savo Island in August.

## SICKNESS CLAIMS MORE THAN WAR

During the summer of 1942 both sides were anxious to occupy two places on New Guinea; one was the spacious harbor of Milne Bay, at the eastern end of the island, the other, Buna, a village with its own airstrip, some 150 miles northwest of Milne Bay on the northern shore of the Papuan Peninsula. The Americans and Australians got to Milne Bay first, in June, while the Japanese were first into Buna, in July. By the time the Japanese tried to land 2,000 troops at Milne Bay on August 25, the Australians and Americans had nearly 10,000 men there to greet them, and after a couple of weeks of fierce fighting, the Japanese reembarked their surviving troops and left the place to their enemies, never to return.

Then, late in September, Australian troops halted the Japanese overland drive on Port Moresby, when the latter were just 30 miles from their destination. Anxious to get to Buna but unwilling to risk their few ships in the reef-strewn, uncharted Solomon Sea (which was, in any case, dominated by the Japanese), MacArthur's planners had to push their troops over the high mountains that had so impeded the Japanese and then down into the malarial swamps along the north coast. About half the supply and reinforcements went by air, the remainder in coastal freighters and fishing craft, which were constantly at hazard from Japanese air attack once they cleared Milne Bay. MacArthur's 30,000 men began their attack on Buna and a couple of neighboring villages on November 19; they ended it on January 22, 1943, when they finally crushed the 12,000 Japanese defenders. Allied battle casualties were 8,500, but from sickness were at least three times as many.

Above: Gato-class boat USS *Tinosa* (SS-283) left Pearl Harbor on May 29, 1945, and, after rescuing ten men from a downed B-29, went on to locate and plot minefields in the Tsushima Straits. She then sank four Japanese merchant ships and damaged a fifth before returning to Pearl Harbor, as seen here, on July 4, 1945.

During most of 1942, Japan's strong submarine force was reasonably successful in its campaign against American warships, especially in the Solomons. Towards the end of the year, however, the army became increasingly insistent that the submarines should be used to run supplies into the increasing number of isolated garrisons at Guadalcanal and elsewhere. Consequently, the submarines seldom took an effective part in the later fighting, and during 1943 they lost 23 of their number.

### UNDERWATER SUCCESSES

The American submarines, however, which had been unable to defend the Philippines early in the war, and which were seldom deployed with the rest of the fleet, ended the year with a small success north of New Guinea when in December the new boat USS *Albacore* sank the old Japanese light cruiser *Tenryu*. All told during the

year the American submarines sank two cruisers, four destroyers, and six submarines, results far better than those of the Japanese.

Of even greater significance than sinking warships was the fact that U.S. submarines spent most of their time attacking freighters, troopships, and tankers. For example, they sank 23 Japanese supply ships during the Guadalcanal campaign and a total of 140 ships of over half a million tons during the calendar year 1942, quite an achievement against an enemy who started the war with only six million tons. Even more remarkable is that this was achieved at a time when there were terrible problems with the reliability of their torpedoes, a problem that was not solved until well into 1943. Eight American submarines were lost during 1942, only three of which were to Japanese attack, while thirty-five new ones were added.

As the U.S. submarine campaign gathered momentum, Japanese merchant ships, which

*Above: U.S. submarines such as these took the war not only as far as Japan, but even penetrated the Inland Sea, which the Japanese had thought to be impregnable. The reason for this formation sailing on the surface is that they are returning home to the United States at the war's end: Flying Fish (SS-229), Spadefish (SS-411), Tinosa (SS-283), Bowfin (SS-287), and Skate (SS-305).*

naval activity was centered, and this had enormous impact on Japan's ability to withstand the American offensive there. Additionally, the submarines sank 17 destroyers and smaller escort vessels in various parts of the Pacific, as well as the escort carrier *Chuyo*.

### A MAJOR LOSS FOR THE JAPANESE

In February 1943 the Japanese became anxious to take the Australian outpost at Wau, well inland in New Guinea, but since they had insufficient troops on the island, they had to bring more from Rabaul. Thus, nearly 7,000 were embarked in eight transports and, accompanied by eight destroyers under Rear Admiral Kimura, they departed on February 28 en route to Lae, a coastal village in New Guinea.

At first, the convoy was shielded by the weather, but it was eventually found by the Americans. In attacks on March 2–3 Major General George Kenney's V U.S. Army Air Force, consisting largely of twin-engined B-25 and A-20 light bombers, sank all eight transports and half the destroyers in the Bismarck

Below: A picture taken from USS *Salt Lake City* (CA-25) with USS *Indianapolis* (CA-35) astern, as they both bombard *Kiska* in the Aleutian Islands in the summer of 1943.

had originally moved independently, had to be formed into small, four- or five-ship convoys, escorted by two or three destroyers or patrol craft. A "Grand Escort Fleet," was created early in 1943 with 40 escorts, and more than three times that number by the end of the year, although it did little to reduce the depredations of the big and very capable U.S. submarines. Meanwhile, the Americans, in contrast, were able to abandon convoys, their merchant ships being routed independently, because the threat from Japanese submarines was so small.

American submarines, sometimes acting in packs of three or four but more often singly, made over a thousand attacks during the year. They launched 4,000 torpedoes and sank 300 ships for a total of 1,800,000 tons. Since Japan built only 800,000 tons of new ships, this represented an overall loss of a million tons. Fifty-two of those ships sunk were in the south and southwest Pacific, where most of the year's

Sea. Japanese shore-based air cover was unable to cope with Kenney's low-flying bombers and his P-38 fighters, although Japanese destroyers managed to save nearly half those whose ships were sunk. The rest died in the sinkings or in the strafings they suffered from MacArthur's airplanes and patrol boats.

Though most of the forces in both fleets were sucked south into the campaign in the Solomons, each fleet also had responsibilities across the broad face of the Pacific. The Americans, resenting the Japanese occupation of two worthless islands in the Aleutians, planned to eject the invaders. Air bases were set up on other islands from which the Japanese on Kiska and Attu could be bombed, despite the almost continual foul weather; submarines patrolled through long depressing fogs; cruisers and

destroyers blockaded, and occasionally shelled, the enemy garrisons.

## DUEL AT LONG RANGE

On March 26, 1943, Rear Admiral Charles McMorris in the old light cruiser USS *Richmond*, accompanied by the heavy cruiser USS *Salt Lake City* and four destroyers, was on patrol near the Soviet Union's Komandorski Islands, when lookouts spotted masts to the north. The Americans closed to make contact and discovered that the masts belonged not only to the heavy cruisers *Nachi* and *Maya*, but also to the light cruisers *Tama* and *Abukuma*, and four destroyers that were escorting two large troop transports. The morning was spent in a long-range gunnery duel and, while McMorris's

Right: Admiral Koga Mineichi was in a staff appointment from late 1937, but after the attack on Pearl Harbor he returned to seagoing duty to take part in the attack on Hong Kong. When Admiral Yamamoto died in an air crash in April 1943, Koga took over as commander in chief Combined Fleet, but was denied any glory as he oversaw the start of Japanese withdrawals in the face of relentless United States attacks. On March 31, 1944, Koga was killed, like his predecessor, in an aircraft crash. His successor was Admiral Toyoda Soemu.

attempt to sink the transports was frustrated, so, too, was the Japanese attempt to get them to Attu, and they retired to their base in the Kuriles. This was the last time they tried to bring in reinforcements or supplies to the islands.

In May the Americans landed and retook Attu after much fighting ashore. Then in August, after a heavy naval bombardment, they landed on Kiska, but nobody was there as the garrison had been evacuated, undetected by the Americans, some three weeks earlier

The year-long Japanese sojourn in the Aleutians was poorly conceived and of minimal practical benefit, except that it led the Americans to commit large naval and air forces, together with some 100,000 ground troops to an inconsequential campaign. Tactically the Americans were the victors; strategically the Japanese were.

In April 1943 Admiral Yamamoto denuded his four operational carriers—*Zuikaku, Zuiho, Junyo,* and *Hiyo*—sending the 170-odd aircraft to join a similar number of shore-based planes of the 11th Air Fleet at Rabaul and nearby fields. From there, they made a series of heavy raids on Allied shipping, first at Guadalcanal and then at Oro Bay, Port Moresby, and Milne Bay, New Guinea. They sank few ships, shot down a few U.S. aircraft and lost few of their own. Then Yamamoto halted his offensive and sent the carrier aircraft back to their ships. Then, in a devastating blow to Japanese morale, he himself was killed on April 18 by a brilliantly conceived and conducted attack by U.S. Army Air Force P-38s on the bomber in which he was a passenger. He was succeeded as commander in chief Combined Fleet by Admiral Mineichi Koga.

Below: A small portion of the naval might of the United States. These are battleships, cruisers, destroyers, and amphibious ships at anchor in Adak harbor during the 1943 operations in the Aleutian Islands.

Previous pages: *Helena* was hit by three torpedoes at about 2:00 A.M., June 6, 1943, and sank quickly, although most of the vessel's crew were able to abandon ship in a well-organized manner. Two destroyers rescued many survivors, but were forced to leave the scene at dawn, with some 275 men still in the water. One group of 88 men reached a nearby island and were rescued on June 8. The remaining 200-odd men reached a different island some two days later, where they were given food by locals but had to hide in the jungle to avoid the Japanese. Informed of their plight, a force of eight destroyers and two destroyer transports steamed to their rescue on July 15–16. Of *Helena's* nearly 900 men, 168 had perished. Here, exhausted by their long ordeal, oil-covered survivors give details of their adventures aboard USS *Nicholas*.

## IN PURSUIT OF AIRSTRIPS

At the end of June 1943, both Halsey and MacArthur moved forward once again, the former up the Solomons to New Georgia Island, the latter into the Trobriand Islands and Nassau Bay, New Guinea. For more than half a year the two would advance similar, but not large, distances, with the aim first of taking and then, more wisely, of neutralizing the great Japanese base at Rabaul at the northeastern tip of New Britain. The general purpose of each invasion was to seize airstrips in order to deny them to the Japanese, to use them for support of future advances, and to use them for raids on Rabaul. Because Halsey's advance was the more dangerous, it was the one that the Japanese opposed with the greater force.

The assault on Munda, New Georgia, led to the night battle of Kula Gulf on July 6, the first in a series in which the reactivated Tokyo Express was challenged by American forces sent to stop it. Rear Admiral Akiyama, with seven destroyers in column, met Rear Admiral Walden Ainsworth, who had the big light cruisers USS *Honolulu*, *Helena*, and *St. Louis* and four destroyers, and the battle opened at little more than three miles' range. On the Japanese side, Akiyama was killed and his flagship sunk, and a destroyer was wrecked on a reef, while the Americans lost the *Helena*. However, the Tokyo

Express succeeded in its mission of landing the troops.

Six nights later, off Kolombangara, Ainsworth once again challenged the Tokyo Express, which on this occasion consisted of the old light cruiser *Jintsu* and five destroyers, commanded by Rear Admiral Izaki. Ainsworth had a force comprising USS *Honolulu* and *St. Louis*, the New Zealand light cruiser HMNZS

Right: Aboard Fletcher-class destroyer, USS *O'Bannon* (DD450), the chief torpedoman adjusts the settings on the quintuple 21 in. torpedo tube mounting. Note that his tubes even have their own crest.

*Leander*, and ten destroyers. The battle opened at five miles, and although the *Jintsu* and Admiral Izaki were lost, the Japanese landed the troops. On the Allied side, one destroyer was sunk and all three cruisers were severely damaged by torpedoes.

On the night of August 6–7, Commander Frederick Moosbrugger with six destroyers encountered the Tokyo Express in Vella Gulf. On this occasion, Moosbrugger used his torpedoes rather than guns and sank three of the four Japanese destroyers at no cost to his own force.

## CARRIER STRIKE IN RESPONSE

The next landing was at Vella Lavella in August. This intensified the fierce fighting that had been going on in the confined waters of the Solomons among island-based aircraft, destroyers, motor torpedo boats, troop-carrying barges, assorted small warships, and occasional submarines.

The Japanese decision to evacuate Vella Lavella led to a night action between nine Japanese and three American destroyers. During the engagement one of the American ships was sunk and the other two damaged, but the Japanese got their troops away.

On November 1, the Americans invaded the northernmost island in the Solomons, Bougainville. The Japanese defenders ashore expected the Americans to attempt to take the whole big island, but all the invaders wanted was space for an airstrip so that fighters could escort bombers over Rabaul. On the Japanese side, the army found itself frustrated, but the navy reacted quickly and Rear Admiral Omori set out from Rabaul to destroy the American transports in Empress Augusta Bay. Omori had the heavy cruisers *Myoko* and *Haguro*, the small light cruisers *Agano* and *Sendai*, and six destroyers. The advancing Japanese force was intercepted on the night of November 2 by Rear Admiral Aaron Merrill with the large light cruisers USS *Montpelier*, *Cleveland*, *Columbia*, and *Denver*, and eight destroyers. With small loss to themselves, Aaron Merrill's ships sank the old *Sendai* and a destroyer, forcing Omori to withdraw. The next morning more than 100 Japanese aircraft from Rabaul attacked Merrill's ships, but without success.

Koga, alarmed by the landing at Bougainville, sent seven heavy cruisers and some lesser vessels from Truk to Rabaul, to which Halsey's response came in a form unused for a year, a carrier strike. USS *Saratoga* and the new light carrier *Princeton* launched 97 planes on the morning of November 5 from the same waters where Merrill had just won his victory. They caught Rabaul by surprise and damaged four heavy cruisers, two light cruisers, and a pair of destroyers. Six days later the two carriers attacked Rabaul again and were followed by a

Above: A camouflaged PT-boat lies at anchor in Empress Augusta Bay on Bougainville.

Above: USS *Minneapolis* (CA36) replenishes at sea in late 1943. The elaborate sea-train could provide the U.S. fleet with virtually anything required to keep the warships at sea for protracted periods; fuel, ammunition, bombs, food, and spare parts.

strike of about 185 aircraft from the new carriers, USS *Essex, Bunker Hill*, and *Independence*. Most of the Japanese ships had already departed, but one destroyer was caught and sunk.

The Japanese retaliated, attacking the *Essex* task force with over 100 aircraft, losing a third of their number, without achieving any hits. Soon, no more big ships, naval or merchant, anchored at Rabaul until the war's end, and that place, once an advanced base from which Japanese offensives could be launched, now became a beleaguered fortress.

The Tokyo Express, however, still had a few runs to make. On the night of November 25, the Express, taking about as many soldiers out of Bougainville as it had brought in, encountered Captain Arleigh Burke's Destroyer Squadron 23 near Cape St. George, New Ireland. Each side

had five destroyers, but Burke's sank two Japanese destroyers with torpedoes and one with gunfire, without any loss to his own.

Rabaul was now under constant air attack, both from the Solomons and from New Guinea, and occasionally destroyers shelled the shore installations. Halsey, with plenty of force to employ, seized the unoccupied Green Islands, north of Bougainville in February 1944 and in March he took Emirau, north of Rabaul.

Though largely unopposed by the Japanese navy, MacArthur was also barely assisted directly by the U.S. Navy. Yet, it was under cover of Halsey's advances that MacArthur operated. In any event, by September 1943, that general had sufficient amphibious shipping to make a combined airborne, overland, and amphibious descent upon Lae at the head of the Huon Gulf.

The next month he carried out an amphibious landing to take Finschafen at the northwestern end of the Solomon Sea. In December he landed troops first at Arawe on New Britain's southern coast and then at Cape Gloucester, near that island's western tip. He was now in control of the Vitiaz and Dampier straits, which led out of the confined waters of the Solomon Sea and he could proceed westward back to the Philippines.

In January 1944 he captured Saidor and Sio, both on the New Guinea side of Vitiaz Strait. In February he made a daring attack across the Bismarck Sea into the Admiralties. His force was too small and it was touch-and-go for a while. But eventually he had those islands and there the United States soon developed the great naval base of Manus. The campaign which may properly be said to have begun in the Coral Sea in May 1942 was now finished.

### THE U.S. SUBMARINE WAR

In 1944 Japan lost four million tons of shipping, some 60 percent of it to submarine attack, rendering her increasingly unable to maintain civil life, far less wage a war. She was also losing on the ground and in the air, and in one brief battle alone, 219 out of 326 attacking aircraft were lost. By August MacArthur had reached the western end of New Guinea; Nimitz had taken the Gilberts and pushed on to Saipan and Guam. The Americans now had an airfield from which the new Boeing B-29 strategic bombers could bomb Japan and the Allies had a base

Left: The huge minelayer USS *Argonaut* (SS-166).

from which to launch the last part of their drive on Japan.

At the beginning of 1944 there were 123 American submarines in the Pacific. They had solved their torpedo problems and they had excellent radar, which was especially useful for night work on the surface. About half the time they worked in wolf-packs and in the course of the year they sank over 500 ships, totaling 2,500,000 tons. This, combined with the work of both ship- and shore-based aircraft, which sank another 1,500,000 tons, left Japan at the year's end with much less than the three million tons of shipping she needed merely to continue her civil life.

Of course, military needs took precedence over the needs of both civil life and industry. People had too little to eat. Aircraft manufacturing and shipbuilding slumped—no surprise when 1944's imports of iron ore were only one-third of those in 1941. Oil was scarce for everyone. Because of the oil shortage, the Japanese fleet moved first to Tawi Tawi, near Borneo's oil fields, and then to Lingga Roads, near the Sumatra fields. Even so, ships steamed too infrequently to keep up their training and pilots flew too seldom to gain and hold their skills.

In addition, submarines sank a substantial part of the Japanese fighting fleet. The full scoresheet would take up a great deal of space, but a

Below: A U.S. Navy submarine comes alongside in Pearl Harbor after another war patrol.

few selected examples will give the flavor of what happened.

In February USS *Skate* sank the new light cruiser *Agano* off Truk; in March USS *Sandlance* sank the old light cruiser *Tatsuta*; in April the *Bluegill* sank the *Yubari*, another old cruiser, while USS *Flasher* sank the cruiser *Oi* in July. The escort carrier *Taiyo* fell victim to USS *Rasher* in August and that same month the light cruisers *Nagara* and *Natori* were sunk by USS *Croaker* and *Hardhead*, respectively. In September the escort carrier *Unyo* was sunk by USS *Barb*. In October, USS *Ballao*, operating on the fringes of the Battle of Leyte Gulf, sank the already damaged light cruiser *Tama*, while

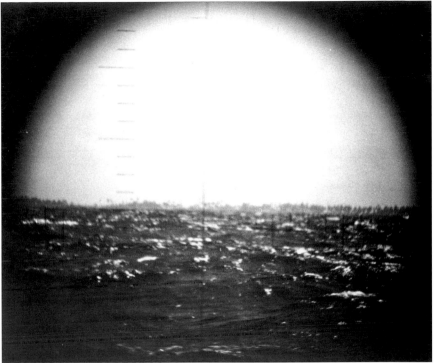

*Bream* damaged the cruiser *Aoba*, although the latter made it back to Japan.

In November USS *Archerfish*, lurking in Japan's Inland Sea, sank the world's largest aircraft carrier, the *Shinano*, just a few miles from where she was built, while the *Spadefish* sank the escort carrier *Shinyo* and USS *Sealion* the old battleship *Kongo*. The heavy cruiser *Myoko* was so badly damaged by USS *Bergall* that she never sailed again, while the *Kumano*, ambushed by a wolf-pack of four, was beached and the wreck was destroyed by air attack. In December the large carrier *Junyo* was severely damaged by USS *Sea Devil* and *Redfish*, and barely made port; that same month the *Redfish* sank the *Unryu*, another large carrier. Apart from those major warships, U.S. submarines also sank 30 destroyers during the year, USS *Harder* alone accounting for four of them (although she did not long survive the last one). Moreover, American submarines were also able to play a major part in the great naval battles of that year.

These successes cost the Americans 19 submarines, including six lost through accidents. By the year's end they had 156 submarines in the Pacific. In contrast, the Japanese, who lost 57 submarines that year, accomplished nothing.

Meanwhile, British submarines working out of Ceylon and, later, out of Fremantle, Australia, and helped by aircraft, closed Japan's supply route through the Malacca Strait to her forces in Burma. One submarine, HMS *Tally Ho*, sank

Above: A submariner's periscope view of the island of Kwajalein.

the light cruiser *Kuma*, and another damaged the light cruiser *Kitakami*.

## NIMITZ THRUSTS STRAIGHT ON

General MacArthur had tried to get his New Guinea campaign, aimed at returning to the Philippines, approved as the main American line of advance. But the combined chiefs of staff, while not disapproving his campaign, also approved Admiral Chester Nimitz's proposal to thrust directly across the Central Pacific with his now powerful marine divisions and amphibious force, protected by his new carriers.

Nimitz opened in November 1943 with an amphibious assault on the Gilbert Islands. Marines landed at Tarawa, soldiers at Makin Island, on November 20. Makin was not difficult but Tarawa was. The Japanese defenders were numerous, tough and determined, and their fortifications were excellent To compound the marines' difficulties, an unexpectedly low tide forced them to wade 600 yards between a coral reef and the beach through heavy defensive fire. The preparatory bombing and naval gunfire support from many ships, most notably the old battleships, was heavy and very impressive— from a distance. But the gunners and aviators tended to believe that the spectacular visual effect of their fire was matched by the physical results on the ground and this by no means always so. As a result, the marines had to fight a bloody battle before overcoming their foe.

The Americans learned their lessons from Tarawa and applied them in the Marshall Islands, their next objective, which were invaded on January 31, 1944. The main targets, undefended Majuro and heavily defended Kwajalein, quickly passed into the competent hands of the marines. On February 22 the marines were landed 300 miles farther west, at Eniwetok Atoll, after a heavy bombardment, and they soon won control.

## TWO DAYS TO SINK 200,000 TONS

The seizure of these atolls provided the Americans with anchorages, airstrips, and staging areas, which served as springboards for further advances, while simultaneously denying these same assets to Japan. While the amphibious force, marines, and soldiers were occupied with the issue at Eniwetok, nine carriers under Rear Admiral Marc Mitscher attacked the Japanese naval base at Truk in the Carolines, some 700 miles from both Eniwetok and

Right: Amphibious landings were a joint Navy/Marine Corps event. Here the landing on Tarawa is watched on November 20, 1943, by Major General Julian C. Smith, USMC, Commanding General 2nd Marine Division (foreground with binoculars) and Rear Admiral Harry W. Hill, U.S. Navy, Commander Amphibious Group Two, Fifth Amphibious Force (helmet with two stars).

Rabaul. Admiral Koga had withdrawn his fleet, but in two days and a night, Mitscher's aviators sank 200,000 tons of shipping and destroyed 275 aircraft. A similar raid on Palau at the end of March led to the sinking of another 130,000 tons of shipping.

All these operations in the Central Pacific were conducted by the Fifth Fleet under Vice Admiral Raymond Spruance. Later, when Admiral William Halsey took his turn at command, the force would be called the Third Fleet, but the ships and the men were the same, no matter what the organizational label. "MacArthur's Navy," as the Seventh Fleet under Vice Admiral Thomas Kinkaid was sometimes known, consisted of different ships and men.

Now, while Spruance's men paused, Kinkaid's moved ahead. After MacArthur's aviators, under Major General George Kenney, had gained control of the air, on April 22 Kinkaid's amphibious sailors landed troops at Hollandia, New Guinea, 200 miles to the westward of the Japanese army's now bypassed fortress at Wewak. On May 17 MacArthur's men invaded Wake and then, in order to get a site suitable for a heavy bomber base, they landed on Biak Island, 350 miles beyond Hollandia, on May 27.

Admiral Koga had recently been killed in an airplane crash and his successor, Admiral Toyoda, responded to the Biak invasion with an attempt to reinforce that island with troops from the Philippines. Toyoda was frustrated in two attempts, first by a false report of a U.S. carrier and then by the presence of a superior Allied cruiser and destroyer force, so he decided to send a force built around the huge battleships *Yamato* and *Musashi*. But before those ships could get to Biak, Spruance began his attack on Saipan and in order to meet the greater threat from the Central Pacific, Toyoda was forced to call off the Biak operation, a firm indication of how far the strategic initiative had slipped out of Japanese hands.

In July MacArthur, still looking for airfield sites, landed at the island of Noemfoor and then, on July 30, he occupied Sansapor at the western end of New Guinea. It had taken him a year and a half to get out of the Solomon Sea; but then he

Above: USS *Maryland* (BB-46) firing her forward 16 in./45 guns. *Maryland* was completed in 1920 and underwent major updating in the 1930s, but by the middle of the war she was a bit old and slow for modern fleet work. But, like other elderly battleships, she found a major role in fire support for amphibious landings, where her 16 in. guns could make a considerable difference in the land battle.

had reached the other end of New Guinea in only half a year more.

## USS ENGLAND SINKS SIX SUBMARINES

The Japanese planners knew that an attack by Nimitz's forces was imminent and, having assessed that it would be aimed at Palau, in May they placed a strong barrier of submarines north of the Admiralty Islands. In addition, in order to make maximum use of their multitude of island air bases, by early June they had deployed 540 aircraft into those islands, with the majority of them to the south.

When news reached Toyoda of Spruance's preliminary bombardment of Saipan he sent his main force, the First Mobile Fleet under Vice Admiral Ozawa, to unite with the island-based aircraft to destroy the U.S. Pacific Fleet. Ozawa's command, most of it at Tawi Tawi, consisted of five fleet carriers and four light carriers, with 430 planes on their decks, as well as an assortment of battleships, cruisers, and destroyers. He set sail on June 13, met the ships from the aborted Biak expedition on the 16th well to the east of the Philippines, and continued northeast. Unbeknown to him, he had been sighted and reported several times by well-placed American submarines and his opponents were expecting him.

That was not all the bad news for Japan. The Americans had found most of the Japanese barrier submarines as well as a number of those on supply missions to nearly forgotten garrisons, and of the 25 submarines at sea had sunk ten. Six of these fell victim, one after the other, to one small ship, the destroyer escort USS England, in one of the most remarkable antisubmarine operations by a single ship in the entire war. Seven more were sunk by other ships within the next few days and it was clear that the Japanese naval command had simply thrown these submarines away, because this so called "barrier" accomplished absolutely nothing for Japan. At the same time, Spruance's fast carriers under Vice Admiral Mitscher (Task Force 58) were busy destroying the Japanese aircraft on their island bases. In consequence, Ozawa was to be left largely on his own.

On June 15 Spruance's amphibious commander, Vice Admiral Richmond Turner, began to land marines and soldiers on Saipan, supported by seven battleships and seven escort car-

riers, as well as many cruisers and destroyers to support the men going ashore.

Spruance considered the task of Mitscher's nine carriers and six light carriers (with 891 aircraft embarked) to be primarily the protection of Turner's transports, so he kept his carrier admiral under tight control. Ozawa's pilots, hastily trained to replace the great losses, were inexperienced, while Mitscher's were largely veterans. So, while Mitscher had the advantages of numbers and experience, but was tied to the transports, Ozawa had the advantages of the offensive, of having a choice of objectives, and of having longer-ranged planes, enabling him to find and strike his enemy before the latter even knew where he was. And he had the advantage of the wind, which blew from the east, a significant factor considering that while Mitscher's carriers had to turn around in order to launch or recover their aircraft, Ozawa's simply kept going, for east was where they were heading.

## JAPAN LOSES 219 AIRCRAFT OUT OF 326

On June 19 Ozawa launched his strikes, four in all, against the American carriers, which still had failed to find him, but their crews did see his planes coming and were ready for them. As a result, the defenses, mainly Hellcat fighters, but

Left: Battleship USS *Iowa* (BB-61) uses her secondary armament of twenty 5 in. guns to bombard the island of Saipan, July 1944.

Far left above: Two Yamato-class battleships were commissioned; *Yamato* (1941) and *Musashi* (1942). Displacing 69,990 tons (full load) and armed with nine 18 in., they were the largest battleships ever built. They were also total failures, whose brief careers were ended by U.S. Navy aircraft using bombs and torpedoes; *Musashi* on October 24, 1944; and *Yamato* on May 7, 1945.

Far left below: The destroyer-escort, USS *England* (DE-635) was tiny compared to *Yamato*, but her achievements were far greater. While on patrol in the Pacific, May 19–26, 1944, *England* sank Japanese submarines *I*-16, RO-106, RO-104, RO-116, and RO-108, and then joined other DEs in sinking RO-105. This success was helped by the hidebound attitude of Japanese commanders, but it was a very impressive feat, unparalleled in any other navy.

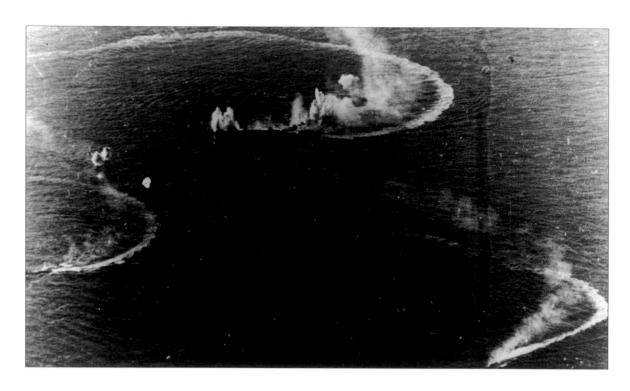

supported by the fleet's antiaircraft guns, shot down 42 out of 69 in the first raid, 97 out of 128 in the second raid, 7 out of 47 in the third, and 73 out of 82 in the fourth. In return, the Japanese achieved little, their only success—and a very minor one at that—was to obtain a hit of no consequence on the battleship *South Dakota*. While Mitscher's fighters were defending the task force, his bombers were again attacking the Japanese island air bases, destroying about 50 more aircraft, so Ozawa could get no use out of them. All this activity cost the United States just 29 aircraft.

Meanwhile, Ozawa's fleet ran right into the submarine USS *Albacore*, which torpedoed and sank his flagship, the large carrier *Taiho*. Sixty miles further, the Japanese fleet encountered another submarine, USS *Cavalla*, that torpedoed and sank the carrier *Shokaku*. Both U.S. submarines escaped unharmed.

Despite reports from the submarines, the American carriers did not find Ozawa's remaining ships until mid-afternoon of the next day, by which time they were a considerable distance away. Mitscher, knowing that his planes were going too far and would come back in the dark, launched anyway, dispatching some 216 planes. They sank the large carrier *Hiyo* and a couple of oilers, and damaged the carriers *Zuikaku* and *Chiyoda*. Ozawa was now down to 35 planes on his few surviving flightdecks and having suffered a major defeat he headed for Okinawa.

Meanwhile, Mitscher turned on all his ships'

lights to help his pilots find their way home and most of them did, although not necessarily to the right ship. Even so, about 80 planes were either forced to ditch or crashed on deck, but almost all of the pilots and crews were saved. So ended the battle.

With the sea battle over, full attention was paid to Saipan, where fighting lasted well into July. Among the thousands of Japanese to die there was Vice Admiral Nagumo, Ozawa's predecessor in command of the carrier force, who had been sent to an inconsequential post with headquarters on that island.

## A BASE FOR MAINLAND RAIDS

Guam and Tinian were invaded almost simultaneously, on July 21 and July 24 and, while Tinian fell quickly, the recovery of Guam was tougher but in three weeks that island was safely back in American hands. As soon as possible Admiral Nimitz moved his headquarters there from Pearl Harbor.

Far beyond Singapore, in the Indian Ocean, peace reigned. Neither Japan nor Great Britain, because of her Atlantic and European campaigns, could find the ships with which to make war effectively, although there were frequent skirmishes, particularly involving German U-boats and Japanese submarines. In April and May 1944, the American carrier USS *Saratoga* spent a brief period in the Indian Ocean. During this time the USS *Saratoga* combined with the

Left: The mighty 14in/50 guns of battleship USS New Mexico (BB-40) bombard Japanese positions on Guam, as part of the pre-invasion fireplan; July 14-20, 1944.

British HMS *Illustrious* to attack oil targets at Sabang and Soerabaya in the Dutch East Indies. In July the Royal Navy's *Illustrious* and *Victorious* carried out a similar mission at Sabang, while gunnery ships, most notably the new French battleship *Richelieu*, shelled targets that were on land.

All this offensive activity on the part of the Allies led, in August 1944, to the establishment of a base from which to launch the final part of the drive to the Japanese mainland. The taking of Saipan and Guam in the Marianas put the B-29 bombers within range of Japan and the raids on the mainland could begin in earnest.

Left: Nothing caused Allied crews greater horror than the introduction of Japanese suicide tactics. Here, a Japanese pilot makes his final dive on USS *Sangamon* (CVE-26), but, while some such attacks inflicted immense damage, most missed, as, astonishingly did this, the aircraft hitting the sea some 25 ft. from the carriers hull.

### RETURN ENGAGEMENT:
### THE PHILIPPINES AND LEYTE GULF

The Philippines, MacArthur's ultimate goal, were the next target, but first a number of preliminary air strikes and landings had to be made. Admiral Halsey had relieved Spruance and the fleet was now called the Third Fleet, while Mitscher's carriers were now designated Task Force 38. In September Halsey struck at the Philippines, destroying 200 Japanese planes at a cost of only eight of his own. He saw that it

would be possibly drop any preliminary operations and land directly at Leyte in the Central Philippines.

President Roosevelt, Prime Minister Churchill, and the combined chiefs of staff, meeting in Quebec, concurred, as did Nimitz and MacArthur. Leyte would be invaded in mid-October.

In the meantime, and without difficulty, MacArthur took Morotai, a small island south of the Philippines, wanted for an airstrip site, while Nimitz's marines and soldiers landed at

Right: Landing craft were originally designed to land men, vehicles, and equipment, but they also proved to be very useful weapons platforms. This craft is launching rockets in the prelanding bombardment of Peleliu; September 15, 1944.

Left: Landing Ship Tanks (LSTs) were ocean-going vessels. Here, LSTs operated by the U.S. Coast Guard are beached amid the surf on the island of Leyte and the troops have stripped down in order to fill sandbags to construct a causeway to speed up the unloading.

Peleliu and Angaur in the Palau Islands east of the Philippines. This was a difficult proposition and took a while. More usefully, Ulithi, an undefended atoll in the Northern Carolines, was seized and its lagoon immediately put to use by the fleet. Halsey sailed from there in early October and struck Japanese air bases successively on Okinawa, Luzon, and Formosa (now Taiwan), destroying some 350 Japanese planes in the process at a cost to his force of 89 planes down and no ships sunk. Two cruisers were damaged by Japanese aerial torpedoes, and offered to Toyoda as bait. The latter sent aircraft, including his partly trained carrier air groups, but no ships, and the crippled cruisers made it to safety.

MacArthur made his dramatic return to the Philippines on October 20 and by the end of that day more than 60,000 American troops were ashore on Leyte. The Japanese naval response was powerful and consisted of four separate squadrons, each under a vice admiral. Vice Admiral Ozawa was in nominal command but in practice each of the commanders ran his force with little reference to the others. The Japanese carriers were in home waters, while the battleships and cruisers were in Southeast Asian waters. American seizure of the Philippines threatened not only to perpetuate the split, which was both operationally and tactically unsound, but also to deny oil to the ships in the north and ammunition and supplies to those in the south.

## OZAWA'S DECOY CARRIERS

Ozawa had four carriers, but they had only 116 aircraft between them, manned by inexperienced aviators. It was, therefore, planned that his force would serve as a decoy to draw off the American carriers, while the unmolested battleships and cruisers rushed in to destroy MacArthur's transports in Leyte Gulf. In the event, the Japanese were too slow and most of the transports had already disembarked their troops, discharged their cargo, and departed before the Japanese could bring off their attack.

In addition to his carriers, Ozawa had two

Above: Amphibious craft approach the beach in the invasion of Leyte. U.S. forces became extremely well-practiced in such large-scale landings, which were masterpieces of control and coordination.

old battleships, three light cruisers, and nine destroyers, which departed the Inland Sea on the evening of the 20th. Two days later, two groups sailed from Brunei Bay in Borneo: Kurita, with five battleships, ten heavy cruisers, two light cruisers, and 15 destroyers; and Nishimura, two old battleships, a heavy cruiser, and four destroyers. Meanwhile, Shima was coming down from the Ryukyus with two heavy cruisers, a light cruiser, and four destroyers. In all, the Japanese force totaled 64 ships, supported by some 300 aircraft, comprising those with Ozawa's carriers, plus the land-based aircraft on Luzon and Formosa.

Ozawa came down northeast of the Philippines, making himself as conspicuous as possible, while the others approached through the South China Sea. Nishimura, with Shima in his wake, sailed through the Sulu Sea towards Surigao Strait, the southern entrance to Leyte Gulf, and Kurita sailed west of Palawan, en route to San Bernardino Strait, whence he could plunge south outside Samar and then into Leyte Gulf.

U.S. submarines made four separate sighting reports on Ozawa's progress and two on Shima's, but they also took direct action. Thus, while Kurita was west of Palawan on October

23, USS *Dace* sank his flagship, the heavy cruiser *Atago*, and damaged a sister, the *Takao*. USS *Darter* sank another sister, the *Maya*, though the submarine itself was wrecked on a reef shortly afterwards and *Dace* rescued her people. Overall, however, these submarines gave the fleet commanders a very good idea of what was approaching.

Vice Admiral Thomas Kinkaid, commanding the Seventh Fleet, had hundreds of amphibious ships needed to land MacArthur's army, and to provide it with supplies. He also had the scores of warships necessary to escort these lumbering transports, and then to provide the troops with gunfire and close air support, which amounted to six elderly battleships, as well as escort carriers, heavy and light cruisers, destroyers and destroyer escorts.

### NO FIGHTER COVER FOR KURITA

Admiral Halsey, commanding the Third Fleet, was responsible for protecting the invasion force from naval attack and for destroying as much of the enemy fleet as possible. To achieve this, he had eight carriers and eight light carriers, with about 800 aircraft between them, as well as six battleships and a substantial number of cruisers and destroyers. His ships were in four task groups, one under Vice Admiral John McCain, and the others under Rear Admirals Frederick Sherman, Gerald Bogan, and Ralph Davison. All had worked hard and McCain's group, which included three carriers and two light carriers, was on its way back to Ulithi for rest, repair, and replenishment. The other task groups were deployed east of Luzon and Samar, Sherman in the north, Davison in the south, Bogan in between.

On the morning of October 24, Japanese planes from Luzon attacked Sherman's group. Most of the planes were shot down but one hit the light carrier, USS *Princeton*, which was so badly damaged that she eventually exploded, causing many casualties, including hundreds aboard the cruiser USS *Birmingham*, which was about to take *Princeton* in tow. A destroyer was also damaged. Ozawa, too, launched a strike on Sherman's ships, but lost most of his planes without scoring any hits.

Meanwhile, the carrier, USS *Enterprise* of Davison's southern group found and attacked Nishimura's force, without much result, while 42 aircraft from USS *Intrepid* and *Cabot* of Bogan's group made the first of the day's attacks on Kurita in the Sibuyan Sea, between Mindoro and Luzon. The latter had hoped for fighter cover from fields in the Philippines but it never materialized. *Intrepid* then made a second

Left: At 9:40 A.M., October 10, 1944, escort carrier USS *Princeton* (CVL-23) was hit by a Japanese 550 lb. (250-kg) bomb. The resulting fire was almost brought under control with help from cruisers USS *Birmingham* (CL62) and *Reno* (CL-96). But, at 3:23 P.M., the magazine became so hot that bombs exploded, blowing off the stern and killing hundreds of men.

attack, with 35 planes. In the afternoon the USS *Lexington* and *Essex* of Sherman's force attacked with 68 planes, followed by a smaller attack later by those same two ships, and then one each by the *Enterprise* and *Franklin* of Davison's group, and by *Intrepid* and *Cabot* from Bogan's. As a result of all these continuous and determined efforts the huge battleship *Musashi* was sunk, the heavy cruiser *Myoko* was so damaged she had to be sent back to

Left: The cruiser USS *Birmingham* (CL-62) approaches the burning carrier USS *Princeton* (CVL-23) to render assistance. Moments after this picture was taken the carrier exploded, causing great loss of life on board both ships. *Princeton* was then abandoned and finished off by U.S. torpedoes.

Singapore, and a number of other ships were hit. Most importantly, Kurita was forced to turn back to a westerly course.

## HALSEY COMMITS ALL HIS SHIPS

At just this time Ozawa's decoy carriers were sighted and they were what Halsey had been waiting for, so he ordered all three task groups, plus McCain's, which had not yet reached Ulithi, to head north. Their orders were to strike as soon as possible the next morning and nothing was left behind to guard San Bernardino Strait. But, unbeknown to Halsey, when Kurita found that there were no more air attacks, he turned eastward once more, heading for the strait. Night scouts from the *Independence* provided some warning of this, but the reports were discounted by Halsey and Kurita transited the San Bernardino Strait at midnight, without a single American submarine or aircraft to notice.

Meanwhile, Nishimura was pushing up Surigao Strait and 39 motor torpedo boats in

groups of three successively first reported his progress and then attacked him, but scored no hits. Nishimura was in column, with four destroyers, the battleships *Yamashiro* (flagship) and *Fuso*, and heavy cruiser *Mogami*. At 3:00 A.M. it was moonless, dark, and calm, when out of the darkness came five U.S. destroyers that launched a devastating torpedo attack. Hit amidships, *Fuso* broke in two, a destroyer was sunk, and *Yamashiro* and two other destroyers damaged. Six more U.S. destroyers then attacked, hit the *Yamashiro* again, and finished off one of the crippled destroyers. Despite its damage, *Yamashiro*, accompanied by *Mogami*, and one last destroyer plodded on. Ahead of them were six old American battleships, eight cruisers, and nine destroyers, all under Vice Admiral Jesse Oldendorf, who was in command of U.S. forces in the strait that night. Oldendorf's ships were armed mainly with shells suitable for support of troops ashore, not for engaging armored ships, but the Japanese had only two armored ships,

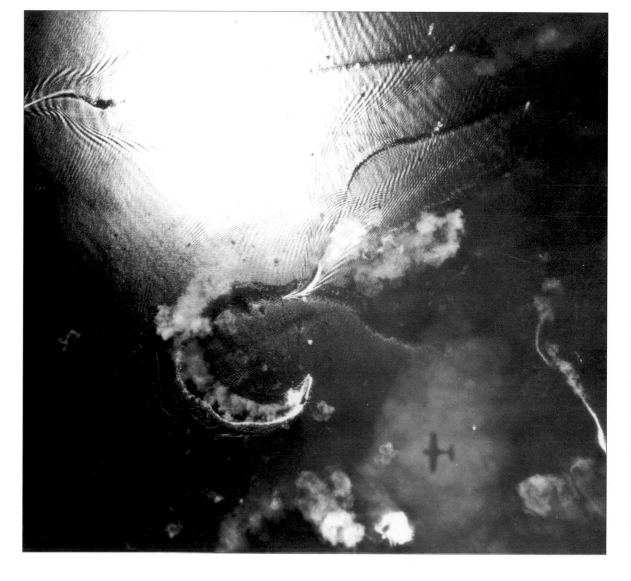

Right: Japanese ships desperately twist and turn to evade U.S. air attacks during the battle of Leyte Gulf. (Note the shadow of the photographer's aircraft in the cloud below.)

one of them severely damaged, when the U.S. ships opened fire on them at 3:51 A.M. The *Yamashiro* was soon blazing from end to end and *Mogami* badly damaged when the U.S. destroyers launched their torpedoes, as a result of which *Yamashiro* went down.

Admiral Shima, 60 miles astern of Nishimura, encountered the motor torpedo boats and his light cruiser, the old *Abukuma*, was badly damaged by one of their torpedoes. He sailed on, saw the gunfire and blazing hulks ahead and, after launching torpedoes at long range, retired. One of his cruisers, the *Nachi*, collided with the flaming *Mogami* but was little damaged. Indeed, his ships suffered no further damage as they made their way to safety, but the crippled *Abukuma* was found and sunk the next day by Army B-24 bombers.

## CARRIERS HIDE IN THE RAIN

Oldendorf now sent his cruisers down the strait, where they finished off a destroyer and hit the *Mogami* yet again, before being recalled. The battered Japanese cruiser was then attacked by planes from Rear Admiral Sprague's escort carriers, and the exhausted crew was then taken off by other ships and *Mogami* allowed to sink.

As the sun rose on October 25 six American escort carriers, screened by three destroyers and four destroyer escorts, were steering north, fifty miles east of Samar. They were the northernmost of three similar task groups intended to support troops and protect amphibious ships from air and submarine attack. Commanding these ships was Rear Admiral Sprague in USS *Fanshaw Bay*, the others being USS *Saint Lo, White Plains, Kalinin Bay, Kitkun Bay,* and *Gambier Bay*. These U.S. escort carriers had barely half the speed of a fleet carrier and carried only about a third the number of airplanes, and some of those were in the air when Takeo Kurita's force appeared dead ahead.

Sprague immediately turned eastward into wind to launch his aircraft, and ordered his ships to make as much speed as they could and to make smoke to hide themselves; they also hid in every patch of rain they could find. While their aircraft were roaring off the decks, armed with whatever was available, the escorts—the destroyers *Hoel, Heerman,* and *Johnston,* and the destroyer escorts *Dennis, John C. Butler, Raymond,* and *Samuel B. Robert*—surged ahead to attack the enemy.

Kurita, in the huge battleship *Yamato*, ordered a general attack. His ships, the battleships *Nagato, Kongo,* and *Haruna*, eight cruisers, and eleven destroyers, forged ahead, believing they were attacking one of Halsey's task groups of big carriers and cruisers. They reached past Sprague and forced him to run south, away from the wind. Splashes from their huge shells towered over the small carriers, and occasionally a shell bit deep into a target.

Despite their total superiority of force, the Japanese were taken aback by the fierce attack of Sprague's pilots, who used bombs, torpedoes, rockets, and machine guns, and when their

Above: Carrier Division 25 under surface attack during the Second Battle of the Philippine Sea. Two destroyer escorts and carrier USS *Gambier Bay* (CVE-73) lay a smoke screen.

Below: Japanese carrier *Zuiho*, photographed from a U.S. Navy plane during the Battle off Cape Engano; October 25, 1944. Shortly afterward the carrier was hit many times and sank.

Previous pages: Kamikaze hits USS *Suwanee* (CVE-27) during the Battle of Leyte Gulf on October 25, 1944. The aircraft impacted the flightdeck near the bridge island, opening a gash in the deck; damage was increased when the aircraft's bomb exploded. Within two hours *Suwanee* was operating her aircraft, only to be hit again the following day, but this, too, was overcome. The gallant carrier then returned to the United States for repairs under its own steam.

weapons were gone made dry runs. They were also confused by the charge of the escorting destroyers, which launched torpedoes in profusion and fired their guns at anything visible.

Given their power, it was scarcely surprising that the Japanese sank the carrier, *Gambier Bay*, the destroyers *Johnston* and *Hoel*, and the destroyer escort *Samuel B. Roberts*. But, astonishingly, the Japanese ships failed to close their targets, and then help came for Sprague's beleaguered ships from aircraft of the other two escort carrier groups.

## WHERE ARE THE BATTLESHIPS?

After nearly three hours of this, Kurita suddenly reversed course and, eventually, headed back to San Bernardino Strait, having paid a high price for this somewhat timorous performance, and having lost the heavy cruisers *Choka*, *Chikuma*, and *Suzuya*, while the *Kumano* was damaged. However, the battle did not end when the opposing sides lost sight of each other and American carrier-based planes continued to attack Kurita's ships.

Then Japanese shore-based planes arrived on the scene to attack the American ships, and now the Japanese introduced the most fearsome weapon of the naval war—the suicide plane, or kamikaze. One destroyed the *Saint Lo* and others damaged the *Kalinin Bay* and *Kitkun Bay*. The southern group of escort carriers was also hit by kamikazes, with severe damage to the *Suwanee* and *Santee*. The latter was also torpedoed by a lurking submarine, the I-56, but survived.

At this moment Halsey, racing north, was nearing Ozawa off Cape Engaño, the northeastern point of Luzon. Night search planes had kept track of the Japanese, who were also steering north, and at dawn Halsey's ten carriers launched 180 aircraft. The first attack sank the light carrier *Chitose* and a destroyer, and the second damaged the light carrier *Chiyoda* and the old light cruiser *Tama*. By this time Halsey was getting calls for help from Sprague and Kinkaid, but he pressed on. He did, however, send McCain's five carriers, which were still far to the southeast, to Kinkaid's assistance. Ninety-eight of McCain's pilots, launched from 340 miles—

Right: Battleship USS *New Jersey* (BB-62) and carrier USS *Hancock* (CVB-19) ride out a typhoon off the Philippines on December 18–19, 1944. *New Jersey* was the second of four Iowa-class to be completed, the finest battleships of the war.

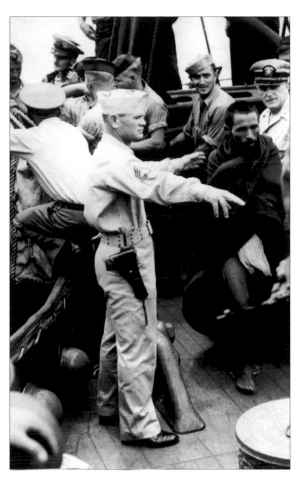

too far away—attacked Kurita's ships, which by then were retiring, but with their light bomb loads they did little damage and a second strike by 53 planes did no more.

Admiral Nimitz, who was at Pearl Harbor reading the message traffic, then asked Halsey where were the fast battleships that everyone had assumed to be guarding San Bernardino Strait. Halsey, with Ozawa's ships only 42 miles distant, turned his six battleships around and headed south with them, along with Bogan's three carriers, but by the time they got to San Bernardino Strait, it was too late—Kurita's force had passed through.

Admiral Marc A. Mitscher, left behind with seven carriers, continued north. Marc Mitscher launched 160 planes, which sank the big carrier, *Zuikaku*, while another strike finished the smaller *Zuiho*.

After a final strike accomplished nothing, Admiral Mitscher sent some cruisers ahead, which sank the damaged *Chiyoda* and a destroyer, while *Tama* later fell victim to a U.S. submarine. The remainder of Admiral Ozawa's depleted force reached home.

Left: It was not often that Japanese became prisoners, preferring instead to commit suicide, but this man has been captured and is on his way to be interrogated aboard USS *New Jersey* (BB-62) on October 24, 1944.

Left: USS *Kitkun Bay* (CVE-71), a Casablanca-class escort carrier, prepares to launch Avengers during the Battle of Leyte Gulf.

Above: One of the duties pulled by submarines that continued until the end of the war was rescuing downed U.S. airmen. USS *Tang* (SS-306) picked up a total of 22 downed fliers off Truk, including the three seen here, on its second patrol in April 1944 .

## KAMIKAZES—ALL THAT IS LEFT

The disasters for the Japanese fleet showed no sign of letting up. The next morning, October 26, Kurita's ships, now back in the Sibuyan Sea, were still barely within range of Bogan's and McCain's aircraft, but the latter hit hard and sank the light cruiser *Noshiro* and a destroyer. Next, a Japanese transport group, carrying 2,000 troops to Ormoc Bay on Leyte's west coast, was hit by aircraft from the escort carriers, which sank the old light cruiser *Kinu* and another destroyer. The only reply came from the Japanese kamikazes, which hit the *Suwanee* again, but she refused to be sunk.

At last, the Battle for Leyte Gulf was over, with the Americans still at sea and ready for more, while the Japanese were beaten and fleeing. The cost to the Americans in ships sunk was seven—a light carrier, two escort carriers, a submarine, two destroyers, and a destroyer escort.

But the Japanese Navy had lost far more, a total of 26 ships—two large and two light carriers, three battleships, six heavy and four light cruisers, and nine destroyers. Never again would a Japanese aircraft carrier go to sea on a combat mission, and only once more would a battleship do so. The once-formidable Japanese force of cruisers and destroyers were reduced to a remnant—only four of the original 18 heavy cruisers, for example, were still afloat and battle worthy. The Japanese submarines long had been beaten. Only the kamikazes, based ashore where their lack of flying skill would not be an insuperable flaw, remained to the once mighty Imperial Japanese Navy.

Because they had a hard time building airfields, General Kenney's shore-based aviators could not take over responsibility for gaining control of the Philippine air, nor could they support the troops and supply ships, so Halsey's and Kinkaid's carrier pilots had to fulfill those missions. This they were not reluctant to do and in early November Halsey attacked Luzon's airfields and harbors, sank the heavy cruiser *Nachi* in Manila Bay, and destroyed over 400 aircraft.

Meanwhile the Japanese resurrected the Tokyo Express to bring troops to Ormoc Bay, and U.S. aircraft, motor torpedo boats, small gunboats, and destroyers engaged in the effort to stop this traffic. Halsey's carriers destroyed one convoy, which consisted of five transports and four destroyers, which were carrying a total of 10,000 troops between them. Another strike sank the light cruiser *Kiso* and five destroyers. Many Japanese aircraft were destroyed, but the carriers *Intrepid, Cabot, Lexington, Franklin*, and *Belleau Wood* had all been hit by kamikazes and needed repair.

## JAPANESE CAN DO NOTHING

On December 7, Kinkaid landed troops at Ormoc Bay and eight days later more troops invaded the island of Mindoro in order to seize airfields to support the next landing, at Lingayen Gulf. This took place on January 9, 1945, and placed MacArthur's army firmly on the road to Manila Bay. It was a grim battle and by January 13, when all the kamikazes had been used up, no fewer than 44 Allied ships had been hit, although only two, including the escort carrier USS *Ommaney Bay*, had been lost, while the Australian heavy cruiser, HMAS *Australia* was hit five times, suffering 116 casualties, but surviving. The rest of the Philippines, and parts of Borneo, were invaded and liberated without further serious loss to the U.S. Navy.

In December a typhoon sank three of Halsey's destroyers and destroyed 146 aircraft. Then Task Force 38, now under Vice Admiral McCain, entered the South China Sea on January 10, with its carriers' flightdecks almost totally filled with fighter aircraft. Having attacked Formosa, the task force, with its oilers, spent ten days in the South China Sea, surrounded by Japanese-occupied territories, but, without losing a single ship of its own, it sank 300,000 tons of Japan's shipping and destroyed 600 Japanese aircraft. The end was clearly in sight for Japan.

## THE DRIVE FOR VICTORY:
## RANGOON TO HIROSHIMA

In February 1945 the Japanese government began efforts to end the war, working through the Soviet Union, which was still neutral as regards the Pacific war. But the Japanese authorities did not know how to end the conflict and the Soviets did little to help. So the war dragged on, reaching its peak of death and destruction with Japanese kamikaze attacks on U.S. and Allied ships, and with American fire raids on Japanese cities.

By early 1945 the American submarines had sunk most of Japan's deep-water merchant ships . In the remaining months the submarines passed on an increasing part of their work to shore- and carrier-based aircraft, which could strike at shipping in harbors and shallow waters that submarines could not reach. But, mainly as a result of the submarines' activities, no oil reached Japan from Southeast Asia after March, although some Japanese traffic continued to run on domestic routes and across the Sea of Japan to Korea. So, feeling deprived of targets, in June nine American submarines braved the thick minefields to enter the Sea of Japan, where they lost one of their number, but sank 28 enemy ships. Other submarines took on reconnaissance and lifeguard tasks, and in the latter role they rescued 380 aviators, whose damaged B-29s could not return to their fields after bombing targets in Japan.

At the end of March, the B-29s took on, as a side job, the mining of Japanese coastal waters and straits, thus aiding the effort of the submarines in strangling the empire, without causing death or destruction ashore.

The submarines also continued their work against what was left of the Japanese navy. Submarines sank several destroyers and about 40 escort ships in 1945, but there were very few larger targets left. In April USS *Charr* and

Below: These two-man submarines were built in a large drydock at Kure, Japan, but were then prevented from leaving when U.S. bombing sealed the gates.

*Gabilan* sank the *Isuzu*, a light cruiser, while, in June, the British submarine HMS *Trenchant* sank the heavy cruiser *Ashigara* near Sumatra. In late July two British midget submarines (also known as "X-craft") entered Singapore harbor, where they immobilized the already damaged heavy cruiser *Takao*.

Japan's submarine fleet, which had had a very undistinguished war, tried to conduct a final offensive in July. The only achievement came when I-58 sank the heavy cruiser, USS *Indianapolis*, on July 29. This turned into a major disaster, since the ship was moving from one command to another and neither noticed that she was missing. As a result, the survivors of the sinking spent some four days in the shark-infested waters, where many more were lost, before being spotted, quite by chance, by a passing aircraft. A fine ship, *Indianapolis* also proved to be one of the last major warships to be sunk on either side in World War II.

## THE FIGHT FOR IWO JIMA

In the Indian Ocean Theater, there were two worthwhile objectives for the Allies' South-East Asia Command—Rangoon and Singapore, both of which could best be taken by amphibious assault. Happily for the Allies, from mid-1943 onwards, the Supreme Allied Commander in the theater was Admiral Lord Louis Mountbatten, Britain's outstanding amphibious leader. But,

though he had an enormous army and supporting air force in India and Burma, he had little in the way of a fleet. Eventually a substantial fleet was assembled, but its big carriers were soon taken away again for operations in the Pacific, while only a small proportion of the promised amphibious ships ever got there.

However, Mountbatten began an overland campaign through Burma's appalling terrain and climate and by May 1945, after fierce jungle fighting, the British and Indian forces retook the capital of Burma, Rangoon. The East Indies Fleet, commanded by Admiral Sir Arthur Power, supported army operations along the coast, and also destroyed what Japanese shipping remained in the Andaman and Nicobar islands. On May 16, five British destroyers under Captain M. L. Power ambushed the Japanese heavy cruiser *Haguro* and a destroyer in the Malacca Strait and, although the destroyer escaped, the cruiser was sunk.

Meanwhile the Americans continued to make territorial advances.

About halfway between the Marianas, where the B-29s were then based, and their targets in Japan there was an airstrip on the tiny Japanese-held island of Iwo Jima, a four-and-a-half-mile-long pile of volcanic ash inhabited only by 23,000 Japanese soldiers. The airfield was used by Japanese fighters to harass the bombers on their way to and from Japan, and the Americans decided to invade, partly in order

Below: Landing Ships, Medium, Rocket (LSMR) taking part in the preinvasion bombardment of the island of Pokishi Shima in March 1945.

to deny it to the Japanese, but also for their own use, both as a base for fighters, from which they could escort the bombers, and for the bombers to use in emergencies.

As a prelude to the landings, the island was subjected to a prolonged bombing by the U.S. Army Air Force, supplemented by shelling from ships at sea. This bombardment lasted only three days—the marines had asked for ten—and then, on February 19, some 30,000 men stormed ashore, with many more to follow. Thus began one of the hardest fights in Marine Corps' history, and only on March 16 was the island declared secured, although sporadic fighting lasted until May. It was of the Marine Corps fighting on this island that Admiral Nimitz said, "uncommon valor was a common virtue."

The U.S. Navy's part in this struggle was to put the marines ashore and then to keep them supplied with ammunition, food, fuel, and replacements, and to provide close air and gun-fire support. In the latter role, the old battleship, USS *Nevada*, a veteran of Pearl Harbor and Normandy, played a very distinguished role. The Japanese made unsuccessful attempts to break up the assault with kamikaze attacks and inflicted severe damage on their favorite target, the carrier USS *Saratoga*, and sank the escort carrier, USS *Bismarck Sea*. But that was about it.

The Japanese lost all 23,000 in the defense of Iwo Jima, and in taking it, the Americans, of course, aided their bombing effort over Japan, and saved hundreds of airmen in crippled aircraft. Whether that was worth the 7,000 dead and 22,000 wounded is a question that can only be asked with the benefit of hindsight; at the time the goals appeared both attainable and worthwhile.

Before the battle on Iwo Jima had ended, the next invasion, that of Okinawa, had begun. But first, in February and March 1945 the fast carrier task force under Admiral Spruance and Vice Admiral Mitscher made several raids on Japan. The March attacks on the airfields in Kyushu, Japan's southernmost island, cost the Americans heavily, because Japanese bombers succeeded in damaging the carriers *Enterprise*, *Yorktown*, and *Wasp*. In addition, one bomber obtained two hits on the *Franklin* as she was launching aircraft, and the resulting damage killed more than 800 of the *Franklin's* crew. But, in spite of being more severely damaged than any other ship which survived in World War II, *Franklin*

was brought to safety by her officers and men, although she had to go to New York for repair because West Coast shipyards were full of damaged ships.

Air strikes by Task Force 58 began on Okinawa on March 23 and gunfire strikes the next day. An anchorage was seized in the Karma Recto, a small group of islands fifteen miles west of the main island on March 26. The invasion of Okinawa, which began on April 1, was commanded by Vice Admiral Richmond Turner, whose forces included 1,300 ships and craft, and 182,000 marines and soldiers, with over 100,000 follow-up troops.

The landings went easily, for the Japanese had learned not to contest an invasion on the beaches against the power of American naval gunfire and close air support. But the operation soon turned into a difficult slogging match, which lasted until the end of June.

## THE LAST RIDE OF BATTLESHIP *YAMATO*

It was at Okinawa that the British Pacific Fleet, built around the Royal Navy's heavy carriers, joined the U.S. Pacific Fleet. This British fleet was commanded by Admiral Sir Bruce Fraser, who was based first at Sydney, Australia, and later at Guam, while commanding at sea was Vice Admiral Sir Bernard Rawlings in the battleship HMS *King George V*, and commanding the aircraft carrier squadron was Admiral Sir Philip Vian. That squadron consisted of the new carrier *Indefatigable* and the veterans *Illustrious*, *Victorious*, and *Indomitable*, each with about

Above: USS *Tennessee* (BB-43) was badly damaged at Pearl Harbor but was repaired and rejoined the fleet. Here the ship wreaks revenge on *Okinawa* on January 4, 1945. The Landing Vehicles, Tracked (LVT) in the foreground are completely dwarfed by the huge vessel.

Above: The Japanese suicide attacks placed a tremendous responsibility on the antiaircraft gun crews, not least because incoming aircraft presented them with only a small cross-section target. Here crews man 40-mm guns aboard USS *Hornet* (CV-12) while operating off the Japanese mainland. Note the piles of empty cases, bottom right.

Their fuel tanks contained almost all the oil reserves still available to the Japanese navy, but, even so, that was sufficient for only a one-way voyage. The intention was that the vessels were to beach themselves and fight until they were destroyed by the Americans.

However, the Japanese plan was foiled because they were seen and reported by U.S. submarines and the following day, when still only halfway to their destination, they were set upon by aircraft from Admiral Mitscher's carriers. *Yamato*, *Yahagi*, and four of the destroyers were sunk and the remaining four destroyers returned to Japan with what few survivors they had been able to rescue. It was an ignominious end for what had, only three years earlier, been one of the mightiest surface fleets in the world.

60 aircraft. These ships made several attacks on Japanese oil targets in Sumatra before going into the Pacific where, operating first under Admiral Spruance, they were designated Task Force 57 and then, under Admiral Halsey, Task Force 37.

During the Okinawa campaign their mission was to keep the Japanese air forces on Formosa from supporting their army on Okinawa, which they did by continued bombing and strafing of airfields on some islands in between Formosa and Okinawa, though at great cost to their own air groups. Moreover, each of the carriers was damaged more or less severely by kamikazes, although the armored flightdecks of the British carriers gave them far greater protection than the unarmored decks of the U.S. carriers.

After about two weeks *Illustrious*, which had painful wounds from earlier campaigns, was replaced by HMS *Formidable*, and in June HMS *Implacable* joined the fleet. In July and August these British ships joined in the attacks on Japan proper.

Aside from the efforts of the 100,000 troops defending Okinawa, the Japanese response to the attack on the island was almost entirely a matter of suicide attacks on the American fleet from the air. There was however, one suicide effort from the surface, when the battleship *Yamato*, the light cruiser *Yahagi*, and eight destroyers sailed on April 6 for Okinawa.

## CONSTANT THREAT OF DEATH

The kamikazes made ten main and many minor attacks in April, May, and June. Over 1,400 suicide planes took part in the main attacks, often accompanied by bombers. They damaged Spruance's flagship, USS *Indianapolis*, on March 30, forcing the admiral to transfer his flag to the old battleship USS *New Mexico*. That ship, in turn, was hit by a kamikaze on May 12, but was able to remain on station for two weeks more. Then, on April 6–7, some 355 kamikazes and 341 other aircraft attacked the fleet, sinking three destroyers, a Landing Ship Tank (LST), and two ammunition-laden freighters, as well as damaging seventeen other ships, some so badly they were scrapped as soon as the war was over.

Though no other kamikaze attack at Okinawa was so damaging as the first one, by the end of June no fewer than 21 ships had been sunk by them, mostly in Okinawan waters, and 66 others severely damaged. No big combatants were among those sunk, but there were plenty of them among those damaged.

British and Japanese sailors had already proved that they could endure, and it was at Okinawa, and especially on the radar-picket stations, that the American sailors showed that they, too, could endure. These pickets were at their exposed stations around the island to give warning of air attacks headed for the ships gathered at Okinawa, which were there to support the U.S. Army intent on conquering the island. And the army and marines were ashore to conquer the island in order to provide airfields, harbors, supply dumps, and

Left: A kamikaze has penetrated the antiaircraft defenses and hit USS *Bunker Hill* (CV-17), May 11, 1945.

Above: Japanese cruiser, *Tone*, is destroyed in Kure Harbor by U.S. carrier-borne aircraft from the Third Fleet. A large scouting cruiser, *Tone* had four twin 8-in. turrets forward (a very unusual arrangement), leaving the quarterdeck clear for catapults and hangars for six aircraft.

staging areas for the anticipated invasion of the Japanese homeland.

Thus, the role of the radar pickets was absolutely vital—as the Japanese well knew— and for three months their crews endured never-ending danger, with the threat of death always present, and the action, when it came, particularly intense. For example, during one period of one hour and twenty minutes the picket destroyer, USS *Laffey*, was subjected to 22 separate attacks. She shot down eight of her attackers, but six more crashed into her, and four bombs also scored hits. More than a third of her men were casualties but, despite all this, her crew brought the *Laffey* home and she served for many years afterwards.

### THE JAPANESE SURRENDER

By the end of June, Okinawa was in American hands. The fleet, now under Admiral Halsey, and centered on fifteen carriers, put to sea from Leyte Gulf on July 1. Ten days later came the first of a series of carrier-based air raids (and,

beginning four days after that, shore bombardments) on mainland Japan. Partly these were intended to supplement (or, perhaps, to rival) the B-29 attacks on industrial targets and partly to sink coastal shipping and surviving Japanese warships. On July 16 the British, with three carriers, joined the attacks.

Immobile for the lack of fuel and their crews largely disbanded, Japan's surviving warships were moored in shallow water. On July 24, those ships at Kure and Kobe on the Inland Sea came under attack by Task Force 38, which launched 1,747 sorties. The new carrier *Amagi*, the old battleships *Haruna*, *Ise*, and *Hyuga*, the heavy cruiser *Aoba*, and the light cruiser *Oyodo* were all destroyed or damaged so severely they settled to the bottom, much as had the U.S. ships at Pearl Harbor in December 1941. Other warships were damaged and fifteen merchant ships and auxiliaries were sunk. On July 28 the heavy cruiser *Tone* and eight auxiliary ships were sunk.

On August 6 the first atomic bomb was exploded over Hiroshima, and the second three days later over Nagasaki. That same day the Soviet Union declared war on Japan and aircraft and motor torpedo boats of the Soviet Pacific Fleet attacked Japanese shipping in Korean waters, while amphibious landings were carried out on the northeastern coast of Korea in support of the advancing Soviet army.

Meantime, Task Forces 37 and 38 continued strikes on Japanese shipping and airfields until August 15 when Fleet Admiral Chester Nimitz ordered them to cease hostilities. However, for another ten days Soviet naval forces launched amphibious attacks on southern Sakhalin and on the Kurile Islands, all of which were successful despite, in some cases, strong opposition.

On September 3, the war in the Pacific Theater which had begun in December 1941 with the infamous attack on the American fleet in Pearl Harbor formally came to an end on the deck of the American battleship USS *Missouri* lying at anchor in Tokyo Bay. General Douglas MacArthur signed the document for the Allies, but it was aboard a U.S. Navy battleship that he did so.

Below: General MacArthur made the Japanese delegation sign the surrender documents in view of the crew of USS *Missouri* and many invited guests on September 2, 1945. It was a carefully calculated and very public humiliation.

# Chapter 5

# THE WAR ON LAND

JAPAN'S PERIOD OF CONQUEST after its devastating attack on Pearl Harbor was marked by ruthlessness and skill. Within months Japan had achieved all of its initial objectives in Southeast Asia and the Pacific: Singapore had fallen; all of Malaya and most of Burma, and all of the Netherlands East Indies had been overrun; the islands of the central Pacific were in Japanese hands and the line-of-communications to Australia was under threat. The Japanese seemed irresistible, until the great U.S. naval victory off Midway Island. Meanwhile, the war within a war that centered on China's vital link with the outside world, the Burma Road, was fought with a savagery rarely equaled in World War II, and in some of the world's worst fighting terrain. In the islands of the Pacific it took the American forces almost three years to retake what the Japanese had taken in six months, and the campaign was marked by very heavy casualties on both sides during the famous island-hopping battles. Finally, fearing even greater casualties in an all-out offensive against the Japanese homelands, the Americans resorted to using the dreadful atomic weapon to bring the conflict to a close.

Right: Marines of the 1st Marine Division advancing across Okinawa in May 1945. The Pacific land campaign, recapturing one Japanese-held island after another, saw some of the bloodiest fighting of World War II.

More than a decade before the outbreak of war in the Pacific, a 1929 U.S. Army staff study observed that, at the beginning of each of its major conflicts, the United States had found itself unprepared and "this condition has eventuated in some cases in humiliating and disastrous reverses." Not even the most farsighted military strategist, however, could have foreseen the staggering defeats and disasters that the United States was to suffer during the first half year of the war against Japan.

As described in the naval section, the Pacific war began on December 7, 1941, with a surprise attack by Japanese carrier-borne aircraft on the major American military and naval base at Pearl Harbor, in the Hawaiian Islands. Within hours of that attack, Japanese forces moved to knock out the other principal American bases in the Pacific, with the island of Guam, in the Marianas, being occupied with ease, but a second attack on Wake Island, farther east, brought a sharp reverse.

Wake is a tiny V-shaped atoll in the central Pacific, and in December 1941 it was manned by a defense battalion of 450 U.S. Marines under the command of Major James Devereux. The battalion was 50 percent under strength, but it had some useful artillery in the form of six 3 in. antiaircraft guns, as well as some 5 in. coast defense guns and a squadron of Grumman F4F Wildcat fighters attached. After repeated bombing raids, a small Japanese invasion force of about 500 men, escorted by eight cruisers and

Below: An aerial view of Wake Atoll taken later in the war when it was under attack by U.S. bombers, shows the horseshoe-shaped atoll consisting of three islets. In December 1941 the garrison comprised 450 marines, plus some 75 men from the U.S. Navy and the Army Signal Corps. In addition, there were some 1,500 civilian contractors' workers building a new airstrip.

destroyers, approached Wake Island on the morning of December 11. Holding their fire until the enemy had closed to only 3,500 yd., the 5-in. batteries on Wake suddenly opened fire on the Japanese and, despite the fact that much of their range-finding equipment had been disabled in the bombing, the marines' fire was accurate and deadly. Four 5 in. shells ripped into the Japanese flagship, the cruiser *Yubari*, which limped away under a cloud of smoke, while the destroyer *Hayate* was almost blown in two by a 5-inch salvo and her sister ship *Oite* was damaged. Two transports and another destroyer were also hit and by 0700 the entire Japanese squadron was in full retirement. The few remaining planes on Wake pursued the task force and inflicted further damage, sinking the destroyer *Kisaragi*.

The Japanese had lost over 500 men and

two warships sunk and more damaged, but they moved quickly to make good their losses. On December 22 a much larger task force, which now included two aircraft carriers and six heavy cruisers, escorted a new assault force of about 1,200 men to Wake Island. At about 0230 in the early morning of December 23, Japanese forces began landing on Wake. The marines resisted fiercely, but by daylight it was clear that the enemy had succeeded in landing a superior force that the Americans lacked the means to repel. Several isolated American positions were still holding out and one Japanese landing force at the extreme western tip of the island had been virtually annihilated, but Major Devereaux and Commander Cunningham, the senior marine and naval officers present, respectively, decided that further resistance would be useless. A relief expedition from Pearl Harbor with additional

Above: Wake was defended by a squadron of Marine Corps Wildcat fighters, who put up a superb resistance, inflicting considerable damage on the Japanese forces, including sinking two destroyers.

Above: Men of the elite special landing forces who spearheaded Japan's drive across the Pacific.

troops and aircraft had turned back a few hours before and no further relief attempts could be expected. So, at 7:30 P.M. in the morning—and having done all, and more, that he and his men could be expected to do—Major James Devereaux left his command post with a white flag to find the Japanese.

The surrender of Guam and Wake gave the Japanese control of the American lines-of-communications across the Central Pacific, and the Commonwealth of the Philippines, whose defense was the responsibility of the United States, was now virtually cut-off from reinforcement. The one remaining possibility was to send relief forces from the south, but the swift Japanese conquest of Borneo and the Dutch East Indies soon made this route extremely perilous, if not impossible.

During the 1920s and 1930s American strategists had tacitly recognized that in a war with Japan the Philippines would probably fall before a relief expedition, which would have to fight its way across the Pacific, could reach the islands. It was hoped that the defenders would at least be able to hold the entrance to Manila pending the arrival of the American fleet, but the small size of American forces in the islands made even this a doubtful proposition.

During 1941, however, as American war materiel became more plentiful, the defenses of the Philippines had been steadily augmented with modern tanks and aircraft. Most notable among these was a small force of Boeing B-17 heavy bombers, then the most modern in the world, and American military planners believed that they would serve as a powerful deterrent against attack. In addition, General Douglas MacArthur who had assumed command of all American and Filipino land forces in the islands in 1941, believed that the Philippine army of some 100,000 troops, together with the U.S. Army garrison of some 23,000 troops, would be sufficient to put up a successful defense of the entire archipelago. Scrapping the old defense plans, MacArthur expected to meet all enemy attacks at the beach-head and force them back into the sea.

The first days of war quickly demonstrated the hollowness of MacArthur's assumptions. As a result of a series of mistakes, delays and miscalculations that, to this day, have never been adequately explained, MacArthur's air force was caught on the ground by Japanese bombers many hours after word of the Pearl Harbor attack had reached the Philippines. Over half of the modern aircraft, together with part of the repair facilities, hangars and fuel storage areas, were destroyed.

On December 22 the principal Japanese invasion force, the 14th Army, commanded by

Lieutenant General Homma, landed on the shores of Lingayen Gulf, on the island of Luzon, about 100 miles northwest of the Philippine capital of Manila. It was followed two days later by the Japanese 16th Division, approximately 7,000 strong, which landed at Lamon Bay, 70 miles southeast of Manila.

In both areas the defenses swiftly crumbled. MacArthur quickly realized that he could not hope to defend all Luzon and that if he attempted to defend Manila he would be caught between the closing pincers of the Japanese forces advancing southeast from Lingayen Gulf and northwest from Lamon Bay. On December 23, therefore, MacArthur declared Manila an open city and ordered his forces to withdraw into the narrow peninsula of Bataan lying between Manila Bay and the South China Sea. Just off the tip of the Bataan peninsula was the island fortress of Corregidor, which guarded the entrance to Manila Bay, and here MacArthur established his headquarters.

Meanwhile, American and Filipino troops under the command of Major General Jonathan Wainwright were fighting a desperate battle to cover the retreat of MacArthur's forces into Bataan and to gain time for the preparation of defenses there. Stubborn fighting and good luck on the part of Wainwright's troops, combined with a halfhearted pursuit on the part of the Japanese who were preoccupied with the capture of Manila, resulted in the successful withdrawal of the bulk of MacArthur's forces into the Bataan peninsula.

The defenders of Bataan occupied positions at the base of the peninsula in the rugged jungles on either side of a high mountain, Mount Natib. To the west, between Mount Natib and the South China Sea, were three Philippine Army divisions and a regiment of Philippine Scouts under Wainwright.[1] On the east, or Manila Bay side, of the mountain, were four more Philippine Army divisions and another scout regiment under Major General George Parker. In the rear, in reserve, was the so-called "Philippine Division" made up of scouts and other regular army troops, plus some light tanks and the heavier artillery.

All of these forces were short of food, while stocks of all types of supplies, particularly medicine, were very low. MacArthur's ill-fated plan to defend all of the Philippines had necessitated the stocking of forward defense positions with large amounts of food and equipment, but once the invasion began and these positions collapsed there was little time and insufficient transport available to move these supplies back to Bataan.

---

[1]The Philippine Scouts were tough, well-trained Filipino soldiers, who formed a part of the regular U.S. Army and not the Philippine army.

Above: Battered Wildcats on Wake atoll testify to the battle for the island. The fighters that survived the first attack inflicted damage out of all proportion to their actual strength, but were eventually overcome by sheer weight of numbers.

The supply problem was further complicated by the unanticipated presence of over 25,000 civilian refugees on the peninsula. By January 5, 1942, MacArthur's forces on Bataan were already on half rations, and these were to be reduced still further in the coming weeks.

The first Japanese attack against the defenders of Bataan began on January 9 with Japanese assaults on both flanks of the American line, all of which were repulsed. Other Japanese units, however, were able to infiltrate between Parker and Wainwright by crossing over the supposedly impassible heights of Mount Natib. Emerging behind Wainwright's forces, they set up a road

block on the only usable road, while other elements threatened to outflank Parker. With their lines-of-communication thus threatened, the American defenders withdrew to a more defensible position farther down the peninsula, known as the Bagac-Orion line.

There now began two weeks of vicious fighting during which Homma attempted to penetrate the new line by frontal attacks and to outflank it by an amphibious assault against the so-called "points" that were narrow fingers of land pointing out into the South China Sea at the southwest corner of the Bataan peninsula. A heterogeneous force of sailors, marines, and

Below: A Japanese officer leads his men during the taking of the island of Borneo.

Left: The Japanese armored corps was not particularly strong and its tanks were of generally poor quality. This is a Light Tank Model 35 Type Ha-Go.

Below: A pause in the advance toward the Bataan front in March 1942. Despite all the preparations, American resistance to the Japanese proved to be ineffective.

Above: Japanese troops throw up a hasty defensive position while a tank goes forward to destroy a British machine gun nest, which is holding up the advance. They are in the streets of Johor Baharu, the southernmost town on the Malayan Peninsula, and once it has been taken only the narrow straits will separate them from their goal of Singapore.

Right: The city of Singapore was subjected to many air raids, which the very few RAF fighters and inadequate antiaircraft guns could do little to resist. Here, yet another civilian casualty is carried away along Bras Basah Road in the heart of the city.

Wainwright replaced MacArthur and Major General Edward King took over the command on Bataan.

During March Homma was reinforced with an additional division and other infantry elements as well as more artillery and on April 3, the Japanese renewed their attacks. The American-Filipino defenses, manned by men near the starvation level, rapidly crumbled and on April 9 King had no remaining option but to surrender his forces on Bataan.

The island of Corregidor and the smaller islands of El Fraile (Fort Drum), Caballo (Fort Hughes), and Carabao (Fort Frank), which together guarded the entrance to Manila Bay, still remained in American hands, but the

grounded airmen, together with elements of two scout regiments, managed to contain the Japanese landings near the beach-head and then wiped them out in the so-called "battle of the points."

Meanwhile, a complete Japanese regiment had managed to slip through the American defenses on the Bagac-Orion line and form two defensive pockets behind Wainwright's corps. In a hard-fought series of actions, lasting until February 17, the Americans finally succeeded in destroying the pockets as well as a Japanese relief force that had attempted to reach them.

By now both sides were exhausted. The Japanese had suffered over 7,000 casualties and had about 10,000 incapacitated by tropical diseases. American casualties had been somewhat lower, but the physical condition of the Americans and Filipinos was far worse as a result of their long days on an inadequate and unbalanced diet. Then, in late February, MacArthur was ordered by President Franklin Roosevelt to leave the Philippines and proceed to Australia where he was to assume command of a new South-West Pacific Theater.

Left: Japanese infantry on the outskirts of Kuala Lumpur, the capital of the British-administered Federated Malay States. The local houses, made entirely of timber, burned all too easily.

Japanese at once began an intense air and artillery bombardment of these positions. Designed for naval defense, most of these islands had their batteries above ground, where they were easily pinpointed by Japanese observers on the high ground on Bataan or in spotting planes. On May 5, having destroyed most of the artillery on Corregidor and its satellite islands, Japanese forces landed on the southern end of the island. The American defenders, supported by the remaining artillery, inflicted heavy casualties on the attackers but the outcome was never seriously in doubt. By the morning of the 6th the last American reserves had been committed and the Japanese were closing in on Wainwright's underground command post and the hospital in the Malinta tunnel. At 10:00 A.M. Wainwright radioed Washington that he had regretfully decided to surrender.

By the time that Wainwright went to meet Homma, Japan had achieved all of its objectives in Southeast Asia and the Pacific. Singapore had fallen and all of Malaya, most of Burma, and all of the Netherlands East Indies had been overrun. The islands of the Central Pacific were in Japanese hands and the line of communications to Australia threatened.

## A BRIEF PAUSE FOR BREATH

Both sides now undertook a revision of their strategies and also reorganized their forces. At the start of the war in the Pacific, the American, British, Dutch, Australian, and New Zealand governments had all been involved in defending their territories and possessions against the

Right: Following the capture of Corregidor in May 1942, General Jonathan Wainwright is forced to broadcast his surrender message under the watchful eyes and ears of a Japanese interpreter.

Far right: Japanese soldiers haul down the United States flag on Corregidor following the island's capture in May 1942.

その乃を撤旗隊を

advance of the Japanese. After a few weeks they had established a unified command—known as ABDACOM (American, British, Dutch, and Australian Command)—under the British General Sir Archibald Wavell to coordinate the defense of Southeast Asia and the western Pacific against the Japanese. With the fall of Malaya and the Dutch East Indies, however, it became clear that the Allied forces in Southeast Asia and the Pacific could no longer operate as a single command. Thus, with no Dutch territo-

ries in the Far East remaining unoccupied by the Japanese and the Netherlands themselves occupied by the Germans, that left only American and the British Commonwealth, and these agreed to establish separate spheres of responsibility in the war effort against the Japanese forces, but, of course, with mutual support as and when required.

The American joint chiefs of staff were assigned responsibility for the Pacific Ocean, including Australia and New Zealand, but they

Right: Japanese picture of Japanese medics treating the leg of an Australian soldier, who is leaning against a rubber tree somewhere in Malaya. Cans of corned beef and vegetables have been placed prominently to show that he is not short of food. In reality, the scene was set up for propaganda purposes, and the Japanese provided little food and virtually no medical care for their unfortunate captives.

Previous pages: Japanese troops cheer their capture of Corregidor on May 6, 1942. They are standing on a huge 12 in. coastal defense gun, almost certainly one of those in Battery Hearn. As in Singapore, the guns on Corregidor were impressive in appearance, but failed to deter attack in practice.

did not, as might have been expected, establish a single supreme commander for the Pacific. MacArthur, a soldier of almost legendary stature in the United States, was already on the scene and was the logical choice for such a command. Yet the campaign against Japan in the Pacific would obviously require the use of large naval forces and the United States Navy was unwilling to entrust the command of its fleet to MacArthur—or, indeed, to any army officer. The U.S. Navy, on the other hand, had no officer of

the prestige or seniority of MacArthur to offer as a candidate for a single Pacific command.

The outcome was a decision by the Joint Chiefs to divide the Pacific Theater into two commands. MacArthur was designated commander in chief of the "South-West Pacific Area," which comprised Australia, New Guinea, the Bismarck Archipelago, the Solomon Islands, the Philippines, and most of the Netherlands East Indies. Admiral Chester Nimitz, of the U.S. Navy, was designated

Below: Wounded American and Australian soldiers lie on litters in a New Guinea village on December 21, 1942. The fighting on New Guinea was particularly bloody and was made the more difficult for the Allies by the dense jungle, extensive swamps, and hot, humid climate.

Commander, Pacific Ocean Areas. Nimitz's areas encompassed most of the Pacific Ocean, except that which was part of MacArthur's South-West Pacific Area, and included Hawaii, New Zealand, and the many small islands of the South and Central Pacific, most of which were in Japanese hands.

While the Americans were reorganizing, the Japanese high command had been pondering its next move. Two lines of action appeared especially promising. One was to continue their advance on the large island of New Guinea, directly north of Australia. Japanese forces had

landed at Lae and Salamaua near the narrow southeast "tail" of New Guinea known as Papua in March and Japanese planners now decided to seize Port Moresby on the southern side of the Papuan tail as well as the Solomon Islands chain to the west of New Guinea. From these positions they could menace Australia directly, and also increase the threat to its lines-of-communication with the United States. The second course of action was to extend the Japanese defensive perimeter in the Pacific by seizing Midway Island, east of Hawaii, and some of the Aleutian island chain, southwest of

support for the expedition. The Americans, who had by this time broken the Japanese naval code, already knew of the impending invasion and sent Rear Admiral Frank Fletcher, with a task force built around the carriers *Yorktown* and *Lexington*, to intercept the Japanese. The ensuing Battle of the Coral Sea (May 7, 1942) frustrated Japanese plans to seize control of southern New Guinea, but, despite this setback, preparations for the Midway operation still went forward.

The Americans, again alerted to Japanese intentions through reading their code, rushed reinforcements to Midway and the Pacific Fleet under Fletcher deployed north of the island. In the Battle of Midway, June 4, 1942, the Americans held the island, while the Japanese fleet suffered major losses, although a small diversionary landing on the remote and unimportant islands of Attu and Kiska succeeded. The Battle of Midway deprived the Japanese of most of their formidable carrier striking force. It was, as Sir Basil Liddell Hart observed, "the most extraordinarily quick change of fortune known in naval history." The Japanese advance in the Pacific was slowed to a crawl and the initiative soon passed to the Allies.

Alaska. Planning and preparations for both these new projects commenced at once.

## THE SECOND PHASE OF JAPANESE ATTACKS IN THE PACIFIC

The attack on Port Moresby got under way at the beginning of May 1942. A troop convoy carrying the invasion force started from the Japanese base at Rabaul escorted by a small carrier, four heavy cruisers, and some destroyers, while two large carriers, with more cruisers and destroyers, provided general "over-the-horizon"

Below: A section of the men from the Royal Australian Regiment passing two knocked-out Japanese Type 95 Ha Go light tanks.

## WAR WITHIN A WAR: INDIA, CHINA, AND BURMA

The term "World War II" is something of a misnomer, since there were really two quite separate wars, one in Europe and a second in Asia, whose fortunes were linked by the fact that the United States and Great Britain (together with other allies) were involved in both. In Asia and the Pacific, American strategy for defeating Japan was simple but sound: to hold the over-extended Japanese perimeter, which by 1943 embraced parts of eastern China, all of the Dutch and parts of the British empires in Southeast Asia, the Philippines, and numerous Pacific islands, and then to concentrate on thrusting at the heart of

Japanese power, Japan itself.

In the meantime it made sense to encourage any opponent who could attract Japanese forces away from its Pacific flank and wear them down. British India was one obvious choice, although at the time the Americans rated British fighting power and determination there very low. In addition, (and despite their own involvement with the Philippines) the Americans were emotionally anti-imperialist and quick to suspect proposed British operations as veiled attempts to reconquer their lost territories.

By contrast, the Sino-Japanese war had been festering for years, and although important parts of eastern China were sporadically under

Below: Throughout the Allied campaigns in the Pacific and India/Burma, the war in mainland China dragged on. Here Japanese sentries gain warmth from a boiler during the advances in the winter of 1942.

Japanese control, so vast was China, and Chinese strategy was so suited to its circumstances, that Japan could not "win" in any conventional military meaning of the word. Thus, for the United States to assist China made strategic sense and was also politically shrewd, because there were strong ties between the Americans and the Chinese, particularly through the missionaries, and such a policy had a large measure of public backing.

The basic American plan, therefore, was to provide the Chinese with American advisers and weapons, to modernize their ramshackle rifle-and-bayonet divisions, and to mobilize China's manpower effectively, with figures of 20, 30, or even 50 divisions being discussed. But the Americans, with their magnificent self-confidence and idealism, underestimated the many and diverse difficulties.

First, there was the intractable complication of the relationship between the Nationalists and the Communists, which varied from, at best, mutual antagonism and mistrust to, at worst, outright civil war. Next, there was the appalling state of the Chinese army, which was, in most essentials, a 19th century peasant horde. All these were made worse by the corruption at all

levels of the Chiang Kai-shek Nationalist regime. Also, one of the few factors on which all Chinese could unite was their chauvinistic and xenophobic reaction to the brash, thrusting, and impatient alien "advisers." Finally, the Chinese concept of strategy totally disregarded time, which made it fundamentally opposed to the American urge for rapid and tangible results.

In the event, United States aid and the operations of the U.S. 14th Army Air Force kept the Sino-Japanese conflict in being, albeit at great

Above: Albert C. Wedemeyer succeeded Joseph Stilwell as commander of U.S. forces in the China-Burma-India Theater and also as chief of staff to Chinese Generalissimo Chiang Kai-shek. He was responsible for overseeing the vast amount of aid provided by the United States to China in its war against the invading Japanese.

Left: The Japanese occupation of those parts of China it had overrun was neither benevolent nor enlightened, and memories of the experience bedevil Sino-Japanese relations to this day. Here, a village garrison (right) forms an honor guard for an infantry regiment as it passes through.

material cost, and despite a marked reluctance on the part of Generalissimo Chiang Kai-shek to take part in any Allied operations; after all, he had enough to contend with inside China, without getting involved in external problems.

There was also the U.S. Army Air Force lobby, which considered that China offered better scope for a purely air strategy. Air support for Chinese troops would enable them to hold the Japanese, and if a defensible zone could be established in eastern China then American air power could be exerted on Japan from that direction as well as from the Pacific.

The main proponent of a land strategy was

Lieutenant General Joseph Stilwell, of the U.S. Army, a ruthless man of uncommon ability and determination, and deeply versed in Chinese ways. Stilwell had been caught up in the debacle in Burma in 1942 and after reaching India on foot had assembled as many Chinese troops as he could collect at Ramgarh, where they were organized and trained along U.S. lines. This corps was to prove the most effective—indeed, the *only* effective—Chinese formation. General Joseph Stilwell was commander of all U.S. troops in the theater, chief of staff and adviser to Chiang Kai-shek, and the *de facto* commander of his Chinese corps. In addition, the 1943

Right: The Ledo Road was a triumph of United States military and civil engineering. It was also a major challenge for every truck driver who drove along it taking aid to the Chinese, or returning in an empty vehicle to fetch more. The infamous stretch shown here includes twenty-one curves, of which the most ominous is the lowest, with the road passing along the lip of a vertical cliff.

Anglo/U.S. Quebec Conference had appointed him deputy commander of all the Allied forces assembled in Southeast Asia under Admiral Lord Louis Mountbatten.

Whichever strategy, air or land, was adopted depended on an uninterrupted flow of supplies to China, but after the sea routes had been lost and the Burma Road cut, the only link was a costly and tenuous airlift from India, which had to fly over mountain ranges up to 12,000 ft. in height—known as "The Hump"—to avoid Japanese-held territory. The chosen American operational goal, therefore, was to clear and secure the extreme north of Burma using

General Joseph Stilwell's Chinese troops, and then to drive a road and fuel pipeline from Ledo via Myitkyina to China, a huge project and typically American in its size and scope.

## BRITISH PLANS

The British in India viewed the American plan with an irritating degree of cynicism, basically because they did not believe that the Chinese would fight. Nevertheless, they themselves had to perform a delicate balancing act, not least because the power and wealth of the British Empire was more apparent than real, as a result

Left: General Joseph Stilwell served in China for thirteen years between the wars and learned the language. He returned to China in February to become chief of staff to Chiang Kai-shek and commander of U.S. troops in the Burma-China-India area. Stilwell disliked the British intensely, but it was the friction with Chiang that led to him being called home in October 1944. Here he shows that he is not too grand to clean his own personal weapon, in this case a Thompson submachine gun.

of which much of what they could do depended upon American goodwill and support. In addition, the British-Indian empire, the base from which any operation must be mounted, was a powder keg, with the power of Indian Nationalism growing every year and the events of 1919, when there had been a serious rebellion in the Punjab, were never far from British minds. As a result, a substantial part of their armed forces were locked up in India in internal security duties, which had little or nothing to do with the war against Japan.

Nevertheless, the British were determined to reconquer Burma and Malaya in order to wipe out the humiliation of their defeats in 1942–43, but they were doubtful of the feasibility of a long land advance back into Burma through a country riddled with disease, without roads, but with large, wide rivers and mountain ranges covered with tropical rain forest. To the British, a sea-strategy that would strike directly at Singapore or even Sumatra came more naturally and so seemed preferable. Above all, the British commanders in India were determined not to

Right: A controversial soldier, Orde Wingate originally made his name in the Middle East, where he became a fanatical Zionist supporter (although not a Jew himself) and helped raise the *Haganah*. The British removed him from Palestine, and on the outbreak of war he went to Ethiopia to help restore Emperor Haile Selasse to his throne. In 1943 Wingate organized, recruited, and led the first Chindit expedition in operations behind Japanese lines. This gained Churchill's attention and he was given the means to lead a second expedition, in the course of which he died in an air crash.

Previous pages: Wingate briefing for the second Chindit expedition. Standing beside Wingate is the charismatic and courageous Colonel Phil Cochrane, USAAF, commander 1st Air Commando Group. His air commando was, in effect, a small air force, including C-47 transports, CG-4 gliders, C-64 Noorduyn Norsemen light transports, a large number of light aircraft, and even the first YR-4 helicopter. Close support was provided by P-51A Mustangs and B-25 Mitchells.

challenge the Japanese in the field again until they had re-equipped and retrained the British-Indian army and, perhaps the most important of all, reinspired it with self-confidence. However, none of this was viewed by the Americans with any sympathy, and, as far as amphibious adventures were concerned, they held the whip hand since they controlled the supply of landing craft.

As a result, a succession of operational plans were made, each of which was modified after much debate and then discarded as an even more attractive plan was put forward. Here it is only possible to concentrate on what actually happened, which was that, in 1944, the Japanese took the initiative and committed military suicide when they gambled on the assumption that the ferocity, combat skill, and self-sacrifice of the Japanese soldier could overcome all obstacles of numbers, weaponry, supplies, and geography, and so they crossed the River Chindwin and attacked the British 14th Army at Imphal/Kohima.

## THE CHINDIT ADVENTURE

The Allied plans for 1944, as they eventually took shape, were for Stilwell's India-based Chinese force to operate south from Ledo, mov-ing along the Hukawng valley and then east to the key objective of Myitkyina (pronounced Mitchee-nah), so clearing the way for the U.S. Army engineers and laborers following behind them to build the road and pipeline. This was already well under way by the beginning of the year. In support of this the British were to launch a large air-transported force of, initially, some 14 specially trained battalions (split into 28 "columns") to cut all Japanese supply routes to the north along the line Bhamo-Indaw—the celebrated "Chindits."[2]

The Americans were somewhat depressed at this stage of the war by what they saw as a lack of inclination on the part of the British to get on with the war or even to fight, except, perhaps, at some remote date in the future. To them—and to Churchill chafing at the bit in far-off London—the plan for this raid into Japanese-held territory was bold, imaginative and, above all, aggressive. In addition, the plan was made more attractive by the fact that its originator, the guerrilla warfare expert Orde Wingate, was an eccentric, dressed oddly, and behaved quite unlike anyone's traditional picture of a British

[2]The name was taken from the *Chinthay*, a mythical griffin-like beast, half-lion and half-eagle, which served as the gate guardian at Burmese temples.

Above: British Chindit infantrymen firing a 3 in. mortar. Senior British commanders in India were reluctant to see so many of their best units being transferred into Wavell's Chindits but were given direct and unequivocal orders to cooperate by the British chiefs of staff in London.

Above: Everything involved with the Chindits was air transportable, even including the mules! This one is being forced/coaxed into one of Cochrane's C-47s.

Army general. Thus, the Americans agreed to the plans with great enthusiasm and made the whole operation possible by providing the necessary resources to carry it out, especially an "air commando" of transport, strike, and light communications aircraft.

Even so, all did not go well, mainly because there were divided minds and divided objectives. The conventionally-minded British high command in India was alarmed at seeing so many of the best British units converted into quasi-guerrillas and objected to the whole project, but were forced to agree to it by direct and unequivocal orders from Churchill and the British chiefs

of staff. An additional complication was that on the U.S. side, Stilwell had one disastrous disqualification for high command in this particular alliance—he despised and hated the British, and was incapable of cooperating with them.

It should be mentioned, however, that Stilwell was placed in a series of very curious command positions. As outlined earlier, he was a deputy to Mountbatten the supreme Allied commander, which made him senior to British General Slim, but the latter was commander of all Allied ground forces operating against the Japanese, which included Stilwell's Northern Combat Area Command, and thus Stilwell's

Above: Chindits crossing the river Chindwin watched by some bemused Burmese boys in their canoes.

operational superior. In addition, Stilwell was chief of staff to Chiang Kai-shek, as well as being the national commanding general of the U.S. China-Burma-India Theater. It would have taken a man of exceptional tact and diplomacy to coordinate all those competing demands, but the aptly named "Vinegar Joe" was blessed with neither of those qualities—just one example was that his nickname for Chiang Kai-shek, the man he was supposed to be serving, was "the peanut"!

The inevitable result was that what should have been one single, closely controlled operation diverged into two imperfectly coordinated

ones. Wingate cannot be blamed for much of this, because he was killed in an air crash shortly after his operation began, although there is considerable evidence to show that he himself was more concerned with demonstrating how Burma could be reconquered using his peculiar methods than in playing second fiddle to Stilwell. In the event, and despite the great bravery and endurance of the soldiers on the ground, neither Wingate's nor Stilwell's activities much influenced the outcome of the war in Burma or in China.

In the Chindit operation itself the honors were about even between the Japanese and the scattered "columns" who landed in their midst. The Chindit 77th Brigade scored two notable successes at Mawlu and Mogaung, while the 14th Brigade (less conspicuously) and the 3rd West African Brigade operated successfully to the bitter end. The 16th and 111th Brigades were both heavily defeated, and the 16th was evacuated complete at an early stage. The Chindits were worn out more by long marches, short rations, lack of rest, and disease than by enemy action.

There is an often overlooked postscript to the Chindit campaign. At the end of the Chindit operation proper, the 3rd West African Brigade was under Stilwell's command, protecting his right flank, but they reached a stage of physical exhaustion that required that they had to be replaced. The new formation was the 36th British Division, commanded by Major General Francis Festing, which was flown into Myitkinya, then marched south to Mogaung,

Right: A great and much-loved leader, Sir William Slim, commander XIVth Army. He commanded the Burma Corps with great skill in the retreat from Burma into India in March–May 1942, and also avoided a disaster in the Arakan. Promoted to army commander, he revitalized, reorganized, and retrained his troops, and then led them back into Burma, where they thoroughly defeated the much-vaunted Japanese army.

fighting their way through against determined Japanese resistance—and all at the height of the monsoon, something previously considered impossible. They reached their objective, Pinbaw, and took it on August 28, but knowing that more was possible, Festing obtained Stilwell's permission to continue for a further 50 miles, pushing the Japanese out of one delaying position after another as he went. Without belittling the achievements and courage of the Chindits, it is worth noting that 36th Division was a standard infantry division, made up mainly of British units, who were simply well-trained, well-led, very aggressive, and brimming with confidence— as a result, they were very successful.

The Chindit operation proved a tragic failure, bedeviled by conflicting aims, by being organized for one role and employed in another, and by its mission being altered in mid-operation. It has excited controversy ever since, the Chindit veterans maintaining that their failure was due to misuse, while orthodox soldiers counter that it was an expensive diversion that achieved little in proportion to the large numbers of casualties. On the credit side it had offered timely proof to the Americans that the British really were prepared to fight the Japanese and offered the chance of Anglo-American cooperation in a theater where relations were strained and tainted with suspicion.

Unfortunately, the opportunity was missed as a result of Stilwell's violent Anglophobia.

## THE JAPANESE OFFENSIVE

In the meantime General Sir George Giffard, and his subordinate, Lieutenant General William Slim, in command of the 14th Army, had been methodically reorganizing and strengthening their positions west of the Chindwin River and in the Arakan, when the Japanese struck. Their first attack, in February 1944 in the Arakan, was a diversion intended to draw the 14th Army's reserves away from the Imphal front, and was delivered with the utmost vigor. The result should have sounded a warning note for the Japanese, since at the battle of the Nyakyedauk Pass in the Arakan they met the revitalized British and Indian troops, and their offensive was, first, savagely handled, and then thrown back. The Japanese did, however, succeed in their aim of drawing Slim's reserves away from the vital Imphal sector, but never guessed that it would be possible to fly a whole division north again to meet their main thrust over the Chindwin River.

In fact, the Japanese had made two serious errors. They had underestimated their enemy and his ability to recover from the earlier disasters and retreats, and they had failed to keep

Left: Orde Wingate and American airmen await the arrival of more aircraft at a Chindit position inside Japanese lines.

Below: Chindit infantrymen moving through very close country. Not only was movement very exhausting in such conditions, but it provided ideal hiding ground for Japanese snipers and ambushes, hence the extreme alertness of these men.

abreast of military development. Thus, in March 1944, when they crossed the Chindwin in strength to challenge an expectant 14th Army, they were still an all-infantry army belonging to a previous age, without heavy artillery—they took with them no more than 17 light guns—or tanks, with little air support, and relying almost entirely on animals and coolies for transport. The undoubted courage and combat ferocity of their soldiers proved incapable of balancing the material superiority the British now possessed, and even this was underestimated. In particular, they judged the British and Indians by the hastily expanded wartime units they had met and

Right: A Chindit soldier moves through a Burmese village.

Previous pages: Colonel Cochrane's air commando included light aircraft whose primary task was to land at short, improvised strips in the jungle and evacuate the wounded. This proved to be a great morale booster.

defeated in Malaya and Burma, and failed to realize that British and Indian soldiers were among the finest in the world, with a tradition of courage and devotion, which were at the very least equal to their own. Thus, in 1944 the Japanese were taken by surprise when they encountered the same soldiers, fighting from

well-prepared positions, and lavishly supported by guns, tanks, and aircraft, and who were not prepared to budge.

The result was the extremely hard-fought battle of Kohima-Imphal, which, nonetheless, had moments of great anxiety for both sides. The Japanese had mounted their offensive without any real reserves and without regard for the massive intervention by the Chindits or Stilwell that was apparent in March, and elected to fight with over-extended communications and a large river behind them, on ground of the enemy's choosing already well stocked with supplies. They themselves were to be starved for ammunition and food.

Above: In the center is Brigadier Michael Calvert, a Chindit commander and a great admirer of Wingate. He later commanded the SAS in the Netherlands, and then raised the Malayan Scouts on SAS lines in 1950.

Below: Chindit engineers prepare a railway bridge for destruction during the second expedition.

Right: A mortar section in action during the Battle of Kohima, March–July 1944.

Below: The remains of a Japanese position during the fighting around Kohima/Imphal, in March–July 1944. It has just been captured by troops of 10th Gurkha Rifles who move warily, checking that every Japanese soldier has been dealt with, as a commonly-used trick was to feign death and then try to kill unsuspecting Allied soldiers using a submachine gun or grenade.

The weakness of the British position lay in the fact that their supply routes lay parallel to their front. The Japanese thrusts isolated Kohima and therefore Imphal by cutting the road from the rail-head, and had the Japanese penetrated further they could have cut the railway as well and so starved all the U.S. and Chinese troops supplied through Ledo. (This possibility alarmed Stilwell greatly, as he had no confidence in the staying power of British troops, and he offered to Slim, who refused it, a Chinese regiment to secure the rear areas.) For Slim, therefore, all hinged on holding the Japanese around Kohima and Imphal while his garrisons lived on their stocks or were supplied by air, in order to throw the Japanese in their turn onto the defensive, wearing them out and then destroying them in a series of counterattacks.

Imphal was first encircled at the beginning of April and not relieved until June 22, but in the course of the fighting the Japanese army, which had so confidently crossed the Chindwin, was totally destroyed as a fighting force. The 14th Army had confounded its critics, and to

clinch the point—and regardless of the exhaustion of its units and the onset of the monsoon rains—it then pursued the Japanese remnants. By August 5 the 14th Army was over the frontier and into Burma and by August 20 it was able to announce that there were no Japanese troops left on Indian territory, and that it was still going forward.

In the meantime Stilwell's Chinese had also enjoyed success, and a surprise march led by his Chindit-trained "Marauder" regiment had captured the airfields outside his objective, Myitkyina, in early May. But it was not until August that the town itself fell, as the Chinese-American troops lacked both the skill and the heavy weapons required to dislodge the Japanese by direct assault from a strong position, which they were determined to hold until the bitter end. The new Burma Road was finally opened in January 1945, a tribute to Joseph Stilwell's ruthless determination and to the U.S. Army Engineer Corps. But Stilwell himself, whose relations with the ever-prevaricating Chiang Kai-shek had deteriorated beyond the

Below: A British patrol moves cautiously through long grass, with two scouts being covered by the light machine gun (LMG) section closest to the camera. The actual LMG is the 0.303 in. Bren, a very reliable, accurate, and well-liked weapon, which served the British army very well in every theater during World War II.

Above: A soldier of Merrill's Marauders, Pfc Peter Gugliano, discusses the finer points of his rifle with a soldier from the Chinese Army's 88th Infantry Regiment. Strapped to his pack, the American soldier carriers the famed Gurkha knife, known as a *kukri*, which he has acquired somewhere on his travels.

possibility of repair, was relieved in October.

It is a remarkable tribute to the Imperial Japanese army, purely as a fighting instrument, that while its strategy may have been misguided, in 1944 it fought an offensive operation on one front and defensive operations on two others, and dealt very firmly, for example, with any Chinese units who attempted to cross the Salween River.

The fact remains that the harder they fought in 1944 the riper they were for the *coup de grâce* to be delivered in 1945 by Slim and the 14th Army. From being defeated in 1942, they now gave an astonishing demonstration of how to conduct modern warfare in an undeveloped country over mountains and through the jungle, including crossing two of the great rivers of Asia in the process. Rangoon fell in May and the surviving Japanese troops, after suffering fearful casualties and hardships, were persuaded to surrender in August.

To take World War II in an overall perspective, and with the benefit of a very large helping of hindsight, it is apparent that these huge,

costly and prolonged operations, were—to use a phrase popular in World War I—merely a "sideshow." However, that was by no means apparent at the time and by tying down huge Japanese armies, the British, Americans, and Chinese played a significant role in the eventual defeat of the Japanese.

### FIGHTING BACK IN THE SOUTH-WEST PACIFIC

After the great American victory in the Battle of Midway, the American joint chiefs of staff were anxious to seize the initiative against the Japanese. General Douglas MacArthur, commander of the South-West Pacific Theater, and Admiral Ernest King, Chief of Naval Operations, suggested a campaign aimed at the capture of the great Japanese base at Rabaul on the island of New Britain in the Bismarck Archipelago northeast of New Guinea.

After much discussion and debate over the question of whether the projected operations would be under navy or army control, the joint chiefs of staff issued orders for a three-stage

Above: Merrill's 5307th Composite Unit, Nauhaum, Burma, in April 1944. At the end of a long day during Merrill's march, platoon commander Second Lieutenant Murray is handed a pack of C rations as he leads his men into camp.

Left: Men of 2nd Battalion, 475th Infantry Regiment engage Japanese snipers at Loi Kang on the Burma Road. The unit was originally designated 5307th Composite Unit (Provisional)/ Merrill's Marauders, but on May 17, 1944, it was redesignated 475th Infantry Regiment and was also known as Mars Task Force. The survivors moved to China in March–May 1945, where the unit was disbanded.

operation. The first stage was to be under the command of Vice Admiral Robert Ghormley, commander of the South Pacific Area of the Pacific Theater, and the subsequent stages to be under the direction of MacArthur. In the first stage Ghormley's forces would seize bases in the southern part of the Solomon Islands, southeast of New Guinea. In the second stage Ghormley's forces would advance north through the Solomons while MacArthur's command cleared

the north coast of New Guinea as far as the villages of Lae and Salamaua. In the third stage the two commands would cooperate in an attack on Rabaul itself.

Operations began on August 7, 1942, with landings by the 1st Marine Division (Reinforced) under Major General A. Vandegrift on the islands of Guadalcanal and Tulagi, at the southern end of the Solomons. The marines achieved complete surprise, quickly overcoming

Right: The campaign on Guadalcanal was long and bitterly fought, but many lessons were learned, which were put to good use in future amphibious operations. Here a group of marines from a Marine Parachute Regiment are leaving Guadalcanal to operate on nearby Vella LaVella island.

Previous pages: A sad scene among typical rice fields near the Burmese town of Lashio as a group of soldiers of 475th Infantry carry a dead comrade to his burial. These men fought hard but malaria, amoebic dysentery, and other, unidentified tropical fevers inflicted more casualties than the Japanese.

the small number of Japanese defenders on the islands and capturing the still unfinished airfield on Guadalcanal, which they renamed "Henderson Field" after a marine aviator killed at Midway.

The U.S. Marines' position soon became precarious, however, when on the night of August 9 Japanese cruisers under Vice Admiral Mikawa slipped down undetected from Rabaul and sank one Australian and three American

heavy cruisers, which were covering the invasion convoy. American aircraft carriers covering the operation had already been withdrawn because of fear of air attack, and now the transports and supply vessels were also forced hurriedly to withdraw, even though they had not been completely unloaded. The marines were thus left short of supplies and ammunition, and with little air support. But they possessed two advantages that, in the end, were to prove decisive: they held Henderson Field, which was speedily rushed to completion; and their strength had been drastically underestimated by the Japanese.

As a result of this latter miscalculation, Japanese forces were fed into the island piecemeal. The first detachments were annihilated by the marines in futile attacks on Henderson Field and, in September, a major Japanese effort to seize the high ground south of Henderson was beaten off in the "Battle of Bloody Ridge."

During September and October air and naval battles continued around the island as both sides sought to reinforce their troops. Ashore, the marines fought not only the Japanese, but also the jungle, mud, heat, torrential rain, and tropical diseases. A three-day battle in late October marked the high tide of Japanese efforts to retake the island and this was beaten off with heavy losses by the Americans.

Following this the Americans took the offensive. The 1st Marine Division was relieved by the 2nd Marine Division and two U.S. Army divisions, the 25th and the American. In three more months of hard fighting the Japanese were

Above: Battle-weary U.S. Marines of the 2nd Raider Battalion return from the Makin Atoll raid on November 22, 1943. Intended to eliminate the Japanese garrison and gather information, it was only a qualified success. The surf proved far worse than predicted, the operations ashore were characterized by a lack of command-and-control, twenty-one marines were killed, and nine more were unintentionally left behind, all subsequently executed by the Japanese. But, the Japanese garrison was almost completely eliminated, several ships and aircraft were destroyed, and many valuable lessons were learned.

Above: One type of terrain encountered during the island campaigns. The natural rain forest has been partially cut back, leaving a clearing, which is totally open to the tropical sun. At ground level there are palm trees and bamboo thickets, the latter being particularly impenetrable. The clearings make for good progress in an advance, but are particularly hot, and their fringes provide excellent cover for snipers and stay-behind parties.

gradually forced back to Cape Esperance, at the extreme western end of the island, from which 13,000 were successfully evacuated during the first week of February 1943.

If "Task One" had proven much more difficult than anticipated, MacArthur's "Task Two" was forestalled completely. On July 21 a Japanese force landed near Buna on the northern side of the Papuan peninsula of New Guinea and pushed south across the rugged Owen Stanley mountains toward Port Moresby, the principal town of New Guinea still in Allied hands. By September the Japanese had advanced to within 30 miles of Port Moresby when growing supply problems and incessant Allied air attacks finally brought them to a halt.

Australian forces under General Sir Thomas Blamey stubbornly fought their way back across the Owen Stanleys but were halted by strong Japanese defenses around the villages of Buna

and Gona on the north New Guinea coast. In what was to be one of the most costly operations of the war, in proportion to the forces engaged, Australian troops reinforced by the American 32nd Division gradually reduced the Japanese strongholds at a cost of about some 8,500 killed and wounded and thousands more incapacitated through disease. The Japanese force was almost totally destroyed.

The bloody battles in the steaming, disease-ridden jungles of Papua and Guadalcanal had been far longer and more costly than anyone had anticipated. Yet the Allied victories there had shown that Australian and American troops could engage the Japanese soldier in jungle warfare and defeat him. By the conclusion of the Guadalcanal and Papuan campaigns the initiative clearly lay with the Allies. Both sides had lost heavily in warships and planes, but while the immense industrial capacity of the U.S.

Left: U.S. Marines crouch, ready to play their part in an assault on a Japanese position. Note the primary jungle, with its profusion of trees and dense undergrowth. The latter makes any progress slow, and, unless care is taken, movement can be noisy, warning defenders of their enemy's approach.

insured that its losses would be more than replaced, the Japanese losses could not be made good so easily.

### A TWO-PRONGED STRATEGY

While MacArthur and Vice Admiral William F. Halsey, who had replaced Ghormley as the South Pacific Area commander, prepared to resume their campaign against Rabaul, a debate raged among Allied strategists as to the proper long-range strategy to be pursued against Japan. During the spring and summer of 1943 American forces had cleared the Japanese off the islands of the Aleutians, which they had occupied during the Midway operation, but any further advance along this line was ruled out by the severe weather of the region and the lack of adequate bases. Logistical problems also ruled out any major offensive operations from China, leaving only two practical routes of approach to the Japanese home islands.

The first route was by way of the island chains of the Central Pacific, the Gilberts, Marshalls, Marianas, and Carolines to either the Philippines or Formosa and thence to Japan

Below: Japanese troops on a training exercise in the Marshall Islands in December 1942. The Japanese infantry were aggressive in attack and very determined in defense, but proved to be by no means undefeatable.

itself. This was the route long contemplated in the American prewar "Plan Orange" for war against Japan. This route would allow the U.S. Navy to employ the growing strength of the Pacific Fleet, which by late 1943 had been reinforced with modern fast carriers and battleships. Moreover the Japanese garrisons on the small Central Pacific islands were far apart and could easily be isolated and picked off one by one.

MacArthur and his staff strongly challenged the Central Pacific approach. They pointed out that the old Plan Orange had never taken into account the possibility that Australia would be an ally in the war against Japan. The considerable military resources of Australia and its potential as an advance base could best be exploited by following a line of advance along the coast of New Guinea and then through the Philippines to the Japanese home islands. This South Pacific drive could be supported by land-based air forces, while forces operating in the Central Pacific would be totally dependent upon carrier-based planes for their support.

In the end Allied strategists decided to use both routes. At the British-American "Trident" Conference at Washington in May 1943 it was

Below: Australian troops cross a makeshift rope bridge across a fast-flowing river at Buna in Papua, December 1942.

agreed that MacArthur and Halsey should proceed with their campaign against Rabaul while Admiral Chester Nimitz's force would open the Central Pacific drive with an assault on the Marshall Islands (later changed to the Gilberts.)

A few weeks after the conclusion of "Trident" the South-West Pacific forces resumed their drive on Rabaul. This operation, now called "Cartwheel," consisted of a series of alternating coordinated attacks against the Japanese as MacArthur's forces advanced west along the New Guinea coast and Halsey advanced northwest up the "ladder" of the Solomon Islands.

The campaign began with the invasion of the unoccupied Trobriand Islands, off the New Guinea coast, by elements of the U.S. 6th Army under General Walter Krueger. Halsey followed this up with an invasion of the island of New Georgia, the principal Japanese air base in the Solomons. The landings were accomplished with little opposition but Major General John Hester's 43rd Division was inexperienced in jungle warfare and faced stubborn opposition from the Japanese. A second U.S. Army division eventually had to be committed, and Hester was replaced by Major General Oscar Griswold. Fighting dragged on for almost two months

Left: Soldiers of 2nd Battalion, 165th Infantry Regiment advancing through the surf on Butaratiri Island in the Makin Atoll on November 23, 1943. They are very vulnerable to enemy fire during this phase, but it is clear that the beach shelves very gradually, making it impossible for even flat-bottomed landing ships/craft to get any closer.

Left: U.S. Navy landing ships tank (LST) waiting to disgorge supplies at Leyte Island in the Philippines. A veritable army of men is involved in building temporary causeways out to the ships to enable unloading to begin. In such a situation air supremacy was vital, since otherwise large, immobilized LSTs neatly lined up in a row and hordes of workers would offer ideal targets to enemy ground-attack fighters.

429

Lac and Salamaua in mid-September. One week later a brigade of the 8th Australian Division landed at the port of Finschhafen and held out against determined Japanese counterattacks until the end of October. By January 1944 Allied forces controlled the New Guinea coast as far west as Sio on the Huon peninsula.

The joint chiefs of staff now adopted the "leapfrogging" tactics. This was the bypassing

Above: Amphibious tractors, such as this landing vehicle tracked (LVT) on Bouganville, played an invaluable role in getting men ashore and then moving them around the battlefield.

Below: One of the major innovations of the war was radar. Here the antenna array for an early air detection radar is erected on Bougainville.

before the airfield at Munda was secured and Japanese resistance overcome.

Wishing to avoid a repetition of the "slugging match" on New Georgia, Halsey and his commanders decided to bypass the next island, Kolombangara, and, instead, attack the lightly held island of Vella Lavella. This was accomplished successfully against little opposition and an airfield was constructed for an attack against the island of Bougainville at the top of the Solomons ladder.

Meanwhile MacArthur's forces began their advance along the New Guinea coast, capturing

and cutting off strongpoints and attacking weak ones, which Halsey had employed after New Georgia. MacArthur and Halsey were ordered to encircle Rabaul and destroy it through air attack and blockade rather than by a direct ground attack, which would have proved very costly against Rabaul's 100,000-man garrison.

Halsey's part in the isolation of Rabaul was completed in the fall and winter of 1943 when troops of the 3rd Marine Division landed at Empress Augusta Bay on the west coast of Bougainville. The Japanese reacted violently to the invasion. Planes and ships from Rabaul attacked the invasion forces but Allied planes from New Georgia successfully interdicted most of the Japanese air attacks while carrier task forces, lent by Nimitz's Pacific Fleet, took a heavy toll of Japanese warships at Rabaul. By

Below: Early morning on Bougainville as infantry supported by a tank mop up Japanese who have infiltrated their positions during the hours of darkness.

431

Right: Two aggressive marines on Tarawa in November 1943. The second marine is in the act of throwing a hand grenade, while his buddy, nearest the camera, grasps his carbine and a bandolier of ammunition, ready to charge forward as soon as the grenade explodes.

the end of 1943 the marines had been reinforced by a U.S. Army division, and Allied air bases were in operation on Bougainville. The remainder of the island was finally secured the following spring.

The encirclement of Rabaul was completed at the end of February 1944 when the U.S. 1st Cavalry Division landed on Los Negros Island in the Admiralties. The Japanese forces on the island initially outnumbered the invaders but the island commander fed in his forces piecemeal against the increasingly large American forces. By March 23 the island was secured. Rabaul, with its large garrison, naval base, and airfield, was now surrounded by a ring of Allied bases and left to "wither on the vine."

## ISLAND-HOPPING THROUGH THE CENTRAL PACIFIC

While MacArthur and Halsey had been closing the ring around Rabaul, the long planned Central Pacific drive got under way with an attack on Tarawa and Makin in the Gilbert Islands in November 1943. Convoyed by one of the largest naval armadas ever assembled, under the overall command of Vice Admiral Raymond Spruance, the invasion forces arrived in the Gilberts on November 20. Makin fell with little difficulty but the attack on Tarawa developed into one of the bloodiest battles of the war in the Pacific Theater.

Below: The second wave of marines wades ashore in Tarawa in the Gilbert Islands to reinforce the units already there. Note that even the men in the far distance are no more than waist-deep in the water.

Previous pages: Marines moving forward to take a Japanese bunker during the operations on Tarawa in November 1943. Again, the picture illustrates the devastation created by the pre-landing bombardment from warships standing offshore.

Above: Men of an infantry company of 7th Division, U.S. Army in a temporary halt on Kwajalein, February 1944. The tracked vehicle giving fire support is an M10 Tank Destroyer.

The Japanese had converted Tarawa into a small fortress with a formidable array of light and heavy guns protected by concrete bunkers. The entire island was ringed with beach defenses and antiboat obstacles. Yet the island's most deadly defense proved to be a shallow coral reef where many of the landing craft carrying the assault troops of the 2nd Marine Division ran aground, forcing their occupants to wade ashore under murderous fire from the Japanese.

By nightfall on the first day almost a third of the marines on the beach had been killed or wounded, but the remainder hung on tenaciously and the following day, with the help of reinforcements, pushed back the Japanese defenders. In three days of hard fighting the marines cleaned out the enemy bunkers and pillboxes and virtually annihilated the defenders. Almost 3,000 casualties were suffered by the marines in the battle for the tiny 300-acre island.

Despite the appalling casualties, the Tarawa campaign proved of considerable value to the U.S. Marines and Navy in improving their techniques of amphibious warfare. The lessons learned on the subject of air and naval gunfire support, the need for better communications

arrangements, and the need for improved amphibious assault vehicles were to stand the Allies in good stead in later campaigns in the Central Pacific. In addition, the seizure of the Gilbert Islands gave Nimitz's forces air and supply bases to mount their assaults against the Marshall Islands, next on the schedule of the Central Pacific drive.

The campaign in the Marshalls proved unexpectedly easy compared with the ordeal of the Gilberts. Nimitz directed Spruance's invasion forces to bypass the most easterly islands and attack the atoll of Kwajalein, in the center of the island chain. On February 1, 1944, after a three-day air and naval bombardment, an army and marine division of General Holland M. Smith's V Amphibious Corps landed on different islands of the atoll. Japanese resistance was stubborn but ineffective and the atoll was secured in less than a week with relatively light losses. The westernmost atoll of Eniwetok was then attacked by about 10,000 men of Smith's corps reserve.

In order to cover the assault on Eniwetok, Spruance's fast carrier task forces carried out a devastating series of raids on the Japanese fleet

Above: When all else failed and the Japanese were clearly not going to surrender, U.S. troops had no choice but get really close and use the dreaded flamethrowers, as seen here on Kwajalein Island in February 1944.

Left: Parry Island in Eniwetok Atoll was of no strategic significance, but the Japanese defenders fought for every inch of it. Moments after he took this picture, the Coast Guard photographer was thrown into a foxhole by an incoming Japanese mortar shell and his camera destroyed, although the film survived.

base at Truk, in the Carolines on the south-western flank of the Marshalls. Truk was the principal Central Pacific base of the Imperial Japanese Navy and had long been considered an impregnable fortress. The American carrier raids revealed Truk to be surprisingly vulnerable. Half a dozen Japanese warships, many more auxiliaries, and more than 250 planes were destroyed at small cost to the attackers. Eniwetok fell four days later and Truk was unusable as a fleet base for the remainder of the war. Like Rabaul, Truk had been effectively neutralized and could be safely bypassed in the Allied march toward Japan.

The campaign in the Marshalls had proved so successful and been brought to such a swift conclusion that Nimitz was able to advance considerably his timetable for his next objective. This was the Marianas, the long island chain southeast of Japan. Over 1,000 miles from the nearest American air base at Eniwetok, the Marianas formed part of the inner ring of Japan's defenses. From bases on the three large southern islands, Tinian, Saipan, and the former American-held island of Guam, Boeing B-29 long-range bombers could attack Japan itself.

The Japanese were well aware of the importance of the Marianas and committed all their available forces, including the Combined Fleet, which had been kept out of the Gilberts and Marshalls, to defend them. The American invasion of the Marianas began on June 15, 1944, with the landing of Lieutenant General Holland

Above: Marines take temporary shelter behind an M4 Sherman tank during the final stages of the operations on the island of Saipan.

Left: The landings on Guam took place on July 21, 1944, following the operations on Saipan. A lengthy shore bombardment preceded the landings, and, as shown here, the first wave was temporarily pinned down on the beach. These Japanese counterattacks were, however, beaten off and the island finally fell on August 10.

Smith's V Amphibious Corps on Saipan, which was a much larger island than those previously encountered in the Marshalls and Gilberts. Smith's two marine divisions, soon reinforced by the U.S. Army's 27th Division, were obliged to fight their way from south to north on a broad front through extremely rugged jungle-covered country studded with sheer cliffs and narrow ravines. Army and marine commanders sometimes blamed each other for the slow progress of the advance and at one point Holland Smith (a Marine Corps officer) relieved the Army general commanding the 27th Division.

Saipan was finally secured in mid-July at a cost of some 3,126 American and 27,000 Japanese dead. Guam and Tinian fell during the next few weeks.

### THE RETAKING OF GUAM (JULY–AUGUST 1944)

Every island invasion during the Pacific campaign had its own unique characteristics—particularly for those taking part in it—so none can be described as being "typical." However, the re-taking of Guam is described here as an example of the sort of fighting that went on and of the fortitude required of the combat troops.

The Marianas group of islands extend in a 700 mile north-south arc, located some 1,000 miles south of Japan and 800 miles due east of the Philippines. All were former German possessions, mandated to Japan by the League of Nations in 1919, except for Guam, which became U.S. territory in 1901 in the Spanish-American War. When the Japanese invaded on December 9, 1941, Guam was garrisoned by 365 U.S. Marines and was the first U.S. possession to fall into Japanese hands.

The main islands in the group are Saipan, Tinian, and Guam and by capturing these the U.S. forces could both establish air bases from which to raid mainland Japan, as well as using them as a staging-post for the recovery of the Philippines. Guam itself is some 30 miles long and 10 miles wide, consisting of a flat limestone plateau with low hills in the center and mountains in the south. There was a fine anchorage in Apra Harbor with a Japanese-built airfield on

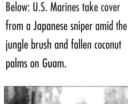

Below: U.S. Marines take cover from a Japanese sniper amid the jungle brush and fallen coconut palms on Guam.

the Orote peninsula, close to the former U.S. Marines' barracks.

The Marianas were occupied by the Japanese 31st Army, with Guam itself being garrisoned by 29th Infantry Division and 54th Naval Guard Force, a total of some 19,000 men. Unlike some Japanese-held islands, however, the defenses were well-prepared, with concrete bunkers, the artillery dug-in, and underwater obstacles laid on the main beaches. Most Japanese defenses lay around Apra Harbor overlooking Agat and Asan beaches, which were the only realistic sites for any landing, since the northern and southern ends of the island were covered with cliffs, while the east coast was protected by a wide coral strand.

The American Marianas operation started on June 15, 1944, when 2nd and 4th Marine Divisions landed on Saipan. Japanese resistance was very stiff and on June 17 the U.S. operational reserve, the Army's 27 Infantry Division, was committed. Japanese resistance ceased on July 7 after almost the entire 27,000 man garrison had been killed. (One distressing event on

Saipan occurred in the final hour when some 8,000 Japanese civilians leapt to their deaths from the cliffs in the north of the island.) The second phase of the operation followed with 4th Marine Division landing on nearby Tinian on July 24 followed by 2nd Marine Division on July 25. This operation was relatively quick and the island had been cleared by July 31. (The airfield built on Tinian was the operational base for the B-29s that dropped the atomic bombs on Hiroshima and Nagasaki.)

The invasion of Guam by III Amphibious Corps, commanded by Major General Geiger and comprising one division and one brigade, had been scheduled for June 18 but, once the fierceness of Japanese resistance on Saipan had been appreciated, it was decided that a larger force would be needed. As a result, the invasion was postponed, the Army's 77th Infantry Division was summoned from Hawaii, and a new plan was prepared.

"Softening-up" started on July 8 and continued for 11 days with numerous carrier-borne air attacks, while the warships lying offshore

Below: An explosive charge is detonated in a Japanese dugout on the Orote Peninsula, Guam, July 26, 1944. Japanese defenders numbered some 18,500, of which all but a handful were either killed or captured. A few roamed the jungles until well after the end of the war, when they were finally persuaded to give themselves up. U.S. losses were 2,124 killed, most of them in the Marine Corps.

fired 28,764 shells of between 5 in. and 16 in. caliber into the island, reaching a crescendo in the final day, with 18,400 rounds plus 9,000 4.5 in. rockets. Many targets were destroyed, but, as always on the Pacific islands, as soon as the bombardment lifted there were still enough Japanese left to make the attack costly for the Americans. 3rd Marine Division hit the Asan beach at 0829 on July 21 and by mid-afternoon held an area some 2,000 yd. wide and 1,200 yd. at its deepest. The Japanese poured in artillery and mortar fire from the hills overlooking the beachhead, causing many casualties, but the hand-to-hand fighting at the water's edge, for which the Japanese had planned, never took place. The Japanese mounted a major counterattack on the night of July 25/26, but failed to clear the U.S. beachheads.

The second landing by 1st Provisional Marine Brigade on Agat beach was hit by Japanese guns as they arrived, costing them some 350 men killed and 24 amphibious tractors destroyed. Nevertheless, they got ashore and quickly penetrated to a depth of 2,000 yd. A platoon of Sherman tanks plus some 3,000 tons of supplies were brought ashore in the first day, with the tanks proving of great assistance in repelling three Japanese counterattacks between 2:30 A.M. and 4:00 A.M. on July 22.

In the hills ringing the northern beachhead the Japanese used caves on the forward slopes for their mortars and the reverse (hidden) slopes for their artillery, causing problems for the marines. Nevertheless, the accurate naval gun-fire support helped the U.S. forces to fight their way up the hills and by July 24 they held the Crestline. On the night of July 25–26 no fewer than seven battalions of Japanese infantry made a major attack, with fixed bayonets and shouts of "banzai" and "Wake up Yankees and die." In the heavy fighting small groups of attackers penetrated into the rear areas, with some even reaching the field hospital where wounded marines lying on beds defended themselves with rifle fire. Eventually the attack petered out with heavy Japanese casualties.

On the southern beachhead 1st Marine Provisional Brigade was counterattacked by the Japanese every night, although these were always beaten off. When a regimental combat team (RCT) from 77th Infantry Division came ashore to take over the southern half of the beachhead, the marines fought their way out of

the beachhead to the north, aiming to join up with the Asan beachhead. They advanced slowly until they had isolated Orote peninsula, which was defended by a Japanese infantry battalion.

This unit subsequently made one of the more unusual attacks of the Pacific war, when the battalion commander ordered his men to drink whatever alcoholic liquor they could obtain, which included beer, Japanese saki and synthetic whiskey. Once they were thoroughly intoxicated, the men made a night attack (July 25/26) on the Americans, laughing and giggling hysterically, lurching about, firing their weapons indiscriminately, and shouting drunken *banzais*. U.S. artillery defensive fire was brought down, together with machine gun, mortar, and rifle fire, and the drunken (and highly dangerous) soldiers were slowly dealt with; at dawn tired U.S. Marines counted over 400 Japanese corpses.

With this disgraceful episode dealt with, 1st Provisional Marine Brigade advanced up the Orote peninsula with fire support from both the fleet and corps artillery, which was now ashore. At first, the Japanese contested every yard, but their resistance cracked on July 27 and by July 29 the peninsula had been cleared; the airfield was in operation on the 31st.

There were still many determined Japanese left and the Americans now pushed them slowly up into the northern end of the island, with 1st Marine Division on the left and 77th Infantry Division on the right. Effective Japanese resistance ceased on August 10.

During the battle 54,891 United States troops landed, of whom 1,440 were killed, 145 were missing, and 5,648 were wounded. The Japanese were some 19,000 strong at the time of the U.S. invasion; 10,693 were killed and 98 became prisoners. The remainder went into the jungle and fought on in small groups, with the last unit, consisting of a lieutenant colonel and 113 others surrendering on September 4, 1945. The last known survivor, Corporal Yokoi Shoichi, emerged only in January 1972.

## MACARTHUR RETURNS TO THE PHILIPPINES

News of the American invasion of Saipan brought Vice Admiral Ozawa hastening to the area, with a large fleet built around nine carriers, to attack the American invasion forces. The Japanese made contact with Spruance's fleet

Previous pages: American soldiers blast a Japanese stronghold on Guam's Orote peninsula. The weapon on the right is an M3 37 mm antitank gun, which was obsolete in its original role in the European Theater, but still suitable for tasks such as this and attacking weakly-armored Japanese tanks in the Pacific campaign.

Left: It gave the U.S. Marines particular satisfaction to recapture their former barracks on the edge of the airstrip at Orote on Guam. This camp had been abandoned several years earlier in the face of what appeared to be Japan's inexorable advance on the Pacific.

west of Guam on the morning of June 19. In the ensuing Battle of the Philippine Sea the Japanese naval air arm was virtually wiped out and, in addition, Vice Admiral Ozawa lost three of his best carriers, while American losses were negligible. The carrier-based striking force, Japan's most potent weapon of the Pacific war, had now ceased to exist.

While Nimitz's forces had been advancing across the Central Pacific, MacArthur, in one of the most brilliant operations of the war, had leapfrogged more than 500 miles along the New Guinea coast, bypassing the Japanese strongpoints at Madang and Wewak, to capture the major supply base at Hollandia. This base was outside the range of Allied land-based air support but MacArthur managed to borrow the fast carrier force of the Pacific Fleet, under Vice Admiral Mitscher, long enough to support his assault on Hollandia and an intermediate position at Aitape. From Aitape MacArthur's land-based planes, under Lieutenant General George Kenney, could support further operations in western New Guinea. So as not to alert the Japanese to his objective, MacArthur directed

that Aitape and Hollandia be attacked at the same time.

In late April 1944, while Australian forces kept the Japanese at Madang occupied, the American 24th and 41st Divisions, covered by Mitscher's carrier planes, landed on beaches east and west of Hollandia. Other forces, covered by Kenney's planes, seized Aitape. Within two days American aircraft were operating from Aitape and on April 27 Hollandia was secured.

The Japanese 18th Army, cut off from its supplies at Hollandia, attempted to break out during the summer of 1944 but the Japanese attacks were beaten off with heavy losses by American and Australian forces. MacArthur, meanwhile, continued his advance westward, capturing Biak Island on June 29 after one of the bloodiest battles of the Pacific war. By the end of July 1944 American forces stood on Cape Sansapor, at the extreme northwest tip of New Guinea, and all Japanese forces on the island had been isolated or destroyed.

Douglas MacArthur now proposed to proceed with his long-planned invasion of the Philippines, but some Allied strategists had come

Above: Australian troops in Aitape, New Guinea. The lead scout is carrying an Owen machine carbine, instantly recognizable by its vertical magazine. Designed and made in Australia, it was a workmanlike and effective weapon, and very popular with all who used it.

Left: A commanding officer's parade for Company A, 2nd Battalion, First Filipino Regiment, at Oro Bay, New Guinea, on May 18, 1944. Filipino troops provided many guerrillas who fought behind Japanese lines from 1942 onward, as well as more conventional troops such as those seen here.

Above: A lone Japanese aircraft flying over the island of Leyte on October 22, 1944. Despite their ever-dwindling resources, Japanese air attacks remained intense against both sea and land targets, with kamikaze attacks serving to make the threat even more severe.

to favor bypassing the Philippines in favor of an attack on Formosa (now Taiwan), followed by an invasion of the south coast of China. In the end, however, considerations of strategy and logistics, the military weakness of China, and the fact that an invasion of the Philippines could be launched long before an attack on Formosa, dictated the decision to proceed with the Philippine attack.

In October 1944 forces from both Pacific and South-West Pacific theaters converged on the island of Leyte, in the central Philippines. Four U.S. Army divisions comprising the 6th Army under General Walter Krueger were put ashore on the Leyte beaches. This was to be the

largest invasion of the Pacific war. The Japanese reacted vigorously and all that remained of the Combined Fleet was ordered to Philippine waters to attack the invasion forces. In the ensuing Battle of Leyte Gulf, the largest naval engagement in history, the Japanese lost most of their navy but almost succeeded in decoying part of the American fleet's fast carriers away from the invasion beaches.

Meanwhile American troops on Leyte were making slow progress against determined resistance. Heavy rains hampered American ground and air operations and allowed the Japanese to slip in reinforcements. But the Americans had

Left: A Filipino boy helping airmen of a USAAF forward control team to load a Landing Ship Medium (LSM) before they depart to take part in another amphibious landing.

also been reinforced. On December 7 the 77th Division made an amphibious landing on the west coast of Leyte, and by the 20th the Japanese were surrounded by three U.S. Army divisions and cut off from all access to the sea. By Christmas Day the back of the Japanese resistance had been broken.

While mopping up actions continued on Leyte the bulk of Krueger's 6th Army moved on to Luzon, landing at Lingayen Gulf, northwest of Manila, on January 9, 1945. General Yamashita, who had commanded the Japanese forces in the invasion of Malaya, now commanded the Japanese army forces defending Luzon, but did not intend to imitate MacArthur's ill-fated attempt to defend the entire island. Nor did he intend to be bottled up in the narrow Bataan peninsula. Instead he concentrated his forces in the rugged mountain country of northern Luzon where they could conduct an effective defensive campaign against the superior American forces.

Japanese naval ground forces on Luzon, only nominally under Yamashita's command, insisted on conducting a stubborn defense of the capital city, Manila, which Yamashita had ordered abandoned. The Japanese murdered tens of thousands of Filipinos and it required almost a month of bitter house-to-house fighting

before the capital was again in American hands. Bataan and the islands of Manila Bay fell by mid-March, but operations against the Japanese strongholds in north Luzon continued until the end of the war.

### THE LAST LAP

With the successful invasion of the Philippines accomplished, Allied forces closed in on the Japanese home islands, the invasion of which was scheduled to begin in November 1945. On February 19, 1945, marines of Major General Harry Schmidt's V Amphibious Corps landed on

Above: General Douglas MacArthur, supreme Allied commander of the Southwest Pacific, surveys the ruins of the Clerk Field Hospital on Luzon Island in January 1945. The Japanese deliberately destroyed the hospital as they retreated and also caused great destruction in Manila in clear breach of the rules of war.

the tiny island of Iwo Jima, southeast of Japan. From Iwo Jima fighter planes could escort B-29s in their strikes against the home islands and damaged bombers could make emergency landings there for repairs and fuel.

Defended by more than 22,000 men, Iwo Jima was probably the most strongly fortified island attacked by the Allies in the Pacific war. Its brilliant commander, Major General Kuribayashi, did not throw his men away on suicide attacks but skillfully and stubbornly defended every yard, so that the island soon became a symbol of carnage and gallantry. Nearly 25,000 marines were killed or wounded in five weeks of savage fighting before the island was secured.

A final preliminary to the invasion of Japan was the capture of Okinawa, a large island in the Ruckus island chain just south of the southernmost Japanese island of Kyushu. Two Army and two marine divisions under Lieutenant General Simon Buckner attacked Okinawa on April 1, 1945. Japanese resistance on land was savage and at sea swarms of *kamikazes* attacked

the invasion fleet supporting the landings. Yet the overwhelming superiority of the Americans in air and fire power and their ability to bring in superior numbers of support weapons, especially tanks, doomed the defenders to defeat. Okinawa was secured on June 22 at a cost of almost 50,000 American and well over 100,000 Japanese casualties.

Allied commanders now began the final planning and preparations for the assault on the Japanese home islands, but this operation was to prove unnecessary. On August 6, 1945, a single B-29 bomber dropped an atomic bomb on the city of Hiroshima, followed by a second on the city of Nagasaki three days later.

Although die-hard militarists in the Japanese government wished to fight on, the sheer destructiveness of the atomic bomb gave Japanese moderates a chance to seize the initiative and end the fighting. On August 10 Japan signified its readiness to surrender, and on August 15 the guns ceased firing throughout Asia and the Pacific. The Allies had reached the end of their long and bloody road to Japan.

Left: U.S. Marines land on the shores of mainland Japan in September 1945.

Below: Marines finally take Kings Hill on Okinawa on May 6, 1945.

*Chapter 6*

# THE WAR
# IN THE AIR

NEITHER THE SHATTERING EFFECT OF PEARL HARBOR—a classically planned and executed air strike—nor the decided early superiority of Japanese aircraft (in both design and numbers) could deter the Americans in the Pacific. They clung on desperately and struck back, first at Coral Sea and then, tellingly, at Midway to win parity in the air. Then began the long haul back across the Pacific, the development of new aircraft, competed at breakneck speed, and the hard-won superiority in the air. The Superfortresses hit at Japan itself, causing much damage to industry and morale, and the kamikaze force had its wild, retaliatory fling. But not even that suicidal fanaticism could compete with the eventual superiority of the American combat aircraft and the training and experience of their pilots, the immense industrial might of the United States which insured a fast and liberal flow of new weapons and replacements, and ultimately the power of the shockwaves from the atomic bomb. While it is true that air power can win territory, but only land forces can hold it, the conflict in the Pacific Theater was initiated, dictated, and decided by war in the air.

Right: A Japanese twin-engined bomber is shot down during an attack on U.S. Navy carriers off Saipan during the Marianas operation on June 18, 1944. U.S. carriers were the top-priority targets for Japanese aircraft, surface ships, and submarines, but despite some successes, they never approached total victory.

There was a remarkable organizational similarity between the American and Japanese air forces at the start of the Pacific war in December 1941. Both sides possessed a naval air force and a land-based air force, but the latter was part of the army, unlike most European air forces that were independent services in their own right. Both the American and Japanese naval air forces operated the best fighters of their respective countries, while the army air forces operated long-range bombers and somewhat inferior fighters. The vital difference, however, was that the Japanese had carefully planned a surprise offensive aimed at seizing the initiative in the air and holding it, while on the other side the government in Washington was obsessed with the desire not to provoke an all-out war with Japan, so the American air forces were deployed in a defensive posture. As the

attack on Pearl Harbor was to show, this tacit yielding of the initiative by the Americans was to have serious consequences for the Allied cause.

For the American Pacific Fleet to play a decisive role in the Central Pacific, the U.S. Navy's base at Pearl Harbor, on the Hawaiian island of Oahu, was vital. But the security of the Hawaiian archipelago was not the only American concern. In the western Pacific lay the Philippine Islands, a republic under American patronage that the U.S. was pledged to defend. An American general, Douglas MacArthur, commanded in the Philippines, American aircraft were based on Filipino airfields, and American troops formed the core of the garrison. In the event of a Japanese attack the American forces in the Philippines were expected to defend themselves until the American Pacific Fleet could come to their aid, force a

Below: A mixed group of U.S. Navy floatplanes at the Kaneohe Bay Naval Air Station on the eastern side of Oahu. This base was attacked by some first-wave aircraft, but was in the direct line of fire for the second wave, which inflicted considerable damage.

decisive naval battle on the Japanese Combined Fleet, and spearhead the counterattack.

The first priority for Japanese planners was to tackle the U.S. Pacific Fleet and with that out of the way the garrison of the Philippines could be isolated and defeated, both of which were essential preludes to attacking the other vital oil-bearing islands of the southwest Pacific. Admiral Yamamoto, the commander of the Japanese Combined Fleet, therefore welcomed the plans to knock out the battleships of the U.S. Pacific Fleet at its anchorage with the use of naval air power.

## Nostalgia governs tactics

Naval theory accepted that the aircraft carrier had come to stay, but the admirals were still beset both in the U.S. and Japan—by strategical nostalgia. The big gun of the battleship had always been the key weapon at sea and was still expected to be so in 1941. Thus, both the American and Japanese navies were simultaneously expanding their carrier forces *and* building more battleships; in the Japanese case, the 18 in. gun super battleships of the Yamato-class. So, just as the first tanks were seen as aids for the infantry rather than as a weapon in their own right, so aircraft carriers were regarded as support vessels for the battleships, their main task being to enable a battle fleet to carry its own air umbrella. But it took the first year of the Pacific war for both sides to realize that carrier fleets

Above: The scene during the attack on Pearl Harbor, with heavy fires raging at the Navy Yard. Nearer to the camera the giant cruiser submarine, USS *Narwhal* (SS-167), in rear and right-hand of automobile, lies undisturbed.

Above: The passenger liner *Argentina Maru* was used as a troop transport for a short period, but in December 1942 she was taken in hand for conversion to a carrier and was commissioned as *Kaiyo* in November 1943. Her aircraft capacity was poor, just twenty-four, and she was used as an aircraft transport and for flight training.

could not only defend themselves but were also the most effective way of destroying their opposite numbers.

By 1941, carrier aircraft had evolved into three major types: the fighter, the bomber, and the torpedo-bomber. The Japanese fighter in December 1941 was one of the best warplanes in the world: the Mitsubishi A6M2 Zero-sen.[1] With a maximum speed of 351 mph it was not only faster but could also outmaneuver anything the Allies could put into the skies for the first two years of the Pacific war, and it was armed with two cannon and two machine guns. The main Japanese dive-bomber at the outbreak of the war, was the Aichi D3A (Val), which had been developed from study of German designs such as the Ju 87 Stuka. The responsiblity for torpedo-carrying was carried out by the Nakajima B5N2 (Kate).

On the other side, the American F4F Wildcat carrier fighter had been operational for over a year before Pearl Harbor, but was no match for the Zero. The Douglas SBD Dauntless was a fine dive-bomber and could take heavy punishment and by the end of the

war had scored the lowest loss-rate of any American carrier plane. On the other hand, the Douglas TBD-1 Devastator torpedo-bomber was a death trap; it was too slow (although somewhat faster than the British Fairey Swordfish) and had only two machine guns as a defensive armament. Only cast-iron fighter cover could have guaranteed the Devastator success and this it seldom had.

In the Philippines the U.S. Army Air Force pinned its hopes on three main types. The most important of these was the Boeing B-17 "Flying Fortress," the world's first operational all-metal bomber, of which 36 were based on the island of Luzon in December 1941. Unfortunately, fighter defense was a quite different matter and depended almost entirely on the Curtis P-40F Warhawk, which, like the Navy's Wildcats, was outclassed on all points by the Zero.

## AMERICA'S FATAL FLAW

The overall American defense was geared to accepted "standards" of warfare, one of which was that hostilities would open with a formal declaration of war. This may have made sense in the early- and mid-1930s but not in December

1941—over two years since the German army had simply crossed the Polish frontier. In the Philippines, the U.S. garrison had its eyes, in the shape of the excellent PBY Catalina reconnaissance flying-boats, while the U.S. Pacific Fleet at Pearl Harbor had the equivalent in the form of

[1]Its official American reporting name was "Zeke" but it was universally known as "the Zero."

Above: This Japanese Zero fighter was captured early in the war, and put through a series of urgent and rigorous tests to discover its strengths and weaknesses.

Left: USS *Lexington* (CV-2) leaving San Diego, California, on November 10, 1941.

Below: The Grumman F6F Hellcat was not the most elegant of fighters, but it was very powerful and extremely successful. A total of 12,272 were delivered between 1942 and 1945, and these destroyed over 6,000 enemy aircraft, of which 4,947 were shot down by U.S. Navy aircraft, 209 by land-based USMC aircraft, and the remainder by Allied Hellcat squadrons.

the scouting aircraft operated by the carriers USS *Lexington* and *Saratoga*—but both depended on some advance warning.

By contrast, the Japanese operated under no such impediment; their only serious concern once the decision to strike had been made was the difficulty in putting a sufficiently strong strike force over the Philippines. All six fleet carriers—*Kaga, Akagi, Hiryu, Soryu, Zuikaku,* and *Shokaku*—were earmarked for the Pearl Harbor operation, which left just three smaller carriers—*Ryujo, Zuiho,* and *Taiho*—for the attack on the Philippines. These had a combined

operational capacity of little more than 50 aircraft—a figure that was halved in windy conditions. The answer was found in an excellent example of tactical ingenuity, in which the range of land-based Zero fighters flying from Formosa was extended by rigorous training that gradually extended the mileage that could be squeezed from the Zero's total fuel capacity of 182 gallons. Eventually, the record for economical consumption was set by the crack pilot Saburo Sakai, who managed to lower his Zero's fuel consumption from 35 gallons per hour to less than 17. This meant that the immense

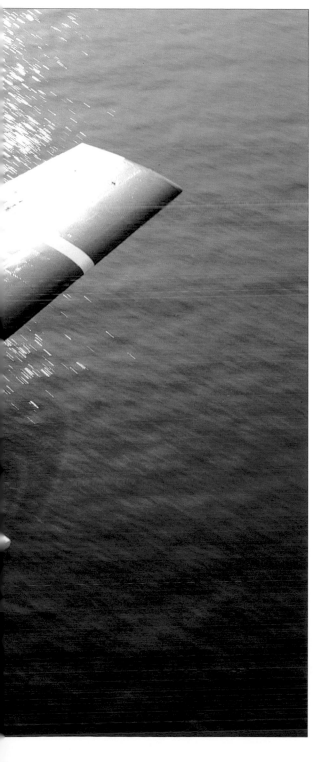

distance to be covered—almost 1,200 miles from Formosa to the airfields of Luzon—could be covered by the Zeros without the need for a carrier force. This transformed the Japanese plan and gave them another surprise advantage over the Americans, who could not believe that the Japanese had any fighters that could hit them direct from land bases. Saburo Sakai and his fellow Zero pilots had the nerve-racking task of cruising at 180 knots at 12,000 ft., barely above stalling speed and with engine speed hovering between 1,700 and 1,850 revolutions per minute. But, for the Japanese planners, this meant that both Pearl Harbor and the Philippines could be dealt smashing attacks at the same time.

Although the main objective at Pearl Harbor was the Pacific Fleet, and that in the Philippines the American air strength, the two attacks were in fact very much alike. First came surprise, so that the attackers would not find American fighters already in the air waiting for them. Next came the suppression of enemy flying activities—the favored initial ingredient of German blitzkrieg attacks from the Polish campaign onwards. Finally, pinpoint attacks would exploit the benefits of the first two provisions and eliminate the key strategic targets.

### EIGHT BATTLESHIPS WERE NOT ENOUGH!

Another point working in favor of the Japanese was the fact that, at this early stage of the war, the U.S. Pacific Fleet did not operate its carriers in close cooperation with the battle fleet. Thus, on the morning of Sunday, December 7, 1941, the two Japanese air strikes were able to make their approaches to Oahu with no opposition whatever from American carrier-borne aircraft,

Above: The Douglas TBD Devastator was the first cantilever monoplane designed as a carrier-borne torpedo bomber and was selected for production in 1936. A total of 129 were delivered and some 100 were still in service at the time of Pearl Harbor. They saw a great deal of action in the early months of the war, but after heavy losses in the Battle of Midway they were phased out of service, being replaced by the Avenger.

Right: The Japanese carrier *Akagi* in April 1939. She was laid down as a battlecruiser, but converted while on the stocks and completed as a carrier, being commissioned in March 1927. She was completely rebuilt between 1935–38, emerging as shown here.

while there was not a single counterstrike of any sort against the Japanese carriers.

The Japanese plan depended on eliminating *all* the capital ships of the U.S. Pacific Fleet and it was left to the discretion of the strike force commander to decide whether or not the warships actually in Pearl Harbor were, in fact, a sufficiently large proportion of the U.S. battle fleet to justify the Japanese showing their hand and attacking.

It would have taken a clairvoyant naval strategist to see that eight battleships, although a superb target, were not enough. Commander Fuchida, the Japanese strike force commander, was thoroughly justified in making his decision to attack. But, it was his chief, Vice Admiral Nagumo, who made the decision to withdraw his carrier force after the strikes on Pearl Harbor and not finish the job by seeking out and destroying the American carriers.

Nagumo's task force included six aircraft carriers, with a total strength of 493 planes; two

Right: The Nakajima B5N Kate served in two forms, the B5N1 attack bomber (seen here) and the B5N2 torpedo bomber. The Pearl Harbor attack force included 103 B5N1s and forty B5N2s. Both types had left service by mid-1944.

Previous pages: Amid the devastation of the Naval Air Station on Ford Island, stunned sailors look in disbelief as the USS *Arizona* blows up.

battleships; three cruisers; nine destroyers; three submarines; and eight tankers to refuel the squadron at sea. The force sailed on November 26 on an easterly course along the 43rd Parallel. On December 2 came confirmation of the order to attack and on December 6 the force turned towards Oahu. The following day, on Sunday, December 7, at 6:15 A.M. (local), Nagumo dispatched the first wave of attackers.

The first of the two Japanese air strikes on Pearl Harbor was led by the air group com-

mander, Commander Mitsuo Fuchida, in person. His force, launched 230 miles from Pearl Harbor, consisted of 50 bomb-carrying Kates, 40 torpedo-carrying Kates, 51 Val dive-bombers, and a fighter escort of 43 Zeros to tackle any interference from the Americans and press home ground attacks. This was followed an hour later by the second wave led by Lieutenant-Commander Shimazaki from the *Zuikaku*: 54 bomb-carrying Kates, 80 Vals, and 36 Zeros. The first wave was actually picked up by American radar on Oahu, at a range of approximately 160 miles, but it was casually assumed that the huge plot on the screen was a flight of bombers from the American mainland that was expected to arrive that morning. Another reason for the ease with which the Japanese gained complete surprise during the run-in was that the Japanese formation was also mistaken for air groups from the carriers *Lexington* and *Enterprise*, which were at sea.

Although the carriers were not in the anchorage, the entire battle fleet was present, and Fuchida commenced his attack at 7:50 A.M. (local time) and his aircraft ranged virtually unchecked until 8:25 A.M. By the time the first wave was heading back to the carriers, the battleships *Utah*, *California*, *Arizona*, and *Oklahoma* were on the bottom, *West Virginia* was sinking, and *Tennessee* was ablaze. The second wave forced the Americans to beach *Nevada* and severely damaged the *Pennsylvania* and *Maryland*. Ground attacks on the airfields wiped out the entire effective strength of the U.S. Navy scout-planes and flying-boats on Oahu. When

Above: Nakajima B5s on a pre-war publicity flight. In the 1930s Western experts were very dismissive of Japan's technical capabilities and achievements, and, in particular, of its aviation industry. As a result, they lulled themselves into a false sense of security and the attacks on Pearl Harbor, Malaya, and the Philippines came as a very rude awakening.

Above: A Nakajima B5N Kate takes off from a Japanese carrier early in the war. The rash of Japanese naval successes in the months following Pearl Harbor tended to disguise the fact that, while a number of U.S. battleships had been eliminated, the carriers had not been touched.

the second wave finally departed to return to their carriers at around 1000, the two waves of the strike force had lost only nine Zeros, 15 Vals, and five Kates out of the total of 354 involved in the operation. This was a crushing victory, but it was marred by Admiral Nagumo's decision not to search out and destroy the two American carriers—a decision that would have fatal results for the Japanese in the sea battles of 1942.

In the Japanese war plan, the attack on Pearl Harbor was a pre-emptive strike in order to win time for conquests elsewhere, and this aim was abundantly fulfilled. After the attack it was impossible for the U.S. Navy to throw any major naval reinforcements into the desperate fighting in the western Pacific, and for a while the Pacific Fleet had to retire to the west coast of the United States. This enabled the Japanese to make a clean sweep in the western Pacific and air power was instrumental in their victories.

Even though bad weather delayed the Japanese strike on the airfields of the Philippines, their pilots were amazed to catch the American aircraft completely by surprise when they finally arrived five hours after the Pearl Harbor strike. By the end of the first day the Philippine air force had ceased to exist as a serious threat. The Japanese were then able to

Left: An Aichi D3A dive-bomber during the Pearl Harbor attack. The Allies rarely knew the correct Japanese aircraft designations, and even when they did, a combination of figures and numbers was fairly meaningless and difficult to remember in the heat of battle. Thus, they were given official nicknames, invariably boys' or girls' first names, and this Aichi D3A, for example, became the much more easily remembered "Val."

Left: This Zero was shot down by U.S. forces on December 7, 1941, enabling it to be examined and analyzed. Designated A6M by Mitsubishi, it was also known to the Japanese navy as the Type 00, from the last two digits of the Japanese year 5700, in which the aircraft was accepted for service. In Japanese this became *Zero-Sen* ("double zero") and Allied pilots shortened it to "Zero," becoming the one exception to the first-name rule.

467

turn to the elimination of the make-shift British battle fleet based on Singapore, which consisted only of the battleship *Prince of Wales*, the battle-cruiser *Repulse*, and a handful of destroyers. Lacking any fighter cover, the force was overwhelmed on December 10, 1941, and the two capital ships were sunk by Japanese land-based naval bombers from airfields in Indo-China. The aircraft involved were two standard types— the Mitsubishi G3M-Nell and the G4M-Betty— both twin-engined machines with long-range striking capabilities.

### FLYING FORTRESS PROBLEMS

Having swept the Pacific of every Allied battleship the Japanese were then able to go ahead with their island-hopping campaign through the Dutch East Indies, for which air reconnaissance and protection were vital. The Japanese retained both from the start and it soon became impossible for the ever-decreasing number of Allied cruisers and destroyers to move without being spotted by Japanese reconnaissance aircraft, most notably the Kawanishi H6K Mavis flying-boat with its impressive range of just over 3,000 miles. Meanwhile, the Zero pilots ground down the dwindling Allied reserves of aircraft in the Dutch East Indies, coping easily with the Curtis P-40 Warhawks and Bell P-39 Airacobras. However, the Boeing B-17 presented more of a problem as its huge size (by contemporary

Above: Sailors desperately try to bring a burning PBY flying boat to the shore, following the first wave attack on Pearl Harbor.

Far left: A moment of glory for the humble garbage lighter, *YG-17* (on right of picture), which without orders or hesitation immediately placed herself alongside the port side of the blazing battleship USS *West Virginia* and stayed there for over twenty-four hours, using her hoses to help bring the fire under control. She maintained this position despite repeated explosions from ammunition. When the fires aboard *West Virginia* were under control on the morning of December 8, *YG-17* turned her attention to the burning USS *Arizona*.

Previous pages: A Nakajima B5N2 Val, laden with a torpedo, takes off for the second wave of attacks.

Japanese encountered P-36 Mohawks and Brewster F2A Buffaloes during this phase of the campaign, which shredded the last Allied pretense at fighter protection in the East Indies. By March the Japanese were already regrouping their crack fighter units at Bali before sending them east to Rabaul en route to the next target—the east coast of New Guinea, where hastily-seized airfields were to be the bases for

Above: The Curtiss P-40 Warhawk was one of the USAAF's front-line fighter at the time of Pearl Harbor.

Below: A very unusual design, the Bell P-39 Aircobra had just entered service at the time of Pearl Harbor.

Previous pages: The Japanese attacks on December 7 were extremely well focused, as seen in this shot of Wheeler Army Air Field.

standards) and high speed caused much confusion at first and the gunsights of the Zero proved generally ineffective, causing many a capable Japanese pilot to misjudge his attack and miss completely. The B-17's ability to take punishment, plus its high defensive firepower, were other points that the Japanese had to discover the hard way.

The Allies' chances of retaining a foothold in the Dutch East Indies were finally destroyed on February 19, 1942, by a wild day of dogfighting over Java which cost the Allies over 70 fighters. It was the sort of day's fighting of which the German Luftwaffe had dreamt during the Battle of Britain. Apart from the P-40s, the

the planned conquest of the vital Allied base at Port Moresby in New Guinea.

Between April and August 1942 New Guinea saw an intense air campaign, with the Allies operating from Port Moresby and the Japanese from their fields along the New Guinea coast. Physically separated by the Owen Stanley mountains, both sides came in for heavy air raids, with the Allies favoring attacks by the twin-engined Martin B-26 Marauder. During this phase the Japanese fighter wing based at Lae became the most successful Japanese air unit of the Pacific war—but its victories were hollow since thousands of miles away the first carrier-versus-carrier battles of the war were taking place and not only reversing the flood of Japanese victories but also enabling the Allies to go over to the offensive.

Below: The crew of a naval Mitsubishi A4M Betty awaiting the start of the next mission. Their aircraft had a long range, which was achieved at the expense of poor defensive armament.

Above: The Boeing B-17c. Such aircraft took part in many of the early actions in the Pacific war; they were reasonably effective against land targets but their antishipping missions were generally unsatisfactory.

## A BATTLE OF ERRORS

The first carrier clash, which took place in May 1942, was part of the fight for New Guinea and was fought by the Allies to thwart an amphibious Japanese assault on Port Moresby. Tactically the Battle of the Coral Sea (May 4–8, 1942) was an extremely confused affair and both sides made mistakes that could have been disastrous, but that they were not was due primarily to inexperience on both sides in this novel form of warfare. American pilots sank the small Japanese carrier *Coho* but missed the much more important targets, the fleet carriers *Zuikaku* and *Shokaku,* while the Japanese immobilized the American carrier *Lexington,* which was then lost because of inexperience in damage control. Both sides put in wildly inflated victory claims; identification was bad

on both sides and at one stage in the fight Japanese aircraft even tried to land on the American carrier *Yorktown*!

The result of the Battle of the Coral Sea was that the Japanese lost a small carrier and were temporarily deprived of their best fleet carriers (*Shokaku* had been damaged and the air groups of both had been heavily depleted), but the U.S. Navy had achieved its strategic aim by preventing the Japanese from taking Port Moresby, albeit at the cost of losing the *Lexington.*

This temporary stalemate in the South-West Pacific was followed by Yamamoto's attempt to force the decisive battle of the war by attacking an island objective that the U.S. Navy could not afford to concede. This objective was the island of Midway, westernmost outpost of the Hawaiian group. By attacking Midway,

Left: The view aboard USS *Hornet* (CVA-8) as the pilot of one of Doolittle's B-25Bs hauls his heavily laden aircraft off the forward end of the flight deck. The B-25s were at maximum gross weight and all were parked on the deck, which meant that the first to take off had only a very short run, but all got off successfully.

Left: Doolittle's force was formed entirely from volunteers, and their sixteen aircraft were the reliable and effective North American B-25C Mitchells, powered by two 1,700 hp R-2600 Wright Double Cyclones, which carried a 3,000 lb. bomb load. After attacking Tokyo, the bombers flew on to China, although not all arrived successfully.

Above: The Japanese carrier *Shoho* is hit by American torpedoes during late morning attacks on May 7, 1942.

Previous pages: Despite heavy antiaircraft fire, a Japanese torpedo bomber scores a direct hit on the carrier USS *Yorktown* (CV-5) at the Battle of Midway, midafternoon June 4, 1942. *Yorktown* had already been hit by three bombs in the morning, but had been repaired and was underway again when this second attack arrived. The carrier suffered two torpedo hits, which opened a huge gap in her port side and her captain, assessing that she was about to capsize, ordered his crew to abandon ship.

armament, taking place on a crowded flightdeck and under the threat of imminent attack, caused chaos, and the American dive-bombers caught the Japanese carriers absolutely cold. As a result, three of the carriers—*Kaga, Akagi,* and *Soryu*—were set hopelessly ablaze, but the surviving carrier, Hiryu, managed to launch a counterstrike

Yamamoto was convinced that he could lure the last units of the Pacific Fleet to destruction by the guns of the Japanese battle fleet and he expected no opposition from American carriers, which he believed had been neutralized during the Coral Sea fight. Thus, he was confident that his carriers would have surprise on their side in the initial smash at Midway's defenses.

American code-breakers, however, had unmasked the Japanese plan and superhuman efforts in the shipyards sent a carrier force to sea. This consisted of *Yorktown,* frantically patched up in 48 hours in Pearl Harbor after returning from the Coral Sea, *Enterprise,* and the new carrier *Hornet.* Admiral Chester Nimitz, well aware of the terrifying superiority of the Japanese task forces committed to the Midway venture, relied on surprise to ambush the Midway attack force and the all-important Japanese carriers.

So, with both Yamamoto and Nimitz certain that they would surprise their opponent, the two fleets approached each other in what would be known as the Battle of Midway, which took place on June 4, 1942. Nagumo quickly realized that the first strike had not neutralized the island's defenses, so he ordered his carrier planes to prepare for a second attack. While the aircraft were being rearmed he discovered that American carriers were in the vicinity and ordered his aircrews to prepare for a strike against the new menace. These rapid changes of

that crippled *Yorktown* (which was later sunk by a Japanese submarine). However, *Hiryu* was subsequently eliminated by another American strike (on June 6).

Thus, the Battle of Midway wiped out the Japanese carrier supremacy at a stroke, although almost as important in the long run was the Japanese loss of some 250 aircraft and their practically irreplaceable crews.

## FIGHT TO A STANDSTILL

The next stage of the Pacific war opened in August 1942 when the Americans seized a

Below: At the Battle of the Coral Sea, USS *Lexington* survived early damage, but following internal explosions she had to be abandoned and sunk by torpedo.

foothold in the Solomon Islands by landing on Guadalcanal. The Japanese, based on Rabaul, were swift to counterattack and the result was the six-month ordeal called the Battle of Guadalcanal. This struggle was unique: a land campaign that depended entirely on sea and air power. The Japanese cruisers and destroyers were supreme by night, while American naval air power retained a tenuous command of the sky by day. Two hard-fought carrier battles—the Eastern Solomons (August 24) and Santa Cruz (October 26)—resulted in a tactical draw that passed the ball to the night operations of the surface warships. The Japanese lost the light carrier Ryujo and another crippling percentage of

trained carrier aircrew; Japanese submarines torpedoed the carriers *Wasp* and *Saratoga*, and torpedo-bombers sank the *Hornet*. In these two battles the American and Japanese carrier forces fought each other to a momentary standstill.

The last key naval battles in the Guadalcanal saga were the First Guadalcanal (November 12–13), the Second Guadalcanal (November 14–15), and the Tassafaronga (November 30, 1942). By the time the Japanese finally conceded defeat and had evacuated Guadalcanal (February 7, 1943) the Imperial Japanese Navy had lost the equivalent of an entire peacetime fleet: two battleships, an aircraft carrier, five cruisers, twelve destroyers, and

**Below:** The crippled carrier USS *Yorktown.* Note the rescue boat, bottom right, and the two Grumman F4F Wildcats still parked on her flight deck, immediately abaft the island.

eight submarines. Most of the fighting had been orthodox naval warfare: visual clashes between surface ships, almost entirely by night. But these engagements had been fought because the opposing carrier forces were unable to settle the issue by day. It was the last time that carrier units of the Japanese navy were able to tackle their opposite numbers on equal terms.

During the Guadalcanal fighting the Japanese pilots got their first real taste of the new aircraft that would, in time, reverse the Zero's superiority forever. The Grumman Avenger torpedo-bomber had just entered service in time for the Battle of Midway. The Grumman carried a power-operated dorsal

turret and was an unpleasant surprise. The Japanese ace Saburo Sakai barely escaped death when he dived his Zero onto a formation of Avengers, believing that they were Wildcats. Badly wounded, he managed to retain consciousness and return to Rabaul.

It was also during these campaigns that the Grumman F6F Hellcat showed its effectiveness. It remained the standard American carrier fighter to the end of the war, and enabled the American pilots to meet the Zero on virtually equal terms.

### NO PARACHUTES—BY CHOICE!

A great advantage for the Allied machines that tangled with the Zero was their superior protection for the pilot and fuel tank. Magnificent though it was in many ways, the Zero was a death trap if hit in the fuel tanks. Another significant Allied advantage was the development of aircrew recovery. Air-sea rescue remained rudimentary on the Japanese side, depleting their vestigial reserves of trained aircrew still more.

Ace pilots like Sakai, Ota, and Nishizawa preferred to fly without parachutes—simply because they found the harness irksome and felt that they could better become part of their machines without it. It was, however, untrue that Japanese pilots were deprived of parachutes in order to make them fight; on the contrary, there was a standing order that parachutes should be worn, but this remained a matter of personal preference.

The year 1943 saw the Allies in the South-West Pacific take their first long step along the road to Tokyo, pressing home their counter-

Above: Japanese carrier *Hiryu* burns fiercely during the Battle of Midway on June 5, 1942.

Above: During the second Battle of the Solomons on November 16, 1942, a Douglas SBD Dauntless flies past burning and abandoned Japanese transports, which their crews were forced to beach on Guadalcanal.

Right: A Japanese torpedo plane flies low over U.S. cruisers as it lines up to attack an aircraft carrier lying dead in the water (off left of picture).

offensive in New Guinea and fighting their way along the Solomon Island chain to Bougainville and the doorstep of Rabaul. In this phase of the war no carrier battles took place but there was plenty of air activity. One of Yamamoto's last acts was to order the air reinforcement of the Solomons. He stripped the carrier air groups of strike aircraft and launched a massive air offensive on the Allied forces in the eastern Solomons in April 1943. It was a failure, due to the changing balance in combat efficiency between the Japanese and American pilots.

On April 1, the very first day of the offensive, eighteen Zeros were shot down for the loss of a mere six American fighters. Yamamoto's pilots also grossly overestimated the damage they were inflicting, and when Yamamoto called off the offensive in mid-April he believed that the fighting two weeks ago had sunk a cruiser and two destroyers and that his aircraft had shot down 175 Allied machines. In fact, the Japanese had sunk only one destroyer, one tanker, an antisubmarine trawler and a merchantman, and had damaged an Australian minesweeper.

The failure of Yamamoto's air offensive was in contrast to the success of Allied bombing operations against Japanese attempts to reinforce New Guinea. In March 1943 the Battle of the Bismarck Sea had been fought—36 hours of intermittent bombing attacks against a Japanese convoy from Rabaul. This convoy consisted of seven transports, eight destroyers and a collier, and it carried 7,000 troops. By nightfall on the 3rd all the transports and four of the destroyers had been sunk and over 2,000 of the troops were lost—a crushing victory for the bombers. Only five Allied aircraft were lost in the attacks.

Then, on April 18, 1943, Yamamoto was

Above: Douglas SBD Dauntless dive-bombers aboard the carrier USS *Ranger*. The Dauntless sank more Japanese ships than any other Allied aircraft, stopped the Imperial Japanese fleet at Midway, and played a major role in the battles in the Coral Sea and the Solomons. It was very popular with its crews, who preferred it to its successor, the SB2C.

killed by a long-range ambush flown by P-38 Lightnings out of Guadalcanal. Intelligence of his movements had been culled from wireless interception, and the Admiral was shot down while flying from Rabaul to Buin. Removing Japan's greatest naval strategist, the man who had warned that he had absolutely no confidence of victory if the war should last more than a year, was a great asset to the Allies in the Pacific. Most battles involve thousands, and some perhaps even millions, of troops, huge amounts of equipment, and massive firepower on each side. The skirmish that took place over Bougainville in the Pacific on April 18, however, lasted for just a few minutes and involved fewer than 100 men in 26 aircraft. For the price of one

P-38 lost and six damaged the Americans had scored a victory over the Japanese equivalent to any battle, and the effects were felt for the remainder of the Pacific war.

## 270 KILLS IN TWO DAYS

In November 1943 the American drive in the Central Pacific opened with the assault on the key atolls in the Gilbert Islands, Makin, and Tarawa. The next objective was the Marshall group of islands with the main objectives being neutralized by massive preliminary air strikes. After the taking of Kwajalein in the Marshalls by February 4, carrier aircraft strikes pounded the Japanese Combined Fleet's anchorage at

Previous pages: Following the prewar dearth of intelligence about Japanese aircraft, it became imperative to gather as much information as possible. Here members of a USAAF Technical Air Intelligence Team inspect an abandoned Japanese fighter near Lashio in Burma.

Truk for two days, sinking two cruisers and four destroyers and accounting for no fewer than 270 Japanese aircraft. The assault on Eniwetok, the last objective in the Marshalls, was made with no intervention from the Japanese and the Marshalls campaign was over. The atolls of Wotje, Maloelap, Jaluit, and Mili were left isolated, and under sporadic air attacks—the Americans found that these bypassed Japanese garrisons were ideal for giving their raw pilots combat experience without undue risk.

The Japanese had no such facility. Frantic efforts to train more aircrews, including sacrificing all the finer points of combat experience at the disposal of the seasoned instructors, failed even to keep pace with losses. The Japanese

Above: Australian infantrymen conduct a nontechnical examination of a Mitsubishi Zero fighter, which they captured during the assault on Lae in New Guinea, September 1943.

Left: Japanese navy Mitsubishi G4M Bettys attacking U.S. transports (to left of picture) during the Guadalcanal campaign. U.S. ships are sending up a hail of antiaircraft fire, but the two Bettys on the left and right of the picture are flying at wave height and passing underneath it the fire.

Previous pages: An F6F has crashed aboard USS *Enterprise* during the Gilberts campaign and Lieutenant Walter Chewring climbs the side to assist the pilot.

High Command could afford to lose the Gilberts and Marshalls but the next obvious objective on the Americans' list, the Marianas group, was vital to the defense of the Japanese homeland. The all-important battle of the Central Pacific would be fought for the Marianas—the battle for which Japanese naval strategists had always yearned. To this end every effort had been made to reconstitute a fighting carrier fleet.

Only two veteran fleet carriers were left— *Shokaku* and *Zuikaku*—one new fleet carrier, *Taiho*, had been commissioned and there were

Above: The USAAF's Lockheed P-38 Lightning possessed good firepower, high speed, and, of great importance in the Pacific Theater, long range, which was increased yet further by underwing drop tanks.

Left: One that did not make it. A Japanese torpedo bomber has been hit by a 5 in. shell from USS *Yorktown* and veers away, shedding its torpedo as it does so, on December 4, 1943.

Far left: The remains of the Betty transporting Admiral Yamamoto, which was shot down by USAAF Lightnings in April 1943.

also six light carriers; between them the Japanese carriers could operate 432 aircraft.

The opposing carrier fleet—Admiral Marc Mitscher's huge Task Force 58—consisted of 15 carriers with a total of 800 aircraft, and this was quite separate from the invasion fleet for the Marianas, which had its own air umbrella of 300 aircraft aboard 12 escort carriers. The disparity was, however, not just quantitative, because the Americans were also far ahead qualitatively as well in matters such as crew experience, training, maintenance, and servicing.

Above: On return from attacking Rabaul, USS *Saratoga's* deck crew gently ease a TBF's rear gunner with a shattered knee out of his turret.

Right: SBD Dauntless dive-bombers from USS *Lexington* attack a Japanese radar station on the island of Ulalu, April 29–30, 1944.

## TERRIFYING ODDS

Despite the terrifying odds against them, the Japanese were confident. Admiral Ozawa, commanding the Japanese fleet, grouped his vessels into two task forces, and planned to fight the battle at long range, but he was never allowed to do so. The Battle of the Philippine Sea took place on June 19–20, 1944. From the start every aspect of the Japanese plan was wrecked by superior American tactics and numbers. Ozawa had planned to catch the Americans between the hammer of his carrier aircraft and the anvil of the land-based aircraft from the airfields on the Marianas. But the latter were never able to intervene as Mitscher's fighters easily coped with the feeble attacks by the Japanese land-based

aircraft. Then the Japanese carrier strikes were savaged by Grumman F6F Hellcats, successors to the Wildcats, 50 mph faster, and with two additional heavy machine guns.

The Japanese carriers were shadowed by American submarines, which passed on accurate sighting and position reports to the American carrier fleet. In one extraordinary incident, a Japanese pilot in the act of taking off from *Taiho* spotted a torpedo streaking towards his ship and instantly dived his plane onto it—an act of great courage and sacrifice, but it did not save *Taiho* from being hit by another torpedo. At first, no serious damage seemed to have been done and *Taiho* steamed on, but, apparently unnoticed, lethal fuel fumes began to build up in her hull. At 12:20 P.M. an American submarine torpedoed the *Shokaku*, which sank six hours later; and as she was going down the *Taiho* blew up as the fumes finally ignited.

While Ozawa was shifting his flag to the cruiser *Haguro*, his last air strikes against the American fleet were being massacred. Some 373 Japanese aircraft had taken off from Ozawa's carriers on the 19th but only 130 returned. With the Japanese land-based aircraft losses added in, the overall Japanese loss was around 315, while the total American losses for the day were only 23 aircraft.

### FRENZIED DOGFIGHT

On the 20th, the fleets were still in contact and a mass American strike of 131 aircraft set out to finish the job, which led to a frenzied dogfight

Above: Flight deck crew aboard USS *San Jacinto* (CVL-30) arming a TBM Avenger with a torpedo during the Battle of Leyte Gulf on October 25, 1944.

Left: Aboard cruiser USS *Birmingham* (CL-62) in Task Force 58, crew members are spectators and can only watch the contrails in the sky with amazement as U.S. and Japanese aircraft slug it out in what became known as the Marianas Turkey Shoot, on June 19, 1944.

Above: The continuous and violent activity in the Pacific makes it too easy to forget that there was another important campaign being fought in India and Burma. Here a USAAF P-47 Thunderbolt and RAF Hurricane are about to carry out a joint attack on Japanese positions in Burma.

over the battered Japanese fleet, in which the number of operational Japanese fighters was reduced to a mere 35. However, the American strike only managed to inflict heavy damage on *Zuikaku* and the seaplane carrier *Chiyoda*, but it was enough and without any operational carriers left Ozawa had no option but to retreat to Okinawa, leaving the American fleet free to cover the conquest of the key Marianas, Saipan, Tinian, and Guam.

The loss of the Marianas was an important milestone in the defeat of Japan. The result of Ozawa's defeat, plus the knowledge that the enemy was now at the gates of Japan with a vengeance, finally saw the frantic development of more modern fighters.

The three most important types were the Kawanishi N1K1-J and N1K2-J *Shiden* (George), the Mitsubishi J2M3 *Raiden* (Jack), and—best of all—the Mitsubishi A7M2 *Reppu* (Sam). All four types finally abandoned the old Zero formula and offered Japanese pilots multiple cannon armament and armor protection. The standard *Shiden* had four 20 mm wing cannon often augmented by two 7.7 mm machine guns; its maximum speed was 362 mph at 19,360 ft. and its service ceiling was 35,300 ft. A total of 1,435 *Shidens* of all versions were completed before the end of the war.

The *Raiden* was a light interceptor that was unpopular with its pilots on account of engine troubles, structural failures, and poor visibility; Saburo Sakai also thought it "flew like a truck" compared to the old Zero. Only about 730 *Raidens* were built instead of the 3,700 planned. The *Reppu* on the other hand was a sensational machine with a story even sadder than that of the German Me 262 jet. It could out-fly any fighter the Americans had and could operate at

over 40,000 ft.—but only eight of these machines were completed by the end of the war. American bombers had wrecked the production lines, which should have turned the Reppu out in thousands. Thus, even in the last months of World War II Japan's navy pilots were still relying on the Zero, with the odds as heavily stacked against them as the Luftwaffe on the Eastern Front, and with the agonizing knowledge that adequate weapons existed but too late and in insufficient quantities.

Then, after Japan lost the Marianas a new menace faced the Japanese homelands: constant air raids by the biggest bomber of the war. This was the Boeing B-29 Superfortress, powered by four massive 2,200 hp Wright Cyclone engines. It could make 358 mph at 30,000 ft. and normally carried 12,000 lb. of bombs over a range of 3,250 miles. The B-29 gave the Allies a weapon with which the long-awaited, regular bombardment of Japan could be realized.

## THE FIRST RAIDS ON JAPAN

The first B-29 raids on Japanese targets were made from China, a country that had battled on

Left: Seen from USS *Birmingham* (CL-62) during the Battle of the Philippine Sea, twenty-three Grumman F6F Hellcats fly overhead to intercept incoming Japanese bombers, June 1944.

against the Japanese invaders ever since 1937 despite millions of casualties, the loss of all its key ports, and Japanese occupation of thousands of square miles of strategically important territory. Early and vital aid had come in the form of an airborne "foreign legion" of volunteer fighter pilots: Claire Chennault's American Volunteer Group, the famed "Flying Tigers."

Chennault's men proved so important to the Chinese war effort that a major crisis arose, with bitter arguments between the American ground forces adviser, General Stilwell, who argued that the Japanese could only be defeated in battle on the ground, and Chennault, whose contention was that the key to victory over Japan lay in the air. In the event, the Allies were able to operate

Right: An SB2C Helldiver (successor to the much-loved SBD Dauntless) is launched from USS *Hancock* (CV-19) for a strike on Manila Bay on November 25, 1944.

Previous pages: Corsair fighters of a Marine Corps squadron are silhouetted by the lacework of tracer shells from Marine-manned antiaircraft guns during a Japanese raid on Yontaon airfield, Okinawa, on April 16, 1945.

from airfields in western China and it was from there that the first Superfortress raid on Tokyo was flown in June 1944. After a brief period of suspension the raids were resumed in November, this time from the new American bases in the Marianas. They met with little or no resistance over Japan, for no home-defense force had been created as of yet.

The increasingly heavier B-29 strikes began with a vengeance in December 1944. Every major city of Japan received pitiless fire raids. Japanese aviation factories were a major target from the start and the supply of new aircraft never rose above a trickle.

The Philippine Sea debacle was the last time that a Japanese carrier force met the American fleet head-on in battle, but it was not the last occasion that Japanese carriers put to sea. This occurred in October 1944 when the Americans landed at Leyte in the central Philippines. A complex Japanese naval plan was ordered into operation, which was aimed at decoying the American carriers away from the landing

Above: This is Tokyo after repeated "conventional" raids by U.S. bombers during 1944 and 1945. These raids killed much greater numbers of people than the atomic bomb attacks on Hiroshima and Nagasaki.

Below: A Boeing B-29 Superfortress makes an emergency landing on Iwo Jima following a raid on Tokyo in March 1945. This particular aircraft was the first B-29 to land on the island.

Previous pages: A pilot is invested with the ceremonial headband prior to a kamikaze attack. Despite the enormous sacrifices made by these brave young men, in the final analysis the results were not as substantial as they had hoped.

Below: A kamikaze pilot approaches the battleship USS Missouri. However, he failed and hit the sea.

beaches while a concentrated Japanese battleship force got in among the landing fleet and destroyed the men on the beaches. The result was the Battle of Leyte Gulf (October 23–26, 1944)—a four-day epic that was the closest the Combined Fleet ever came to winning a major victory over the U.S. Pacific Fleet. Air operations dominated throughout, and the total Japanese insolvency in air power was decisively proved.

Admiral Ozawa's carrier fleet consisted of four carriers with a pitiful total of 118 aircraft. This meager parody of the superb task force which had struck at Pearl Harbor in December 1941 was now nothing more than a decoy duck to lure away the carriers of the American 3rd

Fleet. The prime movers in the plan were the battleships: five of them under Admiral Kurita, intended to break into Leyte Gulf through the San Bernadino Strait, and two under Admiral Nishimura, were to form the southern claw of a pincer movement by steaming through Surigao Strait and attacking from the south.

## THE FLEETS MEET HEAD-ON

The Battle of Leyte Gulf consisted of four main engagements. The first, Sibuyan Sea, saw the savaging of Kurita's battleship force as it approached the San Bernadino Strait. Repeated American carrier aircraft attacks throughout the

24th finally sank the giant battleship *Musashi*, but failed to halt the advance of the Japanese battle fleet. The second phase, Surigao Strait, was an orthodox night battleship action in the Strait that smashed Nishimura's force and averted the danger from the south. The third, Samar, saw Kurita's battleships surprise the light American escort carriers off the coast of Samar and put them to flight, only to throw away a decisive victory by withdrawing at the moment when it seemed that the fleeing carriers must be overwhelmed. And the fourth, Cape Engaño, saw the inevitable destruction of Ozawa's decoy carrier force by Admiral Halsey's pilots.

Leyte Gulf was the greatest naval battle of World War II and was a clear-cut defeat for the Japanese. But it also ushered in a unique type of air warfare: the kamikaze strike, flown by dedicated pilots determined to sacrifice themselves by becoming human bombs and taking an enemy warship and its crew with them when they died.

The mentality behind the kamikazes staggered Western minds and is still usually misunderstood. The legend itself was deep-rooted in the lore of Japan, for the kamikaze was the miraculous cyclone (the word literally means "divine wind"), which had scattered Kublai Khan's invasion fleet in 1281 and saved Japan from a Mongol invasion. The kamikazes of

Below: Marines from Air Group 31 were the first into Japan, where they found a hangar full of these suicide bombs. These devices were suspended underneath a bomber, which delivered them to a dropping-off point from which they commenced their one-way journey.

Above: Hiroshima, a few days after the detonation of the atomic bomb on August 6, 1945. Without this and the second bomb on Nagasaki, the Japanese government would have held out, forcing the Allies to invade. Judging by the resistance on the Pacific islands and adding the fact that this time it was the sacred homeland that was being defended, the human cost of such an invasion would have been far greater than that caused by the two atomic bombs.

World War II did not see themselves as fanatical suicides, their motivation being "one man, one warship"—an equation that offered Japan the only chance of whittling down the vast American superiority in late 1944 and 1945.

A kamikaze strike consisted simply of aircraft, single- or twin-engined, armed with bombs, which were given fighter escort to the vicinity of the American fleet to be attacked. The kamikaze pilot would then seek to crash his plane into an enemy warship—a carrier for preference. The ideal point was the flightdeck elevator, so that the exploding plane could create a blazing inferno in the carrier's hangars. Aircraft used for such attacks were almost always standard types with minimal modifications. The only specialized kamikaze aircraft to be developed was the Yokosuka MXY-8 Ohka (Cherry Blossom), which was known to the Americans as the Baka, or "fool bomb." This aircraft was essentially a manned, stand-off, rocket-powered missile and was carried like an outsize torpedo beneath a bomber. The Ohka was released at about 50 miles from the target at a height of some 27,000 ft. and then glided at about 200 mph until the pilot had positively identified a target. He then fired his three solid-fuel rockets for the final dive onto the target at 570 mph, where, provided he hit, the 2,645 lb. high explosive would cause devastating damage.

Throughout the war there were examples from time to time of pilots deliberately crashing their machines onto enemy targets, presumably having been desperately wounded or in the private knowledge that they stood no chance of survival. This was not the prerogative of Japanese pilots only. But the Japanese kamikaze was different, because not only was it officially approved, but it was adopted as a deliberate tactic, using specially trained volunteers and aircraft provided for the purpose.

The first kamikaze raids are accepted to have occurred during the running fight off Samar in the Battle of Leyte Gulf, when a land-based Zero crashed through the flight deck of the light carrier *Saint Lo* and sank her. In the last two major campaigns of the Pacific war, Iwo Jima and Okinawa, kamikaze raids took over as the spearhead of the Japanese air defensive.

At Okinawa, the battle that carried the Americans to the very doorstep of Japan, about 1,900 kamikaze sorties were counted (compared to 5,000 sorties by normal bombers). Their total score off Okinawa was 24 American ships and landing craft sunk and 202 damaged (which included four British).

When they actually hit a target the effect of a kamikaze was quite impressive, but such successes remained very low. This was in part due to the fact that the pilots' flying skills were very poor, but also because it needed skilled pilots to single out the really important ships to be attacked and then crash their aircraft on the most vulnerable spot. The experienced pilots, typified by Saburo Sakai, respected the motivation of those who actually flew such sorties, but regarded the kamikazes as a waste of invaluable human and material resources.

## THE FINAL CHAPTER

By the last months of the Pacific war Japan's chronic shortage of aircraft and of fuel to fly them was making itself felt. Nevertheless the Allied planners knew that intense kamikaze activity was only to be expected as they prepared for the last battle of the war: the decisive invasion of the Japanese homeland. Fortunately for all concerned, however, such an invasion was made unnecessary by the Japanese acceptance of surrender terms in August 1945.

This acceptance was forced upon them by the two atomic bombs that were dropped on Hiroshima (August 6) and Nagasaki (August 9). Both bombs were delivered by a single B-29 flying from the Marianas, and were air bursts with a nominal explosive power equivalent to 20 kilotons (20kT) of conventional high explosive.

The morality behind the use of these two atomic bombs against Japan has troubled some sections of humanity ever since 1945, but three facts are inescapable. The first is that without them the Allies would have had no option but to carry out an amphibious invasion of the Japanese islands. The invasions of the Pacific islands had been bloody and the defending garrisons had almost invariably fought to the last man and the last round, at tremendous cost to both the Americans and to themselves. Japanese plans found after the war showed that an even more strenuous defense would have been made for the homeland, which would almost certainly have resulted in huge loss of life for the Japanese and the invading Allies, alike. That invasion would have been accompanied by ever heavier strategic conventional bombing by B-29s, which would also have resulted in tens, if not hundreds, of thousands of Japanese deaths.

The third fact is that the bombs used at Hiroshima and Nagasaki possessed only a tiny power compared with the weapons later developed in peacetime, the most powerful *known* warhead having had a yield of 60 megatons (i.e., equivalent to 60 million tons of conventional high-explosive).

The two atomic weapons that were dropped on Hiroshima and Nagasaki served not only as a deterrent to die-hard Japanese leaders who wanted to fight on to the bitter end, but over the years, since 1945, the memory of their effects has proved to be the most decisive strategic deterrent in military history.

Below: The final act in a long and bitterly-fought war, as U.S. Navy carrier planes fly in salute over USS *Misssouri* (BB-63) and other U.S. and British warships in Tokyo Bay on September 2, 1945.

# INDEX